Gender as Soft Assembly

Gender as Soft Assembly

Adrienne Harris

THE ANALYTIC PRESS
2005 Hillsdale, NJ   London

Published by
The Analytic Press, Inc., Publishers
Editorial Offices:
101 West Street
Hillsdale, NJ 07642

www.analyticpress.com

The case material in chapter 10 appeared originally in the author's chapter, "Relational Mourning in a Mother and Her Three-Year Old After September 11," in *September 11: Trauma and Human Bonds*, edited by S. Coates, J. Rosenthal, and D. Schechter (The Analytic Press, 2003).

Library of Congress Cataloging-in-Publication Data
Harris, Adrienne.
    Gender as soft assembly / Adrienne Harris
        p. cm.
    Includes bibliographical references and index.
    ISBN 0-88163-370-4
    1. Sex (Psychology). 2. Gender identity. 3. Psychoanalysis. 4. Developmental psychology. I. Title.

    BF175.5.S48H37 2004
    155.3'2—dc22

                                                        2004051994

Printed in the United States of America
10 9 8 7 6 5 4 3 2 1

For Robert Sklar

Contents

Continued

Acknowledgments

A book requires a host of helpers. There is the particular solitude in clinical work and writing that produces in me the need for community and conversation. In that regard, I have been blessed with amazing colleagues. Above all, my work is tremendously indebted to the original group of people gathered together by Stephen Mitchell to launch *Psychoanalytic Dialogues,* a group in which thinking about and evolving relational theory was always encouraged. Steve Mitchell and Emmanuel Ghent, above all, mentored and inspired and supported this work. Lewis Aron, Neil Altman, Anthony Bass, Philip Bromberg, Muriel Dimen, and Jody Davies are colleagues who have provided a crucible of hard work, fun, invention, and opportunities.

The other journal that is intellectual home to me is *Studies in Gender and Sexuality.* The people who began that journal have been the closest companions and the deepest sources of influence and inspiration: the editors Virginia Goldner and Ken Corbett, along with Susan Coates, Nancy Chodorow, Jessica Benjamin, and Muriel Dimen.

Because this book is in the Relational Perspectives Book Series, series editors Stephen Mitchell and Lewis Aron read many drafts and pushed me to speak clearly no matter how complex I wanted to make things. I have a particularly strong tie to Lewis Aron, with whom intellectual and professional collaborations go back now over 20 years. We have engaged in a steady evolution of projects that have been fruitful sources of growth and learning for me.

Friends, colleagues, and family read and critiqued chapters of this book. My thanks to Beatrice Beebe, Muriel Dimen, Susan Coates, Bob Sklar, and Nancy Chodorow, along with Lew and Steve.

I also want to acknowledge the help and influence of many colleagues, intellectual comrades, and mentoring figures: Glen Gabbard, Sam Gerson, Rita Frankiel, Lynne Layton, Roy Lilleskov, Shelley Nathans, Maureen Murphy, Donald Moss, David Olds, Barbara and Stuart Pizer, Ellen Rees, Karen Rosica, Roy Schafer, Sue Shapiro, Doris Silverman, Steve Solow, Elizabeth Bott Spillius, Donnel Stern, Ruth Stein, Elisabeth Young-Bruehl, Lynne Zeavin, and staff and friends at the Austen Riggs Center: Gerald Fromm, Craig Piers, John Muller, Jane Tillman, and Ed Shapiro.

At The Analytic Press, I have had the great good fortune to have received careful editing and assistance of a caliber that is absolutely unique in contemporary psychoanalytic publishing: Thanks to Paul Stepansky, Eleanor Kobrin, Nancy Liguori, and Joan Riegel.

Thanks to Alexandra Todorova for scrupulous editing and bibliographic help.

To my family—Kate, Justin, Lorna, and Norah (and I will sneak Rosie into this list) and above all to Bob Sklar, a model of writerly discipline and so many other matters as well—much love and thanks.

Gender as Soft Assembly

Introduction

I want to engage in a cross-disciplinary dialogue about the *develop-ment* of a "relational" subject and to make this dialogue meaning-ful to clinical psychoanalysts. The developmental story I want to tell is one that braids bodily and intrapsychic life with historical and social forces. My interlocutors come from academic developmental psy-chology, from the cognitive sciences, from linguistics and philosophy of mind, and from the wide-ranging practices of gender theory, feminism,[1] and queer theory.

The theoretical music being composed can be dark or light. Some writers are caught up in the losses and emptiness of identity, some in the deep enmeshment of body and psyche, and some in the sliding and playful paradoxes of performance and authenticity. All the writers and theorists I engage with in this book struggle with both the necessity and the instability of many powerful but unsatisfying binaries: self–other, inside–outside, male–female, performed–real, core–variation, empty–full, body–mind, intrapsychic–interpersonal, essence–construction.

For me, the most powerful psychoanalytic writing maintains a scru-pulous vigilance over two contradictory pressures on meaning making. First, we have to notice the power in organizing polar structures: mom–dad, boy–girl, gay–straight, connected–separate. These formations give coherence and heft to our experience. Simultaneously, we have to no-tice the great creative potential released when these polarities are deconstructed. Each organizational form yields particular pleasures and constrictions. There is the deep expansiveness that comes from recog-nition and belonging, and there are the quirky spurts and frissons when the unexpected, the transgressive, the novel emerge into view. This may, indeed, be one powerful developmental process—the dialectical movement from coherence through differentiation to new integration. It is a process one sees in all the great developmental theories: Piaget, Werner, Vygotsky, Baldwin, and in the psychoanalytic developmental theories: Freud, Winnicott, Fairbairn, Loewald, Klein.

In this book, I look at development through the lens of relational psychoanalysis. Hardly more than a decade after Greenberg and Mitchell (1983) first outlined the relational model as an alternative to classical theory, in particular to American ego psychology, Aron (1996) wrote a historical summary of the evolution and emergence of this powerful perspective that has altered the theoretical landscape of psychoanalysis.[2] He notes that there are a number of different ways to describe this history and that the unique theoretical integrations depend greatly on the institutional and personal history of the writer. It is perhaps one of the hallmarks of relational theory that it has fostered many distinct and creative ways of making use of the relational two-person, intersubjective approach to considering clinical treatment and forms of psychic life.

Writing this book about development caught me up in a demanding developmental crisis of my own. Simply put, I am rooted in several distinct language worlds: clinical practice, social theory, and developmental psychology. I believe that language and speech (in oral or written form) always carry myriad object relations. Speech is always dialogic even when it is part of self-reflection or self-regulation. There is always a listener even if that listener is hidden or latent and not even clear to the speaker. So, when people from different disciplines try to speak to each other, the struggle is to make the ideas from an other, foreign mode of work—work addressed to another, less visible cast of characters—seem more like the familiar talk of close kin.[3]

One of the earliest developmentalists, James Mark Baldwin (1904), considered an interdisciplinary approach essential to the understanding of a person's growth both as an individual experience and as a socially mediated process. At my most optimistic, I operate out of the deep conviction that Baldwin articulated over a century ago, namely, that cross-disciplinary integrations are crucial to theory building. At its most troubling, my predilection for synthesis is an insistence on sitting in the middle of traffic.

To my chagrin, I find myself writing a book that depends on three ideas that have often aroused antipathy in an audience of clinical psychoanalysts. First, I take up the question of developmental models at a time when there is a wide range of questions about the utility or status of developmental theorizing. Second, I try to stay mindful of the political or ideological dimension of psychoanalytic theories. The presence of values, power, and social regulation is always hovering at the edge of my consciousness, clinical or otherwise. It is one aspect of my interest in social constructionism and postmodernism, both different ways of understanding the presence and function of the analytic "third."

Third, this is a book about theories and the cross-talk among theories in different disciplines: psychoanalysis, developmental psychology, language studies, and feminism. Let me take these problems up in turn.

WHY STUDY DEVELOPMENT?

This project began with the wish to rework early experiences in my own professional and intellectual formation as a developmental psychologist in the light of what I later learned in analytic practice. I was trained to think about development with a strong functional emphasis, development as a dynamic, dialectic, transformational process. Structure and the more straightforward descriptions of stages take a back seat. The emphasis on process, self-organization, and function is fundamental to developmental psychologists like Baldwin, Vygotsky, Werner, and, in certain respects, Piaget.[4] They were all, in different ways, interested in the questions of what led a system to alter and disequilibrate, what was continuous and what was transformed. How did development cycle and oscillate between external and internal poles, between simplicity and complexity?

In this book I explore how learning to speak, developing a mind, or becoming gendered are always understood to be emergent in context and therefore neither solely social and interactional processes nor reified into simply endogenous experiences. Minds and bodies, words and thoughts, are always constituted in histories. Historical, social, biological, and intrapsychic processes are always interacting, overlapping open systems.

Generated in the philosophical light of James (1890, 1910) and Peirce (1955), these ideas[5] can be traced in developmental psychology over the past century sometimes as a minor thread, sometimes in the mainstream. In my view, these ideas are key for relational psychoanalysis, a theory in which meaning making is an interactional, co-constructed experience. Contemporary developmental researchers are increasingly interested in telling developmental narratives that weave together the cognitive, the social, and the emotional domains of experience and embed these phenomena in complex multiply intersecting interactions (see, for example, Cicchetti and Beeghly, 1990; Cicchetti and Cohen, 1995; and Cicchetti and Toth, 1996 for "state of the art" readings of developmental theory and research).

The Vygotsky scholar William Frawley (1997) puts it succinctly:

> Social and computational mind come together in the way certain parts of language, perched on the mind-world boundary, are used by computational minds to mediate inside and outside during thinking. Individualism could not but be right on one score: the direct mechanisms of mind are internal. But we simply cannot tell the tale of the management of thinking, metarepresentation, inhibition, recovery from breakdown, self-talk, stance in problem solving, theory of mind development and breakdown, and the frame problem as an inside story [pp. 270–271].

There is a need to integrate computational mind with social mind and I want to address that imperative here.

This Vygotskian perspective, which I share, is less focused on the individual as simply endogenous and less dominated by old splits between reason and emotion and strictures of positivism and empiricism. It is very evolved and alive in contemporary developmental work in the cognitive domain and in the domain of social psychology, personality development, and developmental psychopathology and in studies of language development.[6] One common characteristic of all this work is the determination to integrate complex intrapsychic process with field theories that stress the constituting power of context and relationships. It is this aspect of the work that makes for such good potential conversation with relational theory.

Within psychoanalysis, Fonagy and Target work for a synthesis of developmental psychopathology, philosophy of mind, and attachment theory (Fonagy and Target, 2002, 2003; Fonagy et al., 2002). Fonagy's model of the development of reflective functioning traces the evolution of capacities for self-regulation and self-reflection from the relational interactive grid of being thought about, felt about, and imagined. The relationship becomes both the container and the product of mind. Representation carries the object relation and is the outcome of its particular forms and evolutions. This is very akin to Vygotsky's more general model of the dialectical interpenetration of dialogue and cognition.

An important developmental model for me in this book comes from chaos theory, with its particular application to the study of development, nonlinear dynamic systems theory (Thelen and Smith, 1994). Known under a number of different names (complexity theory, nonlinear dynamic systems theory, chaos theory), this point of view privileges open systems, self-organization, and dynamic prospects for change and re-equilibration. I will use the terms somewhat interchangeably but I retain a fondness for the term "chaos theory," although principles of pattern, regulation, and unfolding really are the characteristics of the system. The term "chaos" suits my rhetoric, my aesthetic, perhaps. I want to privilege the unsettled, the unpredictable, the nonlinearity as a deeply important aspect of psychoanalytic developmental theories.

I think the encounter of chaos theory with relational psychoanalysis is a marriage made in heaven. But it is also true that the details of the prenup are still being worked out. It is one of the great potentials of the nonlinear dynamic systems approach that there is plenty of room for plasticity and for biology to interact with information and contexts in the world (social or physical). But these factors are set in terms of process, not prestructured outcomes. And that makes a lot of difference. This book is a kind of progress report on this marriage, its potential for creating an interesting home in which to look at the development of gender and of symbolization.

If there is a rich, century-long tradition of work in child development that centers on dialectics, integrated systems, and multiple lines of development, there is also a well-developed critical discourse about development both in psychoanalysis and in developmental psychology (Harré, 1984; Henriques et al., 1984; Broughton, 1987; Chapman and Dixon, 1987; Chodorow, 1992; Cushman, 1995, 2000; Lewes, 1995; Lesser, 1996, 1997; Coates, 1997; Magee and Miller, 1997; Dimen, 1999; Meyes, 1999; Reisner, 1999; Corbett, 2001b).[7] I try to stay in dialogue with this critical discourse, with which I both agree and disagree. There is a widespread concern that our treatment of adults not fall prey to the distortions of what Mitchell (1984) referred to as the "developmental tilt." Meyes (1999), for example, has cautioned against a reductionist parallel between developmental process and analytic process. A number of psychoanalysts (Wolff, 1996, 1998; Green, 2000) urge that we remain open to conceptions of developmental process without equating analyzing with parenting or regression in adult treatment with conditions of infancy.[8]

The critique of a too-easy assimilation of psychology has often been

joined to a general distaste for empiricism and observation, a distaste
that must surely go back to the era of Bowlby. Primarily by European
and British analysts, there is a critique of the importation of developmental *observation* into our theory making (Breen, 1993; Green, 2000).
Drawing so heavily on observation leads, it is feared, to a domination of
reality over an appreciation of the unconscious. This is often seen as a
particularly American problem, whether ego psychological, relational,
or interpersonal.

   The critics of developmental theory also take up the opposite point,
namely, that theories of development can be too adult centered, too
dominated by some idealized or normatively defined endpoint of development. Developmental theory is sometimes viewed as a kind of
Trojan horse within which cultural norms and ideologies are smuggled
into unsuspecting psychoanalytic models (Schwartz, 1995, 1999; Dimen,
1996b, 2002). The impact of these critiques cannot be underestimated.
It is tempting to dismiss critiques of normative or dominating prescriptions in our theories as "politically" driven attempts to enforce ideological purity. But at the heart of these critical commentaries on
developmental models is an ethical concern. These critics (see Layton,
1998; Altman, 2000a, b; Cushman, 2000, for example) make a demand
for analytic self-consciousness about the norms and controls and sur-
veillances that can unwittingly reside in theory and leak into practice,
despite our claims for neutrality.

   Yet, as Hoffman (1998) has so movingly noticed, the new focus on
the subjectivity and self-consciousness of the analyst/theorist can never
be a matter of absolute certainty. Vigilance always partially fails. Immersed in both culturally driven theories and structures of power that
can never be perfectly transparent to us, the analyst/theorist carries
much that is unknown and unconscious into studying and working clinically. It is for this reason that the project of making theory must be
collective. Only in collegial dialogues, which are difficult to establish
except in conditions of trust and safety, can analysts elaborate and
struggle to integrate all that is carried in our theoretical and personal
baggage.

   In matters of gender and of sexuality—so much the focus of psychoanalytic theorizing—there is a particularly strong potential for ideology to be imported seamlessly into theory. One well-remarked danger
in developmental theory is that a prescribed set of psychosexual arrangements is legitimized at the expense of variation and alternative
developmental trajectories and outcomes. Lewes (1988, 1995) and

Chodorow (1992) have critiqued this linearity. One of the subtle ways this legitimation is achieved is that the particular stands in for the general or generic. In gender or sexual experience, the generic form is invariably the masculine and the heterosexual. It is as though gender and sexuality always come with brand names—male, heterosexual—and then what is proposed as description slides and shades subtly into prescription.[9]

Some analysts argue that the whole developmental project, even the whole concept of a model, is so flawed, so contaminated by ideology, as to be unusable (Fuss, 1991, 1995; Schwartz, 1995, 1999; Lesser, 1997). A different strategy is to posit a gay gene, or homosexuality as a separate line of development (LeVay, 1993; Isay, 1996). This has been a strategic attempt to draw on the power of a developmental account but to shift the ground to work against the conventional forms of pathology. But as Dimen (1998, 1999), Corbett (2001a, b), and others have suggested, this project so constrains and biologizes ideas and concepts of sexuality as to be as foreclosing as any of the more normalizing theories.

Psychoanalytic theorizing about development manifests a very strong tendency to proliferate a number of distinct developmental lines. Often these lines of development seem canalized and linear (A. Freud, 1946, 1965, 1966; Tyson, 1986, 1994; Tyson and Tyson, 1990; Lichtenberg, 1993). I argue that this focus on distinct and predictable lines of development creates a kind of Balkanization of development, with bodies of knowledge and developmental skills or capacities produced as a series of disconnected silos.

Following Ghent (2002), I suggest that motivational systems are not blueprints but outcomes. This is certainly the working premise of this book, and it is certainly a feature of nonlinear, dynamic systems theory and its applications to problems of motivation. Ghent asked us to give up our ideas of growth as a process moving through a series of distinct motivational pathways. Motivation is thus not a *before* phenomenon, not a press on behavior or fantasy or experience. Rather, motives are emergent from simple infant capacities. Thus, from unidimensional, narrow-gauge actions that arise in rich interactional matrices, a child very quickly develops needs and wants. Often retrospectively these wants are experienced as already present from the beginning, but this experience is a construction. In this way chaos systems theory addresses one of the concerns of many critics of developmental theory, namely, that the desired normative adult outcome is foreshadowed and predicted from the beginning. Developmental theorizing that already knows the endpoint, preset at the outset of growth, is not actually a developmental theory.

Reisner (1999), approaching the developmentalists' search for origins from another angle, argued that developmental theory is myth driven, creating stories of origins often masked as science.[10] Faced with such criticism, one has two choices: abandon myth making altogether or self-consciously elaborate myth or myths as part of the social and narrative forces underlying growth. To take, in other words, an interest in narrative or hermeneutic truth (Spence, 1982, 1992, 1994; Schafer, 1992; Fajardo, 1998).

An intriguing and hopeful trend in recent psychoanalytic work is an expansion of the range and types of myths we draw on. More and more, psychoanalysts are noting both the cultural contexts in which different myths emerge and the range of gender-specific kinds of narratives we might tell. There are the stories of Jocasta (Olivier, 1989), of Persephone and Demeter (Kulish and Holzman, 1998; Holtzman and Kulish, 2000), of Artemis (Harris, 1985), of Oedipus's maternal neglect (Kohut, 1977). One can tell the oedipal story in reverse by focusing on Laius's assault of Oedipus (Pollock and Ross, 1988). Even within the Western tradition of classical mythology there is more than one story. And once we attend to the variability and culture-bound nature of myth and story, concrete or universal lines of development recede in prominence. Myths may organize solutions and understanding of common problems of growing and living, but the arrangement is more kaleidoscopic than linear and monolithic.

This expansion of myths and metaphors raises the question of what a theory should be able to do. Thinking of a theory as a narrative or as a metaphor is already a move away from theory as a deductive instrument predicting outcomes. Yet we also know that even apparently benign theoretical "stories" can form different types of prisons. A developmental story can be an imprisoning container, or it can be a map for new space and freedoms.

The longing and determination to map new spaces certainly motivates practitioners of chaos theory, who exhibit a considerable commitment to freedom. Stuart Kauffman (1995) describes the particular feature of chaos theory's computational form:

> The theory of computation is replete with deep theorems. Among the most beautiful are those showing that, in most cases by far, there exists no shorter means to predict what an algorithm will do than

to simple execute it, observing the succession of actions and states
as they unfold. The algorithm itself is its own shortest description.
It is, in the jargon of the field, incompressible [p. 22].

The implications of this idea are that the behavior of these unfolding
nonlinear systems would never be predictable by some general law. There
is no "covering law model," as Alicia Juarrero (1999) notes, and this
difference in her view, shifts theory away from deductive and deterministic cause-and-effect explanations. Theories no longer need to function as the latest newly evolved creatures in the intellectual food chain,
devouring weaker and aging competitors. I hope to put in question the
model of theory as imperialist conqueror of the opposition either within
or across boundaries.

Within psychoanalysis, the dominant model of the theorist is as
authority, the magisterial one who knows. Sometimes the one who knows
grounds his knowledge in medicine. Stepansky (1999) has noted the
shift in medical speciality as metaphor for analyst: analyst as surgeon
(Freud) changing to analyst as obstetrician (Ferenczi). Relational theory
was founded on the hope for a revolution in matters of analytic authority,
a revolution grounded in a critique of magisterial knowledge (Mitchell,
1993). I want to set in play a number of other metaphors and terms for
theory and for theorist—theory as transitional space, as landscape, as
social field. Theorist as farceur, as spy, as double agent, as cointerlocutor.
These images contest the traditional metaphors of theorist as entrepre-
neur, as revolutionary, as anarchist, as military campaigner.

Marcia Cavell (1988, 1993, 1999), a philosopher/psychoanalyst who
is attentive to the contradictions and problems in pragmatism's and
relational theories' absorption in hermeneutic enterprises, reminds us
that we argue for a truth we cannot know foundationally but that we
believe we apprehend. The truth we strive for is a necessary third term,
though one on an ever-receding horizon. It is this perspective that offers an alternative to the caricaturing of postmodernism as merely nihilistic or simply a fetishizing of text and its effects.

I connect postmodern preoccupations with the relational interests
in analytic subjectivity, which is not a refusal of meaning making but a
decentering of it. If you accept ambiguities and indeterminacies, both
in the subject and the object of study, it is not that you are adrift in
some sea of relativism but that you are suspicious of claims of exhaustive knowledge. These suspicions surround the worry that it is power
that is often more at stake than reason.

Cavell (1988), drawing on Davidson, finds her way to a balance of objective and subjective knowing:

> The concept of mind requires us to abandon the dualism of subject and object altogether as epistemological terms. Of course you and I see things differently, if that means that we have different attitudes toward the same things in the world. Talk about a point of view presumes a common coordinate system on which other perspectives can be mapped [p. 873].

Once we have linked up speaking and thinking in this way (and there is a grand philosophical backdrop to this from Davidson, Wittgenstein, Vygotsky, and the pragmatist tradition of James), we have a model of mind that is both ineradicably private and ineradicably social (Cavell, 1993, 1999).

Too linear, too silolike, too normative, too prescriptive, too ideological, too invariant, too infantilizing, too behavioral: the scope and range of critiques of developmental theory are daunting. Many of these criticisms of psychoanalytic developmental theory making seem compelling. As a feminist, I have made them myself. The problem for me is that no aspect of psychoanalytic theory seems free from most of these dangers, although developmental theories are particularly vulnerable to, and saturated with, cultural norming.

For some writers (Phillips, 1995, 1999; Corbett, 2001b) the project of developmental models is suspect, interesting, impossible to resist. I put myself in their camp. For all the difficulties and reservations about developmental theory and research, I continue stubbornly to hold on to the belief that both are crucial to any psychoanalytic project. I am most interested in a theory of development that is illuminated by local practices rather than by overarching universals,[11] developed within the broad outlines of a social constructionist perspective. Only when we give up the idea of a "core" or "true self" will we be able to try to braid together the intrapsychic, the social, and the interpersonal. One argument against both social constructionism and interpersonal theory is that the individual is left too shallowly structured, without depth or complexity. But the great potential in chaos theory is to see complexity and coherence and structure as *outcomes* of interaction, subtly but powerfully elaborated in early developmental interactions. This theory would not function like a predictive engine but, rather, would be the ground for a conversation, a circulating set of metaphors. One of my goals here is to reconsider developmental theory in the light of the important and telling criticisms to which such theories have been subjected.

RELATIONAL THEORY AND FEMINISM ARE SO POLITICAL

One of the hallmarks of a psychoanalytic approach is that intense immersion in clinical practice requires periodic bouts of self-conscious worry and self-examination. This idea is built into all psychoanalytic education and practice. A critique of authority is one link between relational theory and feminism. And this questioning of power links both to postmodernism. Within these three perspectives there has been a steady development of questions that destabilize our certainties about the objects we study and interact with and shake up our own convictions of what we "know."

My worries, growing out of my own immersion in feminism and critical theory, center on the values, ideological forces, and hidden presuppositions that creep into clinical work. I believe that, regardless of one's theoretical perspective, normative biases and values wash through even the most carefully titrated forms of analytic listening. Interest in coconstructed meaning making and the presence of analytic subjectivity in patient process has been a consistent and steady thread through the narratives of relational psychoanalysis. This is one way of defining the force of the community or the "analytic third." The question of community values (Greenberg, 2001), using or abandoning "the book" (Jacobs, 1991; Hoffman, 1992; Renik, 1993, 1996; Aron, 1996), the status of enactments (Smith, 1999) are very much alive for contemporary analysts. But the notion of the "third" is not exactly stable: sometimes it is an emergent property in the development of the analytic couple (Aron, 1991, 1992, 2001; Ogden, 1994; Benjamin, 1998); sometimes a limit on experience provided by the symbolic register or the word (Lacan, 1977; Muller, 1996), and sometimes an interlocutor with whom we are all engaged (Greenberg, 2001; Spezzano, 2001).

While trying to pay attention to the multiple relational matrices we are embedded in as analysts, I have drawn on one metaphor to think about the whole range of an analyst's or a theorist's functioning— I imagine that we are embedded in a series of overlapping and interacting psychic envelopes (Anzieu, 1989, 1990; Guillaumin, 1990). We live inside the permeable and the impermeable membranes of particular treatment dyads. But we are also enveloped in institutions, subcommunities, and our own analyses and training relationships, envelopes that are lived in material reality and in the imagination. Along with these living, breathing envelopes, we all swim in a rich acoustic, oral, aural stream of words, ideas, and affective states. Analysts live amidst multiple reveries and dialogues through which cultural and professional ideas and ideologies flow into our clinical process.

An analyst is like a railroad switching station, organizing and processing communications and internal dialogues in which aspects of the third must be operating while simultaneously immersed in the clinical conversation. Clinical work is perhaps always best imagined as a complex series of overlapping envelopes and conversations. Benign or insidious, clear or confused, conscious or unconscious, the multiple functions and multiple states of the analytic third put flesh and bones into the idea that there is power in certain sites of knowledge and healing (Foucault, 1965). This concern, that regimens of control coexist with care and insight, has been one of the particular pressure points on theory and practice, pressure emanating from feminism and from queer theory.

Another metaphor often brought to bear on thinking of the role of authority and rule in healing practices is that of prison, a metaphor that we owe principally to Michel Foucault. Foucault is often positioned in psychoanalysis in a notorious, even lurid, light. Projected as the poster child of postmodernism at its most nihilistic, Foucault (1980) can be stereotyped as the experience-distant theorizer and fetishizer of madness and outlaw sex. But I locate Foucault right at the beginning of his attempts to understand both psychiatry and madness. There we find him not in an airy Parisian apartment worrying about literary and historical texts but in the daily, difficult work of a psychiatric hospital. It is a site familiar to many of us, a place where the tugs and pulls of institutions, economic pressures, clinical judgment, and care, are often in terrible, irreconcilable tension.

In an interview, Foucault (1988) described the work he did at Hôpital Ste. Anne in the 1950s while studying psychology. The work led eventually to his analysis of madness and the clinic. He was more identified with patients than with doctors and functioned somewhere between doctor and patient. He felt, he said, a malaise that only gradually crystalized into a historical critique. His situation was thus both like and unlike that of those of us who are usually both doctor and patient and who must therefore address our practices as places of coercion and subject production as well as healing. We carry the knowledge, the hopes, and the uncertainties that come from being on both sides of the couch. The anguish we may feel is that our work can be a site both of surveillance and of resistance.

To attempt a Foucauldian approach to one's own practices and discursive traditions is to try to analyze power and interests that are at work in the very processes in which we are simultaneously enmeshed. This conception of analytic work as occurring within a set of relational matrices of intense mutual (though asymmetric) interaction has always been a potent feature of relational theory. The work of Altman (1996, 2000a), Lesser (1996), Cushman (2000), and others (Botticelli, in press) exemplifies extensions of this approach beyond the clinical dyad and into the world while maintaining self-criticism as a kind of internal gyroscope. I think it is a desirable effort to make.

Interest in the social forces that flow through our theories, our work process, and our ways of listening leads some of us to social constructionism (Hoffman, 1991, 1992), which is the overarching theoretical umbrella in which I would situate this work. This perspective embeds the individual and the discourses of natural and social science in which people are made comprehensible to themselves and others in social and historically contingent processes.

The social constructionist perspective argues for a light hand, a provisional way with theory claims. Gergen (1985, 1994) says of social constructionist theories that they are mute on the subject of ontology. This approach is not antireality or antiempirical. But, since there is no easy way to get between words and the objects or actions they refer to, foundational claims of truth and any privileged relation to reality are put in doubt. In the current intellectual climate, where intersubjectivity and coconstruction in some form coexist with serious and "successful" attempts at approaching objectivity, how subjectivity and objectivity intersect is among our most compelling preoccupations (see Hoffman, 1991, 1992; Aron, 1992, 2001; Benjamin, 1998; Friedman, 1999, 2002; Hanly, 1999; Eagle, 2001; and Hanly and Fitzpatrick-Hanly, 2001 for serious struggles with these concepts).

Let us see how that mixed focus on subjectivity and objectivity might look clinically. An analysand is chronically late, usually only five or 10 minutes. He always arrives rushed and upset (with himself, with me, with time, with the external world). Framed as an analytic couple by a variety of interlocking beliefs and knowledges (Davidson, 1980; Cavell, 1993, 1999), we both know where my office is, the routes to it, the time of the session. There is usually an exquisite calibration of the degree of lateness with some pressing, external event. Time is both held in chronometric reality and toyed with. Time's meaning, and thus its phenomenal feeling (endlessly open, rushed and full, gaping or cramped), is deeply subjectively and intersubjectively coconstructed. Over time we developed an almost ritualized scene. There would be the look on my face, welcoming or wary. Then, in reaction, there would be his body language, abject and shamed. We both seemed always poised to conduct transactions of shame and anger. Often there seemed the threat, or the hope, of some sadomasochistic outbreak.

There are many clinical and dynamic issues we can parse out: the refusal of reality, the allure of sadism and abjection for both of us, the wish for a kind of violent finding of the other, the despair that reality would not conform to wish. All these experiences were there to be absorbed in an understanding that requires both objective and subjective knowing. Time, as a developmental underpinning, as both an objective experience and a fluid subjective site of meaning, is a process I explore in this book.

In social constructionist theory, what something means and what matters in a theoretical enterprise is agreed on through dialogue (multiple dialogues) and not through authoritarian fiat. There is, in the social constructionist perspective, a continuum of method across the hermeneutic, social, and natural sciences because all involve interpretation. These are the ways that an intellectual or professional community practices theory. The nexus of power and knowledge in which theory emerges is a series of negotiated dialogues or exchanges. It is the dialogic process that a social constructionist is interested in. Within this perspective, it is easy to idealize dialogue as a democratic process.

Social constructionism may certainly bear that utopian hope, but, as any clinician sitting through case conferences or undergoing institutional training knows, there is an inevitable weighting of certain kinds of authority within any institutional setting devoted to the various projects of meaning making. Ann Fausto-Sterling (2000), deploying historical method and an informed scientific reading of the medical literature on intersexuality, makes this case. Even such apparently unassailable physical phenomena as genital size and formation turn out to be interpretable and thus prey to social, political, and ideological values.

Diagnoses, clinical strategies, values, interpretations, timing, and management are all adjudicated through a social process in which power (which may derive from many obvious and not obvious sources in a professional community) plays a crucial role. Certain terms come to be "deeply sedimented by use" (Gergen, 1994) and have great purchase and power in wide common understandings; but, at a given historical moment or gradually over time, these terms become intensely contested and unstable. It was precisely this immersion in the powerful mutations of gender categorizing, appreciated through feminism and psychoanalysis, that led me to rethink questions of development.

Within psychoanalysis are terms and concepts descriptive of gender and of sexual life that have deep barnacled meanings that have become highly contested. Many of our most passionate debates, influenced by feminism and other social theories, have tried to address the fluidity or solidness of many of these concepts. Thomas Kuhn's (1962) model of scientific revolution describes paradigm shifts as dramatic reorganizations of ways of knowing. A social constructionist approach adds attention to the many social and historical forces inside and outside any discipline that affect what counts as real, what matters, and what terms mean. Many forces in social life, mostly movements of liberation within the last 30 years, feminism and queer theory in particular, have affected our psychoanalytic understandings of gender and of sexual practices and sexual life. Social constructionism applied to psychoanalysis illuminates the impact of history both on the individual and on theory making itself.

Yet there is some utility as well as some importance to our engagement with these intellectual movements (see Fairfield, Layton, and Stack, 2002, for a major text on postmodernism for psychoanalysis). The "postmodern" subject is, above all, a traumatized subject, someone whose consciousness and subjectivity has been fractured and rendered incoherent through the embedding of that subject amid economic, political, and ecological discord and contradiction. Charles Taylor (1989), looking at modern identity from a historical perspective, argues that interpretation and meaning structures are necessary for anyone's sense of stability and selfhood and that, at many levels in contemporary life, these systems of meaning and comprehensibility, embedding narratives of identity, have broken down. Alienation, splits, disoriented dissociated states are the hallmarks of the postmodern character and certainly frequently encountered in our consulting rooms.

Psychoanalytic work drawing on postmodern ideas could be a site where intellectual practice and clinical practice coexist and interact in uniquely meaningful ways. Using postmodernism clinically is not like operating some low-flying theory plane zooming over miles of literary text and gleefully deconstructing everything in sight. We sit in rooms where we are embedded in dialogues and experiences of suffering and confusion, and there we must entertain many contradictory ideas. There is the indissolubility of the subject and object of knowledge, but there are also splits and fissures within subjects. There is the force of all social interactions in the constituting of persons and the complexities of power in intellectual and therapeutic practices.

As clinicians we have an increasing sensitivity to the indeterminate quality of affective and sometimes passionate exchanges in analytic life. More and more we can tolerate indeterminacy about whose mind, whose body, whose unconscious is mixed up and intertwined in an analytic pair. I think a postmodern sensibility attuned to the issues of power in healing practices has a role to play in the development of our clinical understanding. This dimension, power, is never simple or simply patriarchal and never fully free of these historical forms. It is not so easy for us to absorb. We often want to keep clinical work as a free space. But we cure with contaminated tools. We are embedded in structures of money, hierarchy, and power, and we must keep a double vision in play. Psychoanalysts practice subversion and hegemony in every hour.

TALK BETWEEN DISCIPLINES

If I insist on sitting at the busy, not very well regulated crossroads of developmental theory, social theory, and psychoanalysis (with occasional detours to philosophy and neuroscience), it is probably a good thing that I have become so involved in thinking about chaos theory. The kind of interdisciplinary traffic jam I am describing means that clinical work or theoretical work is always occurring in conditions of potential or actual disequilibrium. All the areas of work that I draw on, those I consider necessary if not sufficient elements in developing theoretical narratives or clinically useful concepts, are under intense critical scrutiny and revision.

Writing this book has been an opportunity for me to draw together different traditions and areas of work that I have been involved in and cared about for the past 30 years. It is an attempt at synthesis and reconfiguring, not a break with the past to produce some novel developmental theory. I hope to clear some space, a kind of transitional space where I can work within a relational framework and can reflect on and make use of developmental processes.

Daniel Dennett (1991) offered a metaphor for his efforts at theory making that I find particularly pleasing. No home runs, no "swinging for the fence," but some honest base running. Actually he said aggressive base running. But to temper this macho metaphor let me offer another, more humbling image. Local, historically specific theory is theory with a limited shelf life. Schafer (1997) made this point by suggesting that an analyst must live in multiple necessary fictions, the partial fiction of the autonomous observer and the partial fiction of embedded subjectivities. No single approach is all-encompassing; each sets limits, and perhaps the best a social constructionist theorist can do is be content with knowing "an epistemological and methodological grounding can never be the sort that precludes alternatives or skepticism" (Schafer, 1997, p. 12). The dialectic between objectivity and subjectivity must be kept in tension.

Preoccupation with the status of our knowledge comes up for many relationalists in the context of discussions about analytic authority. Hoffman (1998), Aron (1996, 2001), and Pizer (1998, 2001), along with many others, explore the tension of functioning with conviction alongside curiosity and a sense of mystery. Interest in clinical work as a form of making and creating new stories sits counter to the conviction that one knows. Britton (1995, 1999), for example, considers knowing to be a kind of symptom. Belief, in a certain sense, he argues, operates from the depressive position. This echoes Phillips's (1995) idea that symptoms are really simply matters of conviction, although these convictions can often reach extreme and desperate heights. Perhaps one might say that pragmatism, in general, functions from the depressive position, requiring the melancholy understanding that what feels true can sometimes be driven by what has usefulness.

Our theory making outside the consulting room and the theory making we do inside when we interpret to patients might be imagined in the way Bion (1962) thought about knowing. Curiosity and the claim to know could be kinds of loving and attaching, but also forms of devouring and acquiring. To practice from the depressive position entails living with the tension between certainty and indeterminacy, as well as with the tensions of loving and hating that become implicated in modes of knowing and being known.

This difficult prospect has been targeted in discussions of modernism and postmodernism as guiding spirits of psychoanalytic theorizing (Dyess and Dean, 2000a, b; Fairfield, 2000, 2001; Mitchell,

2001b). I have often thought that we think postmodern but practice in the enlightenment because we are embedded in multiple world views. We live in hybrid paradigms. Jamesian pragmatism can take us a long way in not reifying and colonizing those we work with and learn about, recognizing that we routinely fall short of this ideal.

Such a process at work within psychoanalysis is most prominent in the study of gender. Freud initiated a century-long investigation with his provocative question, "What does a woman want?" This was neatly turned by feminist critique (Irigaray, 1985; Kofman, 1985; Benjamin, 1988, in particular) into questions of women's desire, "Do women want?" and "How do they want?" The feminist challenge was designed to put into question the assumptions of classical psychoanalytic accounts of femininity. We might frame the contemporary approaches to gender and sexuality as a set of questions. What do gender and sexuality serve? What are the multiple and often paradoxical functions of being someone or loving someone in some way? But as these questions are raised in the light of new theory (feminist, relational, queer, postmodern), the practice of theory and the stability of categories and concepts are also put in question.

Sometimes my images and metaphors for the project of interdisciplinary work come from the world of landscaping: maps, bridges, overlapping and convergent terrain, or eclectic gardens. Sometimes I think of multivoicedness, a participation in many conversations carried on in different styles and genres. More recently, I have been drawing metaphors from chaos theory to think of systems of theory as "softly assembled," multidimensional, fractallike phenomena; emergent and shaped in particular histories, environments, and contexts. Developmental psychoanalytic theory is, I would say, a hot point in the wider theoretical system of psychoanalysis. In the eccentric language of chaos theory, a developmental model could be a strange attractor.[12]

Though the translation tasks can be formidable, there are problems investigated in child development that could be of interest to psychoanalysts: the problem of discovering other minds, learning and being inducted into the representational systems of your family and culture. Psychoanalysts are very interested in how to conceptualize the way a person becomes gendered, becomes a self, becomes intentional. One task in this book is to make this translation from developmental psychology useful to analysts and to show how the nonlinear dynamic systems perspective opens up profoundly interactive models for many developmental processes. Because the focus in chaos theory is on real-time, context-sensitive, interactive constructions of individual experience, the biological always within the social and vice versa, the match with a psychoanalytic process is very strong.

In this book I am attending to the intellectual and theoretical side of the conversations we are embedded in. Caught up, sometimes happily, sometimes unhappily, in this integrative process, I developed and worked on these chapters with a number of colleagues, but most crucially and demandingly with Steve Mitchell. As I let this work brew slowly, incorporating the reactions of and interactions with other people, I always imagined an ample expansion of time for maturation. Thinking about development across several distinct disciplines, translating between different languages and ways of conversing, I was certainly aware of the need to evolve painstakingly what Mitchell did so powerfully and apparently effortlessly: to synthesize.

I would never have imagined that I would write this introduction in the shadow of Steve Mitchell's death. One of the intriguing aspects of his unfolding work is its continuing transformations. An early critic of the "developmental tilt" in certain object relations theories, Mitchell (1984) was concerned about the potential to infantilize adults in treatment if a developmental approach is taken in too reified and concrete a form. Yet in his penultimate book, *Relationality* (Mitchell, 2000), his ongoing interest and immersion in Loewald and his appreciation of the emerging work on attachment made me feel that he was exploring a new interest in processes of development.[13]

ORGANIZATION OF THE BOOK

Because, as I have been suggesting, interdisciplinary cross-talk is difficult, I decided to begin with what is familiar to clinical psychoanalysts, questions of self and identity, and to move from there to problems in metaphors for self and self and other, including the issue of temporal versus spatial forms of metaphor. From there I can lead into chaos theory as a way to figure developmental process. I begin by thinking of the multiplicity of self, an abiding feature of relational theory, and tying this to contemporary models of mind, to ideas of language and to change process. Chapter 1, on multiplicity, takes up one implication of a widening theoretical space for development: that the individual is to be understood not in a summary manner as an unchanging continuity of core self but as a complex site of multiple states in various stages of editing. I think of a multiply configured model of genderednesses, reactive to the multiple dialogues—personal, social, and institutional—in which gender is constituted and maintained. Shifts and transformations in a patient's gender experience are shifts on a continuum of dissociative splits.

In chapter 2 I take up the question of time as a feature of developmental theory. Developmental theories and the research tradition in academic psychology have always had a workmanlike relation to time. Freudian and neo-Freudian theory on sublimation and the retrospective organization and reorganization of symptoms and experiences (*Nachtraglichkeit*) suggest a more complex, less linear idea of time and temporal markers in experience.

Chapter 3 outlines the main aspects and potential power of chaos theory or nonlinear dynamic systems theory as a theory of development. I will draw on empirical studies of motor development to illustrate key concepts of this perspective: nonlinearity, the role of context, disequilibrium and transformation, strange attractors, the central focus on variation, and the function of complexity. I will apply many of these concepts to gender and sexuality in a later chapter (ch. 6).

In the second section of the book, I explore the history of constructing gender in psychoanalysis, the relational turn, and the potential use of chaos theory as a point of view on the construction of forms of identity and of forms of love, gender, and sexuality. In chapter 4 I draw a retelling or narrative line for the study of gender in psychoanalysis. I look first at ideas of gender made on and through the body and then at ideas of gender made through attachment. I am particularly interested in tracing the conflicts around activity and passivity in the construction of femininity and the complex ways terms like femininity and masculinity ebb and flow in our construction of genders. I introduce chaos theory as one interpretive gloss on these materials.

In chapter 5, through an examination of the contradictory phenomena of tomboy identity, I introduce the issues surrounding developmental work and the potential in chaos theory. I see "tomboy" as variously an identity, a self-state, an alter, an aspect of gendered but also ungendered life, and an aspect of sexuality or a defense against it.

In two subsequent chapters I examine chaos theory as a way of modeling gender and sexuality (chs. 6 and 7). In chapter 8 I review the contemporary psychoanalytic literature through the prism of chaos theory. The analytic work stresses intersubjectivity; the interplay of intrapsychic and interpersonal, bisexuality, and multiplicity of genderedness; and the newer voices of transgender and intersex persons as they are entering the dialogues about gender and sexuality.

In the third section, I explore the research and theoretical traditions in developmental psychology that interact fruitfully with relational theory. In chapter 9 I illustrate this perspective with examples drawn from empirical research and clinical work. I look at chaos theory as a lens for early cognition and representation, for motivation and for early dyadic life. In chapter 10 I use an extensive clinical account of relational mourning to illustrate a chaos theory application to development, the dynamic skills theory of Kurt Fischer.

I am betting on the notion that, at this moment in our field, we are in one of those fascinating "edge of chaos" situations Kauffman (1995) has conjured. A system poised to change, to reorganize in unpredictable but patterned ways.

The current discussions on forms of intersubjectivity and social constructionism are illuminating. We have now a continuum of constructionisms—humble, critical, radical, social—all serious attempts to conceptualize the force, the effect, and the epistemological status of the object world, particularly the world of social objects. This is an interesting and, of course, also a poignant moment to present a progress report on relational approaches in psychoanalysis. After nearly 20 years' work, there are two perhaps opposite impulses. On one hand, relational psychoanalysis is carrying increasing amounts of hardware: journals, institutions, and the like, paraphernalia associated with aspirations to be a paradigm. This new and established status brings up all the difficulties of reification, hidden interests, and power. On the other hand, we are currently in a period in psychoanalysis of considerable theoretical fluidity, and it is possible to see the emergence of many intricate connections and conversations with other theoretical traditions.

Ruefully, the social constructionist in me has also to notice that any developmental theory saturated with history and conscious and unconscious relations of power and cultural force is doomed to become obsolete. Theory has a limited shelf life. But developmental theory is a transitional object I still cannot do without. Let me see what I can do with it.

Relational Developmental Theory

CHAPTER 1

❦

Multiple Selves, Multiple Codes

In a growing sector of contemporary psychoanalytic thought, the joints of the mind are located at the borders between different versions of self. Conflict is now envisioned between contrasting and even incompatible self-organizations and self-other relationships.

—Stephen A. Mitchell

*M*itchell (1993) took his inspiration and language for thinking of self and selves from Sullivan.[1] From the beginnings of relational theory, discontinuities and variations in self states and self-organization have been center stage. Following Sullivan (1953, 1964), Mitchell tended to think of the rigidity or singularity of self as a kind of illusion. Looking in a more finely grained way at how people speak, look, move, and interact, one sees subtle as well as gross signs of manifold selves. Multiplicity and the intersubjective construction of self and other go together.

Many relational theorists have been developing a picture of an individual in a relational context as an interweaving of subjectivities and self-states, as containing inevitably multiple centers of narrative gravity played out along multiple complex time lines.[2] In the works of Ogden (1989, 1994), Bromberg (1996a, b, 1999, 2001a), Davies (1996a, b, c, 1998a), Slavin (1996), and Pizer (1998, 2001) and in work on gender and sexuality (Dimen, 1991, 2000; Goldner, 1991; Harris, 1995, 1996b, 2002, 2004; Benjamin, 1997, 2002; Corbett, 2001b, c, d; Dimen and Goldner, 2002) multiplicity is the unremarkable developmental

25

outcome in human subjectivity.[3] These models of psychic functioning are embedded in a very particular kind of developmental theory, with multilinear lines of development and considerable indeterminacy. Mind and evolving mind is perhaps more like Dennett's (1991) description of consciousness as multiple strings of narrative in various stages of editing and interweaving.[4]

Dennett uses the term Cartesian theatre as a metaphor for models of mind that treat mental representation as hierarchically organized and centrally managed. He intends the term somewhat derisively to capture the notion of consciousness as a kind of executive director. He does not think that minds are structured like a top-down corporation, run by some executive, homunculus-like CEO that oversees all activity from a central vantage point. Dennett is critical of a perspective on mind that places the individual somewhere as an audience member reading experiences off some centrally located screen and then applying meaning or significance.

To use a metaphor from the world of espionage, conventional cognitive theory views the mind, or central processor, as the spymaster "running" the hapless agent. Dennett, it seems to me, pulls us away from the notion of mind as solely endogenous and stresses social action and collaborative interpretive practices as the stuff of subjective experience. These generated fictions of who we are and what we mean are as real as it gets. And it's real enough. Moreover, these fictions are both intrapsychically and socially maintained. There is a great deal of interesting clinical writing, across many theoretical perspectives, that takes up the complex, not fully determinable understanding of what each participant in an interaction is contributing. Whose mind is it? Whose feelings are these? We understand that in analytic dyads we hold and hoard our experience. We are subjects and objects. We project, disown, appropriate, or colonize. Analytic work is often a matter of negotiating multiple potential pathways through complex, multiply determined minefields. It is often unclear who in the room and who among the many ghosts that haunt any clinical dyad enters and disturbs and coconstructs the interpersonal field.

In Dennett's (1991) Multiple Drafts model of consciousness, "all varieties of thought or mental activity . . . are accomplished in the brain by parallel, multitrack processes of interpretation and elaboration" (p. 11). Editorial processes overwrite, alter, emend, and endlessly revise the sensory input such that it makes no sense to think of a single narrative or a "canonical" form of experience.

Dennett is a particularly interesting figure for relational psychoanalysis because his philosophy of mind is sharply counter to an idea about consciousness that dominates our field. He is opposed to a view of mind as having intrinsic, nonrelational properties through which external objects, or internal ones and affective or sensory states, are essentially apprehensible. His method, *heterophenomenology,* gives the subject "the constitutive authority to determine what happens in your subjective world, what it is like to be you" (p. 77). This lived, experience-near conception of subjectivity is the ground material of many psychoanalytic conversations. It is a paradigm shift in both philosophy and psychoanalysis in that *causes* of behavior are abandoned in favor of *reasons.*[5]

Dahlbom (1993), a colleague of Dennett's, organized a critical volume of essays assessing Dennett's ideas. In that volume, the essays by Dahlbom and by Rorty are fascinating glosses on Dennett's work. Like all "reading" of texts, they alter the "Dennett" they read. Dahlbom gives Dennett a big shove toward social and interactional theories of mind. Dennett, he argues, "is inviting us to apply 'postfordism' to consciousness, to give up thinking of mind as a centralized bureaucratic organization and begin thinking of it, rather, as a decentralized, flexible, organic organization" (p. 164). In this approach, what Dahlbom calls "postfordism" is a practice in which mind is not seen as a kind of rationalized factory. Mind is material not natural and its materiality includes internal and external phenomena. Materialism, in this context, includes the artificial and the social as aspects of mental and intentional life. In this spirit, Dahlbom brings Dennett closer to a social constructionist position and asks that Dennett appreciate the force of the social field in constituting human intentions.

Within relational psychoanalysis, Bromberg's (1996b, 1998a) writing on multiplicity has some kinship with Dennett's heterophenomenology. Bromberg lives in multiple theoretical spaces or, to follow one of his signature metaphors, stands in the spaces between different realities. His particular integration of the interpersonal and the intrapsychic leads to a clinical focus on the surfaces of language and speech practices, the genres, styles, and idiosyncrasies of human performance as the registration of internal worlds. Actually, the term surface does not capture Bromberg's masterful accounts of the shifting psychic realities that shape the interpersonal relationship, each state expressed and elaborated through its own unique experience-near style of being and talking. Bromberg's clinical attention is often directed to the fascinating shifts (in analysands or analysts) in affective tone. Laughter, silences, heightened moods, uncanny feelings of one kind or another guide Bromberg to salient interpersonal moments where change seems immanent or in progress.

In a similar vein, Spezzano's (1993) work on affect gives interpersonally constructed feeling states and emotional experience a central or "superordinate" position in thinking about individual character and interactional transactions. He writes:

> Narcissistic representational arrangements are multiply determined solutions to universal developmental problems. These are dyadically and triadically conflicted affective-relational problems. Each solution is unique but all involve attempts to deal with the affect of excitement, the inevitability of mutual affective influence and the need to use others to regulate one's affective states [p. 179].

Jody Davies, in a series of theoretical and clinical papers, demonstrates the movement from play to horror, from comedy to tragedy, that comes from both taking and living this perspective on multiplicity. Davies (1996a, b, c, 1998a), extending her work on particular conditions of abuse (Davies and Frawley, 1992) and their sequelae, considers more generally a relational model of mind in which multiplicity is key.

> The internal integrity of experience evolves out of an ever-present, yet constantly changing, system of affective, cognitive, and physiologically based self-experiences in ongoing interactive and dialogic discourse with a host of significant internally and externally derived objects [p. 196].

Her metaphor for these processes is the kaleidoscope, an image that captures the emergent, reconfiguring organizations that draw sometimes on internal states and sometimes on external or interpersonal situations. As in chaos theory, pattern and coherence emerge and self-organize, but processes of fluidity and reorganization are much more center stage. She acknowledges that this process of state shift appears with most ferocity and power in very traumatized persons. Yet the phenomena of shifting self state is ubiquitous. Her clinical examples allow a vision of psychic experience that is both transpersonal and internally fissured. The boundaries of self and other are more fluid than fixed.

The developmental models I use—variations of chaos theory and complexity theory—all privilege *variation* over the statistical concept of central tendency, a focus on the average or mean values of any behavior or experience. Because I am interested in variation within individuals as well as between people, I use the term soft assembly to describe the protean, multipathed but planful and patterned unfolding of experience, such as becoming gendered. Multiplicity offers a certain psychic flexibility that, in relation to shifting objective and social contexts, is distinctly adaptive.

MULTIPLICITY IN A RELATIONAL CONTEXT: DISSOCIATION AND PERFORMANCE

Experiences of multiple patterns of relatedness arise in early dyadic and familial life. Shared minds, from the earliest period, are crucial to the evolution of the individual mind. Multiplicity is part of identity formation over the life span. The picture of early attachment now so elaborately developed at the intersection of clinical psychoanalysis and developmental research gives a picture of early patterned interaction that, in a multimodal, multiply configured way, is quickly and complexly developed. Intricate entrainments (Sander, 1988, 2002), hidden regulators (Hofer, 1984), and RIGS (Stern, 1977, 1985) give us a picture of the developing child as a constructive, transformative participant in complex gestalts that will vary with context, coparticipant, and setting. These patterns are both robust and idiosyncratic. Even as researchers are identifying types of relational patterning—secure, insecure, and disorganized—it is equally important to see both individual and cultural variation (Lyons-Ruth, Cicchetti, and Toth, 1992; Lyons-Ruth, Alpern, and Repacholi, 1993). Attachment is not one modal phenomenon but, rather, is multiply configured, routed through variable pathways, and culture sensitive.

In the research program of Beebe and Jaffe (Beebe et al., 1992, 1997, 2000; Jaffe et al., 2001), subtle but distinct patterns of relatedness and rupture and repair arise in highly context-sensitive forms. Interactions with caretakers, with researchers, and with strangers show variation and continuity. Later in this chapter I illustrate this variability from the world of child language research, where multiple speech codes register the multiplicity of relational patterns within which the child is functioning. The cross-cultural data are equally intriguing (Rothbaum et al., 2000). Cultural valences on dependency and autonomy have some shaping effect on patterns of relatedness. Context is a multilayered

phenomenon that includes parental character, interactional and systems dynamics, the relational landscapes within the family and broader
cultural formations. (See Seligman, 1999a, and his colleagues' intricate
observational work on early relational patterns as the site for dynamic
conscious and unconscious transmissions.) The vicissitudes of
subjectivities emerge within socially and ideologically drenched dyadic
systems moving back and forth between love and hate, empty and full,
melancholic and mourned.

Fischer's (1980; Fischer, Ayoub, et al., 1997; Fischer and Bidell,
1998; Fischer and Watson, 2002) dynamic skills theory is a developmental model that draws on dissociation and multiple pathways. Fischer
sees the development of "skill"[7] (telling stories, constructing a self, solving problems, resolving emotional, relational puzzles à la oedipal
struggles, etc.) within four broad constructs: (1) Development always
has many components. Any skill is uniquely made of multiple aspects
and experiences uniquely coordinated. We might evoke the language
of chaos theory and think of strange attractors as evolving in manifold,
fractal space. (2) Different aspects of any person's mental/social experience exist and coexist in states of mutual regulation, and this coordination is both interindividual, that is, between people, and intrapsychic.
(3) In any individual one would likely see multiple levels of functioning,
and it is certainly a key idea with regard to psychopathology that one
think not of arrest or fixation or immaturity but of unique configurations. Dissociation and the organization of fragmented internal worlds
is a skill, a survival skill—and what a novel intervention into the conventional ideas of psychopathology this is. (4) Finally, any developmental process is both socially mediated and context sensitive.

Cultural theorists like Butler (1997a, b, c) speak a very different
language but are addressing many of the problems that compel
developmentalists like Fischer as well as relational psychoanalysts.
Subjectivities are founded on various turns, Butler argues. "Turns" here
seems to be a multidirectional process of splitting. There is the emerging into awareness of self-reflection, what Fonagy and Target (1996,
1997) now term "the interpersonal interpretive mechanism," a capacity
to turn on one's own mind that is inextricably linked to the social practices of mentalization of others that the child is embedded in.
Mentalization of the child can shade subtly or dramatically into processes of regulation. The origins of self-regulation can lie in interactions
of harsh submission and shaming or in interactions of attunement and
containment.

This is one way to think about a process that has interested Butler (2000a), the appearance of internalized voices of shame, abjection, and self-regulation. She is also interested in what we could term the turn of the subject toward the law or the state, a turn toward some other that mirrors and reflects prospects for identity and development. We can also see a multiplicity of mental functions along the lines of Benjamin's (2000a, 2002) ideas of thirdness.[8] For Butler (2000a), these turns are inflected through many longstanding projects in philosophy of mind. From a relational perspective, she is describing a multidimensional process in which mind/body/psyche is the emergent outcome of multiple, dynamic contacts with other minds, general and specific, and with emerging fractionated aspects of our own minds.

Dissociation

Almost all relational theorists draw on some concept of dissociation to describe multiplicities of experience and self-state at intrapsychic as well as interpersonal levels. I am considering dissociation more particularly at a phenomenological level. That is, I am speculating about the experience of multiple modes of knowing, of the paradoxical experience of knowing, and not knowing, and of the subjective sense of having a doubled or fragmented vision. Rivera (1989) has noted that in considering traumatic experience the problem is less in the multiplicity of experience than in the degree of disconnection. Multiple self-states may coexist happily or unhappily, subtly or dramatically. Shifts in awareness and consciousness may seem abrupt or fluid, terrifying or ecstatic, comfortable or anxiety riddled.

Slavin and Kriegman (1992) consider the adaptive use of shifting self-states wherein splits are not simply trauma driven events but system characteristics. Those authors see separateness and schisms in the self as adaptive ways to prevent a total immersion in context or relational dyadic experience. Splitting allows an opening, a space for self-reflection and a necessary space for some sense of subjective agency. But what internally or interpersonally triggers shifting states? Defensive dissociation seems one mechanism, but equally a sense of trust and playfulness may occasion an experience of being between spaces, of feeling both multiplicity and authenticity.

Dee is my patient in a long-term psychotherapy in which, over time, we have developed two intertwining storylines. We live out variations of the terrifying disruptions in her early life. But, antiphonally with these processes of rupture, confusion, and alienation, there has always been a deep registration of an abiding, often wordless attachment that she and I feel together. This parallel tracking of multiple experiences—continuity and rupture—can be reproduced in each session by her experience of familiarity and unfamiliarity on arrival. Object constancy coheres and fails. We have learned over time to be patient when sessions begin and Dee feels numb and cotton headed. Rageful, angry feelings are often produced in the mimetic voice of others she is "quoting." A mind in lockdown, a dead face will sometimes open up and function if we can sit together until some emotion emerges for me.

But sometimes we are at a loss to know what meaning system, what narrative world we could be tracking. She speaks cynically of the frustration of handling and reacting to an aging friend. She brings me a tape of a recent phone call, and as she and I listen to the crumbling, shaky voice, I start to weep. I have my own reasons, of course. Dee is upset and immediately tearful too. We have the task of holding the archaic story of a loving, passionate early tie lost to illness, too much disruption, and many later mismatches. Memories of love, very early, procedurally remembered schemes, coincide with later experiences of alienation and distrust. They all belong in this mix that comes into being sometimes in one of us, sometimes transpersonally.

During one session, Dee begins to recount some experiences at a recent medical visit. She speaks in broken, halting syntax. She seems scarcely a competent speaker of English, let alone someone capable of ordering her thoughts. Her accounts of her own body experience are laden with disgust and anguish. Somewhat later in the session she details an experience at work when she had to manage rather subtle interactions among coworkers. She was able to notice her reactions, the process between herself and others. All this was conveyed to me with nuance and clarity. Her speech flowed smoothly. Reflective functioning rather dramatically comes online. We noticed this doubled state together. I, the listener, am often scaffolding her experiences from an only partially shared higher ground of collaboration and connection.

Knowing something, or having a representation or schema of knowledge, is not an all-or-nothing-matter. The concept of partial knowing, of representations as distributed and integrated across multiple systems, means that experiences can be known in many distinct ways. Within one framework, you know something; in another you do not. Nonlinear processing has properties that produce "subthreshold knowledge" (Elman et al., 1997, p. 44) and therefore potentially radical discontinuities in behavior and experience.

Representations of experience are distributed along multiple sites within a complex system in which there may be shared sites for distinct representations and different levels of integration for single experiences. Representations of experience might be available or unavailable under particular conditions, and so the capacity for self-reflection would fluctuate and change, depending on intrapsychic and interpersonal contexts. There is, therefore, a neural parallel for the kind of variegated, fragmented experiences of consciousness and awareness that is described clinically and personally in phenomenologically salient language.

Trauma theorists have been saying this all along, citing work on the context dependency of memory and on the impact of dissociative states on a sense of ongoingness or wholeness in an individual (van der Kolk, 1995, 1996). Would not affective states and anxiety play a role in how representations are organized and activated? The phenomenological experience of feeling dissociated is often an odd, doubled state in which you feel that you simultaneously know and do not know. You feel that something in your reflective capacities is disrupted. A divided experience of watching yourself act, think, or move is an oft-described state of reaction to great danger or difficulty. It is just this kind of split consciousness and shifting representational status that chaos theory and nonlinear dynamic systems theory models and psychoanalysis are particularly good at describing in vivo.

Sandy, unlike Dee, usually feels herself to be having an ongoing coherent experience in her sessions. But there are dramatic, not predictable, always unsettling glitches in her functioning and our process. Sandy's progress in analysis and her relation to her work and to others is susceptible to unexpected and dramatic flights. We had been working for some time on her relationship to the art she makes. We had developed a set of metaphors for this relationship. She neglected, abused, and abandoned her art. Rather than think just in the language of writer's block or artistic paralysis, we found a more active language of damage and punishment. Sandy could report and trace experiences of delight and confidence followed by disorganization and sleep states. She would fall into a kind of amnesia in which she forgot what she cared about, what she had done in the past, what had mattered to her. After a session of considerable liveliness and processing, Sandy would come back with a stony face and absolutely dead eyes to tell me she was a hopeless case.

Now she details a very typical scene. A boss has asked her to help him with something that is, strictly speaking, not appropriate to her situation. She cannot say no, for fear of hurting him and for fear of retaliation. As she describes the experience of sitting side by side at work with this person, I feel simultaneously that she could be describing a scene from *Nosferatu*, where the vampire pulls every ounce of will and energy out of the victim. I feel myself sinking, too; so, of course Sandy is almost simultaneously victim and vampire. Her face is closed and scrunched up like a little fist. Somewhere within the session we talk about her need to continue the hopeless task of caring for broken others, and I ask if that has been played out between us. Do I have to learn again that nothing I do with her, nothing we do together, matters? This makes her tearful and worried. It would be terrible to hurt and deplete me.

Yet this pattern of hopes and dashed hopes has a frightening tenacity. She and I can also stand from time to time on high ground and reflect on why at crucial moments when she might preserve herself, her work, her sense of integrity, she seems to, in her words, "go off-screen." These self-states—mesmerized possession, frozen hopelessness, delighted playfulness, attuned concern—live in one-person and two-person schemes. Sandy and I fall into various performances, and find moments of reflection and respite.

Performance

A tricky question regarding multiplicity is authenticity. Here is a paradox: Psychoanalytic theory places a great premium on "realness," on true self as states of very basic comfort and security for a child. Alien selves (Fonagy, 2001; Britton, 1995, 1999), or false selves (Winnicott, 1971) are the outcome of interpersonal processes of neglect, gross distortion, and parental projection that cannibalizes the child's mind and being. On the other hand, without imaginative mentalization and parental fantasy, we understand how compromised the child's imaginative, reflective potential is. And the developmental picture shows an early appearance of protoforms of fantasy and pretend and an emergent capacity in children through toddlerhood for the appreciation of pretend. At what point in the spectrum of interactions does imaginative mentalization turn into coercion?

I find it useful to think in the language of chaos theory and nonlinear dynamic systems to imagine some unpredictable organizing and self-organizing experiences that can emerge only when the context becomes propitious, as in a good treatment. A self or selves emerge to organize shattered processes and affect states into new forms. The alter is both mnemonic, that is, from the past, and fantastical, that is, drawn from the imaginary potential world, a hoped-for world that must also be mourned. Alters are, like genders, necessary fictions, enactments, but not the posturing false-self role of a hired actor. Rather, alters draw on our deep capacities as improvisers, whose performances depend on authentic, deeply felt affective capacities.

Gender is often deeply and idiosyncratically involved in these hot spots of contested authenticity. Phenomena like gender built on particular body-based psychic states are crucial points for intergenerational transfer of anxiety or affective charge. Genderedness is one particularly acute register of local trauma and of the more broadscaled traumas of social and historical change. Developmentally and historically, gendered states and selves can come to function like a magnet, a strange attractor to manage, express, and organize relational transactions, meanings, trauma, and defense against trauma.[9] Gendered selves thus often bear the markings of complex interpersonal business. Gender is a particularly vulnerable and volatile carrier of many self-state experiences, both those that are noxious and those that are idealized. Gender can feel from inside and look from outside like a fortress, a rigid armor. Gender can feel fully authentic and fully inhabited or seem to be an alien falsehood, a caricature, a parody. One's gender or genders can feel porous or solid, reified or flexible.

Even when some dissociative states are involuntary reactions to trauma or its reenactment or to self-regulation, the performative aspects may not be altogether absent. I was led by a patient's associations to an extraordinary passage in Faulkner's (1931) novel *Sanctuary* where Temple Drake lies in the barn, awaiting the arrival of Popeye and knowing she will be raped. She drifts off into a dissociated dream state in which she plays with the image of herself as a boy and Popeye's surprise when he discovers this. Several clinical experiences with a tomboy state in certain girls has made me think that, for some women, the boy persona is an alternative to remembering, erasing the dangerous experience of femininity. Body ego, the embodied state, one's gesture, one's mimetic activities, operate as a background condition for seeing and being seen (Harris, 1996a, 1998a). One's body ego, including the gendered body, becomes a condition for perception and engagement. Shifting multiple identities including embodied identities, are thus one mechanism for managing interpersonal space and also for managing memory and affect.[10]

Graham Bass (2002) has described a clinical encounter with a patient whose self-states shifted along dimensions of body, gender, and age. Is the analyst a passive witness, a voyeur even? Bass describes himself sometimes as witness and sometimes as cocreator. Sometimes gender as an aspect of the patient's alters seems to be a useful fiction and sometimes a life- or death-dealing force. How do we hold these different possibilities together?

An alter coheres self-states in a meaning-making narrative, often with a distinct time line and chronology. As in any coherent structure, these selves may be transient or permanent, stable or evanescent, rigid or flexible. These are the islands of subjectivity that I believe are not uniquely the outcome of traumatic and pathological experiences but, in more coherable forms, arise in any subject. Culture theorists speak of multiple subject positions. Reviewing work on memory in relation to disavowed memory of abuse and trauma, I found in the contemporary cognitive literature evidence for the organization of memory in a constellation that includes both an affect state and a self-experience (Harris, 1995). Agency or authorship may operate like a nugget around which memory and feeling can cohere.[11]

Is an alter a kind of museum relic, dusty, kept hidden and then brought out for exhibition? Is this early self state historical truth or narrative truth? In what way might we be speaking of agency? I think we have to hold to the paradox of authentic/performed. Old disavowed states, imaginative fantasies, and modes of being and speaking appear in a newly found amalgam. Alters contain both a kind of carbon dating of the past, those traumatic elements never forgotten (Yovell, 2000) and also new creations, dramatized rogue subjectivities (Grotstein, 1999).

One problem in considering the question of multiple self-states and the related questions of agency and authenticity is that we have saddled ourselves with a metapsychology that is both overly moralizing and unrealistically Cartesian. Winnicott's (1960) term the "false self," although it captures the adaptive compliance in being of object use to another, commits us still to a split between the socially emergent and the personally authentic, a split that the constructivist perspective seeks to heal and critique. The idea that one "performs" gender does not mean that gendered life is false, even if constructed (Goldner, 2003). Among the old-fashioned ideas we might need to give up are outmoded models of acting and performance. If we enact or perform gender, or genders, if these are self-states that can shift and change, then we probably need to think of acting gender as a Method actor's performance: credible and realistic and authentic.

Something like this kind of theory of acting and performance is embedded in all theories of transference. It seems to me that Loewald (1980) had a performance theory of technique:

> The psychoanalytic situation and process involves a re-enactment, a dramatization of aspects of the patient's psychic life, created and staged in conjunction with and directed by, the analyst. . . . Seen in this light, psychoanalysis shared important features with dramatic art. Aristotle defined tragedy as 'the imitation of action in the form of action' [p. 353].

This aspect of speech as performative is one of the points Bakhtin (1986) intended by his idea of envoicing, or the polylogue of all speakers. To think about performance, authenticity, and multiple self-states, let us turn to the question of speech more directly.

SPEECH REGISTERS, LANGUAGE, AND MULTIPLICITY: BAKHTIN AND VYGOTSKY

Relational psychoanalysts have produced a capacious account of psychic states and the normal or usual multiplicity of self-states in psychic functioning. Surprisingly often, analysts note a shift in state signaled by a shift in speech register. It is often very productive in a session to ask oneself, Who is speaking? Who is being spoken to?[12]

In this section I call on work in child language, the linguistic theories, and their application in Bakhtin (1968, 1981, 1986) and in the seminal ideas of Vygotsky (1962, 1978) to explore these phenomena: multiplicity in speech registers as an unfolding developing process. Multiplicity is grounded in preverbal constellations and takes on unique and powerful elaborations as language comes online. With the capacity to use language to express and hold multiplicity, psychic life takes on even more deeply its mesh of endogenous and historic/social elements.

The power of an analyst's attunement to speech appears in Ferenczi's (1931) clinical paper on seeing the child within the adult in treatment, a paper firmly committed to a concept of multiplicity. Ferenczi was an astute listener to speech styles, and in an early paper on semiotic styles he argued for the specificity of speech registers as a guide to both the shifting state of the speaker and the affective tension in the experience (Ferenczi, 1911, 1931, discussed in Harris and Aron, 1997). Ferenczi (1931) noted a shift in language use with a patient at a certain moment within a regressed state. The adult male patient saw and responded to Ferenczi as a grandfather. Ferenczi reported that he met and matched the patient's style of talk. In psycholinguistic terms, the code switched: "I said nothing to him for the moment about transferences, etc, but retorted in a similar whisper: 'Well, but what makes you think so?'" (p. 129). And in a footnote the translator notes that both the patient and the analyst have shifted pronouns from *Sie* to the more intimate and familiar *du*.

My interest in the mother-child narrative as a fusion of emotional, social, and cognitive projects led me to work on an integration of Winnicottian object relations theory with the linguistics of Michael Halliday, Vygotsky, Trevarthan, and Bakhtin (see Harris, 1992). Because these linguists embedded speaking in processes of thought and social life, it was possible to reintroduce the question of development into studies of language acquisition. These theorists are attentive to a duality. We acquire language and language acquires us. We are inserted into and at the same time we obtain some command over the experience of speech. But there is no seamless fit between speech and self, text and subjectivity. The relation of speaking and being, including being a particular gender, is one of excess and gaps.

Vygotsky's (1962, 1978) interest in the intersect of speech and thinking focused on what we would call metacognition, a form of knowing he called co-knowing, and a form of consciousness and self-consciousness he thought of as a multiply configured system. Reflective functioning was a very particular capacity, derived from the social experience of being known, spoken to, thought about. Metaconsciousness would be both representational and instrumental, part of a system of action and regulation.

Frawley (1997), discussing Vygotsky's model of mind, refers to levels of subjectivity: unconscious, conscious, and metaconscious, with the social dimension shaping the latter two forms. The Vygotskian self is therefore private and public, social and personal, conscious and unconscious. A Vygotskian child emerges with an intentional or aspectual self, a formation born of social relations and what I think analysts would term intersubjectivity.[13]

From developmental psycholinguistics we know that speakers shift both dramatically and subtly in and out of different linguistic codes.

Rosemary Perez Foster (1995) has been describing the experience of bilingual treatment, the switching of languages and the complex psychic processes available or unavailable in this move. That is simply the most extreme code switching; even within one language, all speakers change the style or genre of their speech. The best-documented codes have been the study of what is called the baby register, that is, the way adults talk to children. It turns out that this shifting register—its tempo, its intonation patterns, its pragmatic features—are used intuitively by all speakers (Snow and Ferguson, 1977). Even older children shift register when speaking to younger children.

This work has implications for analytic dialogue (Massey, 1996). Just as a parent or older child intuits or construes or constructs the state of the child listener and what the child can absorb and process, this sort of imaginative construction of the other occurs within analytic spaces as well. Some code switching may be an unconscious response to imagined or perceived states in the other person, whether analyst or patient. The code switch signals the state shift.

Bakhtin's (1981, 1986) interest, which is so useful for psychoanalysis, was to consider speech utterances embedded in dialogue and functioning at the intersect of person and other, person and culture. Oral speech genres, or types, Bakhtin felt, are beyond taxonomy and highly diverse. They are carried in accent, rhetorical style, and the intersect of pragmatics and syntactic form, intonation, and rhythmicity—in short, all the sensuous materiality in signs.

In several of the clinical experiences Bromberg (1994, 1998a) describes, laughter is one hinge for shifting from one state to another. Laughter is an interesting process to think about. In Bakhtin's (1968) terms, laughter—the comic as genre—is part of a new and powerful shift in cultural terms from the epic to the novel, a shift that reflects a change in the experiences of subjectivity and identification in literary texts. Laughter, Bakhtin suggests, is one of those experiences that disrupts hierarchy and makes for more intense and closer contact. Laughter invites exploration and play, and, in the suspended feeling of unrealness and theatricality, anxiety and fearfulness may feel more manageable.

In sessions, laughter, singly or shared, is perhaps a moment of safe, shared playful space in which something new can happen. A patient carried as a precious memory the experience of being read to by her father. As he read the saga of Piglet and Pooh carried away on a rushing river, father and child were carried on a stream of shared laughter, playful, wild, rhythmic. Perhaps the spoken story is a form in which the primary process of laughter and love was supported. On the other hand there are many regrettable clinical moments when a mistimed joke or laughter can be cruel and humiliating, when it is a speech genre of crudeness or of delicacy.

Bakhtin's (1981, 1986) perhaps most powerful ideas have to do with the polyglot quality of all speech experiences.[14] Any speaker—and we have seen that even very young children operate in multiple genres and registers—deploys a range of modes of speech tailored to context and to function. Dennie Wolf (1990), following children's unfolding narrative voices, noted that from early conversation there is a heterogeneity to a child's speech, even in proto forms. Children employ code and voice shifts, mimetically reproduce styles of talk they are exposed to, and speak as another. Wolf's work, replete with rich examples of multivoicedness in children under four, connects this speech skill, pragmatics one might say, to the emotional and social task of becoming a person. Becoming a person thus turns out to be a matter of becoming a fluidly multiply and distinctly configured set of persons.

RUDIMENTARY MULTIPLE SELF-STATES EMERGING FROM PARTICULAR CONDITIONS AND PATTERNS OF BEING (SOCIAL AND INDIVIDUAL)

Code switching arises in plenty of internal dialogues. I am often surprised at how frequently these shifting states have a call-and-answer format. There are temporal and dialogical rhythms. A woman trying to describe some difficulties in her work reported a sequence of instances when she went to buy something she needed for a project. She felt enlivened and enthusiastic in this activity but, in her words, had done herself in "by the time she gets to Starbucks." Tracing out the minute-by-minute internal transactions, we could hear two voices, but two voices in a call-and-response dialogue. "You selfish greedy thing. How could you?" "But I need this. It's not for me. It's for my work." She replays this nasty duet. There is an enthusiast who happily collected the material for her work and there is a sour, bitter one who tore the enthusiast to shreds for the various crimes of greed, excitement, and agency. Shifting self-states, to be sure, but also dialogic partners whose historic routes were in a highly charged, sad mother–daughter duet.

In the clinical duet, the woman alternated between, in one scenario, living out this dynamic, trying to breathe life into me, and worrying about a counterattack if she developed vitality on her own behalf. Loewald (1962c, 1972) beautifully captured this sense of transference enactments as a strange "near future" event. A nuanced insight he developed is that life from the past (transference) is lived as an about-to-be future, an impending experience due soon to arrive and wreak damage.

Bakhtin's (1981) linguistics are irreducibly intersubjective. There is always a "listener" and an "addressee" in speech, and it might be that changing speakers is one of the boundaries of an utterance. But the other to whom we speak is fictional in many ways—the one we imagine, the one we wish for. It may be quite illusory to focus on change of speaker as a genuinely stable boundary.

We have experiences of this paradox in analyses. In transference you "speak" to another in the analyst, a "fictional" other you have constructed. This "fiction" may capture many aspects of the analyst and so we think that in speaking we co-construct these identities or subject positions. In many analytic discourses the boundaries between speakers can be experienced as permeable, in a delightful or in a terrifying way. "Empathic understanding" can feel like an assault to a patient: the fit in meaning required for dialogue may be excrutiatingly tight, or it may loosen and allow for interpretive space. There will be varying degrees of tolerance for meaning indeterminancy. Since our speech is often filled with the words of others, speech can seem like a permeable or material skin, a site of merger, that may feel dangerous or desirable.

Bakhtin (1986) noted that often, when one takes in the speech of another, it is set off with ironic tones. It is as though through the other's speech a form of internalization were occurring, and we may attempt to keep the other at the boundary, not fully taken in. Bakhtin was describing the different ways that speech can support or collapse the symbolic register. This perspective embeds the transmission of ideas, propositional thought, and interpretations in a stream of utterances that may or may not be marked psychically as separate and distinct parts of separate body–minds.

Even the most gifted analysts probably practice in mixed dialects, expressing distinct states of being and feeling in interaction. Bakhtin (1981) saw all utterances as taking shape and meaning in a dialogic and communal situation. A single speaker, marking his discourse uniquely, producing a kind of signature, is also masquerading in the words and signifiers of others, other cultures, other speech genres. All speak in distinct and multiple speech registers or genres, and even then there is no certain distinction between what any signifier, however social, means to speaker and listener.

This view of the inherent conflict in speech use and meaning making makes the exchange of words in analysis a site of change in yet another way. Bakhtin saw in this process of decoding conflictual meanings as a possibility for apprehending difference and alterity. It is interesting that the Lacanian-inflected cultural theorists who draw on this idea stress the despair and emptiness at the alienated heart of identity, whereas Bakhtin, more in the direction of Levinas (Levinas and Lingis, 1974; Hand, 1989), saw the possibility of genuine respect for otherness in this encounter.

MULTIPLICITY AND TRANSFORMATION

If multiplicity is normative in identity and central to the process of developmental change, a number of hypotheses follow. Mutative action emerges in the spaces. Shifting self-states occasion potential disequilibrium. Multiplicity is at the edge of chaos.

In Melvin Feffer's (1983, 1988, 1999) theoretical account of cognitive reorganization and transformation, a child must have experiences that oscillate between polar schemes through which an experience of the world or of others is organized.[15] This cognitive transformation is also well described in the work on embodied mind and enactment by Varela, Thompson, and Rosch (1997). Their central preoccupation is with what they term a middle view, that is, a middle ground between inner and outer, between objectivism and subjectivism. Their view keeps clear that the mind is embodied, that the mind and self can never be fully separate from the world, and yet discontinuity of world and reflection also thrives. Like the work of Bromberg and Feffer, their project is an attempt to heal the Cartesian split between the subject and object of knowing while leaving space for conflict and mutation out of conflict.

Psychoanalytic work provides many distinct and important examples of this oscillating experience out of which change and new forms of knowing and experiencing arise. Moreover, there is a rich body of theory, across many orientations, about the conditions in which conflict can lead to knowing, not fragmentation. Feeling states, anxieties, experiences of safety or danger, conditions and contexts in relationships—all present possibilities for psychic change organized along these principles. Thelen (1986, 1995; Thelen and Smith, 1994) uses chaos theory or, in her preferred term, nonlinear dynamic systems theory. She models development not as a concrete, preformed ladder over which an individual scrambles, but as a set of pathways, each of whose particular form and achievements are the outcome of emergent interactive process, not hardwiring. The implications of this model of emergent functions for general psychoanalytic theories of development and the microdevelopmental theories—that is, theories of what happens in the room in the course of treatment—are provocative. Bromberg (1996b) describes microdevelopmental processes in a sequence of hours or minutes within an analysis. Betty Joseph (1989, 1997) sees change not as an achievement but as a process organized through "constant minute shifts" in the session. These ideas are an encouragement to abandon the moralizing pressure in our work for psychic change. We could also abandon the tendency to see change mapped simply against linear growth with preformed or predetermined models of outcome.

Small shifts in consciousness or experience can have subtle or massive implications for reorganization, which is variously stable or unstable. Thelen and Smith (1994) suggest that we think of subjective states in interpersonal experience as a kind of "softly assembled" set of behavioral attractors, stable or unstable depending on the task and the environment and forming complex multidimensional systems of a particular task in a particular context. Variability is the expected condition, not the site for pathology. Craig Piers (2000) argues that pathology, within the chaos theory model, is, in fact, defined by rigidity. A system, such as a biological system like the heart, that functions with a rigid, invariable pattern, is often a morbid system. So pathology switches valences, in a sense taking up residence in a singlemindedness and rigidity of pattern, not in error signals. A little noise within a system is apparently healthy.

Conceptualizing change and new experience is one of the most daunting challenges for a developmental theory in which radical constructivism is a guiding principle. If a child's activity (mental and sensorimotor) is the source of knowledge, how is new knowledge that is not predictively set up or blueprinted noticed? Feffer's (1999) analysis of this process is reprised in contemporary connectionist modeling and chaos theory, of which nonlinear processing is a central feature. Using a classical experimental study from Piaget, the conservation of volume, Feffer describes a child who cannot conserve, who does not recognize that the sausage-shaped clay refashioned as a ball is the same clay. Stuck in this nonconserving state, the child has constructed two paradoxical and contradictory realities. The clay is the same clay when the shape changes; and the clay changes when the shape changes. Immutability and discontinuity remain as polar, oscillating constructions.

The extending and consolidation of these polar schemes, like container–contained, victim–abuser—what Feffer terms "quantitative consolidating differentiation"—eventually become regular and patterned enough such that a new qualitative reorganization becomes imaginable. There is a transitional period between the stage when the child is nonconserving (seeing the object as changing whenever the shape is changed) and the stage when the child is conserving (seeing the object as unchanged in volume when the shape changes). This transitional experience is one that clinicians can resonate to when a patient seems to function on two distinct parallel tracks. Often the analyst is experienced as both an old and a new object. In my earlier vignette, Dee and I live out these kinds of contradictory experiences. I am continuous and reliably familiar for her. And on the other hand, I am an unstable object. Each new entry into the room, each new meeting can seem to her unsettling and unexpected. There is object constancy and yet often there is not. When we can be together on the higher ground of shared reflection about our process, these oscillating distinct processes reorganize into a more comprehensible gestalt of both/and not either/or. The shifts in states between gender-polarized complementarites and states of subject-object mutual recognition (Benjamin, 1995) in periods of transition constitute a comparable process.

The connectionist position considers that all that is needed is an expanding short-term memory capacity for conflict and reorganization to be managed in a new organization. In a psychoanalytic model we would add the requirements of conditions of safety and affective harmony as the inevitable accompaniments of such emergent reorganization. This seems another instance when a dialogue across disciplines would be extremely fruitful.

In modeling change, the connectionists and proponents of Thelen and Smith's (1994) synergetics provide a number of distinct trajectories. Linear change, nonlinear change, models that describe asymmetry, and models in which change can temporarily or permanently reverse will all occur. What is experienced as a burst of growth may be a slowly emergent process experienced with a sense of illusory suddenness.

The unpredictability of nonlinear change, like the difficulties in specifying the causes of some novel or emergent event in a session or in a patient's ongoing experience, may require a new way of writing and thinking about mutative action in psychoanalysis. A sudden shift in experience, a dramatic change in the patient or in the analytic relationship, may signal that the system is disequilibrating and altering in that moment. Or it may only summarize and reflect slow changes ongoing for some time. The "new" event in the consulting room, involving an individual or a dyad, may be more like a screen memory than a site of change. The implications of this, I think, are that we must use caution in claiming a mutative effect of either the dramatic enactments or the powerful resonant interpretations.

Thelen's (Thelen and Smith, 1994) model of change predicts that a perturbation in the system provokes reorganization and repatterning. The polarities of unity and separateness, of multiple and shifting self-states, have themselves to be embedded in a complex context, in a relational matrix, or in a set of matrices. These polarities live and move and function in a set of social experiences. All self-states contain and express a set of object relationships. Shifts in self-state alter and reconfigure the internal landscape and world of object ties. These shifts in memory and internal world arise from what Fairbairn (1952) conceived as a person's loyalty to bad objects, the dilemma of many patients who experience any movement away from a deeply grooved self-state as a dangerous separation from those others to whom that self seemed attached.

Many repetitions of change, followed by a return to both an old state and an old object tie, can eventually lead to more tolerance for the doubleness of experience, the fort/da of self-states in the service of losing and finding all the key figures in the internal world. These conflicting self-experiences brought into sustained awareness are thus the source of transformation. The analytic work sustains experience within the spaces, between the self-states, so that conflict can come into awareness.

This model of change and reorganization based on emergent experience of multiplicities of self seems to me a helpful way to think about transference, or, more exactly, the analyst's countertransferential apprehension of the patient's transference. The analyst must be performing identity in the context of shifting self-states to be able to act in the transference. He or she often lends the full range of the analytic instrument to the evoked scenes played out in the consulting room with relatively little overlap into the rest of the day. And, for an analyst, the shifting countertransference experiences can be striking within hours let alone throughout a day.

Analytic work often seems a kind of ongoing altered state or states, a kind of deep meditative practice embedded in powerful scenes and performances. In fact, the analyst probably spends considerable time in a kind of doubled state of awareness, a suspended disbelief (Mannoni, 1980). Mimesis, the playing out of experience in an emotionally truthful way, is a requirement of transference held in suspension and tension with a more strategic, objectifying experience of self and other. This is a more fleshed out rendition of Loewald's (1975) performance theory of therapeutic action, the artistry in the work. Like any artist in any medium, an analyst must be lost in the material and be in control of it. This is what makes analysis so compelling and so dangerous.

Both transference and countertransference are always a doubled self-state, a partial knowing. In analysis it is the polar scheme of the constructed object (the analyst) that does or does not react as one expects. In the analytic dyad, the procedural organization, or security operation, works and fails to work at the same time. Over time, as this polar scheme, which is actually a double set of role/reciprocals, consolidates, the possibility for a new organization appears.

Fonagy and Target's (1997) model of change process follows a comparable developmental trajectory. When an analyst can contain evacuated, unprocessable elements of thought and address the meaning of these experiences for and with the patient, an experience of partially shared minds begins in the dyad. In many striking clinical examples, Fonagy and Target demonstrate how intolerable this is for many patients. Mind is better fragmented than synthesized. The intersubjective context begins to provide conditions for the patient to process thoughts differently. Psychic change is less about the contents of mind than about functional organizational capacities. Changes are procedural. The trajectory Fonagy and Target are outlining proceeds toward held, flexible multiplicities, with hierarchies and with contradictions. This kind of processing is the outcome of an experience of a functioning other-mind sharing experience. Benjamin and Aron (1999) describe this process as thirdness.

Fonagy and Target (1997) illustrate the use of shifts in mental states as the site of mutative work in analysis. They follow a patient–analyst dyad through a repetitive oscillating pattern. In a clinical vignette in which analyst and child play out a scene in a father–daughter game, the playfulness of the "pretense" allows emotional freedom. Their exuberant attachment dramatically collapses when the "play" is pierced by the analyst's speaking in a different register and of a different interpersonal scheme. The doubleness of the experience, the genuineness of play, and the starkness of loss is intolerable as a gestalt. The pattern decomposes to two irreconcilable scenes. The painstaking work of analysis is to gain the emotional fortitude to keep in mind such oppositional understandings and experiences.

Oedipal and postoedipal are perhaps early and repeated concentrations of multiplicity. From a number of relational writers—Benjamin (1990, 2002a), Bassin (2002), Cooper (2003), and Davies (2003a, b)—and from Fogel (1998), holding a more classical position, there is a renewed focus on oedipality. From the Kleinian tradition, the doubleness in oedipal situations is also explored. Ron Britton's (1992) account of the shift from paranoid/schizoid to the depressive position in the oedipal phase is a powerful example. The child's rival in one construction is the beloved in another. Another aspect of analytic work consists of enabling the analysand to bear knowing this doubleness and to organize the separated constructions as simultaneously immutable and discontinuous. Bearing this knowledge of this intertwining of love and hate in relation to significant others is always an emotional as much as a cognitive condition. We could extend this to many dyadic experiences: the one you love and who loves you destroys you by disappearing. The container figure also refuses projections and leaves you isolated.[16]

CONCLUSIONS

The concept of a core or unitary self may be our field's teddy bear, our transitional object. Our fluidity and uncertainty, the movement within and between persons, is often difficult to sustain. The more chaotic and dissociated the self-states we are asked to embrace and live, the greater the drive for certainty and conviction. So much theorizing and so much technical procedure work off deterministic models. Since even hermeneutic and social constructivist models hold out the hope for increased coherence and consolidation as the aim of treatment, it is not without anxiety that one imagines a form of psychoanalytic theory in which questions are asked, more narratives worked and reworked, and determinacy remains unresolved.

Fairfield (2000, 2001) suggests we are functioning in various degrees of hybrid, multimodal states. I think so. Gender, as I suggest, comes in traditional, enlightenment, modernist, and perhaps postmodern forms. I often feel that we practice Enlightenment and think postmodern. Fairfield has created postmodern analysis as a kind of horizon effect with immediate, on-site consequences to undermine our sense of mastery or omnipotence. My holy grail is pragmatics-driven conversation and dialogue.

Timelines and Temporalities

Dread is just memory in the future tense.
—D. W. Winnicott

For Loewald, feelings of past, present, and future are constructions that create a sense of before, now and after, and provide answers to the questions, What happened? What is happening? What will happen? Each of the concepts—past, present and future—has no meaning in itself. Past in relation to what? Present in relation to what? They imply each other, and create a subjective sense of connection, a narrative scaffolding for organizing experiences.
—Stephen A. Mitchell

Memory, as recollection for instance, manifests psychic time as activity; it makes the past present. Anticipation makes the future present. When we speak of object presentation, drive representation, a concept of time is implied in which 'present' is understood as an active process—to present something.
—Hans Loewald

Thrown into being-towards-death, Dasein initially and for the most part flees from this more or less explicitly revealed thrownness. The present arises from its authentic future and having been, so that it lets Da-sein come to authentic existence only by taking a detour through that present.
—Martin Heidegger

Only the future, not the past is packed into the present.
Without the embeddedness in context and history that
feedback accomplishes in open systems, there is an
arrow of time but no history.
                                        —Alicia Juarrero

Given an emergent event, its relation to antecedent
processes become conditions or causes. Such a situation
is a present. It marks out and in a sense selects what has
made its peculiarity possible. It creates with its unique-
ness a past and a future. As soon as we view it, it
becomes a history and a prophecy.
                                        —George Herbert Mead

*I*n this chapter I explore the complex ways that time and temporality function in relation to distinct and multiple self-states and to
development. I connect multiplicity to heterochronicity, the experience of variable, multiple, distinct experiences of being in time and
being ongoing. I am intending to flip the pattern, making, as in an
Escher engraving, the unremarkable remarkable, making time the variable not the norm. Here temporality is the main event in focus, not the
backdrop. When time is liberated, as it were, from its casing as a linear
frame, complexity in intrapsychic and interpersonal life opens up.

I find myself drawn to one of the projects Loewald (1972) identified: the power of time to structure psychic life. The model of shifting
and multiple self-states is enhanced by expanding our metaphors, en-
twining metaphors of space with metaphors of temporality. Mitchell
(2000) cast the evolution of his thinking about coconstructed subjectivities
as a shift from spatial to temporal metaphors: "Thus, internal object
relations, the internalized interactions with others that are the lattice-
work of mind, are bound together in time. Time is the basic fabric of
the psyche" (p. 45).

Perceiving and apprehending time weave together experiences of
subjective and objective time but do so in an intersubjective context.
Time experiences are social as well as intrapsychic. Time—marked or
unmarked, empty or full, slow or syncopated—takes its shapes and meanings in relational contexts. Solitary time and shared time may seem to
be very different.[1] In enactments and in transference and countertransference matrices, complex arrangements of time, history, and generational place can come to life.

Shifting self-states can often be tracked through changes in speech registers and shifting body states (Bromberg, 1999, 2001b). These body–mind/speech states or representations inevitably draw on time, timing, and temporality in unique and unusual ways. People carry their histories and their experience in and of time in gait, in modes of relating, in body motility, in gestures, lexicon, and syntax, in rigidities, and in rhythms that dance through speech and bodily life.

A patient who has carried a long-held set of anxieties and inhibitions remembers from childhood his parents' admonition to hurry up, get moving. He responded to this demand with a kind of oddly dissociated lassitude, a foggy drift that covered depression and anxiety. This style of movement, this diminished, blanketed motility, has been reworked and reconfigured in many forms over a lifetime. He has a body ego as constructed memory, a memory filled with dialogue and interaction, and, crucially, a memory with tempo. These are memories of a conflicted early relationship carried as a personal rhythm to which, despite the pain and conflicts in that history, he has nonetheless clung.

There are many rich examples of the way speech registers the subtle involvements that a patient has with time, going back to Ferenczi (1931). Remnants of the mother tongue appear in an analysand's verbal productions, which echo powerfully in the analyst's countertransference, cuing him to a profound disruption in generational relatedness in the patient (Sapisochin, 1999). A patient in analysis begins to notice that, under certain conditions, intonation patterns, the accents of childhood, a Midwestern burr suddenly erupt in his speech. A woman recalling the way she continued to speak about a childhood accident years later realized that she still conveyed the experience in a very childlike syntax, "I got bit by a dog" (Harris, 1998a, p. 53).

Many relational analysts present clinical work in which both patient and analyst are seen as inhabiting lives lived in multiple timelines, sometimes well coordinated, sometimes not (Bromberg 1996b, 1998b, 1999;[2] Slavin, 1996; Davies, 1998a; Mitchell, 2000). This might be a way to translate Dennett's (1991) conception of consciousness as multiple narratives in various stages of editing and development.[3] Along with experiencing these micromoments of temporality, patients and analysts are in the flow of ongoing time, of aging, and of historical context. There are cohort effects and generational differences. We live defiantly, anxiously, or unconsciously in relation to the social and biological markers for actions and achievements within our social and familial groups. We speak of biological clocks ticking, although these clocks tick differently in different eras and in different cultures and in the light of different technologies. A whole range of issues can render age markers labile: technology, diet, cultural conventions, escalations in education, economic power.[4]

We have anniversary reactions, some organized around ritualized holidays or events fixed in the calendar, some triggered by changing conditions of weather and light. Often our reactions are organized through some metrical or rhythmic sensibility that simmers just out of reach of conscious apprehension. All these experiences—a constructed nostalgia, a dreaded future, a past that won't stay in the past, a future foreshortened, a refusal to live in time—are available to clinical listening and watching.

At the same time as we know these often wildly fluctuating and historically mediated, subjective experiences of time, time's uniformity and linearity are aspects of personal life that we, as industrialized Westerners and as analysts, count on. It seems that time's calculus is both general and idiosyncratic, and our temporal sensibilities are revealed as both made and given, a construction that is intrapsychic and interpersonal while operating in relation to objective experience.[5]

Loewald explored his interests in the fluctuating subjective experience of time in several papers (Loewald, 1962a, b, c). He commented that time can be simultaneously suspended, flowing, fragmented, and always reciprocally related. He meant to convey that any time sense, past, present, or an anticipated future, was always experienced in relation to other time states, always relative. But he also saw temporality as a lived experience, as an aspect of memory or representation. Time replaced space for Loewald as a metaphor for internal structures.

When Loewald spoke about the transference experience in relation to time, he very nearly described a doubled or multiple state of awarenesses. A unique quality of being in a past experience, experienced as present, characterized the transference states. Time, he wrote, is "an active agent in psychic life" (Loewald, 1972, p. 145) operating on representations and memory in the course of analytic work and transference experience. Time for Loewald was a linking and a fragmenting agent signaling shifts in awareness and subjectivity, but also an integral part of any memory or state.

Among his most interesting insights is his thinking about transference experience as from the past but set in the near future, the *about to be*. Typically for Loewald, oedipal dynamics mixing primary and secondary process, and forming in relation and in reaction to id, ego, and superego, can be described in temporal terms. These dynamics are lived internally and interpersonally in the transference. "The superego then would represent the past seen from a future" (Loewald, 1962c, p. 47). The past is carried as an experience that is about to happen.

There are echoes and strains of Heidegger in the deeply subtle interest Loewald has in temporality. Even the cadence of Loewald's prose when he writes about time has some of the oddly trancelike mind-shifting effects of repetition that occur in Heidegger (1962). Loewald is following, I believe, Heidegger's project to describe existence as a "be-ing towards death," as an experience that is always poised in relation to an oncoming future, an experience that carries a kind of ethics that Heidegger (1962) termed "care." His immersion in Heidegger gave Loewald a certain attunement to the complexity of living in time, the attention to how and in what way an embedded experience of being can be ruptured by denial, by reification, by objectifying experience.

Hoffman (1998), from a different tradition, focuses on some of the same issues: the carrying or miscarrying of awareness of mortality, of limit, into psychic life. Fear of mortality is Hoffman's particular inter-vention in the social constructionist perspective and on relational inde-terminacy. Mortality is Hoffman's sole universal, and much psychic fortressing keeps at bay the conscious experience of being toward death.

The topic of time and timelessness appears occasionally in the psy-choanalytic literature of the 30s and 40s (Yates, 1935; Lewin, 1946) and then sparingly thereafter (Orgel, 1965, 1976; Arlow, 1984, 1989; Akhtar, 1995). The dominant preoccupation seemed to be to examine the di-chotomy time–timeless. Those authors saw the workings of unconscious phenomena in the particular quality of a ruleless, endless suspension of ongoing life.

There is a timelessness that appears in dream states and fantasies and, ominously, in life arrangements. Often time and timelessness are embodied, a marker of psychosexual stages (Abraham, 1923), and the refusal to live in time may be considered a preoedipal fusion with the mother. Disorders of time conception are linked to disorders in object constancy, particularly to early disruptions in mothering. Akhtar (1996) notes the complex relation of nostalgia and idealization, the pushing of hope into an out-of-reach future. Bassin (1994), in a different context, has linked nostalgia with melancholy and with difficulties in separation. Timelessness as merger, as a dreamy union, or as bottomless pit bears the inevitable mark of the mother.

A number of authors refer to one of Yates's (1935) cases in which a powerful mother–daughter battle, replicated in the analysis, was fought over time. Time seemed alternately food, feces, bodily substance, a co-coon, space for creativity, and space for separation. Time was something to be hoarded and something hurled to injure others. Many of the struggles were enacted through the patient's love of and use of music. Temporality and rhythm became bound into the deepest preoccu-pations in the patient's life. Yates concluded with some insights that, in the light of infancy research and the work of Hofer (1995) on "hidden regulators" in parent–child interactions, seem remarkably familiar to a clinical listener.

> 1. That all that is most fundamental to a person's apprecia-tion of time and rhythm originates in a pattern laid down at the breast period, when the body supplies the rhythm.
> 2. That where there is gross disharmony between the child's and mother's time, a degree of aggression is aroused which influ-ences all subsequent time relationships, first excretory, then genital and then passing on to the relationship of work and pleasure and to sublimations as a whole.
> 3. That it is essential for achievement in any sublimation in-volving creative activity for a certain tension of repetition and cli-max to be reached, that this can only be borne when the restitutional element, the purposive and rhythmic repetition, dominates the un-controlled crisis first seen in the crying of infancy [p. 348].

We can cite here the work of Hofer (1984, 1996) on hidden regu-larities of pattern and interaction, Sander's (2002) idea of transegrity and rhythmicity, and the work of Beebe et al. (2000) on vocal rhythm matching. Their study of temporality and rhythmicity is one of the most substantial empirical grounds for Beebe and Lachmann's work on the implications of parent–infant patterning for adult treatment (1994, 1998, 2002).

Thinking of time experience in the light of chaos theory draws on these polarities of time and timeless but expands the repertoire of timedness. Chaos theory's application to problems of development leads to an emphasis on diversity, on multiple pathways and variations in how experiences are constructed and evolve. Time is another source of variation. In the turn away from monolithic, single line developmental accounts, time comes into play in a number of different ways. Multiple developmental trajectories may carry unique and distinct timelines.

Shifting self-states and representations, or to use the terms of chaos theory, strange attractors arising out of unique and emerging distributions and patterns or activation and interrelatedness, could yield up different experiences of time and timing.

ATTENTION TO TIME IN THE CONSULTING ROOM

I try to pay attention to emotionally charged late arrivals, to the rhythms of entry and departure (using tempo and space as interlacing metaphors), silences and the dangers of silence, the varying experience of full and empty hours. Time here is carrying subjective experience in the context of its objective chronometric status, but often the experience of timedness is intersubjective. There are analytic couples who seem attuned to the rhythm of the hour, both expecting its diminution. Yet both can get lost in an hour. Moments when the *analyst* loses a sense of the time frame can be powerfully illuminating. An hour that is unconsciously truncated or one when time spills over reveals some rippling process in the dyad or in the individuals.

I have an analysand for whom my announcement that the time is over for the day is always a surprise and elicits a startled "Oh" every hour. What premature rupture is being repeated? I listen for the repetition of certain rhythms—hope or dashed hope, energy or a drift into despair—all conveyed in the temporal rhythms of speech in real time. A session might begin with a strong sense of complaint and grievance and lead either to soothing or to disappointed emptiness. Temporal flow here is a kind of memory. These are all aspects of distorted time perception, some signal that psychic life—its anxieties, misattentions, preoccupations—have affected both the patient's and the analyst's sense of being in time.

These experiences of shifting states involving timedness and speech arise in an intersubjective space. As analysts, we are drawn into ways of being in dyadic space and time, a task we execute well or badly. Misattunement can spoil or provoke change in a treatment. In ways we are often not fully conscious of, we draw on the pragmatics of speech (its functional rules of use) to "find" or recognize the experience the patient is conveying. Mirroring gesture or speech will always capture something about the individual living in time. And frequently the metaphors of space and time reverse and interact. A patient at the beginning of analysis complains I am too fast. Slow down, she insists. But she is expressing both a fear of spatial impingement and a fear of abandonment. Our speech together comes slowly to connect us in relation to time and space.

I feel the presence of multiple developmental timetables in my work with a young woman whose family was seriously ruptured when she was six and an older, bullying brother was eleven. She described a rare reunion of the original siblings with the mother, whose actions had fractured the family. She arrived at the reunion to find her brother hiding behind the door. He then jumped out, shouted "Boo," and pulled at her hair and sleeve. She was 37; he, 42. Neither can acknowledge the stunning loss they suffered as children. She submitted to her brother's childish bullying in a state of dissociated, numb silence. Each registers the trauma and the behavioral style of each is like some form of carbon dating marking events that no one in that scene can stand between the spaces to notice. This body talk, unmatched by anything symbolic, is particularly acute for my patient in the presence of her mother. There she is often brimming with feeling, but speechless. From the calmer site of the therapy room, she can barely describe her experience and cannot really speak of its significance.

STOPPING THE CLOCK

I first began to pay particular attention to unique, quite subjective, often quite eccentric experiences of temporality after reading an essay by Karen Maroda (1987) about her work with a patient who appeared to live outside time. Maroda connected this behavior to narcissism; it seemed to be a kind of refusal of or blindness to the reality of temporal flow. It was a particular refusal to live by rules, to be regulated, in a kind of grandiose suspension of the traffic of time and space. It is sometimes connected to endless and suspended mourning, a refusal to absorb loss. It is also a particular kind of dissociated state. Living outside time appears isolated but may carry hidden relational configurations, old loyalties to the buried and the unburied.

Reading Maroda's paper very much influenced my work with a young woman, Bella, a woman who remained in frightening ways immobilized, grief stricken and hopeless. A striking pattern in her life was the wish to get rid of people, a pattern equally poised against her fervent wishes for attachment and merger with other figures, living and dead. She was constantly deciding whether or not to break up with a changing but continuous cast of boyfriends. Perhaps, she would say to me, I should just throw him away. Or not. She could sound angry, disappointed, dissatisfied, and fearful of connection. This remarkable fort/da[6] of boyfriends seemed to me to be conducted in the kind of time-suspended state that Maroda described. The obsessional elements of back and forth, doing and undoing, carry huge portions of anger and excitement. And there was certainly an intense affective charge in the endless jettisoning and reacquiring of partners.

But the way Bella spoke about these relationships and her own quandary about action had a strange mixture of lawlessness and deadness, of traumatized dissociation and willfulness. While there were many moments of transformation in our process together, I date an important shift in the treatment to a turn in me in the wake of an enactment, one that plunged me unexpectedly into an experience of time. A typical pattern emerged in which Bella caught me up in a scene of crisis-laden anxiety, plunging both of us into a kind of timeless autistic/contiguous state (Ogden, 1989) that was both limitless and acute.

Autistic/contiguous is the term Ogden devised to describe a psychic position, distinct from the depressive position or the paranoid/schizoid position, states of being that describe the internal individual psychic outcome of various thwarted or enhanced early relational patterns. Autistic/contiguous describes states of being that seem shapeless or oddly unnarratizable, sensory, archaic body weather that both defends and suggests the collapse of defensive structure. Procedural knowing, some of the relational patterns Stern (1985) describes as early schemas, objects known by their impact and sensory effect not their distinct objectness: all these ways of describing archaic, preverbal, nonverbalizable states would count as aspects of Ogden's autistic/contiguous position. Analytic relationships bound into this position often feel curiously physical and concrete. Mitrani (2001) uses the term "adhesive" relations to describe kinds of contact with patients which although nontactile can feel gluey or abrasive. The patient is stuck like a shape to the analysis not even to the analyst as a person. Time, in such situations, can feel suspended and deadly.

Bella left me a desperate phone message for help but was then quite unavailable for a return call. I could feel with anguish the ensuing destruction of my own peace of mind and my freedom to work for the rest of the day. I could also feel that my state was a register of the experience she so often described, that of anxious, time-trapped disability.

I was set up in a moment of ruptured going-on-being. I could not continue the narrative of my own day. I lived in a moment of endless waiting at the edge of a precipice. The clock was ticking, but nothing could move forward. I was immobilized and anxious.

In processing this experience, we were able to metabolize together the state of hers that had been evacuated so brutally into me. We could hold together her mixture of fragility and destructiveness, her anger, and her despair. This process of attending to subjectivities in the other was enhanced by the knowledge that damage had occurred. I suffered when I felt lost in time. I believe that the realities of time may have been made more palpable through the link she and I could make between her act and my pain. Her agency here was enhanced and grounded in a relational matrix of self and other, both of us subjects, because I survived an attack but not without damage. I also believe that this experience was part of a changing experience of time, perhaps through the diminishing of omnipotence in both of us.

As Bella grew and changed in her therapy, it seemed to me the sense of timeliness and temporality was one of the most profound signs of her transformations. Her life "commenced." The preciousness of relationships and the insubstitutability, permanence, and fragility of this life, in this time, became clearer to her. Lovers were no longer fungible. She mattered, so they mattered. She seemed to me more capable both of sadness and of depth of commitment.

Suspending time was a way to suspend relatedness, so that no more loss occurred or was registered. Like other patients who with improvement come to live in more speeded-up dynamic timeliness, this woman often felt to herself young and old, suspended in childhood and in aging. This odd double-timed experience is typical of people for whom there has often been a lot of precocious development (Corrigan and Gorden, 1995). The hyperspeed of certain developmental tasks often leaves broad areas of functioning atrophied and unformed. One of the odd sequelae of early precocity is that over time the accelerated pace of development becomes becalmed; the precocious child or adolescent may as an adult be both old and young, washed up and never started.

One of the poignant facts of such treatments, it seems to me, is that the recognition of time occasions the recognition of losses that are not recoverable, an experience that all of us can be understood to flinch from. Awakenings to chronological and objective time in the course of treatment can be excruciatingly painful, and dissociation can be a welcome relief from the burden and the suffering of knowing that time is lost and unrecoverable. The weight of expended time can easily swamp the little boats of change set off in analytic waters.

Disruptions in sense of time and time passing are often an aspect of mourning. A patient returned from a visit to the crash site of her husband's plane, shot down in Vietnam 30 years before. A tentative site had been identified by reconnaissance maps and records sent to her by the Pentagon. She told me that, as she stood in a newly planted rubber tree forest with bits of plane debris still being dug out of the ground, she had the thought, "There is a 28-year-old man lying on the floor of the jungle, and I got old." When she returned to New York, she had a dream in which, for the first time, this age difference was represented. The dream registered restructured psyche as restructured time.

This treatment experience taught me a lot about the variability in time sense, and the effect of securing some coordinates of time and space on psychic structure and memory (Harris, 1996b). The patient and I are of the same generation, and, when she first came to see me and I heard her story, I thought that perhaps I could help her because I was now old enough and the war far enough away. My own under-standing of postwar suffering, was, I hoped, sounder and deeper than it would have been when I was younger. In the course of the therapy, a loss that had been inassimilable began to have a history. The death of her husband came slowly to be in the past, though that process was dramatically altered and consolidated with my patient's courageous trip into a charged geography and a recontextualized time.

As we explored the experience of this trip, I began to realize that she and I lived and yet did not live in the same time scheme or history. Images of the war are completely vivid for me. It is a time-sharpened, intense period. She, on the other hand, never watched a newsreel or the television. She looked up Vietnam in a library encyclopedia and found it was a French protectorate. Terrified and struggling to hold a family together in the absence of her husband, for her Vietnam was a black space from which tapes and letters appeared until they stopped.

We were both haunted by Vietnam but in radically different ways. In my imagination, the Vietnam she had stepped into was alive and potent. It had never left a kind of presentness in my mind and memory. For her it was a blank space filled by a death, a ritual, a place in time and in mind, not beautiful but terrible, doomed, and murderous. In-terestingly, her journey through time and space altered an internal world. I think, among other things, it allowed her a more thorough internal-ization of the lost man, his accomplishments and powers and confidence, and also a differentiation experienced first in the jungle, when time, age, and change were finally taken in.

What I have also understood from this work is that suspended time sense and suspended mourning are never simply personal. Many factors went into the altered time and age sense of this patient, and many factors isolated her in her grief. Her own dynamics and family trauma, along with the American culture's staggering difficulties in creating a social space and public ritual for grieving and atonement, shaped how and where and when this death and this phenomenon we call Vietnam could be experienced.

COUNTERTRANSFERENCE TIME

In Winnicott's (1947) suggestion that there is hatred in the end of the hour, there is a curious indeterminacy. It is probably as much the analyst's trope as the patient's. Winnicott's speculations about analysts' motivations for work show how much the ideal of work from the depressive position may be lost in the more oscillating states of love and hate. Winnicott was sensitive to the difficulties that analysts face in accepting the complexity of their motives to heal and work.

There is increasingly in analytic writing an openness to describing the working process and emotional engagements shimmering in the dyadic lives of analyses. Bromberg's (1998a, b, 1999) work is particularly powerful in creating a capacious ground for analysts' self-reflection and acceptance of the complex, mutually inducing and shifting experiences of psychic and social reality.

Time and money, we all learn in approaching questions of technique, are analytic flashpoints, places where the frame, the container, safety, and reliability are made and contested (Dimen, 1994). The analyst's time is leased (or is it sold?) by the hour. Can you lease time? Analysts practice in industrialized regulated time: this representation of time as homogenous, rectilinear, and empty derives from the experience of manufacturing work and is sanctioned by modern mechanics, which establishes the primacy of uniform, rectilinear motion over circular motion. Taylorism (the application of time/motion studies to enhance factory efficiency), the stopwatch, the material forms of time registration—all developments of rationalized industrial work—come to have constitutive force in our experience of being in time. The idea that time, including analytic time, is empty by nature and must be filled like a production quota is eerie to think of. Ogden (1995), describing a particularly deadening experience with a patient, takes his pulse and watches the second hand on his watch. We must "fill" our hours.

It is all these layered experiences of being in time that an analyst confronts in conducting clinical work—as work, in daily time, in extended practices over time. While many clinical vignettes detail patients' worry over separation and absence, De Urtubey (1995) has written a provocative set of speculations about the analyst's experience of absence. Breaks in analytic work evoke fear as well as respite. De Urtubey imagines that, as the analyst unpeels and disentangles patient psyches, many fears may emerge. Separations are complex psychic surgeries, dismantling temporarily the tendrils of projective and introjective tissues binding an analytic couple together. She speculates that Freud's fears of vacation time as creating a loss of patients is carried by many analysts today. It entails fears of the end of psychoanalysis as well as the end of one's livelihood. And, she suggests, behind these fears lurk our fears of mortality. There is the dread of time stopping.

The analytic workday is not only unique but also constituted within the history of labor and exchange. There are the parameters of the session and the rhythms of an analytic day. Throughout the workday the analyst is caught up, organized, and reorganized in unique and shifting entrainments. It is interesting how often certain themes or interests echo in different hours across a single day. How much do the analyst's subjectivity and ways of listening structure a day's material across different treatments? In the language of chaos theory, we might think of the analyst over a day as a kind of strange attractor, disequilibrating and reorganizing on the rhythm of the hour as the relational context persists and changes over time. Analyst and analysand coexist in a strange paradox of timed and timeless experience.

TIME IN DEVELOPMENT

Time functions as one of those crucial but apparently unremarkable features in developmental theory. Time was always, in standard developmental research design, a linear axis across which change was plotted, predicted, and noticed. From the perspective of psychoanalysis, if we are to think about time as a complex, constructed, multiply structured experience, developmental theory needs an altered model and a more diverse use of time factors. In fact, a number of researchers have been interested in addressing this problem.

In a series of experiments and data analyses, Schaie and Baltes (1975) developed a way of distinguishing cohort effects, age effects, and testing effects. They did this by comparing data gathered cross-sectionally with data gathered longitudinally and made these comparisons across different historical epochs. In studying developmental change, they found that there can be cohort effects and age effects. Ten-year-olds in a computer-literate era live in a multidimensional psychic/social space that is quite different from that of ten-year-olds who came of age during the Vietnam era or during the Depression. From the developmental studies using these methodological techniques, a complex picture of individuals in history and in multiple time frames emerges.

The intertwining of two kinds of timelines has been a preoccupation of Fischer and his colleagues (Fischer et al., 1997; Fischer and Bidell, 1998; Fischer and Watson, 2002), who look to the intersection of macro- and microchange processes as a site of developmental growth. Within any individual's patterns of development there will be local skill development. But, looked at from a greater distance and with less finely grained observation, at the more macrolevel, there will be unique developmental clusters. There is in most people a web of skills such that capacities seen from one vantage point are not present at another.

All these ways of thinking about individual and group development point to the limitations of a perspective of either linear stages or simple developmental lines. Piaget (1955) tried to account for this phenomenon by a concept of *décalage*, in which unequal and asymmetrical developmental patterns emerge. But this nuance in his thinking seemed to disappear in the Americanization of his theory into a linear stage model. This critique of developmental lines is coming into view from a number of perspectives (Coates, 1997). Chaos theory and nonlinear dynamic systems approaches treat time in a number of different ways. Complexity, it is argued, arises in real-time iterations. Continuous and dynamically transforming feedback and reentrant mappings of many skills and processes take place over time. These processes are emergent. Given the multiple pathways and the variation in contextual and local constraints, there will also be a multiplicity of time scales. Pacing, tempo, the unfolding of process all arise in quite individualized ways.

Using De Marneffe's (1997) work on children's apprehension and construction of experience with their own genitals and doll play and the integration of these experiences with gender naming and identity, Coates has very cogently critiqued the focus on developmental lines. She argues for a complex, multidirectional experience of time's effects and no simple prediction of gender identification from the experience of bodily state and body differences. She also calls into question the time line that would trace a body's transformation into psyche and doubt the need to consider in a simple linear way the preverbal as the precursor to the verbal.

In a micro sense, time and timing are crucial developmental phenomena in many developmental processes both intra- and interindividually. Timing, rhythm, and temporality are at the heart of the observational attention of many infancy research programs (Beebe, Jaffe et al., 1992, 2000; Jaffe and Beebe, 2001). Sander (1988, 2002) sees rhythmicity as vital to the mutual entrainment of parent and child. Internal working models (Bowlby's [1959, 1960] terminology) and RIGS ("representations of actions that have been internalized"; Stern, 1977) are best imagined as dynamic *gestalten*, including elements of tempo and rhythm as ways of being self-regulated and related. These aspects of early experiences of being timed, of "going on being" (Winnicott's term) in time, and of the rhythms of interaction enter the procedural memory of the child and enter, with complex potentials, into the clinical dyad (Knoblauch, 1997, 2000; Beebe and Lachmann, 1998, 2002).

Rhythms and patterns of intonation, keyed to face and body rhythms, are central to speech processing and the kind of attentive listening that many researchers believe is a fundamental precursor to the development of some registration of intentionality in others. Speech rhythms and tempo are also part of solacing aspects of language and its particular fitness for regulation (Horton, 1984). Songs and stories carry meaning but also the acoustic memory of a parental voice. This is very much part of Kristeva's (1980) idea of the maternal chora, the material qualities that adhesively live in a child's mind and speech.

NARRATIVES AND INVENTIONS
OF PERSONAL CHRONOLOGY

Many critics of developmental theory are wary of placing certain powerful end states as part of the original motivating factors in a child's development. These critics worry over the tendency to produce gender or desires, particularly heterosexual desires, as normatively the engine of development from the beginning. Gender and desire flower and cross pollinate, and then, Laplanche (2002) argues, they are retrospectively installed as originary. Stein (1998a) has developed a comparable view balancing the complexity of child immaturity and adult mentalization and libidinization in the service of a deeply enigmatic outcome. What this means is that subjectivity is, in a certain sense, constituted with a "false" time line, a founding moment that is actually retrospectively structured. It is interesting to think that what haunts us was set up as an idea of the unrecoverable past.

With the idea of *Nachtraglichkeit*, psychoanalytic theory has thus issued a particularly acute challenge to any simple conception of time or its linearity in development. As experience unfolds and becomes part of what is fed back into memory schemas, memories alter and reconfigure. Powerful affects from contemporary experience enter and rework memory. An ever-altering and renewing developmental narrative takes shape.

Memory, encrypted identifications, and powerful attachments can all produce an experience of time, history, and generation that is multiply configured and conflictual. One of my patients, with considerable shame over money, has found herself, not surprisingly, in a predicament in which this shame over poverty is being inflamed and reactivated in a hurtful, self-defeating way. When we trace the history of her experiences, it seems that this experience of shame has been both disowned and reproduced over several generations. Despite her life experience of late 20th-century affluence and prosperity, a part of her lives as a rural child of the Depression; she is excruciatingly aware of the humiliation of parents living on nothing, scraping by. To receive anything from her family makes her feel like a thief. There are many ways of understanding this experience. It is a representation of neglect and emptiness that registers experiences of care in the context of significant maternal depression in her actual childhood.

But I think it is also a species of the kind of identification that Abraham and Torok (1994) speak of: encrypted identifications, a historical anomaly conveyed across the generations covertly, unconsciously. This woman's shame is connected to an exquisite tie to a troubled, vulnerable, shame-ridden father, himself caught up in painful matters of loyalty and identity. Time is present and structuring in psyches in unique intergenerational processes where history is reproduced in a certain way but quite unconsciously. Seligman (1999a, b) describes the mechanics of this transmission. In intrapsychic terms, my patient lives in several cohorts. She often radically misconstrues the possibilities and resources in her and in her surrounding relationships. A shameful dispossession occurring two generations earlier is being relived relentlessly in the present.

Time appears in developmental narratives in unique configurations when it is cross-linked to the psychic presentation of class. Aspects of class and ethnic history can be carried in psyche as a living remnant of some obsolete past. It is difficult to psychologize class with its citational and material reference points and its locus in economic and social life. Class experiences, in relation to family of origin and to achieved adult position, may present multiple timelines.

I suggest that we can think of class in psychological terms as multiply configured and carrying unique configurations of time. It is encompassed, but not exhausted, by considerations of ethnicity, origin, and status, current and historical. If we think of class as always having a past, present, and future time dimension, we can see that there are actual and imaginative moves in some of the lives of women like my patient. The class you were born into and the class position you live in may operate in complex tension.

Relating this time dimension to class, I am thinking of two patients who resolutely live middle-class, and in one case highly affluent and professionally successful lives. One man carries the early familial anxiety about sufficient food in a regimen of austerity and deprivation in which rage and pride are equally mixed. This cramped Brooklyn childhood, with parsed-out treats and a child's desperate and overmanaged longings and frustrations, lives on in ghostlike form in his suburban home. The second person, whose birth temporarily plunged the family into dependence on welfare, carries obscure but palpable reactions of shame that appear like a changing weather system that is both inexplicable and inevitable. Sennett and Cobb's (1972) phrase, "the hidden injuries of class," seems relevant here.

Remnants of individual experience seem hauled from another generation, the child state in certain patients being intergenerationally transmitted, sometimes over quite a long span. We think of these formations as carried in the nonverbal, affect-laden somatic and sensory experiences that we now term procedural knowing (Kihlstrom, 1989, 1990; Bucci, 1997, 2001, 2002) as well as in more accessible secondary processes in images and narratives. Sennett and Cobb (1972) wrote movingly about the way familial oedipal dynamics can become distorted by matters of class. Interviewing working-class parents and children 30 years ago in Boston, Sennett and Cobb traced the pain of going beyond a father when education, prospects, and position stack the deck against the parent.

These affective states and the chronic dynamics that underlie them are not, of course, unique to families and children in economically constrained circumstances. But they do suggest the power of material conditions starkly to mark the psyche and for those markings to cross generations. We might think of class as having layers of conscious and unconscious meaning, living as encrypted or secret identifications long after the material conditions that shaped them have altered.

GENDERED TIME

Timelessness becomes an embodied experience and, interestingly, can become a gendered one. Wolfenstein (1996) ascribes this feminizing of the unconscious and process and timelessness to the *male* imaginary. His point of view is amenable to chaos theory. The human requirements to metabolize vulnerability and the pain of necessary losses and separations becomes genderized. Gender in this way is a defense against psychic pain. A longing for love subtly changes into a longing to be (and vice versa).

Butler (1990) makes a similar point from a slightly different angle. Lived gender carries the signs of lost love. Identifications as bodily states (or as temporal experiences) hold the residue of longings. For many people, the eternal is feminine, the historical is masculine. The point Wolfenstein (1996) makes is close to that which Grand (1995) developed in relation to traumatic memory, particularly memory of sexual abuse and incest. Our language and narrative tropes for articulating an experience of trauma become subtly gendered. A feminized language of victimization and passivity takes on a life of its own.

Gendering time has bedeviled feminist psychoanalytic thinking for decades. Kristeva (1980, 1982) sees some of the conflict as between the capacity for symbolization in any parent–child dyad and the wish to reserve the material experience of mothering as an inevitable source of experiencing maternal omnipotence.

TIME AND SPEECH

Barbara Gold and I (Harris and Gold, 2001), working in supervision on a patient's contribution to dissociated states in the analyst, began to study the disorienting effects of certain usages of speech in the clinical hour. When we analyzed the speech patterns and verbal "strategies" of the patient, a number of features surfaced. We found that the patient often began with some declaration or description that erased any shared history with the analyst. It was as though, by her way of talking, the patient bound the analyst in an endless present, as though hour after hour they were meeting and talking for the first time. The patient lived in a profoundly traumatized state with many suspensions of life process and of a sense of ongoingness.

With a less extreme history, another patient, in late middle age, often begins her hour with a brief resume of how things are going, but it is a recital that is, in subtle ways, quite destabilizing to me. From week to week her description of ongoing life can change dramatically. Things are going well. Then it turns out that "things" are going badly. Terrible problems have persisted and deepened. But, in the next session, the past is accounted for quite differently. The immediate past is constantly revised and re-presented, as though each present moment comes with its own unique experience of the past. The past is an object without constancy, an unfixed and sliding constellation of states and experiences.

As I try to assess the impact of the patient's verbal behavior on me, I think that the patient is imposing on me (inducing) an experience of destabilizing uncertainty. What is real? What to believe? That her relationships are developing? They are and always have been in crisis. Our basic shared understanding of tempo, of the rhythms of life, and of social experience is in a constant state of revision or negation. The patient has cued me directly to be attentive to when she is speaking authentically or when she is avoiding my scrutiny. She has described a childhood of great confusion and murkiness. How disturbed was her mother? How out of control was her alcoholic father? Dinner time she described as resembling a script by Harold Pinter. Her description was difficult to follow, and her words seemed unrelated to the simmering affects and blank gaps in her family's functioning. The experience for me was of unsure footing. I was carried into a reality that could shift on a dime while everyone seemed to be going on as usual.

These experiences are reproduced in the intersubjective matrix through a subtle (unconscious) use of language. In this case, it was the speech pragmatics that were doing this complex psychic work. Rules of speech usage come into play: How is a time line described? How do verb tenses and word choice signal a background fabric to shared experience? From childhood on, speakers develop a capacity to organize communication in the structure of given/new topic/comment (Feldman, 1990). Speakers who are known to each other and are in regular communication carry a shared sense of what they know together and what the stretch of past and future looks like. With my patient, a deeply disturbing experience of herself in relation to others and to her own internal world is endlessly called into question. She and I can count on very little to sustain us in a shared ongoingness.

Multiplicity, temporality, and speech are organized in a subtle construction, or an assembly brought to life in the particular crucible of transference and countertransference matrices. Time disjunction may be signaling psychic disjunction, often subtly carried in speech.

Sapisochin (1999) described a case in which the particular distortion of oedipal longing that was present in his patient foreshadowed a kind of collapse of generational and dimensional space. His analysand began to speak to him in their shared mother tongue. It was seductive speech, acoustically and semantically conjuring up food and maternal care. The analysand was recreating a mother–child pair but an incestuously tied pairing. The analyst felt the regressive pull through speech that brought with it the primary-process affects of his own childhood as well as the patient's. There was a glitch in genealogy, a slip or collapse in historical time that actually went back several generations. A preoedipal tie of the analysand's father and his mother was in the place where an oedipal link could have been forged. The clues to this trauma were carried in speech.

TIME AND TRAUMA

Time, during and after traumatic events, has a complex epistemological status. There is, in many reactions of shock, a sense that the person lives in an extended state of being, poised and frozen in a moment in time that seems to be set just before the traumatic event. This frozen time is expressed as a paralysis in the body. But, as in transference phenomena

(Loewald, 1972, 1986) there is in traumatic experience an often equally inchoate terror of the near future. Paradoxically, the future has already happened. Memory in the future tense.

Cathy Caruth (1996) captured something of this link between loss and time disruption in her essay on Freud's chapter in the *Interpretation of Dreams,* "Father Can't You See I'm Burning?" The dreamer constantly moves between sleep and waking, sleeping so that she can move away from loss, but encountering it in the dream and waking to avoid knowing that a death has occurred. "Immediacy takes the form of belatedness" (p. 92). Caruth is sketching a paradox: the dreamer can neither dream in safety nor awaken to safety. In this oscillating process of waking, and reawakening, and sleeping and dreaming, the dreamer attempts to master an inassimilable reality. He awakens too late to save his child. That "too lateness" is a condition of the death. He is awakened from within the dream by a call from the child—living in the dream—to come in time. In these anxiety-driven moves back and forth in time, a terrible gap is skipped over. In that gap is both death and presentness, together unmetabolizable.[6]

Trauma disrupts experienced temporality both in micro- and in macroterms. Trauma's effects show up in time gaps, in ruptures of sequencing. Time is often an odd aspect of the mysteries of unconscious transmission. On the morning of Tuesday, September 11, one of my patients, Emily, who lives in downtown New York City, not far from the site of the 9/11 attack (Harris, 2004), is awakened by a noise she cannot exactly identify but that she imagines is coming from the street. She gets up, glances at her clock. It is 8:30 a.m., so she closes the window and goes back to sleep. She dreams. A bus is trying to fly. It sprouts wings and starts to rise in the air. She watches but becomes worried that it won't make it. It is unclear if the bus will crash or manage to get aloft. She sleeps on until her phone rings, waking her *again,* but now with the frightened voices of friends recounting the events of the morning. I say again to suggest that the first awakening is through primary process and the second through logic and reality (secondary process), though both levels have their sanities and their madness.

It is several days before she and I can meet in my office. In that first hour, she begins to speak of her impressions and experience. To my surprise, Emily is worried about the tourists. How will they manage? How will they get home? Will they have enough resources? How upset they must be. So out of context. By the third time she has mentioned tourists I ask her about this. In the next minutes she is weeping, and it is very obvious to both of us the minute she begins to explore this that she is the tourist, always in transit, in between, never home.

As I listen to Emily describing her experience of the fallen buildings and all the devastating sights, I realize that I am remembering an experience of the previous night when a patient brought her three-year-old with her when she came to to talk over the harrowing escape they had had from the environs of the towers. What is echoing in my head is a repeated sentence as the child put toy people in and out of a toy ambulance: "Now the twin towers fell. But they weren't really twins." It was the first inkling I had that there might be a psychic animation of the two towers, including the twoness, although these unconscious fantasies would be built very differently by each patient. In Emily's life, a family devastation really did leave nothing standing and left her a kind of permanent tourist.

It is also relevant that my mental association was a communication from a child to a child-part of Emily, for it was at her next session, the following day, that she mapped out the double awakening of that Tuesday morning and the dream. As we work on the dream, she describes the winged bus as a kind of cartoon drawing, a yellow bus with sweet, fat little wings. I tell her that one of my images is from the children's story *Chitty Chitty Bang Bang*, a book whose cover, I seem to remember, has just such a cartoony flying vehicle. Emily laughs. It is a book she read and loved as a child, and she also notes ruefully that it is a book she very much connects to the time of family breakdown.

So Emily is the bus, with its sweet little not-quite-adequate wings, trying so hard to fly. It is a child's bus. It is a tourist bus. We see the remnants and representations of Emily's project of self-cure made in the wake of destruction, and we know that there will have to be breakdown and creation if Emily is to "rejoin her destiny." The contents of the unconscious rupture a sense of time and timelines, and this rupture affects past and future. Emily is a kind of "girl interrupted," poised to fly and to crash. Here, in the sweet frailty of the dream image, the horror is modulated and defended against both outside her window and in her memory.

So Emily sleeps to move away from what is about to happen but dreams of an event that has happened, relations that were ruptured, planes that did crash in the past and in the present. And she awakens to the flying bus, hovering and uncertain; she awakens to a new reality. This is the movement of the dreamer in Freud's essay.

Many "repetitions" of trauma carry the feeling of endlessly returning to an imagined moment just before nothingness.

> Robertson has recorded many cases of young children whose long-
> ing for the absent mother was clearly apparent, even though at times
> so muted that it tended to be over-looked. Of Laura, the subject of
> his film *A Two-Year-Old Goes to Hospital* (1952), he writes: "She
> would interpolate without emotion and as if irrelevantly the words
> 'I want my Mummy, where has my Mummy gone?' into remarks
> about something quite different; and when no one took up the in-
> truded remark she would not repeat the 'irrelevance.'" The same
> child would sometimes let concealed feelings come through in songs
> and, unknown to herself, substitute the name of "Mummy" for that
> of a nursery-rhyme character. On one occasion she expressed an
> urgent wish to see the steam-roller which had just gone from the
> roadway below the ward in which she was confined. She cried, "I
> want to see the steam-roller, I want to see the steam-roller. I want to
> see my Mummy. I want to see the steam-roller."
>
> Another child, aged three years, who had been in the hospital
> for ten days, was pointed out by the ward sister as being "happy."
> He seemed to be amusing himself with a droll game of bowing re-
> peatedly and twisting his head. When the observer stood near, how-
> ever, it was clear that, almost compulsively, the child was making
> the motions of looking toward a closed door and whispering, "My
> mummy coming soon"—though in fact his mother would not be
> allowed to visit for another two days [Bowlby, 1960, pp. 20–21].

Bowlby, describing for an analytic audience in the 1960s the depth
of child grief, would have had no trouble recognizing the lifetime of
modulating and managing the effects of an early hospitalization in a
patient's history. For this man the memory of the absolute absence of
parental figures remains overwhelming. The remembered emergency
and panicky move to the hospital seems more like a kidnapping than a
medical action. The parents remain in memory frozen and shrieking.
There is very little coherent narrative sense of the hospital time, and,
what there is is mostly a fragmented muddle of unpeopled enduring.
There is, we discover, an intergenerational transmission of trauma: this
violent rupture of connection reiterated a comparable moment of violent loss for one of the patient's parents, both losses having occurred at
roughly the same age for parent and child. Perhaps the parent's dissociation during the child's ordeal partially ensured this transmission.

In those examples there is one important aspect of time and trauma:

trauma entails a breakdown. There is a missing piece of time. What we call traumatic experience is often a person's attempt to recover from breakdown. Trauma is by its very nature beyond representation. Trauma, then, is, in whatever form it occurs, an experience against which the processing instrument (mind/body/affect) breaks down. We see the traces of trauma as aftereffects, and we see the effects of trauma in the efforts at recovery, efforts that often distort time.

The effects of the young child's trauma lived on in the family narratives, which were told without any density of meaning or exploration. "He was never the same again" was the doomy, time-referencing family sentence. He cannot quite remember. Did he eat? Did he refuse food? Was he hungry and starving but trying to master the trauma by remembering not deprivation but stoic heroism? As the days go on, time and identity and object constancy start to crumble. And afterward, with time to recover and rework a narrative, the traumatic lost time is never stitched back up. There was no reweaving. There were simply enduring black holes into which timedness had disappeared.

CONCLUSION

Our experience of time is actually an experience of multiple embeddedness (Friedman, 1990; Agamben, 1999). We live in circular and cyclical time, a holdover from classical experiences of temporality. Time is quantified and infinite, endlessly repeating and returning, nonlinear and undirectional.

Time is manifold in so many of our experiences. The temporal rhythms of inner states shift and change. The haunted near future of transference. The moments of interpretive work that stop time and allow reflection backward and outward to the patient's experience. Whether as ecstatic or annihilating endlessness or as experiences of fragmentation, temporality as a living, breathing, altering phenomenon is a crucial element in this picture of multiple coconstructed subjectivities.

CHAPTER 3

⤜ঽ⤛

Chaos Theory as a Model for Development

*I*n this chapter I introduce the elements of chaos theory that I find particularly relevant to descriptions of *developmental* process. Be forewarned. This material is quite abstract, some of the terminology is unfamiliar, and the empirical examples here are drawn from work in developmental psychology. My own immersion in chaos theory has taught me that it takes repeated exposure to this framework to absorb its insights and capacities to represent complexity in a way that will be useful to clinicians. After this initiation I will be revisiting many of these same principles in chapter 6 with applications to experiences of gender and gender development.

Complexity theory, chaos theory, and nonlinear dynamic systems theory: these are designations of a new approach to the study of living systems (Wolfram, 2002). New is perhaps a relative term. Galatzer-Levy (1995), who has argued for the applicability of chaos theory to various problem areas in psychoanalysis, traces a half-century of development in mathematics that has produced a dazzling array of tools and concepts. This approach, he argues, is a fundamental break with 19th-century models in physics, in particular the mechanistic, Newtonian theory on which Freud drew. Others within psychoanalysis making creative uses of this approach include Moran (1991), Fajardo (1998, 2000), Palumbo (1999), Beebe et al. (2000), Ghent (2000), Piers (2000, in press), and Seligman (in press).

In considering nonlinear dynamic systems theory as a potential model for psychoanalytic theories of development, I begin with a number of questions. First, what kind of model is this, and what is the intended level of application? Second, what is the value—rhetorical, heuristic, or conceptual—of interdisciplinary borrowing from the natural sciences? Third, can a general systems theory, developed in the study of biological evolution and the study of physical systems, provoke useful reflection on the ways that social reality, fantasy, higher order cognition, representation, and unconscious processes coevolve in development?

CHAOS THEORY: MODEL OR METAPHOR?

First there is the question of whether, in its application to a psychoanalytic study of developmental process and the experience of gender, chaos theory is most useful as a set of metaphors. Is it a point of view, one of many?[1] Is it, for certain problems, a model that is empirically demonstrable? Chaos theory has staked its reputation on a capacity to model formally many individual and collective systems behaviors through the use of algorithms and complex computational forms. These procedures place a premium on description not prediction. This kind of descriptive modelling fits well with a psychoanalytic project that is looking retrospectively to interpret unfolding experience, with no particular attempt to be predictive. But at the moment, the application of principles of chaos theory to problems of consciousness and human mental functioning, indeed to many agent-based models, often seems more a "scouting expedition," to use John Holland's (1998) phrase, than a fully articulated model appropriate to complex systems.[2]

For many theorists who use some version of chaos theory for work in a wide variety of problems, from biology to neuroscience to economics, this is a new approach to doing human or natural sciences. In the intellectual communities developing chaos theory and its applications, there is an interesting mixture of caution and high-drama discovery. Grandiosity is both regulated and free spirited. There is painstaking observation as well as hell-for-leather revolution. Maturana (1980, 1985, 1999), Casti (1994), Kauffman (1995), Elman et al. (1997), and Wolfram (2002), among others, see this approach as a break from more deductively based, cause-and-effect theories. Learning is learning of pattern, an interaction with contexts and environment that reveals latent patterns, harmonies, correlations. It is more gestalt learning than item acquisition. It is learning that is unsupervised, producing underlying rules rather than just bits of information.

What is unique and striking in the chaos theory perspective is that giving up the more positivist-driven, deductive forms of science does not lead to an inexorable slide into relativism and pure subjectivity. This model makes plenty of space for biology, for genetics, for nuanced observations of experiences of learning and processing.[3] Because such a premium is placed on the plasticity and self-organizing properties of experience, chaos theory offers the potential to hold in complex interaction the organic, the endogenous, the social, and the historical. Another useful parallel between chaos theory and psychoanalysis is that both assure nonlinearity in the course of developmental change.

Alicia Juarerro (1999), a philosopher interested in intentionality, draws on chaos theory and the analysis of complex adaptive systems to propose a logic for theory building different from the conventional deductive accounts. She argues that one implication of these new models is a turn away from top-down, covering law,[4] deductive and abstract causal accounts, and a move toward what she terms a narrative logic of explanation, an explanation that tells a specific story, in real time and with the constraints and contexts embedded in particular histories.

Fajardo (1998) linked nonlinear dynamic systems theories to a hermeneutic and constructivist understanding. This approach to analytic understanding through narrative building, through interpretations in complex cycles that integrate global and local understandings (the hermeneutic circle) is familiar to many psychoanalysts (Schafer, 1992). Working at a metatheoretical level, Fajardo examined the different connections between the hidden epistemologies in psychoanalysis and the comparable forms of research work in psychology.

Nonlinear dynamic systems applications to developmental modeling stress features of asynchrony, gaps, ruptures, and novel integrations. Skills and capacities may exist simultaneously at different levels and arise from many different pathways. There is a constant interweaving and interaction between long-term macro changes and short-term, more micro-level changes. In a complex system with ongoing dynamism, dramatic change arises through disequilibration in the system and then through subsequent reorganizations. There is a crucial point here: these kinds of reorganizations would not be predictable from any original starting point.

Kauffman, among others, places as the centerpiece of chaos theory the capacity of organisms and systems to self-organize, to form what he has called autocatalytic sets, whose dynamic action emerges from coordinated activity, not simply from maturation. Regulation is therefore never solely a top-down phenomenon. Yet the resulting system is not anarchic, but one in which hierarchy is organized and emerges from actions and interactions at lower levels. Dynamic patterns produce hierarchical organizations resulting from changes and reorganizations and new coordinations within or between systems. Many human processes, at the individual, independent, and interdependent social levels, are self-organizing.[5] Baldwin's (1906) speculations on the emergence of thinking are relevant here: "An organism has somehow to acquire the capacity to turn around on its own schemata and to construct them afresh" (p. 14). Something like this capacity, drawing from a dyadic context, must be what enables the reflective functioning (observed and theorized by Fonagy and Target, 2002).

If much of the use of chaos theory still lives, in psychoanalysis, as a set of useful metaphors, there is a considerable body of work in developmental psychology producing rich descriptions of developmental process drawing on chaos theory. For its practitioners in developmental psychology, the nonlinear dynamic systems approach has ambitions beyond making metaphor. The empirical and theoretical work I have made most use of is Thelen and Smith's (1994) application of nonlinear dynamic systems theory to developmental problems that generate distinct, complex, and sophisticated data sets. Learning to walk, the development of early cognitive structures, the development of sensorimotor actions, infant cries, the growth of semantic and lexical meaning: all these human activities, which we generally imagine to be biologically or maturationally driven, can be shown empirically to follow the distinct, emergent, and nonpredictive patterns characteristic of nonlinear dynamic systems.

When these online, real-time developmental experiences (walking, meaning making, social interaction) are studied as dynamic systems, a very different picture of development comes into view, different from the kinds of stage theories or theories of developmental lines that many clinicians and developmentalists are used to. We know most about this focus on co-construction from infancy work, notably in the theoretical approach of Sander (1988). For Sander, it is the multilevel intricacy of systems entrainment that creates the ground for the expansion of individual consciousness and capacity. He has given highly specific developmental details to the kind of general thinking Vygotsky (1962) was doing, in which social scaffolding created and opened individual potentials.

Elman and his colleagues (Elman et al., 1997) have transformed the cognitive neuroscience computational tool "connectionism" into a new and dynamic set of conceptions. Terming themselves "developmental connectionists," they argue for plenty of brain specificity or modularity. But they argue that these phenomena develop. Modal structures, devoted to unique high-order cognitive, or sensory, functions, are the *outcome* not the preconditions for consciousness and thought. Developmental connectionism stresses plasticity, interaction effects, and the active construction of experience.

I would highlight three features of Elman's brand of "connectionism" that are highly relevant to psychoanalytic work on development: modularity, plasticity, and subthreshold knowledge. First, Elman and his colleagues (1997) demonstrate that it is not necessary to propose highly specific "innate" or "domain-specific" microcircuitry to account for complex capacities.[6] The term modularity is often used to claim a context-impervious, genetically driven character for such phenomena as language, gender, and sexuality.

The connectionists' claim is that modularity is an *outcome* not a beginning state. They demonstrate, through the use of complex learning systems, that word learning, sound-pattern prediction, labeling, and the learning of grammatical tenses are evolving competencies, built fast but in real time as an outcome of guided learning with feedback. Edelman (1987) offered this model as a prototype for skills learning as an effect of interactions at many levels in organisms and systems.

The connectionists reserve the term innateness for very restricted, specific uses. "Innateness" may describe constraints on processing, but not highly specific complex content. Representations would not be innate, but constraints on the networks and the architecture of connections that construct representations would be. Other built-in constraints involve timing, although, in this regard, the connectionists note some interesting variations in conventional developmental thinking.

Analysts looking at attachment and developmentalists looking at language development are familiar with the critical-stage hypothesis, a kind of limited window of opportunity for particular developments.[7] Here chaos theory presents clinicians with an interesting paradox. On one hand, highly complex and robust patterns (maladaptive or flexible) can emerge early and powerfully in development and appear to close off possibilities for change. On the other hand, change remains always in potential, dependent on conditions that open space for new equilibria. Some such conditions might be experiences of transference in which both old patterns and new possibilities oscillate in a way that, with careful titration, can lead to reorganization and new learning.

Second, connectionism makes good use of the new findings of plasticity not merely in immature organisms but in adults. The issue of plasticity is certainly related to the first point about innateness and the kinds of critical stage.[8] Plasticity must be involved in the fact that children exposed to a local language will learn it. Deaf children exposed to sign learn that form of communication in ways that are dramatically similar to those by which hearing children learn speech. There is also evidence that deaf children using sign for the visual-manual system of communication use brain circuitry that in hearing children would be used for auditory processing. It is this interplay between emergent use and specificity that characterizes these developmental models.

Connectionism's particular perspective on plasticity (with its limits and its potentials) offers a way to think about developmental process within treatments. This is the kind of process elaborated by Beebe and Lachmann (1998, 2002), who study the transformations of infant self-regulation and self–other regulation in adult treatments. Their clinical examples are often of subtle shifts in the nonverbal weather of the dyad, shifts that open a closed system and permit a new level of entrainment and communication.

Third, from the connectionist work on brain organization, a model of partial knowing, or "subthreshold" knowledge, has been elaborated. For clinicians this is a useful concept with which to think about dissociation. Dissociative states can be endemic in certain treatments, flowing back and forth between both participants in the dyad. Analyst and analysand can come upon the uncanny sense that an experience is both clear and opaque, known and unknown, foreign and familiar. This doubled experience of knowing and not knowing is at the heart of Bromberg's (1996a, 1998a, b, 1999) clinical work. From his clinical examples one can see that many different contexts can trigger a state change which often brings with it knowledge that feels both new and old, eerily unknown and familiar. Humor that leavens the intersubjective context may be one of those delightful modes of disequilibrium, potentially a safe point of transition and volatility. Affect states and shifts in the analyst—odd, inspired mishearings, many experiences at the edge of awareness, perhaps at the edge of chaos—can lead to a radical reorganization of what is known and what can be talked about. Whitmer (2001) proposes that dissociation is a kind of double knowing, one that is dependent on knowledge as dyadically distributed. This idea is central to relational thinking and guides many clinical choices and under-standings (Davies, 1996a, 2001a; Pizer, 1999; Bromberg, 2001a, b).

The mixture of conceptual fluidity and precision in connectionism, and in chaos theory generally, could be the draw for psychoanalysts. If the hallmark of a psychoanalytic understanding is the centrality of mean-ing as it is uniquely and individually constructed (Chodorow, 1999), then it may be useful to have a theory committed to such a high degree of plasticity that complex experience can arise in real time and in par-ticular and unique landscapes. Time is, in this theoretical scheme, a multiform process. This particular kind of plasticity may be a useful concept through which to see individual development as always pro-ceeding along several timelines. This work also addresses an important critique of developmental theory, namely that end points are estab-lished as genetic starting points, the outcome already normalized and expectable.

This new way of envisioning development can allow clinicians to see development in its nuanced variation and complexity, such that developmental process can have some of the subtlety that clinical expe-rience so powerfully reveals. By contrast, a developmental theory de-scribing global, unitary sets of developmental lines flattens and constricts our perspective on human growth.

Fajardo (1998), describing a research project on early infant ego capacity, showed that different explanatory approaches reveal different kinds of data: nonlinear processes are revealed only in particular, fine-grained data sets; linear change appears only at the macro level. Chaos theory, applied to development, produces ideas, experiences, and data sets that match well the variability and nonlinearity we experience in clinical work.

SIX FEATURES OF NONLINEAR DYNAMIC SYSTEMS

My second question in regard to the application of chaos theory to psychoanalysis centers on the matter of interdisciplinary borrowing. Regarding interdisciplinary projects, our field is quite divided. For some, consilience, E. O. Wilson's (1988) term for patterns across disciplines, is exciting and useful. For others, psychoanalytic clinical data should drive theory, and our concerns should remain domain specific. Clearly my heart is with the former approach. I cannot imagine psychoanalysis without also imagining the conversations between theorists interested in *developmental* aspects of psychoanalytic theory and developmentalists. Yet the project of designing useful conversations between disciplines entails many problems of translation, of language, of values, of power and interests. "Hard" science can be a phallic idealization, leading to various forms of "physics envy." For all our postmodern projects and impluses, we are still powerfully creatures of the Enlightenment. We are reassured by empiricism although, we hope, not omnipotently shored up by empiricist determinations.

Here are six features of the nonlinear dynamic systems approach that I believe merit highlighting for clinicians and analysts with developmental interests.

Order for Free

In Piers's (2000) application of chaos theory to the study of mind and character, he describes change that arises from simple processes that attain regularity but not exactly identity. These regularities might be something on the order of the procedural knowing that we observe in people when pattern, prior to language or symbolic representation, settles in. Experience will move toward organization but not stasis. The distinction that Piers notes between experiences that are self-same and experiences that are self-similar is important. Tiny distinctions, not discernable in any statistical sense, are nonetheless sufficient to produce distinct evolving patterns. This is a paradox in chaos theory, the interaction of indeterminacy and pattern.[9]

Rigidity, in a clinical dyad or in a person's character, is a sign of pathology. A fully rigid system might, in fact, be a morbid system. Sadomasochistic dances, oscillating patterns of idealization and degradation, can produce polarized impasses in clinical work that are familiar and deadly. These oscillating, rigid patterns are manifestations of self-same organizations. But a system whose parameters feature similarity among elements, not identity, carries the potential for change and reorganization. Often quite subtle shifts in systems, introducing small elements of novelty and difference, are sufficient for movement and change. One could imagine an analyst and a patient caught in a powerful oscillating system of antagonism and incomprehension. Movement and disequilibrium and reorganization might be possible only when the analyst can keep a doubled experience of entrainment and reflection. There is a wonderful clinical example of this effect of disequilibrium in Britton's

(1992) account of the difficulty certain patients have tolerating experiences of difference in the analyst. "Stop that fucking thinking," a patient shouts at him. Something alive and disequilibrating in the analyst's internal system has disrupted the patient's internal, polarized world of kill or be killed.

Palumbo (1998) suggests that clinical impasses that are fatal to treatment may be those in which the analyst no longer looks for difference in the patient and no longer imagines the patient as capable of growth. More than just rigidity, morbidity has set in. Chaos theory is a useful corrective for clinical pessimism. Very subtle differences, self-similar not self-same iterations, have profound possibilities for the appearance of new experiences. Chaos theory has the illuminating example of the movements of a butterfly in Brazil leading, in a series of iterations, to typhoons in Japan.

Another implication of this model of development is that in any complex system there is both variation built into the system and multiple pathways even if the system initiates in an extremely simple yet rigorous pattern. It is certainly a hallmark of relational theory (Bromberg, 1998a, 1999; Mitchell, 2000) to think of human experience as self-organizing, with organization evolving from relational contexts. Add to this Fischer and Watson's (2002) conception of synchronous and multilevel experience and inevitably human individuality seems to come in multiple or manifold forms.

Nonlinearity

A nonlinear dynamic system is one in which, from simple, describable beginnings, radical, unpredictable differences set in very quickly. One follows the emergence of such a system knowing the components and relative weightings and interactions at the starting point. But within a very few iterations change becomes patterned but unpredictable. Terms like maturation have reduced explanatory power in this kind of thinking. There is always a novel yet organized process of interaction of context and individual (Trofimova, 2000).

Development is not executively planned but built out of experience that increasingly bootstraps more complex experiences from simple rules and functions. When chaos theorists describe this process, they sound a lot like certain hermeneuticists: "The emergent structures exist by means of the parts, but the component parts are present both because of and in order to sustain the whole" (Kauffman, 1995, p. 69). Development enables a child to become increasingly selective across contexts and to use contextual clues in increasingly complex reentrant mappings.[10] This is a theoretical approach in which mobility and stability interact or oscillate and *nonlinear* change occurs in what is termed a punctuated equilibrium. Open systems brim with the potential for change, always susceptible to variation from sources that may be internal or external to the system. Variation produces information. Information, as Palumbo (1998) suggests in a wonderful image, is a form of food or energy absorbed by a system and in this process alters it and is altered by it.

Let us look in some detail at Thelen's (1986, 1995; Thelen, Bradshaw, and Ward, 1981; Thelen and Fischer, 1982; Thelen and Ulrich, 1991; Thelen and Corbetta, 2002) empirical work. She and her colleagues use chaos theory to model skills we might think "prewired," such as infant cry and locomotion. She demonstrates that there is no advantage to thinking of constitutional features as immutable or linearly, predictably unfolding. Descriptive and explanatory accounts of walking as a key exemplar of motor maturation are among the oldest and most robust features in developmental psychology. Their provenance goes back to Gesell (1940, 1946, 1948; Gesell and Thompson, 1934, 1938). Conventional wisdom had it that walking went from reflexive to intentional behavior under the guidance of some central executive brain center. It was thought to be a maturational process driven by neural systems. Hence the development of a capacity to walk would be linear and under a unitary causal program.

Thelen (1995) paints a very different picture. There is no simple isomorphism between brain and action or outcome, but any process in which the organism/individual interacts with the environment requires a coordination of subsystems in patterns that are highly context dependent. Action takes place in a continually changing force field. So what looks like a smooth, automatic pattern, a hand outstretched to catch a ball, for example, is potentially organized and coordinated by many local and variable subsytems. There will be multiple possible pathways to what, on the surface, appears to be a smooth and identically repeating action. Only a body–mind reactive to context, not operating from executive design, could explain an individual's ongoing capacity to move smoothly and skillfully through time and environment: kicking a soccer ball, dancing a waltz.

> For infants as well as for adults, movements are always a product of not only central nervous system but also of the biomechanical and energetic properties of the body, the environmental support and the specific (and sometimes changing) demands of the particular task. The relations between these components is not simply hierarchical (the brain commands, the body responds) but is profoundly distributed, heterarchical, self organizing and non linear. Every movement is unique: every solution is fluid and flexible [Thelen, 1995, p. 81].

Through a series of developmental studies beginning at one month and following individual children over most of the first year, Thelen demonstrated that walking is a multidimensional and multicomponent experience, with subsystems (kicking, balancing, stepping, etc.) all emergent and changing along distinct timelines and along very distinct nonlinear trajectories. There could be sudden phase shifts, reversals and disappearances, at steady growth; and a number of different control parameters seem to affect how this process of walking is enacted by any particular child. Mood, arousal level, motivation, postural and muscular biodynamics, structural properties, and proportions of body type, as well as motor maturation, all play a role. Central nervous system executive patterning is not the only or the dominant control parameter for walking. In fact, it is the unique and context-specific coordinating of subsytems that is most crucial for the appearance and stability of walking.

Walking occurs in a changing force field of movement in real time such that biodynamic challenges more than brain directives are potent sources of organization and stability. If coordination is locally not executively managed, then any system is advantaged by elements of indeterminacy. Even stable behaviors that seem both preprogrammed and consistent over time are actually systems whose open energy is in a constant exchange with the surround. Stability is not equivalent to hardwiring. This is one hallmark of the nonlinear dynamic systems approach to development: goals are emergent not preset. Asynchrony occurs often. Thelen models development as a landscape, not as a staircase or an escalator whose end point is set from the moment of entry.

Nonlinearity is a particular feature marking a distinction from developmental theories that treat time nonproblematically and view developmental lines as arcs of maturational unfolding. It is actually a feature of chaos theory that may be particularly applicable to a psycho-analytic account where time is often quite complex. *Nachtraglichkeit,* the experience where the strange emotional effects appear to move back-ward in time. Later-occurring events reorganize, remap, and sometimes retraumatize earlier events. This is a powerful distinctly nonlinear pro-cess. The variations in how time enters memory and then reenters on-going experience are phenomena we encounter often in clinical work.

A good example of the place and scope of diversity is in De Marneffe's (1997) careful observations of children's use and organiza-tion of bodily experience, gender category names, and gender identity. She has charted a variable set of organizations for individual children that integrates general findings and specific pathways. Her intention was to unpack the too globally conceived mixture of experiences in a child's emerging sense of gender. She found that many factors may af-fect the rate, ordering and unfolding, and construction of the complex experience of gender. De Marneffe noted consistent gender difference in the availability of names for genitals. It is as though girls and boys, with all their individual differences, inhabit different problem spaces when it comes to learning labels for body parts. How this difference will integrate in any child's emerging construction of gender as a body-based identity, as a category of experience, and as an intersubjectively orga-nized self-state is a question answered at the individual level. Coates (1997), discussing this work, argues for the importance of nonlinearity, of multiple and differing developmental trajectories.

Attractors

One of the workhorse concepts in chaos theory is the notion of *attractors.* A crucial aspect of the paradigm shift in nonlinear dynamic systems theory is the shift in focus from structure to function and to process. This requires holding in mind quite a contradictory notion in regard to the concept of attractors. Attractors, in whatever formation (strange, chaotic, periodic, and deeply basined) are described in structural often spatial forms but they are not reified, static objects.

Attractors are points of convergence without being exactly points of gravity and not structures as much as dynamic patterns, sometimes regular, sometimes bimodal and sometimes fractal and strange. Attractors describe qualities of dynamic experience rather than things.

Attractors can be defined as those fixed points in the stream of behavior, but fixed points that are nonetheless dynamic and potentially susceptible to transformation. Attractors can be modeled as deeply troughed or rigid pattern forms or as rather fluidly assemblies that mutate and reassemble in new and distinct configurations. This concept identifies the unique ways that individual experience is unfolding and self-organizing, changing through multidimensional phase spaces and moving along multiple time scales. Metaphoric spatial terms like "basins," "valleys," "eddies in a moving stream" are conjured up to convey the organization of patterns that have global but dynamic coherence and microvariation.

Stuart Kauffman developed the image of lake and basins, with a variety of trajectories flowing into some steadying repository. This image was a means for grasping the relative mix of stability and variation in any state. Piers (in press) has described a variety of attractors, each conveying distinct forms of experience. A fixed pendulum would be a rigid attractor with distinct quite change resistant qualities. Piers (2000) has analyzed character along these lines equating pathology with rigidity. Piers (in press) evoked another striking image for attractors. Imagine the charred ash of a fire. It is a sign that a system has formed, emerged, and transformed. Attractors don't exactly drive a system, they are the outcome of activities of systems in perturbation and movement.

Thelen also uses the image of an attractor as a basin between two hills. Depending on the slope and depth of the valley, an object will be trapped and immobilized in the valley or susceptible to bounces and shifts in terrain. The most intriguing attractor state in chaos theory is the so-called strange attractor, a system always on the edge of deterministic chaos, a state that can be disequilibrated and reorganized in unexpected ways.

I am going to follow in some detail her use of dynamic systems theory and the concept of attractors to describe an unfolding dynamic as infants learn to reach.

Thelen and Smith (1994) think of an attractor and its surrounding basin as a momentarily stable, equilibrated place, a preferred topology or a particular behavioral mode. She also uses the phrase "attractor regime"

> only determined as the system is assembled. . . . There are no codes, prescriptions, schemata, or programs orchestrating the nature of the attractor or its trajectory. As we shall see, under different conditions,

the components are free to assemble into other stable behavioral modes, and it is indeed this ability of a multi-component system to "soft assemble" that both provides the enormous flexibility of biological systems and explains some of the most persistent problems in development [p. 60].

Thelen and Smith illustrate the power of nonlinear dynamic systems in a study of children's learning to reach. From the study of a classic developmental sequence such as that studied by Piaget and contemporary researchers like Trevarthan, Thelen's data suggest that reaching and grasping are neither the innately maturing phenomena that Trevarthan notes nor a simple coordination of perceptual and motor action into higher order schemas. The children Thelen studied found unique and distinctly novel solutions, organized in different attractor spaces, to the problem of reaching and grasping an object.

One child flapped his arms like a wild spring and had to modulate action and in a sense tame the biomechanics of his grasping. Another child sat quietly and had to generate an action, responding to considerable environmental input and handling. Another child thrashed wildly one week, coordinated both hands at another point, and was quite disorganized and not functioning bimanually at yet another time.

Thelen and Smith's (1994) online, real-time registering of a wide variety of measures of action, watching, and reacting yielded a picture of development in which the endpoint, smooth motor action to coordinate reach and gaze, was a global outcome achieved through a myriad of distinct, uneven, and variable developmental pathways.

> A new skill in one domain, a new motor milestone or success at a Piagetian cognitive task—often appears as if the precursors to that skill should be privileged in that domain. But . . . the story is more complex and often surprising. Fat changes motor skills, motor skills change cognitive abilities [p. 277].

There is always a dynamic matrix of distinct domains and skills in any higher order complex behavior. It is these kinds of findings—the multifunctionality of experiences, the variation in developmental pathways, the coconstruction of attractor spaces—that suggest the limits to a theory of distinct developmental lines and implies an advantage to a process-based dynamic model of change and development.

Applying the developmental model proposed here to the evolution of gender draws from Ghent (2002) and from Edelman's (1987) work on motivation and evolving systems. Gender is built on processes that may not initially be gender coded. Gender is a kind of layering that occurs as the child, and the child in relationships, goes beyond those early experiences on which values, in Edelman's sense, are set. These experiences, like Laplanche's (1989) "initial somatic receptivity," might be no more than orientation to food, warmth, and contact.

Development proceeds through a process of "reentry and remapping."[8] The terms reentry and remapping come from Edelman's theory of neuronal group selection. He has described the assumptions of this theory very simply as three steps. First, there is a dynamic (and highly variable) process of selection and organization at the level of neuroanatomy. This selection is constrained by environmental and species conditions. Second, through experience in real time, particular functional circuits are "carved out" (1987, p. 83). This secondary repertory he thinks of as the formation of memory. Then, in a process which for Edelman has the potential to connect physiology to psychology, brain maps formed in the first two steps in the process come into unique interactions via a process he calls reentry.

Yet, quite soon within this system of encircling landscapes, gender will come to be some kind of attractor, some sort of organization in which such seemingly simple matters as food, warmth, and contact may take on unique "gendered" meanings and affect states. The gender imposed as meaning on these experiences may have salience sometimes for the parent, sometimes for the child. The layering of gender into ongoing developmental process is thus a subtle kind of "interpellation" as the culture, via the family, "reads" certain child experiences as gendered. These readings, of course, are local, not universal.[9]

Let me return to the metaphor Piers (in press), uses, describing attractors not as things but as the sign of process. Attractors leave a kind of trace that reveals the system that produced them. Piers used the image of charred remains of a fire as a sign (or index) of the dynamics of fire. In personality one might watch for complexity of pattern, of regularity, and distinct types of action (polarized or fractal) to describe the experience of the subject with old (periodic, polarized) and new (fractal) objects. The attractors do not drive the system; rather the system's emergent activity produces the particularity of pattern and change.

Might this be a way to think about gender as a melancholic structure? Might we not see gender as the charred remains of various fires, set intrapsychically and interpersonally, representing conflicts between loving and being that cannot be fully metabolized and "internalized"?

Gender could be constituted as an attractor, an emergent pattern with particular qualities that depend on the context, the rate of change and movement. Gender as an attractor would be composed of or incorporate a variety of subsystems, but this kind of integration again would be context dependent. Attractors are points of expression of both long-term and short-term change. It is therefore around gender conceived as an attractor that we might observe the interweaving of the long-term historical processes with microlevel transitions and interactions. Gender as an attractor would be a touch point where systems intersect explosively or cooperatively: historical, familial, individual.

Complexity

In a nonlinear dynamic systems model, development is a process of progressive integration in which complexity develops and then is reorganized into higher level but often radically simpler structures (Waldrop, 1992). Development unpredictably yaws back and forth between complexity and simplicity in a way that chaos theorists as well as earlier figures such as Werner (1957) or Vygotsky (1962) easily imagined.[9]

I believe a psychoanalytic project is immeasurably strengthened by exploring the implications of thinking that "dynamic categories are the primitives of mental life right from the start" (Thelen and Smith, 1991, p. 311). Developmental accounts should start from very simple primitives (Thelen's term for orientations to warmth and sound), drawing on the barest minimum needed to start what becomes highly complex developmental cascades. I use "primitive states" in Edelman's (1987) sense: "a richly interconnected matrix that through mutual activation and entrainment construct an ever more sharply defined functional reality" (p. 100).

For developmentalists there is certainly an affinity between chaos theory and the dominant developmental theory of this past century, namely, that of Piaget. But the affinity is not to the Piaget (1924) of reified structures and stages or monolithic cognitive frameworks. Rather the affinity is to the Piagetian concepts of equilibration and disequilibration, the dynamic model of change, and to an underutilized element in Piaget—vertical *décalage*—a concept through which Piaget introduced variation and discontinuity in level of functioning. Thelen's theory is, in a certain way, a critical revision of Piaget. She stresses the dynamic dimension of Piaget's' account of early sensorimotor intelligence. Piaget was able to see that thinking begins with acting. He thus decentered thought from logic and abstraction and instead grounded it in sensorimotor experience.

This view of mind as embodied mind is at the heart of Irene Fast's (1985) integration of Freud and Piaget. She undertook to see a child's way of understanding the world, not as reception or simply a taking in but as an engaged, body-based encounter with objects and others. This is a view of cognition as body based. Action is a mode of perceiving and knowing. As I consider later, this perspective is very interestingly echoed in the work on category formation and language being developed by Lakoff and Johnson (1980) in which meaning is emergent from action, interaction, and body-based life.

An important aspect of chaos theory lies in the paradox between simplicity and complexity. Beginning in a very subtle simple set of behaviors that Thelen refers to as primitives (Thelen and Smith, 1994, p. 311), interactions and individual capacities become very complex within a very few iterations. A number of developmental problems are often defaulted to some explanation of innateness because the developmental curve seems so steep, infant capacities, speech comprehension, and language learning being important examples. It is almost an axiom of Chomskian-based (1965) psycholinguistics that the acquisition of rules comes online too fast to be learnable. Chaos theory, placing a high premium on complexity as a cascading achievement, offers a new way to see many crucial experiences of growth as emergent in a system, particularly, though not exclusively, a dyadic system.

Development in a Relational Context

A number of writers drawing on chaos theory (Fajardo, 1998; Palumbo, 1998; Beebe and Lachmann, 2002; Ghent, 2002; Sander, 2002), have exploited the systems aspect of the theory. This is a model of development that is poised subtly between individual and system, giving ground fully to neither and watching for phenomena that appear only in context.

In contemporary developmental research it is increasingly axiomatic that individuality arises within a matrix of significant others and relational experiences. Sroufe (1990), for example, argues that the self should be conceived as an inner organization of attitudes, feelings, expectations and meanings which arises itself from an organizational caregiving matrix (a dyadic organization that exists prior to the emergence of the self) and which has organizational significance. . . . The self is organization. It arises from organization. It influences ongoing organization of experience [p. 281].

Sroufe's developmental analysis centers a core self in the infant's experience of operating with internal working models. These are models of a relationship not yet a self. Similarly, Sander (2002) describes stage shifts in the first year of life from coordinated sequences of regulation and joined affect first managed by the adult that later allow the child to initiate sequencing. There is a move from repetitive relatedness and patterning to the working model that is person specific and thus a period in which loss or extended disruption of relatedness becomes meaningful. Sander, in a systems-theory conception, sees the child as introducing perturbations in a system to test their impact. He pays considerable attention to what we might term negative action (whether anger based, simply assertive, or aggressive) as an important site for the anchoring of a working internal model of the self.

Sander (1988) and Hofer (1980, 1995) detail the complex entrainments, bidirectional between parent and infant, that enable individual development.[10] These are what Hofer has termed hidden regulators, a host of physiological processes that establish patterned experience from birth onward. The presence of these deeply patterned interactions creates the conditions for the appearance of representations of increasing sophistication and symbolization.

These interactions, relations in context, are the substrate and the ingredients of what become intersubjective processes and reflective capacity. The bodily connection between mother and infant is the precursor to mind as well as to attachment pattern and relatedness. Vicissitudes in these early patterns have an effect at all levels: physiological, perceptual, and affective. The power of this early regulation is such that profoundly important body links are formed even in the presence of toxic aspects of the relational context.

Hofer (1984, 1995, 1996) describes effects that are not only early ways of binding systems but also processes that reappear in relations with adult caretakers and in adult reactions to stress and loss. The work of Beebe and her colleagues (2000) to integrate clinical theory and attachment research mines this idea, that procedural knowing is endlessly reintegrated into ongoing experiences. Lyons-Ruth (1999) and Lyons-Ruth et al. (1992, 1993), exploring the unfolding consequences of disorganized attachment, have noticed the vulnerability, both to ordinary and to extraordinary circumstances, of children who grew up in a disorganized attachment system. In Hofer's (1995) research and in Lyons-Ruth's (1999) theoretical applications to analytic ideas, the evolution and the tenacity of early pattern are salient.

Another view of the relational context is exemplified in Palumbo's (1998) account of cooperating and competing antagonisms in two-person systems. Drawing on game theory, Palumbo models the two-person clinical dyad in terms of shared and unshared assumptions. What is the capacity of the analysand to trust the analyst? How, in the transference, is an antagonistic, resistance mode of interaction interwoven with trusting cooperation? Palumbo's insight is that asymmetry in the analytic dyad is a potential source of change. It is the doubled state of awareness in the analyst, when he or she can decenter from the rigid polarized stasis with a patient, that opens up mutative action. States of multiple consciousness, being stuck and being aware of being stuck, offer the potential to override the rigid, more morbid system's organization, moving a periodic attractor regime into a constellation more like the more volatile, disequilibrating strange attractors.

Transformation and Developmental Change

Chaos theory functions in marked contrast to linear stage models of development. It takes a perspective on change process that is different from that of theories endowing separate developmental lines for particular psychodynamic processes. What attracts me to this approach is that it is a way to put development back into developmental theory, a way to focus on change itself. Variation, movement, and dynamism are the givens of such a system.

Fischer (1980; Fischer and Watson, 1992; Fischer et al., 1997), one of the most important neo-Piagetian cognitive theorists, captures the power of nonlinear dynamic systems theory as a model of change. One of his key interests is in identifying transition mechanisms, and his approach is boldly constructivist. His methodology is designed to watch the interactions and intrinsic relationships between micro- and macrolevels of skill and capacities. Skills cluster and organize in unique configurations depending on social context, biological context, and the time and space needed for any skill's evolution. Knowledge that is, first of all, local and contextual is "gradually consolidated, generalized and related through continual microlevel constructive processes on many fronts" (Fischer and Bidell, 1998, p. 513).

Fischer (Fischer and Bidell, 1998) has identified four aspects of these transitions. First, transitions are characterized by a new capacity to shift focus or to have a kind of double focus. Here we might think of shifting self-states, the standing in the spaces that Bromberg (1996b) proposes, as one site of psychic transformation. Second, as skills cluster, they organize in hierarchical formations. As a child develops competence from distinctive local experiences, simple mappings and representations proliferate. As commonalities emerge, distinctive mappings have to organize into hierarchies through rules of inclusion and exclusion (Feffer, 1988, has worked on a similar model for cognitive reorganization).

A quantitative continuum of skill development is, at some point, efficiently reorganized into a qualitatively different pattern of hierarchy and ordering. This is an example of Kauffman's (1995) "order for free." There is something else to notice in Fischer's model. Change is a response to deepening constraints within a system. As mapping and harmonies of pattern become more integrated, there will be a moment when the system has to reorganize to accommodate the new experiences. Reorganization, the outcome of successive actions and reactions, leads to hierarchy and reflection. Organization is emergent, not imposed from some top-down executive function in the mind. There is local government in the psyche, not a monarchy.

Fischer's third and fourth aspects are dialogic and dyadic, involving the kind of repetition and generalizing that arises when people work on a problem together. He uses the term bootstrapping to describe how one domain's competence can be drawn into change and growth within another. One can track this process in the tremendous change in focus in the field of early cognition, which now is deeply centered on social cognition.

The knowledge in young children that is most vital to understand combines thoughts, feelings, feelings about others, intentions, and an understanding of others' intentions in the context of social relatedness (Bruner, 1986, 1990; Olson, 1988; Meltzoff, 1990, 1995; Fonagy and Target, 1996; Fonagy, 1997). Interest is in how children come to understand and represent others' minds and experiences, a "skill" that draws on affect, perception, cognition, and attachment experiences. Similarly, motor development, cognitive growth, and different affect states and interactive capacities interweave in unique, context-sensitive organizations. This is a perspective antithetical to the idea of separate developmental lines, traced and predictable from some starting point.

Fischer notes that, in a variety of situations and tasks, change is often prefaced by experiences in multiple registers and at distinct levels of competence. Dual or shifting representations can be a maddening and challenging aspect in clinical work as analysands gain and abandon gains in understanding, often within the same hour. Yet it is precisely this doubleness that creates the conditions of reorganization and movement. Strange attractors, to draw from the chaos theory bag of tools, may be the signposts of such transitional moments.

In many important developmental transitions, a child or adult holds dual representations. Developmental change is not a matter of stepping up a ladder but moving through a kaleidoscope, weaving and being woven into a web of meaning and narration. It is as though one lives in conditions in which something is simultaneously known and yet not known. This state of doubled awareness is a conflictual but also a creative moment. This idea can be highly meaningful to clinicians. For example, it is certainly one way of describing the experience of transference or countertransference, a simultaneous immersion in highly charged affective material, an imaginary but deeply felt experience of self and other accompanied by much secondary process and reflective awareness. This perspective on transference, as performed and lived, as a mix of primary and secondary process was articulated by Loewald (1949, 1980). All improvisation has the dual character of free play and order (Knoblauch, 2000, 2001; Ringstrom, 2001a, b).

Fischer's description of bridging sounds remarkably like the working of "a hermeneutic circle" (see Stern, 1996, 1997, for an application of hermeneutics to psychoanalysis).

> In bridging people direct the construction of their own knowledge thereby functioning at two levels simultaneously: They establish a target level of skill or understanding which lies unconstructed beyond their current level of understanding and they use it as a shell for constructing understanding. In this process of self-scaffolding, the target shells that people build are partial and fuzzy, but they provide a framework that directs the search for new knowledge. People then use their activities to gradually fill in components of the shell until they have moved themselves to a higher level of understanding for the new task in context [Fischer and Bidell, 1998, p. 519].

One of the shifts in modern cognition theory, that toward an integrated model of emotion and cognition and toward an appreciation of variability of developmental pathways, is a shift away from structure as reification or reduction. In a sense, phenomena are always understood as living, dynamic action patterns. Structures are artifactual, and a reified rigid system is in essence a moribund system. Human thought, feeling, and action are always self-organizing and in motion.

This material is both highly abstract and, for many clinicians, a new model of analysis. So, I am repeating and elaborating in this chapter ideas developed in the earlier chapter on multiplicity. I will also apply many of these concepts to the analysis of gender in chapter 6. Multiplicity is a key site for change process. Dual representations, doubled modes of knowing and acting, and variable pathways are all constructs that suggest that for anyone multiple or manifold self-states are usual. Coherence is the form a particular dynamic pattern may have from a certain vantage point. But, close in, the variegation in pattern emerges. Skill clusters, self-states, multiple personas: we have different languages for what is being described as a highly useful feature of human functioning. Given that contexts, in particular social contexts, have so much variation, variability in and between individuals seems an effective aspect of human growth.

Kauffman develops these ideas in an exploration of what he terms "the edge of chaos," the phase space in which systems are poised between disorganization and stasis, an optimal moment for movement. I think this concept could be usefully mapped to Fonagy's (1998) concept of the moment of change in a treatment dyad. In an extensive clinical example, Fonagy notes a powerful process in which a patient kept intact an actually quite brittle sense of potency and grandiosity by evacuating or projecting into the analyst any self-experience that was vulnerable, inchoate, or anxious. There were subtle and not so subtle interpersonal communications and strategies through which this patient transmitted grim, unpleasant self-beratements into the analyst. It is a familial clinical moment and one that requires enormous capacity in the analyst to accept, metabolize, and organize into a self-system without collapse or rigid polarization.

Paradoxically, at the point of maximum difficulty there is a moment of potential transformation. It is at the moment where the negative projections, seen as alien, can be evacuated, as it were, housed elsewhere, that the analysand may be available for new feedback. Often this is a moment too chaotic and disorganizing for the analyst to function. But under certain conditions these moments are at the edge of chaos, a point where a new organization has some potential. What makes the difference? In psychoanalytic terms, it is the difference between being able to use a projection as a communication rather than as a defense (Rosenfeld, 1983). Drawing on chaos theory, we might see these moments as potentiated by an extensive experience of being held in mind, being thought about by a listener and thinker who can bear the damaging projection/feedback without disorganizing and who can maintain a hierarchy of understanding and attributions. Perhaps also this moment of potential psychic change must occur because a larger, two-person system has been sufficiently elaborated and the experience of multiple minds and consciousnesses is integratable.

Chaos theory might open up another way of thinking about mutative action in clinical work. We often, rather melodramatically, link intrapsychic change to immediate, short-term actions. We tag the change itself to a moment of interpretation or some local intervention within a session or sequence of sessions. Can we put this process into the language of chaos theory? Does the interpretative event produce disequilibration or does the interpretation register the aftermath of disequilibrium? Does the presence of an interpretation indicate that a transition has already occurred?

Within analytic space, transference phenomena, themselves fluctuating and fluid experiences (Bollas, 1987), might be the registration of long-term molar transitions within which more immediate, short-term microtransitions arise. The containing experience of transference or countertransference operates as a kind of scaffold enabling an analysand to integrate new understandings. In our consideration of the experience in analysis of being and having both new and old objects (Cooper, 2000)—often an aspect of transference states—we might see the presence of a doubled consciousness. It is the experience of several strands of consciousness, multiplicities of experience that may facilitate change as the discrepancies in self-states emerge into awareness.

DEVELOPMENTAL MODELS
AND A PLACE FOR FANTASY

The final question I raised at the start of this chapter is obviously the most difficult. How well can this model address matters of fantasy, unconscious process, and the highly complex interaction of culture and psyche? And at this point, we move from model to metaphor. Thelen and Smith (1994) address the question of nonlinear dynamic systems theory applications to higher order mental processes. They make a strong case for the study of many higher order developmental phenomena (cognition, motivation, affect) as nonlinear dynamic systems, but they acknowledge a shift away from empirical work to conceptual modeling. They draw on what is one of the most appealing and aesthetically elegant aspects of chaos theory, namely, that highly complex behaviors can emerge with dramatic speed from very simple primitives. Or, as Holland (1998) proposes, chaos theory allows you to explore "subtle consequences of the interaction of prosaic mechanisms" (p. 11).

The question cannot yet be, is there a fully articulated, simulatable model for higher order behavior, particularly those involving human consciousness? Rather the question is, can this innovative model stimulate our own creative imagining in psychoanalysis both theoretically and clinically? Moran (1991) has done just that by mapping chaos theory to notions of drive and unconscious process.

One key problem, to judge from the recent volume of work examining attachment theory and theories of infantile sexuality, is that there seems to be no place for unconscious phenomena and fantasy (Widlocher, 2002). There is a longstanding antipathy between certain kinds of psychoanalytic thinking and developmental research (Wolff, 1960, 1996, 1998; Green, 2000) that chaos theory might begin to bridge.

A systems theory approach to development certainly widens and elaborates distinct and multiple pathways, but its very even handedness with regard to developmental outcome carries its own potential ideology. A kind of democracy of possibilities arises in this perspective. There is the danger of a utopian idealization here. The landscapes in which anyone develops are riddled with paradoxes, with interdictions and roadblocks both rational and irrational. There is the particular human draw to excitement precisely where there is transgression, risk, and prohibition. Psychoanalysis is founded on that insight. Psychoanalytic developmental theory takes as a core assumption that certain moments of mismatch are powerfully constitutive of any person's subjectivity. There is the encounter of radically asynchronous developmental systems (mother and infant), an aspect of developmental experience on which Laplanche (1997, 2002) and others have focused much attention. There is the processing of separation and connection. There is the registration of rules and exclusions with the attendant amalgam of shame, guilt, and excitement.

Chaos theory allows us to imagine development along multiple timelines, which sometimes do and sometimes do not overlap and intersect. People are embedded in families and in cultures but also in particular historical cohorts and periods, and all these phenomena carry processes of change with their own distinct movements. No task is perhaps more daunting than that of mapping long-term, macrolevel change to the transmission modes within local institutions, families, and parent–child dyads and the active creative organizations of meaning by the individual.

Developmentalists like Kurt Fischer (1980; Fischer and Watson, 2002) have been arguing that long-term changes must interface with the particular developmental transitions that arise in an individual's life. Particular events (depression, war, rapid technological transformation, migration, genocide) carry a long-lasting, slowly altering radioactivity. The effects may be graphic or subtle, and the intergenerational transmission can be unconscious (Coates, Friedman, and Wolfe, 1991; Apprey, 1996, 2003; Schechter, 2003). We know that many traumatic moments have complex, multigenerational shelf lives.

Thinking from a chaos theory perspective, we will want to understand how these macroevents enter the particular dynamic interactions of smaller systems—individual, dyadic, triadic, familial—and subtly affect many aspects of functioning in the next generation. Certain processes, gender, for example, may powerfully attract and organize historical and social changes that might originally have been either gender salient or gender agnostic. The human task of individuation and differentiation, itself likely to be arrived at through many cultural variations, is in Western culture enabled by gender meanings. This is a particular construction, not a universal. As Dimen (1991, 2000), among others, has argued, gender seems to attract and organize many other phenomena.

Thinking of the prospects of chaos theory, or nonlinear, dynamic systems theory, as a potential space for elements of consciousness, fantasy, and unconscious formations, might be a way to open up discussion of the oedipal crisis, its evolution, its resolution, its precursors, and its aftermath. It is around the oedipal situation, in all its manifestations, that many debates about development, normativity, language, and representation all cohere. An exploration into new bidirectional models for oedipality is taken up in Davies's (2003a, b) work in which a child's identities and forms of desire arise in a crucible of multiple, conflicting systems of desire and containment, safety, and danger.

Gender as Soft Assembly

CHAPTER 4

❧

Gender Narratives in Psychoanalysis

*I*t is increasingly difficult to write with coherence or with innocence about gender as some monolithic, simple, comprehensible
concept. We have to keep putting words like feminine and masculine in irony-conveying quotation marks. With these rhetorical devices
we signal our understanding that these terms have meaning only in
particular and unique contexts and that these contexts shift constantly.

We think and practice and write with such self-consciousness because, in the past 30 years, the experiences knotted into gender identities and sexual life have come under extreme scrutiny. Gender words
and the phenomena they signify have come unglued. Assumed to describe easily and unremarkably various ways of being or loving, gender's
language worlds have been breaking down, breaking open, breaking
free. We use terms like shape shifting, gender morphing—terms from
science fiction and graphic, dynamic, visual media—to convey the complex fluidity of body and psychic life coming under the various rubrics
of gender.

Patients and analysts alike struggle with new and old language,
category terms that carry primary process, charged affective meanings, and words we want to bend to new uses. This seems true at the
level of popular culture, of social and personal life, of clinical experience, and in the shifting and demanding worlds of gender theory and
psychoanalytic theories.

Words bend or they resist. Clinical conversations detail both the
necessary coherence and the troubling gaps and excesses in being a
gender, or having a body, as the following clinical vignettes suggest.
Seen through a relational lens, gender, in these lives and circumstances,

is intersubjectively coconstructed and lived in deep intrapsychic complexity and conflict. Gendered experience bounces off personal history and the larger social history. Gender is more usefully imagined as a function than simply as a structure. Gender functions as a way of doing various psychic and relational tasks in certain ways. For some the traffic of gender is pure pain, for some, a mixed blessing. For some, gender's presence in various psychic functions is rigid and palpable; for others gender seems thin and almost transparent.

JAMIE: GENDER'S HIDDEN TORMENTS AND HIDDEN PLEASURES

The woman I greet for the first time in my waiting room is slouched against the doorjamb. She is scowling, cap pulled low over her face. As I got to know her, I found Jamie to be attractive, enigmatic, easily androgynous in look and style. But along with this pleasing way of being, there was great internal pain and self-doubt. The dilemma she presented was a newly severe conflict over her artistic work, a conflict sharpened after the birth of a son. This conflict seems not the conventional problem of divided loyalties and constraints on time and energy. To her considerable surprise, Jamie feels both delight and confidence in her maternal capacities. When I ask who it was that I met leaning against the door in the waiting room, she is eager to tell me that the sense of herself as boy has been lifelong, intensely felt, deeply important. The person who mothers and the person who writes simply seem to live in different worlds.

Jamie can play with gender but also, almost without warning, feel herself in the grip of a death struggle, within herself and with me. She conveys much of her difficulty with identity and genderedness by her way of talking. Her speech is split among many genres and many registers. Extremely verbal, she has a magical capacity for speech, a comic style. I notice her liveliness and humor when she is engaging me. She clearly feels that her job in therapy is to keep me entranced and interested, to bring me to life. She can describe with intensity and detail a lifelong project of devoted attention to older women who, finally, in gratitude for her lively love, take her in and animate her, clarifying once and for all what she imagines as the limits and potential of her body self.

But everything changes when she speaks of herself, when she is moved to describe her conflicts in terms of her body and her body in relation to others. Her speech is fractured and violent, hateful and hating; the berating of body and mind is overwhelming. She is tearful, confused. The dominant mood in this rumination is hopelessness and horror. Whatever clear, interesting narrative capacity she retains when talking to me, her body talk and body experience fall frighteningly into incoherence.

Her voice and face soften and gleam when she describes her child, but then helplessly she adds that it is unbelievable that this being came from her body. The child is fine and beautiful; she is gross. Where was there space for something lovely to grow? She describes a dream in which a doctor shows her X-rays in which she has two small ovaries with a tiny enigmatic body nestled between them. Will he need to operate? She has another doctor dream at the beginning of her treatment. A woman doctor (the doctor who referred her to me) examines her genitals, tracing her labia, exciting her. Jamie wonders if this is all right. In another dream, I am a therapist working in a perfume shop. I want to sell her a fragrance. Nazi doctor, seductress doctor, and purveyor of femininity: to enter discourse with a doctor or with a woman is to bring the body alive, but also into many dangers—danger of extraction, of theft of the insides of the body, and the danger of enchanted takeover.

Jamie's body is split in ways other than gender or by gender in other ways. Top and bottom are different. Top is strong, defined, liked, female: the bottom is gross, huge, deformed, male. Bad thighs and a dark patch between the legs. The lower body, marked with disgust, is a version of her father's body and of her father's contempt for her adolescent body. When she describes her father, she speaks vividly and intensely. It is a relentlessly negative characterization, but there is the thrill of the description, an odd glee mixed with disgust. I notice that the same lexicon, the same style and tone, the same genre of speech is used for her father and for her own body state. Both are gross morons. Morons, I ask? Stupid, nothing to say. She is speechless. A moron who cannot write or think or speak. If she speaks to me as the disgusting moron, the therapy will surely founder. Her only hope is boyish charm, and this she undertakes through speech but cannot carry this agency into her writing.

There are splits within her experience of masculinity. She experiences herself as the strong, silent sentinel, the caretaker. "I'm standing

at attention. Break the glass and use me. I will take care. It's what I do."
The gross father-self is defined by greed, by a kind of wanton permission
to have and to be, an indifference to others, an object of disgust and
hatred. And, moving around these figures, a charming, seductive boy
who knows how to interest a woman. All this experience lives secretly in
fantasy, in the context of marriage and family life that is precious and
relieving to her and in a relationship with her husband, whose male
body seems to her right, clean, and innocent.

The relational history of Jamie's boy-self is complex and multiply
determined. She held a very early conviction that what would have
rescued her mother from depression was a vivid, lively, helpful boy, a
mama's boy. There are distant, troubling memories of an attentive, preoedipal father. Her gender constellations are more fractal than unitary.

In the midst of intense demands for love and permanent union,
she reminds me that I really am a jerk. She knows and hopes I know
that this is play. "What about my womanliness? Am I not a little bit
pretty?" she insists, at one moment. Yet almost immediately, she founders
on another block. She cannot be in the room as a woman. She reports
that she had very carefully chosen a uniform of cap and jeans and boots.
Even if she must go to considerable trouble to return home from sessions and change into clothes for work or an interview, there is no way
to be a woman in the room with me. So, although I am denounced as
someone interested only in men and able to respond only to the man in
a woman, two women together are simultaneously beyond words and
wonder and hopelessly boring.

For this patient, gender meanings are not only the boiling stew
through which she struggles to find coherence and purpose but also an
access to creativity. Gender is the deeply saturated space where almost
everything that matters to her must be negotiated. Jamie's gender is a
kind of fractal, unstable space where hope and despair conflictually coexist.

HELEN: BODIES OF WORK
WITHOUT A GENDERED BODY

Helen is an accomplished, graceful woman, filled with intellectual and
aesthetic passions around which she has wound a deeply moral understanding of herself and her projects. In a demanding professional world
in which she is a decidedly provocative presence, she struggles with the

questions of corruption, ambition, purpose. At a more hidden level, she is engaged in an equally compelling struggle with neglect and poverty of various kinds, a struggle involving pride, shame, and anxiety, often cast in moral terms.

Helen has solved the problem of access to creativity by bracketing her gender, experiencing it almost as a well-cut suit, architecturally structured and attractive, useful rather than decorative. It is not that her bodily sense is erased, but that its strength and pliability and vitality are foregrounded. What is backgrounded and quite unseen by Helen is the sense of her body as the gendered object of another's excitement. Her own pleasure in her body seems centered on its activity and vitality, not on the interior sites of excitement. Hers is a body to be of service, not always to be inwardly felt. It was not until well into adulthood that her active, owned experience of her body-self encompassed a genital experience.

Her body is a kind of "innocent" instrument, her sensorimotor sensibility not erotized until well into adulthood. Her body state is a mode of perception. The body is for use, not display, and in this notion her artistic and aesthetic senses are mirrored as well. Mostly she does not deploy gender terms in describing herself. She has captured the problems of ambition and her history with the extraspecies metaphor of topdog or underdog.

A woman of achievement, of early promise fulfilled, Helen is a woman who sees herself in a professional lineage of men. She was mentored more as an oedipal son than as a daughter and lives in suspended mourning for an adored, glamorous, and productive father, an adolescent girl's idealized lost father. The oedipal gender-ambiguous offspring to her mentor, Helen appears to shake gender conventions off like an animal shaking off water. She feels a creaturelyness to her body, the gender arrangements and the sexual demand/need of others. She is most comfortable with men. In male mentors the homage to her lost father stays lit. These mentoring relations are often endowed with almost magical properties, eerie, clanging coincidences, and strange parallels. The world of fantasy and magic lives close to the surface, spurring Helen's intense creativity but also a suspended mourning.

Yet another pattern emerges, a triangle of a very particular kind: a powerful, twining connection to a man who is himself enmeshed with an older woman, sometimes sexually, sometimes financially. The older woman is seen as holding the man captive in a corrupt and incestuous trap from which Helen hopes to liberate him. A familial scene surely, but an interesting one, collapsing generations.

As we came to explore these matters more deeply, gender became more foregrounded. Her body sense serves many functions, not the least of which is a suspended melancholy, a young, androgynous, pre-pubescent girl waiting for father, but also an androgyny (not exactly a tomboy, an identity less saturated with gender) that stepped aside from sexual rivalry for oedipal winning as a girl. For Helen the women in her family constitute trouble in different ways. The images of the early maternal environment are of dirt, neglect, incompetence, images that her gleaming, clear-lined aesthetics are designed to repair. Her relations with women are much more difficult and contradictory. She gets bound into cycles of envy and contempt with women perceived to be rich and pampered. She toggles back and forth between the position of degraded, impoverished girl envious of the cared-for woman and the position of a winner, a person of power and accomplishment, living with some contempt for the emptiness of the pampered woman cast against the genuine richness and scope of her professional accomplishment.

Here a shifting self–other constellation ebbs and flows, connects and reverses. Helen lives out a neglected, disheveled relation as child to mother. She has a memory/dream image of a tumble down a flight of stairs. She is a small child but alone, unsupervised, and left alone to recover. But in the family she was also explicitly made into the center of rivalries, triangles of mother, father, and grandmother in varying permutations. Her mother combined neglect with narcissistic identification and the complex envy of a mother that can develop in relation to an oedipal-winner child.

For Helen, precocity was partially a covering for neglect. This mix of potency and destitution is replicated in her current relation to resources. She traverses grandeur and poverty, and the line between ampleness and emptiness can be very thin. This makes for a complex experience for Helen and anyone she is in relation to. Her potency and creativity are palpable, existing in real space. Her convictions of having a moral dimension to her work are deep. And yet, lurking in the background and sometimes in the foreground of her life and work, degradation, economic ruin, and destruction loom.

She particularly loves the myth of Atlantis, the great graceful runner, daughter of Apollo, who must be outrun to be won in marriage. The speedy androgynous girl stoops for the golden apples thrown to distract her. So does Helen carry a covert and worrying gender theory. Willfulness in personal ambition, in the determination to be respected and admired for work, makes for a kind of clarity and insistence that gender and sexuality be irrelevant to judgment and approval. In some way Helen's indifference to gender both is historically structured and is a deep conviction of the toll on her mother and on her parent's marriage that dependency and passivity took.

Helen has contempt for women who use female power; contempt for women drawing on dependence. Certainly there is a disavowed need in her self. Helen has made a virtue of necessity. Precocity or empty neglect and pride, self-berstement, and mental acuity build a structure to encompass fear and emptiness and neglect. Rage and aggression are skillfully tempered into will and work. Activity is kept clear of gender. And clean of gender too.

In the transference, I am sometimes the older woman called on to admire and be feared as envious spoiler, my care complexly welcomed and spoiled. Helen and I have interesting, sometimes exhausting struggles about fees and resources, struggles that I see she is learning to manage better in her life. There is the wish to care for me endlessly and yet to impoverish me, to place me in conditions of dangerous depletion. And there is, inside and outside treatment, a sacrifice to an older woman, often a sharply alternating process whereby a public moment of power and admiration is paid for by private debasement and attunement to an older woman's needs.

CHARLES: GENDER FAÇADES AND A LONGING TO BE "REAL"

In another clinical vignette gender and desire are parsed in a very different way. Charles is a young scientist whose analysis with me is his first treatment with a woman. He has been plunged, to his surprise, into an intense experience that oscillates dramatically between tender dependency and erotic excitement. He can feel "weepy" during or after sessions. He has much to weep about but prides himself on never crying. He imagines that his tears would make me disgusted or angry. This conviction stems from a strong, unsubtle paternal pressure to remain allied with masculinity and stay away from those aspects of family life identified with his mother, viewed by all as disturbed and needy. This is the way he divides the gender world as well. He is both chained and set up by this division. Therapy itself constitutes one of the few points on which he has crossed into the mother-world. Therapy is necessary and must be spoiled.

Over time Charles adopts façades of character and gender through which he functions and produces these personas very creatively in his analysis. Very much drawing on an idealized image of an urbane, smooth-talking father, Charles is genial, agreeable, and apparently eager to please, in particular to please women. But he has become able to notice what a house of cards this is, that he was clinging to a kind of cartoon masculinity, not likely even very real to his father, as a necessary way to distance himself from the mother he longed for and feared.

Being chosen and taken up by his father, while his siblings and mother were consigned to the category of the feminine and the disturbed, gave Charles great relief. But painfully he has had to notice what was airbrushed out of the picture. Charles has a father who is alcoholic, mean spirited, emotionally absent. His father's callous indifference to his wife and his children has rendered masculine identifications virtually useless to Charles. He increasingly doubts his own brittle phallic constructions but fears the slide into emotional turmoil and depression that such shaky structures are meant to forestall.

Even as a child he intuited the shaky mental representation of himself and his family: the unreality of parental speech, the emptiness of family life, the loneliness that was constant and from which he turned to fantasy, and a rich, often lurid internal world. Charles fears that this internal world is often more real than his daily life and relationships, and he has always felt the line between fantasy and reality to be blurry and permeable. His fears of his internal world, its affects, scenes, and meanings, are intense.

When we finally get to hear about them, his fantasies boil with erotic and aggressive scenes, and he is sure that, if and when I learn of them, I will get rid of him. One fantasy he can talk about is the slightly confusing, inchoate sense that "things" can get out of control in the consulting room. What if we both had sexual thoughts in the same moment? These fantasies are sometimes violently sexual and sometimes tenderly erotic. Maybe I would just join him on the couch in a scene that seems right on the edge of erotica and maternal tenderness.

On the other hand, anger and aggression in relation to me are frightening. What if he were angry and wanted to throw me, or actually threw me, out the window? He is not at all certain whether these chaotic, difficult feelings and impulses are in him or in me. And he is equally uncertain what this electric charge, of pain, of excitement, of violence in him and between us, has to do with our relationship or his very charged and unsettling relationship with his mother.

He and I have come to connect the dilemmas in our room to two scenes from his childhood he recalls in vivid dreamscape. One scene is chaotic and fluid; one is charged and crystalline and ominously still. In one, he watches on the sidelines while a maid prepares a bottle for the new baby. The baby is screaming, the maid is awkward, the mother screams. It is a disturbing memory because it is frightening and exciting. When I wonder if it is his screams and his rage that are projected onto these tormenting others (his mother, the new baby), he readily agrees. It is well into treatment before Charles can recall family stories about his own feeding, his rageful hungers, and the anxious decisions whether to feed on demand or on schedule. In his movement from voyeur to actor, his own affective states of longing and fury become more accessible.

In the second scene he remembers, he is in the mother's bedroom. Everything is white: the sheets, her dressing gown. He sits on the edge of the bed and begins to worry. What could happen? Anything. Everything. Sometimes he is a little boy in the scene and sometimes an adolescent. Is this dream or memory? How are these experiences really differentiated? He has memories of repeating dreams in childhood in which the actor–agent relation is reversed. In those dreams, he is asleep in his bed and awakens to the terrifying sound of footsteps coming down the hall toward him. He is convinced the footsteps are his mother's. Longing and terror are completely entangled.

The repetition in his relation with women marks the impossible conflict he is in to feel loving without being a killer or, alternatively, to approach a woman and not be swamped by her passions. It is often as though, as he gets close to a woman, adult states dissolve in a defense against his potency and hers. Under the fear of his troubled, unstable mother lurks the unshakable conviction that he damaged her and will, of course, damage anyone else he comes into contact with.

But if Charles is frightened of being *with* some version of his mother, he is angry and resistant to any idea that he might be *like* her. Gender divides are guarded fiercely, and these divides seem to protect against two possibilities: homosexual longings for men and identifications with the tearful, dependent aspect of his mother. As treatment develops we can trace, in dream and in fantasies, many scenes of half-opened doors— to bathrooms, to bedrooms, to my consulting room, to glimpses into places of mess or excitement. Smell, cloacal or sexual, a life of the body and of passion, all secret elements, the scene behind the façades remain to Charles fascinating and just out of reach.

I am struck by the shifting self-states in our room, shifts that alter gender and generation. Child and grownup feeling states wax and wane, each protecting the other: erotism and aggression enlivening the inter-personal space but also warding off the fall into hopeless and helpless dependency. His boyish child-stance is often consciously a mask against knowing rivalry or competition with other men, but is mixed in with the hopes and longings for an attentive, loving father. Aggression pro-tects against love; aggression is a form of love. Dependency protects against sadism. Agency flows back and forth between us.

In these three examples many questions arise. The treatments and the interactive matrices are not exactly or explicitly organized around the question of gender and sexuality and their relation to boundedness and connection. Sometimes gender and sexuality are the central focus; sometimes I suspect they stand in for other matters and knots in patients' psyches. Sometimes gender seems the solution, sometimes the problem.

We are used to considering body representations as the sites for recording trauma, of experience unsymbolizable. But perhaps a differ-ent point can be made. In the clinical examples, the problem is that very often we cannot find a through-line; the body's and words' incoherencies and volatility are carrying too much excess, too much inexpressible meaning. Speech is often inadequate for framing enact-ment and embodiment.

In thinking of how Jamie, Helen, and Charles use and inhabit gender we have to balance uniqueness and individuality on one hand with the power of cultural narratives of gender, narratives that in our culture draw on and are influenced by the organizing narratives of psy-choanalysis. Gender is lived both as private and public function. We can think of the impact of such cultural forms, including psychoana-lytic understanding, as a working of the microtechnologies of power through which one's body/mind is integrated into psychic organization and into social life. Each of these individuals, in his or her own distinct ways, questions the organizing narratives of psychoanalysis as well as reproduces them and needs them. I make a similar invitation to us as well. We must continue to question the regulatory practices of psycho-analysis around gender and sexuality even as we are enmeshed in and subject to these conventions as well.

THE HISTORY OF PSYCHOANALYTIC GENDER TALK

These clinical conversations sit at the end of a century of work within psychoanalysis seeking to understand, construct, and deconstruct what it means to desire and to be a particular gender. Two quandaries (at least) have bedeviled psychoanalytic theory and practice since Freud: (1) Psychoanalytic work on gender is tipped toward a perhaps obsessional preoccupation with femininity as a mode of life to avoid or to manage or to embrace. (2) Our theories are sometimes clear, sometimes unclear, about the interplay of sexuality and gender. These questions and uncertainties live at all levels: theoretical, practical, and cultural.

It is a well-remarked problem in theory building that there is a dominance of work on femininity in work on gender.[1] Heterosexuality and masculinity are made to appear to be unproblematic, unremarkable. Theory moves to capture the problematic, the special case. And so femininity seems perhaps more "penetrable." Whether this is because of relative power and powerlessness of the two genders and marginal and normative sexualities or whether the anxiety around penetration gets in the way of theorizing masculinity is hard to determine. But as clinicians and as thinkers we are still struggling with the powerful asymmetry of attention to femininity.

Second, there is the question of how to connect gender and sexuality. There is a perspective on sex and gender that reduces gender almost to the status of role or cognitive schemas. Sexuality, from this perspective, dominates the construction and outcome of character. This may be one explanation for the almost total disappearance of gender as a category of interest from Kleinian thought after 1945 (Breen, 1993). From the Kleinian perspective, psychosexuality constructs gender, as though working out a relation to sexuality; produces gender as a kind of byproduct. For the most part, the "sexuality" that is so determinate of experience and psychic structure is a sexuality, described and experienced in relation to the manifest gender of one's object of desire, conceived quite concretely.

From the perspective of feminism and relational psychoanalysis, Dimen (1991, 1995b, 1996b, 1999), Benjamin (1986, 1987, 1988, 1997), Goldner (1991, 2003), and others have critiqued the stranglehold of rigid ideas about passivity versus activity and about concrete visions of sexual difference on the resolution and the preconditions for oedipal development. When gender arrangements are constitutive of sexuality or constituted by it, one has lost all the astonishing revolutionary potential of Freud's (1905) "Three Essays on the Theory of Sexuality," a vision of sexuality as outcome. It is also in queer theory (Lewes, 1988, 1998, 2001; Klein, 1990; Corbett, 1993; Magee and Miller, 1997; Schwartz, 1998, 1999; Butler, 2000a, b; Lesser, 2001) that we find a trenchant disruption of the concretization of sex and gender, the confusion of homosexuality with femininity.

Where gender or sexuality is concerned, we struggle with our own commitments and anxieties in regard to gender arrangements. As analysts we swim in complex waters, with all the eddies and currents of sexual and gender practices that our patients want help navigating and charting. It is one of the unique aspects of analytic work: the instrument of understanding, precision, insight, interpretation is the analyst's own incompletely conscious, rational mind. The unconscious or preconscious aspect of our analytic functioning is paradoxically the flaw in our knowing and the source of our knowing. We come with varieties of blindness—scotomas—in our ways of seeing. Our blind spots arise from our own histories as well as our places in history and culture.

At the same time, our unconscious or preconscious modes of perception and apprehension are like divining rods, instruments only to a degree under our agency or awareness. Apprehension may be one of those intriguing terms, like Freud's (1919) reading of "uncanny," that contain contradiction. We apprehend our patients, and our apprehension contains dread, uncertainty, and the very conditions of all perception. This complex site of sight and blindness is deep in our reading of gender and sexuality. Our own beings—gendered and sexual—become part of the instrument of (mis)understanding. Dyess and Dean (2000a, b) propose a perspective on gender as both constructed and inchoate. They draw on Lacanian ideas of the "real" to notice the unbridgeable gaps of culture and psyche, the limits on structure and rationality.

At any given moment in the evolution of an understanding or theorizing of a concept like gender, we draw from the historical record of psychoanalytic work on gender a particular thread or set of threads. To work on gender development now is to be the beneficiary of extended conversations, full of controversy and contradiction, at the same time grounded in research, in observation, and in clinical detail. In a sense, anyone's organization of such complex and multiple sources must be emergent and context dependent. The selective and not exhaustive historical survey I present here is no different.

Two lines of theoretical work on gender can be traced. First, is the work on gender development in which bodily life as the wellspring and organizer of gender is prominent. This work includes that of theorists who find gender on specific bodily forms, those writers who install "femininity" as a primary body formation organizing the psychic experience of gender (Kestenberg, 1956a, b, 1982; Mayer, 1985, 1995; Richards, 1992, 1996; Bernstein, 1993; Lax, 1994). Some early women analysts saw gender as an emergent rather than an essential property of body–psyche. Even in those earlier evolutions of gender theory, it is the feminine, the world of girls and women, mothers and daughters, that comes into view and under scrutiny.

The second strand—gender formed in the crucible of attachment—begins with the organization of gender development proposed by Stoller (1968a, b, 1973, 1976, 1985) and taken up and developed by Fast (1978, 1979, 1984). In the deepening development of that perspective (Benjamin, 1988, 1992a, b, 2002; Flax, 1990, 1993; Dimen, 1991, 1995b, 2002; Goldner, 1991; Harris, 1991, 2000, 2002; Chodorow, 1994, 2002; Elise, 1997, 1998, 1999, 2002; Layton, 1998; Corbett, 1999, 2001a, b; among many others) we can see psychoanalytic work braided with interdisciplinary interests and with ideology.

GENDER MADE FROM THE BODY:
GENDER AND SEXUALITY

Let us take up this tradition at the point of its inception in the first generation of women analysts. Reread now, they were striking both for close obedience to Freud, who was, in a number of cases, their analyst, but also for the supple, fresh, experience-near quality of the writing and for the prominent place they give to female pleasure. In the early period in psychoanalytic history, two strands of thought were initiated. One is well known to feminists. It is the line of argument that positions femininity as an early protoform of psychic life, locatable on the girl's body. Horney's (1926, 1932, 1933, 1934) work is the most prominent for a contemporary readership. She founded key elements of women's psychic life, envies, and anxieties in some mixture of social constraint and biology.

One strand of work following Horney's unique integration of psyche and culture has had a somewhat marginalized life in the context of mainstream ego psychology (see Notman and Lester, 1988, for an important contribution from that perspective). Person's (2000) work is the most prominent example of this perspective in which cultural matters were braided with drives and conflict. Her work has had an exuberant encounter with feminism and modern gender theories.

What is intriguing to me in the counterperspective, particularly in the writing of Lampl-de Groot (1933, 1982), is that activity and pleasure seeking were considered to be crucial to girls' preoedipal period.[2] Her work may have been neglected as feminist and neoclassical analysts moved definitively away from phallic monism. Yet Lampl-de Groot's most discussed essay on femininity actually struggles with a psychic bisexuality not obviously rooted in anatomy. She tries, not always successfully, to make activity and passivity psychic and not merely natural reactions based on gender. Strongly represented in Lampl-de Groot's work is a sense of a girl's intense, active love, bodily grounded, for her first attachment, her mother, and the narcissistic vulnerability that follows having to give up her mother. Passivity is a reaction to injury and lost love, not a natural attribute of femininity.

By equating boys' and girls' anguish at renouncing loving and being loved by one's mother, but differentiating the intensity of renunciation required of girls and noting that the negative oedipal can eclipse so much of girls' sexuality, Lampl-de Groot illuminates an underdeveloped aspect of girls' gender development, that is, the rupture in homosexual attachment.

A less well known Berlin analyst, Josine Müller (1932), was another early initiator of the primary femininity perspective. Tragically, her fascinating and original contribution was published posthumously. By thinking of femininity in complex terms, her work contains many elements that integrate passivity and activity. She, like Lampl-de Groot, assumes the centrality of pleasure for girls and, interestingly, expands the notion of female bodily sexual life rather than replacing one organ for another. Vaginal sensations, with all the accompanying anxieties and fantasies, have been the primary ground on which contemporary core femininity theorists found gender. Müller rather matter-of-factly proposes, on the basis of observations and case material, that women have two genital organs. She points out that urethral, clitoral, and vaginal pleasures are overlapping and not very distinguishable one from the other. Rather than replacing one site of pleasure with another, she asserts that clitoral pleasure serves a girl's consolidation of genital experience and that pleasure and satisfaction are essential elements in the dissolution of anyone's castration complex.

Kestenberg (1956), reviewing the early history of work on feminine sexuality, cited the Kleinians Brierley (1932, 1936) and Payne (1935) in a similar vein. They saw receptivity as an active incorporation rather than as passivity linked to masochism. They considered feminine sexuality an achievement contingent on coordination and integration of clitoral and vaginal sensation. They actually embraced female activity and strongly privileged the potency of renunciation of the tie to one's mother. This aspect of femininity is much less prominent in theories that either install femininity as primary or focus on the ease or inevitability of same-sex identifications.

The evolution of Kleinian thought on gender development has had intriguing periods of attention and silence. In the pre–World War II decade, Klein's early interest in a stage of primary femininity gave way to the more developed period of her thinking in which boys' and girls' gender development was differentiated solely on the basis of sexual difference. Some of her contemporaries retained an interest in femininity and its relation to a maternal object. Brierley and Payne considered the vicissitudes of female development in the context of anxieties and pleasures in feeding.[3] Brierley is quite interesting about the struggle for integration necessary for girls' development, an integration of early bodily experiences of feeding and weaning. She explored the possibility of displacement and substitution of organs. For Brierley, as for the early Müller and Lampl-de Groot, there is less a transfer of organ pleasure than a blending. She cited Ferenczi on the matter of development as a blending of pleasure and cathexis from different sources.

The danger in female development, then, would have to do with the severity of renunciation of a girl's sources of pleasure. With a telling line, Brierley (1932) summarized a whole set of thoughts about girls' anxieties about aggression and the degree to which self-beratement and self-regulation dominate a girl's internal object world: "A vagina which has acquired too strong cannibalistic tendencies will be afraid to suck for fear of biting" (p. 433).

Rivière (1929), whose work on femininity has an audience of postmoderns, Lacanians, and feminists, was also interested in the fate of a girl's aggression and excitement, but her focus was on the potential for conflict with men and with the paternal authority and its substitutes. She came very close to saying that gender functions as a kind of camouflage, behind which sadism, castrating wishes, competition, and an active phallic capacity continue to function. What is absent from her analysis is the motive to keep and win the mother—the homosexual motive, in a sense.

In the classical focus on the "negative oedipal" (for which we might think of a more descriptive and apt term) there is the potential to rehabilitate the power of female desire and homosexual desire in the girl (see, e.g., Burch, 1996; Davies, 2001b; Elise, 2002). In her early papers on maternality and feminine sexuality, Kestenberg (1956) follows this line of argument, which holds that the earliest forms of femininity are built on active incorporation, the sexuality of insideness and receptivity being in the service of mastery. She also connects early female depression to problems of aggression and sexuality as the tie to the mother is given up. She, like Laplanche (1989), is drawn to the same key passages in Freud's (1910) essay on da Vinci to develop her own riff on maternal erotics.[4]

Kestenberg's (1982) conception of the inner genital, and her overarching project to connect gender to the female body in its specificity, opened up a rich vein of work on femininity and its relation to bodily life.[5] In a series of papers that took off from this basic set of ideas, a new range of possibilities for female sexual life and gender sensibilities emerged. But, as this brief review suggests, something was lost: a focus on activity and pleasure as primary for the girl.

We can subsume this tradition under the rubric of "core femininity," a deliberate separation from the tradition of phallic monism and a focus on the early dyadic life with a mother. There is work on female sexuality stressing vaginal experiences (Mayer, 1985, 1995; Bernstein, 1993); on female superego formation (Bernstein, 1993; Tyson, 1994, 1997); and on female gender identity in relation to genital and pregenital experience (Mayer, 1985, 1995; Kaplan, 1991; Kulish, 1991; Richards, 1992; Balsam, 1996, 2001; Stimmel, 1996; Elise, 1997, 1998; Gilmore, 1998; Kulish and Holtzman, 1998). Mayer wrote about fears of being sealed off; Richards, of the interplay of anxiety and excitement in relation to a girl's experience of her genitals and also about the romance of pain. Elise writes of women who experience loss as a form of incorporative vaginal hunger.

Among the modern neoclassicists, Elise (1997, 1998) takes an approach that is different from these writers stressing core or primary femininity. For one thing, her writing harks back in its freshness and directness and articulation of female pleasure to the classical tradition of the 1920s. In her work, longing and desire and mastery of the body for pleasure return as key interests. This viewpoint is distinct, in tone and emphasis, from the contemporary classical work on core femininity. Perhaps as an unintended byproduct of installing a highly specified gender identity early in girls' lives, this perspective often seems to instill anxiety and shame about sexuality as constitutive and primary. Elise preserves core gender identity but asks us to notice a range of sexual/

psychic/mental practices, usually ghettoized as feminine, that come into play for men and women alike. Penetration as a phenomenon of fantasy, of sexual life, of mental effort, of interpersonal relationships is one aspect of a bisexuality variously loved and feared by men and women.

What is fascinating about the core femininity perspective, aside from its clinical richness and elaboration, is the theorizing of widely variable differences in the female sexual body. The concentration is on women's fear of penetration or of closing over, diffuseness of body state, on one hand, and potent and fierce self-beratement, on the other. Viewed across a number of writers, the whole landscape of the female body is altered: vagina, vulva, clitoris, mons, labia, urethral pressures, vaginal hungers, vaginal terrors. The landscape is richly external and internal.

Yet, despite this renewed geography of the female body with its many potentialities, what dominates these very distinctive approaches is a sense of femininity's anxieties, shames, uncertainties, and often bewildering tensions. Phallic monism often seems simply to have been replaced by vaginal monism, but somehow pleasure and activity seem to have been lost or misplaced along the way. Penetrability and its attendant affects, anxieties, and representations dominated neo-Freudian thinking about femininity, partly as an outcome of a creative attempt to rethink castration in terms of the female body. This dominating, too exclusive focus on the vagina as the designated site of femininity almost inevitably makes the female body one primed for heterosexuality.

Theorists like Kestenberg, McDougall, Chasseguet-Smirgel, Balsam, Kulish, and Holtzman, and Mayer refused to absorb uncritically the application of castration, absence, and lack as the organizing principles of a girl's or a woman's sexuality and in particular her genital experience. They were thus freed to think with specificity and local knowledge about femininity as psychic and as body ego. One of the interesting differences among theorists who want to draw on female bodily life for mental and gender structure is their very different views of the endpoint in oedipal configurations. For some (Balsam, 1996; Laufer, 1996, 1997) the integration of femininity centers on the acceptance of a woman's body as a reproductive body. Sexuality as pleasure or relatedness is much less prominent. For others, feminine identification links to heterosexual attachments and love objects. Considered as a group, these theorists (Chasseguet-Smirgel, Richards, Mayer) seem bound by overall normative prescriptions for development. Heterosexuality, reproduction, and achieved femininity constitute the backbone of clinical judgments and treatment strategies.

The powerful insight of the core femininity/primary femininity analysts was that phallic monism as a restrictive universalizing construct thinned out and homogenized the understanding and clinical insights about femininity. Phallic monism, although a construct and metaphor, also had the disadvantage of the inevitable tumbles from metaphor to material. The phallus/penis distinction could slide and collapse in a way that organized the psychoanalytic conception of the feminine as an absence, a lack. And this lack in a woman's experience came to seem somehow more than the inescapable prohibition through which any sexuality is constituted. Here it may be possible to watch the enmeshment of culture and theory.

Elise's (1997, 1999, 2001, 2002) work on female desire and on male and female fears of penetration and her work on bisexuality begin to get at the power of relational configurations and social life in constituting female sexuality at both a theoretical and a lived level. Elise (2002) has also speculated on the impact of the taboos and constrictions on female desire within the mother–daughter dyad. She takes the idea of diffuseness in female sexuality, an insight that I believe originated with Bernstein (1993), and queries the term. She notes how often the language about female sexuality (in scholarly and in public discourse) often reduces, flattens, and thus minimizes female experience. Why "diffuse" and not "spread"? She comes, in my view, to a political answer to this question by embedding many women's sexual identities and practices in the context of male fears and anxieties about sexuality and about women. Female sexuality too often appears to have to carry the signs of enigma, mystery, and limenality for all sexuality. Gender norms thus subtly enter our ideas of sexuality through our category labels.

It is in the French classical tradition that one finds a particularly rich account of femininity related deeply to bodily life, in particular the early bodily life of mother and child (Chasseguet-Smirgel, 1970, 1976; Kristeva, 1980; McDougall, 1989). Yet one feels about this work that femininity is still seen within a phallic economy, where the maternal figure is either "an inadequate object" easily cast aside in favor of the father (Grunberger, 1966) or a figure split along the lines of phallic/castrated or omnipotent/castrated. The maternal effects on a child's psyche are conceptualized as regressive, engulfing, envy building, or envious attacks. Gender polarities valued and cast in asymmetrical power relations still prevail. The paternal force, in some guise or other, still signifies the rescue operation, the structuring, boundary-making potential for the child. The dichotomies of active–passive are not contested, and the underpinnings of heterosexuality as the developmental endpoint are never put into question.

COMMENTARY

At its best, the work on core femininity, both in France and in the United States, conveyed rich specificity to the fantasies, meanings, and experiences in female life, body, and mind. From my perspective, the limitation in this work is its treatment of the female body as an unremarkable set of facts that speak to and through the mind. The body becomes the site for instilling gender universals into psychic functioning.

An alternative shift in perspective would not so much change any of these clinical observations as change how we imagined their meanings. It is, if you like, a shift from monolog to dialog: body speaks; mind answers; mind and body are always interpenetrating in dialog, coevolving, and differentiating. This does not mean there is no body except for signification or symbolization. Nor does it mean that processes of attachment determine gender and sexuality.

Seeing the body as historicized through mind and interaction simultaneously with mind and psyche evolving out of a social-body interaction cannot help us decide the relative primacy of sex or gender. There will be instances where sexuality works out something about gender and instances when gender works out something about sexuality; or there will be instances when sex or sometimes gender are solutions to other psychic problems, like self-regulation or safety. Many specific constructions will emerge within the life space of any individual. Body–mind is more like a transitional space related to and embedded in the larger cultural and familial spaces in which bodies and minds have highly specific meanings. Within these encircling, interpenetrating spaces identities as embodied and en-minded emerge.

The primary femininity tradition presents a body that is raw and a mind that is cooked. The nonlinear dynamic perspective would be to see mind and body as cooking each other. Bodily consciousness emerges from the particular relational, cultural, and social context in which a child lives. This perspective would not repudiate or reject the conceptualizing of femininity as anxieties, shames, vulnerabilities, diffuseness, fears of penetration, or longings for penetration; rather, it embeds these psychic/somatic/sexual experiences in a matrix that is both historically and contextually placed. The realness of the body, its materiality, its presence *beyond* language does not default to a body *before* language or before social context.

What would it mean to see the body made in history and in relationships? Historicizing the body is an ongoing project familiar to historians and anthropologists.[6] How changeable, contingent, and powerful the ideals and "facts" about the body and the psyche turn out to be can be seen in the historical work on shame, an affect we tend to view as ineluctably private and embodied. This historical approach may be an antidote to the universalizing quality of body talk in psychoanalysis as well as the tendency to see body consciousness and body experience as unremarkably natural and individual.

How do bodies carry and express historical and social forces? Let us consider the study of embodied cognition and feminist theories of the body, what has been termed "corporeal feminism" (Grosz, 1994, 1995; Gatens, 1996).[7] This work in feminism richly elaborates the contributions of context and history through which embodied identities and ways of acting and moving are constituted. Most acutely, this work addresses the construction of gender and gendered bodies with the conscious objective of making the body emergent not given. If Thelen and the developmental connectionists focus on the experience of the individual, the organismic and microprocess aspects of the relational matrix, the corporeal feminists concentrate on the other pole of the relationship: body–mind constructed in and reflected through history. Both perspectives are necessary and interdependent.

Eleanor Rosch and her colleagues (Varela et al., 1992), who are trying to integrate cognitive science, Buddhist practice, and Eastern models of mind, put the problem beautifully. Minds, they write, "awaken in a world" but that world is there before we awaken to it. The world is both before us and yet not separate from us. From this perspective of embodied knowing, the "space" between us and our objects (including each other) is less a gulf than an elastic, living entity whose contours and boundaries can be both stable and fluid. The innerness of mind or body and the outerness of others is never permanently reifiable.

There are many appealing and demanding points in the work of those authors. It stands with a number of approaches against the enthroning of symbolic logic and propositional forms of thinking and abstraction. Varela et al. seek to embody thinking in the living practices of body, mind, and heart. The method of analysis is a kind of embrace of circularity, a living within a paradoxical middle ground that never settles between inner and outer, including both as connected but separate. They argue that, since there is no privileged and unassailable set of mind-independent objects to which any signifier might refer, we cannot really consider mental representation, symbolic or subsymbolic, distinct from the background conditions in which experience is being enacted.

Grosz's (1994, 1995) anti-Cartesian stance is particularly sensitive to the outcomes for the position of woman and femininity within the bifurcated system Descartes established. As Grosz points out, mind–body is a division that tends to devour other divisions: reason–feeling; reason–nature; culture–nature. And all these slide inexorably to the binary man–woman such that woman as a category carries all the less evolved, more "primitive," and archaic elements in human life (see Irigaray, 1985, 1990; Brennan, 1988, 1992; Dimen, 1991, for a similar analysis).[8] Since these dichotomies are built as a hierarchy, the domination of mind and reason over the body and over nature echoes the social hierarchy across genders. Knowledge, including scientific knowledge, takes on a magisterial stance; and bodily life, particularly female bodily life, becomes a crucial object to be known, surveilled, named, and tamed.

A powerful addition to the general schemes of chaos theory is this insistence on the historical specificity of the body.[9] Through the encounter with historically specific tasks of self development, the body will become the site in which particular forms emerge: gait, mien, posture, body type, the outcome of nutritional specificity, diet, exercise regimen, aesthetics of dress, and body presentation. These gestures and habits or styles of being are what communication theorist Ray Birdwhistell (1970, 1974) terms the "tertiary sex characteristics," which, in his view, are what made humans, who are a weakly dimorphic species, into a more dichotomized binary system. To translate Birdwhistell's analysis into our own study of gender, humans' gender plumage makes us more polarized than our bodily states would indicate.[10]

To think about a body as the carrier of history is certainly a way to understand social constructionist aspects of gendered experience. As part of a long-term project to excavate and think about mother–daughter conflicts as they play in women's difficulties with aggression and sexuality and ambition. I have become interested in how the background historical experiences of women stain and are inscribed in bodily life, singular, dyadic, and collective (Harris, 1997, 1998b, 2000, 2002). What I have in mind is a wide variety of experiences, each with its own historical timeline and all creating a web of contextual effects in which any woman grows up and must uniquely come to terms with. Practices of contraception, women's health, and childbirth management; ideas of beauty and motility; space for physicality and sexuality constitute forces of normativity that have real as well as imaginary consequences.

Gail Paster (1993) has written a fascinating account of the relationship of theories of medicine and bodily disease to class-specific and gender-specific constructions of the body. She notes from the outset that our problem in thinking historically and constructively about the body is that

> what goes on within the body "goes without saying" because it goes on daily, habitually, involuntarily, and universally: in this respect bodilyness is the most rudimentary form of self-presence. Hence it seems to fall beneath the threshold of significance into the domain of the merely natural [p. 5].

Her interest, most relevant to psychoanalytic work on femininity, is in tracking the impact of shame as a form of regulation and social control through the medical regimens of the early modern period.

I introduce Paster's work on shame to denaturalize that phenomenon, to excavate shame psychoanalytically as the cover for desire or as the evacuation of feelings in an adult (mother or father) into the female infant's body. There is not sufficient attention to the interpersonal dimension of female bodies and femininity. If relational theory has ignored the body, neoclassical primary femininity theorists do not give relational phenomena any *constitutive* role in bodily experience.

A number of classical analysts have worked on the constitutive force of shame and anxiety in mother–daughter interactions. Gilmore (1998), for example, locates the constituting of femininity in the matrix of cleaning and touching the girl, as well as the anatomical closeness of anus and genital. I would reframe this daily, intimate maternal practice of cleaning as one palpable and powerful (and largely unconscious) site of the transmission of a haunting of gender, where varieties of shame and anxiety in the mother are expressed and projected into the interaction and onto the girl's body. Gilmore's account seems to be a description in which social and psychic, endogenous and interpersonal, live in a complex matrix producing many different outcomes for female body ego and female subjectivity.

It is reasonable to ask, as we do about the sequelae of many traumatic events, large scale and small scale, how bodily consciousness and experience affect the psyche and how historical memory can be seamlessly and unconsciously transmitted. Psychoanalysis has an evolved theory of how, within one's local family dynamics, various forms of sexual and personal life and identity can be both proscribed and encouraged. In connecting this historical material to the contemporary understanding of transgenerational transmission of trauma, I am suggesting that we carry and live out as gender, in conscious or unconscious forms, some residue of historical practices and cultural conventions.[11]

GENDER IN THE CONTEXT OF ATTACHMENT AND INDIVIDUATION

This tradition in the study of gender, in which attachment and object relations play key roles, begins with the work of Stoller (1968a, b, 1973, 1976) and has its clearest elaboration in the work of Irene Fast (1970, 1978, 1979, 1985, 1992, 1993), Nancy Chodorow (1976, 1999, 2002), and Jessica Benjamin (1988, 1995, 2002). Their work initiated and has continued to foster discussions of gender in which the attachments to and individuation from central figures in a child's experience are crucial. While at the beginning of this tradition, the focus was on the mother, more recently, primarily as a result of Benjamin's work (1991, 1992a), there has arisen a new salience for a preoedipal rapprochement father.

Fast views gender through the overlapping prisms of Freudian theory and cognitive theory and sees development as a move from overinclusion to a single gender scheme. Her concentration has been on the development of gender as a category scheme, beginning in the dynamic experience of sensorimotor life. The schemes she describes are bodily and cognitively categorical and move from general and overinclusive to particular and specialized.

A retrospective look at her work reveals an interesting trajectory. Before her articulation of the differentiation paradigm for gender development (Fast, 1984), Fast was interested in action as the origin of self-structure and selfobject representations (Fast, 1970). One of her acknowledged influences, in addition to Stoller, was Edith Jacobson (1968). In her work, set within a Freudian framework, Jacobson cites work on early femininity in which the girl's relation to the maternal body, to an emerging sexuality, was founded on bodily action and relatedness.[12]

Integrating her work on event theory (the idea that experiences are always organized as interaction patterns at differing developmental levels) with a theory of gender development she termed the differentiation paradigm, Fast (1984, 1992, 1993) saw a gendered self or scheme as evolving out of conflict (among schemes) and relationships that over time would move from dyadic to triadic forms. Through this process, gender, initially undifferentiated and embodied, would surface as a body–mind construct in increasingly refined elaborations. While these schemes emerge from interaction, Fast's theoretical writing casts a strong normative light. Gender cleaves along same-sex lines and moves the child's desires through a conventional oedipal steeplechase to heterosexuality. The earlier attention to the active processes of mother–daughter life shades off into a less erotized model of action and sensorimotor experience.

Most recently, with the development of attachment models of increasing sophistication, Fast (1998, 1999), Lyons-Ruth (1991), Tronick (1989, 1998), Seligman (2000, 2001), and others argue for thinking less of the old model of repudiation or separation and more about shifting modes of attachment. In this way one is returned to a very old idea of Freud's (1914): nothing once loved is ever fully given up.

A set of approaches we can term psychoanalytic feminism began to appear in psychoanalytic work on gender and sexuality in the wake of powerful social and political movements addressing the material and social and psychological constructions on women.[13] Poised between social theory, feminism, and psychoanalysis, Chodorow (1976) initiated a reconsideration of gender development, maternal subjectivity, and the fate of attachments in gendered psyches. She has gone on to situate gender in the context of the construction of personal meaning (Chodorow, 1999).

Within relational theory gender as a byproduct of attachment has been best articulated in the work of Benjamin (1988, 1998). This line of argument conceptualizes gender development through the pattern of relationships and the resultant identifications either of gender complementarity or mutual and reciprocal self and other construction. Gender is both vehicle and consequence of the human need to negotiate boundedness and interaction. Gender arrangements may hinder full appreciation of subject-in-object poised in tension with one's own subjectivity.

Benjamin's work is indebted to discussions of questions of subjectivity and subject–object complementarity grounded in philosophy and in Winnicott's theory of object use and aggression in relation to emotional development. Hegel's (1807) account of the master–slave relation and the complementary embeddedness of domination and submission is crucial in Benjamin's (1988) earliest accounts of the difficult trajectory for femininity toward recognition and mutuality. The power of the father as a source of identificatory love (bidirectionally) is an important element in her theory of gender development. She accounts for penis envy as a failure of identification, a thwarting both of agency and of subjectivity.

Benjamin's (1997, 2000a, b, 2002) later writing is caught up with describing the experience of intersubjectivity, and gender per se becomes a kind of category or configuration through which either complementarity or mutual recognition and subject-subject relation arises. I would call this work in the service of a "rights" argument in which Benjamin is interested in the interpersonal and intrapsychic processes through which one subject becomes able to tolerate and find the subjectivity in self and in the other. She sees development as the constant tension and shifting between experiences of mutuality and the collapse into relationships of complementarity in which one person distorts the other under the requirements of unbearable identifications.

The relational tradition of conceptualizing gender, developed in the 1990's (Benjamin, 1988, 1992a, b, 2002; Dimen, 1991, 1996a, 1998; Goldner, 1991, 1998; Gerson, 1994; Davies, 1998b, 2001b; Sweetnam, 1996, 1999; Layton, 1998; Dimen and Goldner, 2002) is an evolving project to study the vicissitudes of gender experience in the light of vicissitudes in patterns of relatedness. One characteristic of that work is the "double vision," an attention to the ideology and normative practices in gender theory and an expansion of the possibilities of identity formation and relational matrices (Layton, 1998). Gender is less likely to be naturalized into an unproblematic body and more likely to be negotiated in interpersonal space (Davies, 1998b, 2001b). It may be fluid or formed (Sweetnam, 1996), and inevitably gender becomes encrusted with many other aspects of psychic life (Dimen, 1991; Dimen and Goldner, 2002). From the joint perspective of family work and psychoanalytic theory, Goldner (1991, 1998, 2003) speaks of the ways that gender may organize as an aspect of an ego ideal, sometimes hopelessly out of reach, sometimes a beacon against collapse and disorganization. Gender may be a defensive fortress or a playful performance.

In my own work, I have come to see gender as an increasingly multiple and layered experience, drawing on attachments that need to be deconstructed to expose both fantasy and preconscious and conscious organizations of genderedness (Harris, 1991, 1997). Gender arising out of attachments must be both concrete and fantastical, public and private. Sameness and difference are meaningful psychological qualities only in context.

COMMENTARY

The developmental story is still being told in too monolithic and too linear a fashion. Same-sex and different-sex identifications and interactions assume a single and too simply categorized identity. Multiple and variable organizations of gender and sexual life grow up in the context of specifically proscribed but also provoked and encouraged forms of being someone and loving someone.

A number of critics have argued that these accounts of gender development depend on an understanding of normative heterosexuality. Chodorow's (1989) essay on heterosexuality as a compromise formation makes a developed and explicit attempt to address the constructed experience of heterosexuality. To do this, she draws on queer theory and on critiques of constructions of homosexuality (Lewes, 1988, 1995).

It is simply too sharp a split to keep so separate the process of loving someone from the process of being someone. Psychoanalysis' most inaugural texts bind these processes of desiring and identifying closely, both in the origins of narcissism and in the work of mourning (Freud, 1917). Yet a kind of theoretical housekeeping sanitizes and cordons off being and loving. Surely this split wards off the anxieties of various homoerotic forms that would then enter normative accounts of identification.

Second, identification is used in too global and generic a sense. The conceptual shift I propose begins with the application of Fast's (1970, 1985) work on event theory and I-schemes to her theory of gender category formation, overinclusion, and renunciation. Beyond our seeing gender identifications as relational patterns and as body based, the whole process of identification needs significant deconstruction. I mean by this more than simply moving away from the concepts of identity founded on autonomy rather than relatedness, the shift that Lyons-Ruth (1999) and others have detailed. Identifications arise through different processes: mimesis, introjection, incorporation, and internalization each yield up distinct forms of identification. Identifications may be global or partial. Some forms of identity may seem fully metabolized and others still undigested and even alien. Powerful unconscious aspects of identification may lie right at the surface of the body or deep in our psychic core.

In this experience, aspects of identity are experienced sometimes as interior, sometimes as exterior, sometimes on the surfaces that link external to internal. Forms of gender emerge in any life space dependent on the interactive matrix within the particular cultural and historic context of all the participants. Gender is yet another structure haunting the subject, the outcome of a complex, sometimes conscious, often unconscious, sometimes fragmentary, sometimes integrated transmission that comes to be housed both inside and outside and on the "surface" and in the depths of any individual. Gender's meanings may be sequestered or broadcast, available or dissociated.

THE POTENTIAL FOR CHAOS THEORY

These two conversational threads in psychoanalysis have some overlap in time, but until recently very little interaction. The traditions, roughly a classical or neoclassical perspective and a relational one, seem too separate, too bound in particular language worlds that do not easily translate or blend. Yet from our contemporary vantage point it is also possible to see that these perspectives also depend on each other, even if this dependency is unacknowledged. (See Dimen, 1991, 1995b, 2002; Ghent, 1989, 1992a, Goldner, 2003; Silverman, 1996, 2000, 2001, 2003; Stein 1998; Chused, 1999; and Goldner, 2003, for examples of this interest in outlining gender development in a more enigmatic, interpenetrating fashion.) This movement toward more integrated models of gender development I take up in chapter 8.

From this contemporary vantage point I want to hold these approaches up to the light reflecting from chaos theory, for a view of development and the study of behavior that has much potential for the analysis of gender. This model of creative and constructive dynamic interaction of constitution and environment is not a rejection of the existing rich observation of gender developments in boys and girls. It is, rather, both an embrace and a re-*visioning* of these observations.

Chaos theory offers a way to think about psychic and interpersonal functions that may sometimes accrue gender meanings but sometimes not. What I mean by that is that I see functions like attachment, identification, and separation as *gender agnostic*. We identify particular human projects, salient to time and context and not universal: developing agency, relatedness, and autonomy, evolving individuality in ways of being and of being sexual. But these projects can, in unique but culturally laden ways, be attached to or implicated in gender meaning and gender experience. In our contemporary, post-Stoller way of thinking about gender development, for example, disidentification with the mother is part of the dynamism of individuation. Gender and separation become enmeshed and linked up, each enabling the other to function. Chaos theory is a model that would view the process of individuation as an emergent phenomenon, not inherently linked to gender but potentially exploitative of it.

One can also use chaos theory to think about theory itself. Gender theory and clinical gender theory might become delicate, fractal, strange attractors, constructed of many different and varying subcomponents. Theories can be shifting and reorganizing in distinct and changing environments. Structuralists call this kind of theory work *bricolage*. You make theory piecemeal.

Social constructionists like Gergen (1985) would see the evolution of gender theory as the multiple sites where terms and concepts are shaking lose the sediment and barnacles in which they have been encrusted. Chaos theory positions volatile moments in process, driven by reorganizations that may be variously motivated. Demands for revision and the making of new landscapes, new maps and new ways of speaking arise from clinical experience, from culture, and from politicized groups that are newly empowered. Our painful condition as analysts is to work both amidst the refreshing vitality of these changes and in the shadow of structures of power and history embedded inextricably in what we do.

Now our understanding of gender development and the role of sexuality as integrating and differentiating from gender experience can be written as a utopian or dystopian narrative. We would have to map gender attractors in the culture and in family systems, as well as within the individual who is constructing gender knowledge (consciously and unconsciously) in the context of action, real time, and endlessly iterative and reentrant processes. Fluidity and multiplicity of outcome and structure clearly can arise; but in considering the landscape in which gender will be construed and constructed, one must remember the contradictions and often lethal consequences of disequilibrium.

For me, it is crucial to include Foucault (1965, 1975, 1980, 1988) as a kind of counterweight to systems theory, with all its abstract power. In the light of Foucault, any landscape in which development grows is actually a power grid with both overt and covert nodes of interest and demand. So the elements of power need to be added to the Waddington-type (1966) epigenetic landscape, allowing us to notice that being a subject entails submission to and rebellion against subjugation.

CHAPTER 5

~∾

Tomboys' Stories

My immersion in chaos theory and the study of nonlinear dynamic systems came out of work I was doing on tomboys. As I began to listen in clinical situations, to reflect on my own tomboy history, and to read, I began to experience a great and persistent difficulty mapping the tomboy to the gender narratives usual within psychoanalysis or within feminism. Tomboys did not seem to be quiet and obedient category occupiers.

Now almost all gender terms and many gender experiences are in flux and under deconstructive scrutiny, and I hasten to say that the term tomboy and the persons or experiences to which the term is applied must surely change and mutate over time. But to begin, recognizing the term's playful and affectionate connotations, I use it to describe an experience of "masculinity" in girls or women. The term must summarize and therefore fail to encompass many experiences. Some of the individual stories are light and playful, some energetic and determined, some dark and terrible. A tomboy state may feel like a ticket to liberation or a bulwark against destruction and annihilation. I mean the term tomboy to slide across both ego-syntonic and dystonic forms and certainly to slide along the registers of symbol, image, or body state.

I feel at the center of a paradox. The tomboy plays with gender conventions, crosses gender borders in pleasure and in pain. She constructs a space between categories, a place to draw a little breath of air. But, looked at from another perspective, some tomboys live embedded in stereotype. Tomboy life can be as airless as a bell jar. Gender conflicts can feel suffocating and rigid. A tomboy identity can feel like a rigid but beloved carapace or a nasty introject worthy only of hatred and expulsion.

131

Alternatively, the tomboy persona can be a claim for action and mobility, a site of doubleness and multiplicity itself. Perhaps one way to think about living a tomboy self is to think of the complexity of passing. Passing, which requires a performer and an observer, is a relational construction in which the disavowed self is also lurking in the shadows, known yet not known. There can be in the presentation and reception of a tomboy self a complex doubling, an experience of enigmatic bi-genderedness.

For some, a tomboy experience can be central to ways of being and feeling sexual, but for others the tomboy persona is a way to manage and constrict desire both as its subject and its object. These shifts go on within one life and across different stories and histories. The tomboy experience often simultaneously refuses conventions and gender coherences and swallows them wholesale. Gender conformist and gender outlaw.

One can see gender bouncing and shifting through the Oxford English Dictionary's definitional history of the etymology of tomboy: "1559: A rude and forward boy; 1592: a wild romping girl; 1700: a bold or immodest woman." A girl who behaves like a spirited or boisterous boy. Over the top even for a boy. Subtly and inexorably as the definition moves through historical time, it takes on transgressive and sexual connotations. And this use of "tom" stretches from the wildness of tom-cat, to the wiliness of Tom Sawyer, to the compliance of Uncle Tom. "Tom" probably also derives from the saint's name, Doubting Thomas, a kind of patron saint of ambivalence and marginality.

What kind of gender identity theory could these stories benefit from? What sort of developmental story could be woven here? How do these stories of women's complex relationships to ideas about masculinity—what I am summarizing as tomboys' stories—illuminate the gaps in our theoretical narratives, force a rethinking? Tomboys' experiences and stories are embedded in culture and gender and language worlds in which they are understood and misunderstood and, in any case, constituted. I have used the variations within and between tomboys to try to destabilize my immersion in psychoanalytic developmental theory, to ask more questions than I can answer.

Although my own identification as tomboy goes back a long way, my professional preoccupations began when I responded to an offer to comment on Coates's (1995; Bradley et al., 1991) work on gender identity. I felt I did have something to say about her work but was just at the beginning of thinking about tomboys. Several months later, I forgot that I had been so diffident and circumspect, and, thinking, Oh this will be fun, I agreed to write a longer paper. At the least, it was a year away.

But over the next months I came to feel more and more beleaguered and uncertain. I felt in over my head but was stoically determined to tough it out. This is one of my tomboy tropes: tough, competitive, stoic, more than a little mindless bravado. One of the most striking adult forms this "jump now, worry later" style took was a decision I made quite spontaneously (i.e., unconsciously) while I was standing on a line at registration quite late in my graduate school career (when immaturity could not be an excuse). I insisted that the University of Michigan men's lacrosse team let me join and play. I was plunged into the fascinating world of Big Ten NCAA sports in the throes of Title IX paranoia. It was 1970.

Tense interviews with coaches and athletic directors followed. I listened to an exhausted-looking woman swim coach describing the fundraising efforts of the women's team: bake sales at swim meet intermissions. I watched the arrogant director of men's athletics signing checks and vouchers for the football players—those gods of Michigan, outfitted with their own new cars and giant playbooks, possessors of nonchalant, sauntering walks into their training quarters for daily practice. Local folklore had it that the Michigan team had an employee whose sole job was to fix or pay the team's traffic tickets.

Such was the fantasy and sense of potency surrounding the male athlete's privilege. The athletic director barely looked up from his desk as he forbade me to join the team until I said, "Well fine, put it in writing." This was the fall of 1970, a brief historical moment when patriarchy was actually fearful of feminism. Title IX had put all federal research funds at risk if it could be demonstrated that sex discrimination existed at an institution receiving federal money. The director and I glared at each other across the suddenly intractable divide of gender, but he did not take up my challenge. I had apparently prevailed.

But then I had to play lacrosse. I had neglected to notice that, while my girls' boarding school played an intense, hard-running, dexterous, stick-handling version of the game, for men it was a contact sport. If macho had plunged me into this trouble, grit and a stoic, tough-girl style saw me through it. By season's end, I had calves that were astonishing, bruises everywhere, and an interesting worm's-eye-view of the power and anonymity of masks and protective padding as well as the particular magic surrounding male athletes. I noticed that the men playing lacrosse (who were divided between protectiveness and fury in relation to me) had a much easier time overcoming the perhaps slender prohibition on hitting girls than I had overcoming the prohibition on hitting anyone. I learned a great deal about rough-and-tumble-play, that signifying symptom of gender identity disorder, and expanded the range of what I could tolerate and bounce back from. I came to feel very pleasurably strong and physically resilient.

The concept of mastery came to have a highly physical cathexis for me. I felt in possession of a body image formed and streamlined away from the objectifying male gaze that stains and maintains so much in female subjectivity. Body imago and self-state were focused and delineated by the impact of flesh on flesh, muscle to muscle, the body mixup and shocks that do not usually arrive for women outside the funhouse or the bedroom. I had never understood the exhilaration and power of physical contact sports, despite a lifetime of those more distal rather than proximal competitions such as tennis or those earlier forms of women's basketball where you could not move or make physical contact. I understood, as never before, how much the physicality of sport was another instance of Winnicott's (1950) concept of the power of well-managed aggression. This can be vicariously felt in any viewing of the current version of professional women's basketball or soccer or women's boxing, but 30 years ago, it was a revelation.

I came to love the experience of getting ready to play or to practice. I was entranced with the intense and particular cathexis of the athlete's body. I could see that penis envy flourished not only in my own aggrieved heart but also within the hierarchy of men. I would watch my male teammates watching the football team's daily progress to practice and see how dramatically my lacrosse guys turned into admiring fans. They were less male, less grown, certainly less magically phallic than the football team, whose bodies and lives and psyches were so mysteriously and intensely attended to by trainers and coaches. I loved being in what I felt were such distinctly male spaces. I liked to be the spy in that world. Retrospectively I can appreciate the mixture of macho/stoic/toughie with curious voyeur. The tomboy as spy and enigmatically as double agent. And as any athletic experience will teach you, sports is a space where a girl's body can have use value and not simply exchange value. Function over decoration.

Sports contains both play and competition, and some of my tomboy life is an intense and combative determination to compete with men. There is often for women a demand to support and take pleasure in voyeurism and attention to male skills and prowess. I respond poorly to these demands, and I can feel that my own tomboy persona is one of my reactions to the internal pressures I feel around competition, where competing seems to entail being able to function in masculine spaces.

Now not all female athletes are tomboys and not all competition is necessarily with or about men. It will take a historical approach to trace out how and in what eras and contexts women doing sports have felt that athletic practices brought either the necessity or the potential of a gender-crossing experience. It is interesting that Rivière's (1929) work on women's anxiety about competing and aggressive striving is viewed in relation to male authority. Neither athletics nor competition needs to be conducted in tomboy mode. Yet it is one of the variations, perhaps both idiosyncratic and generational, in my gender multiplicities. In tomboy experience there can be the rigidity of defense and stoicism. There can be the freedom and excitement that come with a performance that feels somewhat transgressive. And these personae and stereotypes move through history. Yesterday's tomboys give way to today's soccer babes.

Like my trials on the lacrosse team, writing and working on tomboys has taken me beyond where I feel I can easily go. As in playing lacrosse, I find that writing about tomboys turns out to be a contact sport. To work on this topic, I have had to confront theories of development, ideas about gender, identity, and identity formation, and ideas about language and its relation to identity.

TOMBOYS' STORIES

The tomboys' stories and the analyst/listener's interpretive narratives are all tangled in the rules and conventions of gender and gender growth. I like Adam Phillips's (1995) idea that "all symptoms, after all, are states of conviction" (p. 184). Behind one tomboy's "guy" persona is the deep conviction that women are second-class citizens, losers, uninteresting. "Guyness" is the only site of excitement. And, if you press on this conviction, you discover that it is not her own excitement she craves or values. Within this construct of conviction is the notion that only in boy form, only by her carrying and manifesting some elements she would term masculine, will others find her exciting. Within another tomboy's inner experience, there is the horrifying conviction that the "boy," a self-state that feels male to her, is a degraded infantile parasite. For this woman, the avowed identification is a torment. What men and boys get from women, she fervently believes, is unending maternal succor, an idealized, tantalizing maternal breast offered only to boys. But her longings are a source of despair and self-beratement. In her case, infantile longing may have been retrospectively masculinized and enviously hated, an example perhaps of *Nachtraglichkeit*, deferred action and also perhaps an envy of one part of the self for another.

CLINICAL SKETCHES

1. Jeri is a woman with a very strong, lifelong "tomboy" identity that draws much of its style, imagery, and gestures from a powerful erotic tie to an adolescent boyfriend. The intensity of her response to him, her need for him, and her taking in of what she experienced as the essence of his masculine being remain crucial sources of vitality and meaning for her. In sexual fantasies, in her dream life, and in her modes of being in the world, she carries this identification as object and as subject.

Among the early object ties and powerful claims on love and identity that also enter this experience of who she is and how she loves are a number of subtle and often contradictory forces. There is an almost-lost memory of a vital tomboy mother, a memory lost in the debilitating illnesses that ravaged the mother, eclipsing and compromising everyone in her family. There is a disidentification with this ailing mother, a flight to the potent, exciting adolescent boy both as lover and as identificatory object. Curiously, the father in this family is remembered as amply, sweetly responsible, the source of caretaking, feeding, and humor. Yet Jeri can also see that her father sacrificed too much, lived a responsible but anguished and depleted life.

"Masculinity," for Jeri, is sometimes vital, sometimes masterful, sometimes lost, and sometimes ground down in duty. In her adult sexual and emotional life, lived entirely with women, the need to heal and protect a woman, the wish to be the tomboy lover with its roots in her teenage life, and the deeply buried wish for care herself all coexist and organize in a contradictory package. In sexual fantasy, she is often drawn to relive the intense excitement and pleasure she enjoyed with her adolescent boyfriend. In her relationships, she lives out the responsible, caretaking father but also the masterful seducer. She is more usually the source of pleasure than the recipient.

2. Sarah carried a lost tomboy self, a ghostly alter who lived and adventured alongside a depressed and shy girl. This identity was entirely secret, a fantasy of being a boy named John. This boy, who grew and aged as Sarah did, lived a self-determined, powerful, heroic life. He avenged the death of his parents. This element of the fantasy seems intriguing. A murder, a representation of how unparented she felt. But in its reparative aspects, this fantasy carried the conviction that a boy might have thrived in her family.

More poignantly, she imagined that she would have thrived if she had been a boy. A girl at the end of a long line of siblings, mostly girls, Sarah lived as though defeated from the very beginning in her attempts to get attention from her mother. She dreamt once of climbing a very long staircase in order to reach her mother only to find that her sisters had already arrived there, that she was too late. Orphan, hero, adventurer, rescuer, she lived a counterlife inhabited as ongoing fantasy in a developmental progression from depression to a dangerously masochistic immersion in a cult. Trapped in her life, often feeling immersed in a body that she abused, starved, and neglected, she kept a free space as a boy but lived this multiplicity in an unintegratable set of self-states.

The more usual form of lost tomboy is as an age-specific self-state, lively and appreciated at one developmental moment and abandoned or repudiated later on. Gilligan, Lyon, and Hammer (1990) do not characterize the loss of voice and presence and self-esteem as a gender shift, but they do describe many girls' loss of entitlement and agency from the onset of adolescence through young adulthood. Might such a loss not have a gender shifting aspect to it for some women? The lost tomboy represents the potential for being and loving that has been cast away in the face of the need to organize a heterosexual relational identity, a bisexual potential perhaps recoverable in some postoedipal development (Elise, 1997, 1998, 1999; Benjamin, 1988; Bassin, 2002), a loss of multiplicity under the particular developmental demands of adolescence.

Like all psychoanalytically inflected stories, these tomboy narratives hinge identity on both love and loss. Sometimes a tomboy identity carries an "encrypted" identification (Abraham and Torok, 1994), a secret alliance or self-state carried either from some earlier developmental time or from someone in an earlier generation. I am struck by the incidence of a lost tomboy mother, an alive and vital aspect of the mothering figure lost in a variety of circumstances. Sometimes a tomboy identity may then carry reparative hopes, perhaps also atonement. It is usual for a child to believe that he or she is the precipitant of a parent's difficulties. In this way identities and modes of being can carry both the guilt and hope for recovery. And what to make of the "conviction" that a boy would be loved in a family but not a girl? What historical and social forces, what gender asymmetry is carried in this idea, and whose fantasy is it?

3. "So I'd think about praying to be changed into a boy" (Faulkner, 1931, p. 260).

That is Temple Drake's voice in Faulkner's novel *Sanctuary*. A patient reminds me of this passage in the midst of a very tumultuous point in her treatment as she feels poised between the constriction and limits of an asexual boyhood and the imagined terror of being and feeling feminine. Temple is in the barn. She knows she will be raped.

> That was when I got to thinking a funny thing. You know how you do when you're scared. I was looking at my legs and I'd try to make like I was a boy. I was thinking about if I just was a boy and then I tried to make myself into one by thinking. . . . So I'd think about praying to be changed into a boy and then I would pray and then I would sit right still and wait [pp. 259–260].

As Popeye approaches, Temple drifts into a dissociated state, imaging alter identities. She could be an old woman, an old man. And then, almost dreamily, as she floats away from her situation, she imagines amusedly what will happen when Popeye discovers she is a boy.

The patient alerting me to this passage in the novel does not know why or how her tomboy self first appeared. She refers to this experience as "male" and yet feels, quite consciously, even relentlessly woman identified. Perhaps, as Faulkner seems to suggest, being a boy is a way of not remembering, a way not to notice something terrible and frightening. Boyhood, in this case, does not simply express the danger of femininity but forecloses memory and thinking. Certainly the experience of being poised to enter a female space, but terrified and disabled from imagining growth in any direction, transformed my patient into a raging mad person fearing for her sanity.

The triggers for a very dramatic, apparently unexpected psychic shift can be subtle, almost imperceptible. Sometimes I felt we were on the brink of her remembering something, sometimes there was a hint of softness in one of us and sometimes some softness or gentleness that she perceived in my relationship to men. Our interaction would then become the site of abandonment and danger. I became worse than useless. I seemed to be the replication of a woman who refuses to notice danger, a good German refusing to notice "the smell of burning flesh," as she explicitly shouted. The escalation and terror she felt and conveyed to me were powerful. No longer her helpful useful analyst, I was a woman deeply and dangerously ignorant of the life and body-threatening dangers all women face.

This boy self-state (which had both a bullying and a playful side and which existed in concert with other, more adult, functional ways of being) is an identity she despised and felt trapped in. Has it been assembled or organized for the management of trauma and danger? Her family situation includes an older brother who was permitted to behave with considerable, unchecked violence toward her. Although she feels acutely the unfairness of male privilege as it was lived and espoused within her family (and certainly envy is a powerful factor here), there is also the privilege to commit violence that accrues to men.

4. Gendered experience, because of its rich lode of fantasy and because it is such a potent site for projection, is particularly likely to be used in the action of *Nachtraglichkeit,* the retrospective reorganization of early events in the light of subsequent ones. A young woman who had carried physical and psychic scarring since quite early childhood (she was four at the time of a frightening accident) had, over the course of her development, woven together a subtle and complex narrative about the gender meanings of her situation (Harris, 1998a). For this woman the body had become an oddly masculinized suit of armor. She managed her memories of trauma through a regimen of athleticism and bodily ordeal.

Throughout her childhood she had been subjected to a grim series of experiences. There was initially the accident that terrified her and all around her. There were then repeated, painful surgeries that occasioned both physical anguish and shame. These cumulatively traumatic events were experienced and managed as a tomboyhood of adventure and enterprise. Living in a family that privileged self-sufficiency and a demand to control all feeling and responsiveness, this powerful defense against pain and vulnerability became somehow mysteriously caught up with matters of gender. Her body was for her, consciously and deliberately, a nonmaternal body. The horror of pregnancy and mothering, the inevitably humiliating consequences for anyone trapped in that experience, required a stripping of flesh and fat.

The narcissistic pain of her stigmatizing scars and the agonizing memories encountered in any experiences of passivity had to be anaesthetized with more and different pain and buried in a repudiation of femininity. Femininity was organized as a body state, a disfigurement, an affective state that mixed pain and shame and anxiety in a mortifying stew of bad experience. Over time and development, this construction added other themes and disavowed identifications. Powerlessness in the wake of pain and danger was linked to the powerlessness of adult women in her family, in particular her mother, a woman who was held in some contempt in the family for her passivity and who was in publicly shameful ways betrayed by her husband.

Yet my patient's experience of gender was not uncomplicated. There were narcissistic dangers in not meeting some ideal of femininity. For all that femininity was almost synonymous with fat, with ugly scarring, and with needs of many kinds, she could panic if her body slipped too far from something recognizably normally a woman's body. Caught between two regimens—her own mortification of the flesh and the socially driven regulation of look, gait, gesture, and dress—she feels trapped. She is torn between the body she must structure for personal coherence and the adorned, highly produced body she must have for social coherence. She is stymied and frightened.

5. I have to recognize something in my own tomboy story. One key element in this identity is that the stoicism that is part of my tomboy persona has a history in the need to manage physical pain dating from very early childhood. I was by all accounts a brave little soldier, a tough little girl. I can see the identification with a soldier father (away in the war) and a strong, androgynous nanny at whose side I absorbed many tales of a childhood of privation overcome through adventure and grit. Perhaps her stories were her form of dissociation from powerlessness and pain. I took these stories in with relish, along with the usual fare of children's stories in which a child, boy or girl, enterprisingly saves the day. These positive, wholesome stories cover the stoic management of pain, perhaps unconsciously passed across a generation, as well as lived-in reaction to my own life events. In the imaginative living out of tomboy adventure and tomboy mastery, even the memory of pain is banished.

6. I could also reprise elements of the tomboy in the gender experiences of Jamie, a patient discussed in chapter 4. Jamie loved and hated her tomboy self. In fantasy she could take pleasure in athleticism and boyish vitality. Imagining herself to possess the surface style of an entrancing young man she longed to love a woman. Exploring that wish revealed not a desire to please a woman but to be formed and initiated into pleasure and self-knowledge by a woman. Sexual curiosity would yield up identity as much as pleasure. The paradox for me in this nested set of fantasies is that only as a boy could she woo a woman, who would then, in deep, passionate responsiveness, draw her into both being and loving a woman.

Not too surprisingly, these fantasies were difficult to enact. On those few occasions when she lived these hopes out with a woman, the woman's responsiveness to Jamie's boyishness destroyed the entire enterprise. I came to feel that many distinct threads were being woven in this experience. A fantasy that the mother's early love, a wonderful, creative young man, was an endlessly mourned lost love that Jamie could embody. Bringing the woman to life was both erotic pleasure and maternal repair work. Restoring the mother's love by being that love could perhaps bring a woman to life and she could thus live as a woman herself. The confusion of genders was expressing the hope that sexual life can heal and restore a narcissistic fullness to the other and then to the self. Mostly Jamie lived without much hope, convinced that only men were exciting and loveable, a fantasy that could explain her mother's depressions and her listless caring for a girl.

DISCUSSION

A tomboy's masculinity may contain her fascination with men, her fascinated rivalry, or her disavowal and avoidance of men. A tomboy may feel entranced by male power or make fun of it. In a consideration of who tomboys identify with and who tomboys want, there may be instances in which identification and desire lose their stability and distinctiveness. And, to be sure, the tomboy experience can be a carrier or signal for penis envy. Penis envy is a concept undergoing its own transformations. Torok (1970) uses the term to describe a girl's renunciation of agency in deference to her mother. Alternatively, penis envy is the sign of thwarted identificatory love from a father (Benjamin, 1988).

These possibilities must exist along with older ideas: the refusal of castration (Freud, 1925, 1931) and a girl's accurate judgment of social and patriarchal privilege (Horney, 1926).

A tomboy's identity may be as an objectified source of desire initially set in play by a parent (father or mother) or by a sibling. In considering desire and identity as emergent from relationships and relational interpersonal patterns, the desire of the parent, in whatever form, is powerful in constituting sexuality.

The force of parental desire, in whatever guise and to whatever aspect of the child it is directed, has been refocused for psychoanalytic theory by Laplanche's (1997) work on maternal seduction. Although Laplanche's concept of the enigmatic signifier diminishes maternal erotic subjectivity, making her libidinizing of her baby almost an inadvertent act, he does press psychoanalysts to consider the inevitable consequences of parental desire as a necessary component of any subjectivity.

The powerful interplay of conscious and the unconscious experience of passion in the mother–child matrix has been very carefully elaborated by Wrye and Welles (1995). This process can be provocatively called seduction or more neutrally termed sensory enmeshment. It is one potent aspect of the environmental matrix in which gender and sexuality will arise and be constituted (see Stein, 1998a, for a powerful clinical application of this liminal, indeterminate aspect to sexuality and its origins in early dyadic life). This aspect of the early relational dyad inevitably contributes to the emotional temperature and quality of an analytic dyad.

A tomboy's body ego, then, may be libidinized through any of a variety of powerful fantasies and transactions within her relationships. Bion's (1962) concept of parental reverie, the necessary imaginative work that comes to constitute a space both internal and interpersonal for a child, must also be implicated in this process. The tomboy's identity may be mimetically established in relation to the most vital, alive, or free and loving aspects of her primary figures. This masculine self might have been constituted in relation to "masculinity" in either the mother or the father. There is also the fascinating question of how siblings may become implicated in a child's gender construction. Gender shifts may be one way children and their parents organize differentiation in certain families. Not infrequently, a tomboy persona can arise for a girl with bullying older brothers or in families where the boys' aggression, particularly against girls, is unchecked or is exciting and validated.

Some tomboys do a disappearing act at adolescence. Some tomboys may disappear into disguise, as did Riviere's (1929) power femme, that masquerading woman Riviere saw as cloaking her masculinity in a kind of hyperfemme drag. Do they suffer the fate traced in the work of Gilligan et al. (1990; Gilligan and Brown, 1993) on adolescence: the dip in confidence many young women feel and report? Studies designed to refine these ideas strongly suggest that loss of "voice," loss of self-esteem and confidence, is most acute for highly conventionally feminine girls. Being a tomboy protects the self.

Psychoanalysis makes us suspicious of disappeared identities, and rightly so. Is the tomboy a developmental anomaly, carrying the leftover rebellion or expansiveness of adolescence into adulthood? Is she a historical anomaly, living as an internal consequence of the external, socially driven rigidities of gender? In a social world, for example, where athletics are less gendered than in our contemporary world and women's athleticism spread into many venues, would the social aggression and motility of rough-and-tumble play be seen as a gender violation? Would a different history of her body and her body in motion alter the gender implications for a young woman?

A tomboy identity can be moving in time, or it can be fixed. Gender adventure can be made in a state of transcendence or terror. A tomboy jock takes cultural and physical space to move and play and express sanctioned forms of motility and aggression. Tomboy as excess, as conveyer and bearer of jouissance. Tomboy as containing and expressing both genders, both desires, object and subject. Bigendered or crossgendered identities might have a number of meanings and implications. The tomboy may open a space for herself to move and act, at least in her imagination, less rigidly, not be anchored to binary categories, living in the space between masculinity and femininity.

That opening this space is difficult to do is compelling, though contingent on the social and historical contexts. Garber (1995) worries about the reductive elements of bigendering, the organization of experience, in limiting ways, to maintain a representational system organized around either/or. There is, for example, a complex interpretive discourse that develops around female athletes. Tomboy jocks. When and how does a tomboy inhabit free space? The free body space a girl can sometimes find in sports is an important site in preadolescence. Athletics can offer girls opportunities for agency, for a powerful inhabitation of bodily life. Yet reading the discourse about female athleticism in Susan Kahn's (1994) work on the history of women in sports is an interesting exercise because it does reveal a dramatic, fluctuating social anxiety about woman athletes.

In the literature about woman athletes one can see continuing, oscillating fears—fear of an encroachment on masculinity and fear of homosexuality. The historical situation I know most about is the women's baseball leagues in the 1940s. The film *A League of Their Own* sets the conflicts and controls of the players in terms of their need to maintain femininity and to manage female heterosexual sexuality. But the focus on femininity more accurately addresses fears of homosexuality intricately woven into anxieties about "mannish" (that 40s term) players. Now it seems to me that the lesbian text in that film is missing. But lesbians also are missing from the game itself. In reality, Jo D'Angelo, a working-class lesbian, played nearly two full seasons in the league, only to be released unceremoniously not because she broke curfew to hang out with soldiers as did the Madonna character in the film, but because she showed up with a too short, in her words, "butchy" haircut (Kahn, 1994).

In an earlier phase of female athletics, a British doctor, Arabella Kenealy, articulated the fear and fantasies that female athletes could provoke: "A woman who wins golf and hockey matches may be said . . . to energize her muscles with the potential manhood of possible sons, since over-strenuous pursuits could sterilize women as regards to male offspring" (Kahn, 1994, p. 29). This goofy biology hovered around the anxious media attention to Babe Dedriksen, an extraordinary woman athlete who in the 1940s and 1950s achieved great prominence in track and field (the javelin was her Olympic specialty) and in golf. She is probably the premier woman athlete of the mid-twentieth century. Her life was fictionalized in the sports pages as a tale of the tomboy tamed. Her name itself operates like a shifting signifier—the name Babe is stripped of its feminine connotations when placed in connection with Babe Ruth, another sports giant. But this Babe had to be tamed by a giant husband. The gloating headlines when she married: "Babe is a lady now." "The world's most amazing athlete has learned to wear nylons and cook for her huge husband." In what was no doubt journalists' hyperbole, it was said that the Texas tomboy slept with the husband in an eight-foot square bed. Somewhat bitterly, Kahn notes that in Dedriksen's obituaries sportswriters were as admiring of her achievement of femininity as of her achievements with the javelin or the golf club.

Back to penis envy, the inevitable even if unbidden thought that must surface about tomboys. The early midcentury work on penis envy as cross-gender identifications was too singly valenced and too preoccupied with pathology. Masculinity in women has been viewed as a defensive identification with the father, a foreclosing of oedipal disappointments, or as a competitive rivalry with the father. Desire and identifications are anchored as distinct and oppositional processes, a construction that makes heterosexuality seamlessly normative. Within French neoclassical theory (Chasseguet-Smirgel, 1970, 1986; McDougall, 1980, 1989, 1995) masculine identification is seen as the refusal of difference, so that masculinity in a woman is a quasi-psychotic and perverse refusal of reality. Yet the "reality" that is refused is a complex one: is it anatomical reality, psychic reality, or social reality? In a certain way, masculine identification, including masculine protest, paradoxically acknowledges and refuses the reality of paternal or, rather, patriarchal power.

Butler (1990) sounds a cautionary note with respect to this jouissance of tomboy, phallic play. Envious appropriation is always an unstable identification, carrying implications of insufficiency, of the impossibility of full phallic potency in any identity, male or female. Phallic positions, in either a man or a woman, can feel hollow and dissociated, empty and performative, or juicily full and alive.

Masculine protest and penis envy may be opposite forks in the road, or they may be intertwining pathways. Even as bedrock a concept as penis envy begins to deconstruct, to sag, under the demand to carry more theoretical and conceptual freight than even a penis can carry. Torok (1970) sees penis envy and masculine idealization as projective identification intended to allow one to remain loyal to the mother. Idealizing masculinity maintains the division between phallic and castrated and keeps mother and daughter together but on the losing side.

In the most developed feminist revision of this concept, Benjamin (1991) views penis envy as a compensatory attempt to solve problems of separation and rapprochement, the vapor trail of a mutual inability of father and daughter to work out experiences of identity as subjects and agents. But as O'Connor and Ryan (1993) have noted, this analysis never questions the heterosexual underpinnings of the theory.[1] Agency and recognition are endowed through the father such that female subjectivity is still within a masculine cast. And masculinity still comes from the father. And we are certainly still ensconced in the nuclear family, a matter of increasing concern to theorists like Butler, Goldner, Corbett, and others.

To open up the theoretical and practical space for the multiplicity of genderedness and of sexual practices and meanings in tomboys, I draw on Bromberg (1998): "a human being's ability to like a life with both authenticity and self-awareness depends on the presence of an on-going dialectic between separateness and unity of one's self-states, allowing each self to function optimally without foreclosing communication and negotiation between them" (p. 272). In the tomboy's identity, a boy in a girl, a boy and a girl, a girl and more than a girl, a girl whose phallic activities may be dystonic or syntonic are all shifting self-states in play.

As the tomboy experience comes to serve various intrapsychic and interpersonal functions, to encompass and express desire in some people, to build forms of identity in others, the common or *criterial* thread is more phenomenological than categorical. The tomboy self is a girl's or woman's lived experience of what she and the social surround term phallic or masculine. It may be subjectively experienced or objectively salient. It may be obvious or subtle, in your face or private and secret. An example of this cross-identification appears in Winnicott (1971, pp. 72–75). In a well-known vignette, Winnicott describes his own surprise at saying to a patient that, without much salient physical evidence, he was seeing the girl in the male patient.

For some tomboys, their body and vocal presentations serve a crucial function, and the rendering of boy or man or maleness is palpable and visible. For some tomboys, the identity takes on physicality and a bodily form. In a certain way, tomboy experiences are part of a wider range of experiences that effectively problematize the whole idea of "the body" (Grosz, 1994; Harris, 1998a).

I have traced evidence of tomboy selves in a wide variety of situations. Some situations are the normal vicissitudes of interpersonal life in families, with all the potentially eccentric and creative strategies for safety and attachment. Some of these situations are grossly traumatic and destabilizing experiences that would fragment and disorient most people. I realize that the terms tomboy and trauma have been used elastically and summarily.

I hope to show the multifunctional state of these gender constructions, to display the wide variation in the forms and function of what I am terming tomboy as a psychic structure of some form of masculinity in a woman. Not all trauma is resolved or managed by women through a gender move. That particular response to traumatic events is comprehensible in very individual terms for each person. One aspect of tomboy identity, then, may be that activity defends against the danger of penetration and damage. This mode of protection may or may not be initially gendered or sexualized, but may come to be postdated as male or boyish or phallic. A tomboy may oscillate between rigidity and activity as a bulwark against memory or fear of annihilation.

One's body braces the psyche and frames ways of seeing and being seen. If our bodily experiences are, in part, constituted by the gaze of others we may (fruitlessly or successfully) craft our bodies in an attempt to control the gaze of the onlooker. We may try to disappear, or to push ourselves right in the face of the viewer. In the dialectic of seeing and being seen, the body is the receiving and transmitting instrument; and a tomboy, through her body state, rigid and yet softly assembled, struggles in the rough-and-tumble play of visual contact. In fact, one might argue that this claim applies to all women, given that the female body is so strongly objectified in our cultural matrix.

Looking across many life situations and seeing gender structures like tomboy *personae* as multifunctional and multiform, we can appreciate the range and complexity of gender structure in its conscious and unconscious formations. It is this deep richness, so elaborated in culture and history and in family life, that makes gender available and malleable for many different forms of psychic work, including the metabolizing of trauma.

With respect to any of the particular dynamics I have been describing, one has to wonder why any of these activities or internal spaces should be designated as masculine or phallic or somewhere among the many linguistic representations that help regulate and constitute masculinity. Any of the experiences that a tomboy claims for her tomboyhood could, in another person, be happily (or unhappily) ungendered or ego-syntonically feminine. Terms like 'masculinity' and 'femininity' are context sensitive, arising in and taking on meaning in particular life worlds. These terms may be set in single quotation marks to signal both the irony and the qualifications attached.

Feminine qualities or experiences are certainly distinct and different as they appear in a man or in a woman (Blechner, 1998; Corbett, 1999). And, as all the terminology and conceptual structures that adhere to gender begins to shake loose and change, the specificity of genderedness is also likely to change and mutate. Gender terms will, of course, bring their own political baggage into our theoretical discussions and into consulting rooms. It is crucial only that the politics of gender not be imported invisibly and unironically into our understandings. A tomboy's gender construction, desire, and character are not universal or transhistorical forms. The developmental modeling that I think can be useful clinically advances contingent, historically placed claims.

A tomboy, who may be gay or straight, whose doubleness of identity may masquerade or display, may be a wedge into the often seamless connections we make between gender and desire. If sexual arrangements involve constructed genders, constructed body egos in layers of identity both conscious and unconscious, then terms like homosexual and heterosexual and gender category names like boy, girl, man, and woman do not, except as specific practices or as political structures, have much inherent purchase in theory. Butch and straight tomboys alike may live in an erotic world of imaginary or actual boys or girls, men and women. Sexual life may be homosexual or heterosexual in internal fantasy, and fantasy may replicate or defy lived gendered sexual arrangements.

Although there has always been conceptual space in most psychoanalytic theorizing about bisexuality, it is not often richly capitalized on in clinical writing. Elise (1997), concerned that bisexuality remains too frequently a hypothetical construct in psychoanalytic theory, has been addressing this problem. Too often bisexuality is a provisional transitional space to be renounced in various ways. Perhaps it would be helpful to reintroduce here an old idea in psychoanalysis—that nothing once desired or brought into a relation of attachment and longing is ever fully given up. So many of the developmental stories in gender theory use the language of psychic sculpting. Elements of the self are foreclosed, repudiated, disidentified in a kind of psychic Bauhaus aesthetic, "less is more."

Butler's (1990, 1993, 1995a, b) work is crucial here. She notes the melancholic elements in identity that are carried through incomplete mourning; lost attachments and lost loves all remain elements in the internal world, supported or unsupported by psychic and interpersonal and social structures. A tomboy may carry aspects of her identity as a melancholic, ungrieved aspect of her mother's or her father's ideal love. Or in her foreclosed relation to the feminine we might find the ungrieved elements in a homosexual love or a masculine persona connected to her mother or her father.

The distinction Abraham and Torok (1994) make between mourning and melancholia as a distinction among types of internalization is intriguing. Melancholy involves the psychic work of incorporation. As

Abraham and Torok define the term, incorporation entails a concrete fantasy. It is corporeal, signifying a loss still partially disavowed, not yet metabolized into one's own subjectivity. Gestures, mimetically copied styles of physical being, are laced with this melancholic aspect. Butler's argument focuses on the psychic costs of disavowing longings for the maternal primary attachment. We end up being or enacting the figures we are not allowed to love, wearing our hearts on our sleeves. Tomboy identities (as incorporations and internalizations) may be the collectors for a variety of losses, lost loves, and lost desires.

CHAOS THEORY AND GENDER DEVELOPMENT

I have been drawing on dynamic systems theory, the forms of chaos theory particularly developed by Thelen and Smith (1994), to imagine multiplicities of developmental outcomes. Their general-systems approach would see a phenomenon like gender or sexual desire not as a structure but rather as a "softly assembled" set of behavioral attractors whose form and stability are quite variable depending on the task at hand, the context, and the person's life history and experiences. In this approach, variability in pathways and experience is privileged.

Cultural critic Eve Sedgwick (1990) notes, perhaps with some irony, that some people are more "gendery" than others. We could amend her statement to say that gender saturation varies across situations and tasks. And no doubt across cultures and historical time. It is not that everyone has multiple and fluid gender experiences and shifting or labile constellations of experience that come to be gendered. Only that this variation is expectable within the framework of chaos theory.

This proposal would alter (though not dispense with) the normative qualities and features of psychoanalytic theory. Variety in gender saturation would certainly be relevant to the experience of tomboys. The power, density, and meaning of tomboy experiences, expressed through the body, speech, or modes of thought and feeling, would all have unique and individual integrations. For some, it is a ghostly alteration; for others, it is a vital source of growth; for others still, it is sublimated and seamlessly transmuted into self-experience. There are gender divides in some of us, but the maps we make and the boundaries we draw vary in meaning, in intensity, and in function. Gender can function as the bulwark against collapse and deathly danger, or it can seem just another suit.

Many factors make chaos theory, or nonlinear dynamic systems theory, useful for this kind of psychoanalytic work in understanding gender and development. The theory does not begin with a particular commitment to one kind of mental, body–psyche organization. Gender does not inevitably organize sexuality, nor do modes and meanings of desire have a necessary, determinant effect on gender. There are no innate *motives* in this theoretical approach. Rather, motives and forms of life and experience emerge from the immersion of an infant, with only a small repertoire of capacities, in an immediately complex interaction with a social, physical world (Edelman, 1987; Ghent, 2002).

Inherent in this way of thinking about structures is a paradox: human experience is born of deterministic chaos, of the mutual elaboration of randomness and pattern. In this theory there can be robust, ongoing patterns of interaction that begin with the earliest experiences. But these patterns are not outcomes *predicted* from some point of origin. Rather, for any child there is a kind of motivational landscape that begins with minimal initial biases and evolves into a rich set of dynamic possibilities. A psychoanalytic approach expands the landscape to include unconscious phenomena and fantasy about significant other people in the child's life. Here we can invoke Bion's (1962) concept of maternal reverie: the desire of the other, usually the primary parent, is a constituting force in the motivation and emerging capacities of the child. This is in a sense a transpersonal model of motivation.

If gender and sexuality are softly assembled, if the components that enter into the experience of being a gender are variable within a life and certainly across lives, if there are multiple pathways and unique constructions of meaning—it seems likely that we will be much closer to clinical experience than with developmental theories that stress particular narratives, linearity, and distinct developmental lines.

Nonlinear dynamic systems theory has it both ways. There are powerful regularities of patterning in experience. Gender identity can seem monolithic and coherent at one level, but zoom the camera lens in more closely and the fine gradations and variability and unpredictability of emerging processes are much more in evidence. We would not need a concept of core gender identity, certainly not one established or predicted preexperientially. "Core" as a term carries too much weight of bedrock, of depth, even of primaryness. Gender will become a patterned, complex self-state, but under many distinct and idiosyncratic conditions. It is this unique complexity that is obscured by theories that make desire or gender too monolithic. Coherence is an outcome at one level (and not for all people). We don't need to build it into the hardware.

The concept of soft assembly offers the potential for thinking about particular forms of gender life or desire that may be either rigid or flexible. The softness in soft assembly does not necessarily mean flexible or fluid. The terms describe a process of development, not a particular character of psychic structure. Gender can be a rich playground or a desert, a stark cartoon or highly elaborated spaces in mind, body, and life.

Since function and process are more prominent than structure in nonlinear dynamic systems theory, there is a flexibility in the soft assembly concept. Now the structure–function distinction is not a simple one. Corbett (2001b) notes that what we call structure might best be thought of as a very slowed-up, sluggish process. Within chaos theory, structure is perhaps best thought of as a kind of temporary stasis in a dynamic system, a relatively unstable resting point in the ebb and flow of social and personal experience. Gender, in whatever form—rigid, fluid, multiple, or unitary—will only in a particular life enter into certain functions: separation, safety, attachment, mastery, pleasure seeking, isolating.

This is a theory of human functioning that is deterministic but not causal or teleological—a key distinction I want to make among developmental accounts. We do not begin a developmental process knowing already how it will turn out. The end of any developmental story cannot be preorganized from the beginning. The tendency in theories of development to be adultomorphic has been critiqued by Harré (1984), Broughton (1987), Coates (1997), and others. Adultomorphic theory crafts and constrains particular kinds of clinical listening. If our model is organized around monolithic, singular identities based on same-sex and singular forms of desire assumed to be heterosexual—if such a model is considered normative—this grid will organize what we hear and know about a patient. Nonconforming phenomena survive as error or as deviance. Because same-sex and opposite-sex as concepts are unremarkable, they are given the most superficial, almost cosmetic reading and never are submitted to any kind of dynamic deconstruction. This is Chodorow's (1992) critique, drawing on Lewes and others, when she characterized heterosexuality as a compromise formation.

Retrospectively, of course, we may construct a narrative of how anyone became a particular gender or came to inhabit his or her body in a particular and singular way. We can certainly see powerful regularities of pattern in the way a person acts or interacts with others. We can observe how powerfully our earliest modes of interaction constrain ways of being, both being alone and being with another. We are also increasingly able to see how much fantasy and meaning is expressed and elaborated through ways of touching, holding, and talking. A child organizes and constructs an experience of self and self-in-relation in the context of the intense wash of sensory, social, and relational experience. We might think of these interactional patterns as kinds of transgenerational transmissions of normal and abnormal trauma (Seligman, 1999a, b).

By considering a complex phenomenon like gender to be a softly assembled system, we take up gender's meanings within any individual and familial system, its function and form within specific tasks in specific environments. To speak of tasks and environments is to speak at too rational a level. Certainly "softly assembled" gender encompasses behaviors that have conscious, unconscious, and socially interactional properties. Gender and desire would come into their unique and particular forms only in context, context being very broadly construed. Gender and sex would be inseparable from the interpersonal fields in which they are embedded. At the same time, neither gender identity nor forms of desire are reducible to the interpersonal field. This theory makes a place for excess and indeterminacy. Gender and desire would not be linked in preprogrammed or obvious ways.

The implications of this point of view for sexuality have been most powerfully explored in psychoanalysis in the work of Dimen (1991, 1995a, b; 1999), Elise (1997, 1998, 2002), Layton (1998), and Corbett (2001b, c) and in culture studies by Sedgwick (1990) and Garber (1995). It is a perspective deeply indebted to the developments of queer theory, both within psychoanalysis and in cultural studies (Butler, 1990; Corbett, 1993, 1999; Dean, 1993; Dyess and Dean, 2000a, b).

Sexuality expresses and contains multiple functions: self-regulation, interpersonal regulation, distancing or bridging, conditioning safety or potentially destabilizing, courting excitement or danger or sealing it off. Forms and functions of desire would not have an obvious or unremarkable relationship to gender. The assemblage of gendered experience in sexual life is contingent on context and emergent, not preprogrammed. Desire and gender may be set up antagonistically or feel seamlessly enmeshed and obvious. Passivity and activity get separated out from gender constructions or forms of desire, and the configurations and permutations organize in unique and particular ways.

CONCLUSION

A tomboy is only one among many characters about whom we make developmental stories. One of the abiding concerns in this book is that the ideological distortion in conventional developmental and psycho-analytic accounts is not merely that many forms of life are declared nonnormative but that any form of "otherness" from the central story is unfathomably other. If developmental theory is written with wide generality and is so attuned to multiplicity and variation, forms of life we like to keep thickly bounded (gay–straight, boy–girl, sissy–tomboy, identification–desire) are more alike than different in their process of formation while retaining the variability of outcome.

Some of the tomboys' stories in this chapter are stories of tran-scendence and play, and some are stories of danger and loss. I hope the contradictions between play and rigidity are evident and that I have made clear that tomboyhood and tomboy life and tomboy love may operate in many ways. Tomboy as outlaw and as conformist. Tomboy as symptom and as developmental solution. Gender play and gender sickness in the culture and in the individual.

❧

CHAPTER 6

Gender as a Strange Attractor: Gender's Multidimensionality

*I*t is a sunny winter day, and the men and women sitting in my office manage to look both relaxed and intense. There are moments of laughter, occasional jets of excitement, and, from time to time, experiences of intense conflict. I am leading a discussion of a book by Ann Fausto-Sterling (2000), *Sexing the Body*. Drawing on history, biology, and feminism, Fausto-Sterling shows both the fierceness and the falseness of the constructions of polarized sexed bodies. Although we are accustomed to considering the variegations of gender experience, we tend to hold on to the sexed body as a solid phenomenon organized irreducibly as a dichotomy.

Within psychoanalysis and clinical theory, the capacity to think of gender as bent to various psychic functions is indebted to the groundbreaking work of Coates (1990, 1997; Coates et al., 1991) on the way a child's gender can carry and express complex residues of attachment histories, trauma across generations, and crises in parental stability. A child's gender identifications become a conscious and unconscious solution to problems that may be familial, systemic, or intrapsychic.

In search of the same kind of complexity, Fausto-Sterling gently but firmly pries loose the anxious grip we keep on the "concrete" materiality of sexed bodies. She reports on our strange and historically longstanding legal and medical preoccupations with keeping genitals in an orderly and tidy binary. These are as much obsessions as preoccupations, she argues, powered more by cultural anxieties and the demand for social regulation than by medical necessity, anatomical accuracy, or patient care.

Rather dramatically, Fausto-Sterling has drawn on the biological literature to propose a five-sex rather than a two-sex system. She thus makes space for varieties of anatomy and anomaly.[1] The religious right has gone predictably berserk. But so have we in the study group. Technically, I am the teacher in this group, but with this topic we are all subjects and objects of scrutiny. Over the weeks, I feel we are like the brightly colored chips in a child's kaleidoscope, connecting and spinning off, reflecting quietly or exploding with color and movement.

We notice that even this revolutionary five-category system still centers on male and female, although there are more permutations. Someone thinks that the turmoil and fuss over breaking open the two-gender system is, in the end, all about social control. Someone else connects this matter of control to the mad contradictions in the arguments against same-sex marriage. Through the strange logic of conservative ideologies same-sex unions are thought to undermine the institution. How's that? It will somehow destabilize marriage if more people want to marry? What is revealed when you press on this paradox is the not-so-hidden agendas of patriarchy and reproduction as marriage's *substrate*.

For all the creative play in contemporary gender arrangements, it certainly seems that sexual difference and heterosexuality, defined and soldered together at an absolutely concrete level, are still carrying powerful cultural controls. It is this interaction or competition of hegemonic, cultural stereotypes of gender and personal meanings that has propelled the work of Chodorow (1999), Dimen (1991, 2002), and Layton (1998), among others. Deconstructing the entrenched binaries of oedipal and preoedipal constructions is also at the heart of Benjamin's (1998, 2002) more recent work. Binaries are not to be overthrown but analyzed, as Benjamin, unpacking the underlying male imaginaries in psychoanalytic accounts of sexual subjectivity, opts for inclusion and difference in a subtle tension of multigendered identifications.

For many different reasons, we do and we don't want to relinguish polarities of gender and gendered bodies. Some of us like the performance. Some of us believe in the deep, visceral, cellular truth of gender. Within an individual life there can be great pleasure in gender as a deeply inhabited experience, and there can be experiences of gender that seem alienated, false, hollow, coerced. Some of us feel shamed and pathologized by an outsider status. That shame can feel very dug into our psyches. Some of us feel enlivened by the outlaw transgressive space; we love that space for its potential for deep individuality and freedom.

Fausto-Sterling was interested in opening new category spaces, new understandings, so that intersex persons, persons with some variety of anatomical anomalies or ambiguities, would be imaginable and imaginably coherent. Yet, paradoxically, beginning with the liminal, marginal categories of identity, a new and expanded space has been opened for *every* gendered, sexed being. Fausto-Sterling taps into the deep human need to feel coherent, the relief in being mirrorable to oneself and others. This need to feel recognizable lives alongside a need to be known as personally unique. This tension between the needs for uniqueness and cultural recognition or salience lives in all of us.[2]

Even as some of us can be happily delighted with the paraphernalia and feathers of gender, we discovered that, deep down, we hold many different ideas of how body and mind link up. For some, seeing sex or gender as more continuous than dichotomous feels liberating. For others, gender as a continuity threatens the rich texture in gender differences. But, for others, gender markings are simply not critical. If gender has the dimension of "saturation," we can see that we vary a lot in how saturated the colors of gender are for any of us. For many reasons, including the ways members of our study group differ in age, sexual life, history of attachments, and character, we vary a lot in how much we want to play with gender and how angry we feel in the presence (real or imagined) of the gender police.

What are the limits of gender fluidity? How is gender fluidity limited by constraints on body fluidity? True, when we begin to narrate differently about the body, many imaginative shifts in consciousness and body awareness can emerge. Speech practices and gender practices inform and inflame each other. But what happens to fluidity when the analyst gets pregnant or ill or old? How are these material states imaginatively, and yet also concretely, experienced?

An analysand is newly and happily involved in a first pregnancy and spends a lot of analytic time in reveries about her bodily experiences and the multiform fantasies she generates about her baby and their already engaging relationship. But some days she wishes she could leave her belly in the waiting room so that our intense dyadic experience and her precious individuality could be foremost. On other days, she lives imaginatively in a space where there are three of us in the room, sometimes in harmony and sometimes in conflict. The alternation of concrete experiences and fantasy is striking. The facticity of the body matters and does not matter. Dyess and Dean (2000a, b) trace out distinct registers of the body. In only some of these registers does gender matter (or mutter, as Dean [1993] has also argued).

As we follow Fausto-Sterling's arguments in the study group, one of the students articulates his reservations about body and speech with the following anecdote. Monique Wittig, cultural and queer theorist, is quoted as saying, "I have no vagina." In what sense could that be so? Is it that she has no vagina or no "vagina." Is she speaking about the body or about its social construction? Wittig may be contesting the way bodies are claimed by cultures and by signification. She is refusing cultural meaning, not occluding her body. Another student tentatively offers up William James. Perhaps you only have a "vagina" if there is cash value in that concept. Hmm. Pragmatic vaginas.

I tell the group a story in Ursula LeGuin's (1969) wonderful sci-fi novel *The Left Hand of Darkness*. In that novel, one of LeGuin's creative inspirations concerns sex. Sex can occur in her invented universe only when people come into an unusual form of estrus. At those times, when a couple feels drawn together, their genitals morph into an elaborated form. At one time, you might feminize; at another, masculine genitals could appear. "Oooh, a surprise. How interesting," says one person in the group. Another shudders. Since we are now exploring fantasy, we wonder again about the limits of gender-morphing: male fantasies of interiority, female fantasies of thrusting in. A man in the group and the women without children think about the possibility or impossibility of knowing the experience of breastfeeding. How susceptible is the body to fantasy? How resilient?[3]

Fausto-Sterling (2000) pays attention to several lines of argument. She notices the way gender meanings as social and cultural phenomena subtly and seamlessly enter science and thus the "construction" of sexed bodies. She argues that bodies, even in science, let alone in personal life and in culture, resonate and are shaped by many forces of meaning making. Gender polarity moves from the culture by way of science and biological investigations and then subtly and inexorably moves back into cultural reifications. Then a reified, sexed body can explain and underpin gender dichotomies. This might be an example of the hermeneutic circle, where explanations and meanings move from parts to wholes. But it is also a vicious circle that mystifies the social agenda taking root in and through the scientific and medical inquiry.

Fausto-Sterling takes up the history of experimentation and discovery of hormones, often *the* markers for bedrock sex differences. She argues that the incontrovertible effect of hormones on tissue is generic and sex-specific. Yet what evolved in the scientific-medical understanding was actually an inaccurate, sharp segregation of hormones by gender. She suggests that the effect of hormones is better thought of as a general property of growth induction in that many hormonal effects act on both genders. The default to a tight causal link between hormone and gender serves to underwrite strictly bounded, biologically based gender differences. A better way to model this interaction of biology and psyche would be to draw on systems theory and see the effect of hormones on tissue and structures as they are shaped by and emerge in context.

Fausto-Sterling analyzes the role of science and medicine in a process that political theorists name interpellation (Althusser, 1971). The culture, through various intermediaries (parents, teachers, police), steps forward and addresses the individual and in so doing claims and tries to constitute the person in a particular social or familial order. The common metaphoric scene is the policeman who yells out, "Hey you." You, the one addressed, startle and feel guiltily discovered (Zizek, 1989). This example of being constituted by being named is replicated in a million little tendrils of two-person experiences on the way to becoming an individual within a complex, multilayered, multidimensional system. Getting and maintaining a gendered body and a gender is one of these interpellations, working at both a verbal and a nonverbal level. We cannot exactly refuse these categories, though they are assimilated, consciously and unconsciously, in unique ways in any individual.

As Fausto-Sterling (2000) moves back and forth among the roles of scientist, historian, and cultural critic, she creates a big playground with dark corners and light ones, and our group expands and inhabits multiplicities, singularities, polarities, fluidities. We mix and match among a number of identifications and subject positions: gender players, gender police, and gender outlaws. The room throbs with our work, our energy, and our anxieties as we struggle to hold a complexity along many dimensions. For some, gender theory is fun, liberating play; for others it is life and death; and from time to time for all of us it is both. We struggle with utopian and dystopian models.

While we struggle with these theories and ideas, we are also having a struggle with words. We must notice the inheritance of ancient ways of construing gender, the primary-process gunk that adheres to our language and our categories. Our words for body parts, for gendered life, and for kinship relations do not circulate simply and abstractly in the symbolic sphere. This is a point Mitchell (2000) drew from his reading of Loewald, the mix of primary and secondary process, of fantasy and reality that appears in our conceptual language.

The idea that category terms draw from our affective lives, our delights, our shames, and our uncertainties, our somatic experience, and our cultural and interpersonal experience, is very much part of the new thinking about speech and language (Lakoff and Johnson, 1980, 1999; Olds, 1992b, 2000; Litowitz, 2001). The quandary of unconscious meanings and archaic personal and social history barnacled to our ways of speaking about sex and gender is very much the project of queer theory (Butler, 1990, 1993, 1998; Corbett, 1993, 1999; Magee and Miller, 1997). We are placed at the center of a paradox. Of course, when we pay attention to the complexity of our clinical and our personal experience, we put in question the generic and the abstract. But the uniqueness of our particular life-worlds always also bears the undertow of archaic forms of stereotype and phobic hatreds.

There is always some danger in the tight, close-grained clinical and personal focus as we privilege the clinical over the theoretical. In the consulting room and in personal life we need to be very open to gender play. But we must also pay attention to the culture as it surrounds the clinical setting and permeates consulting rooms, bodies, and minds. Playgrounds and prisons usually have guards. Rules carry their attendant shames, anxieties, and guilts and are joined in a very combustible interaction with gendered and sexed experience. Gendered experiences may radically code and color affective states. Dimen (2002) has been attending to the regulatory practices in psychoanalytic theory and clinical listening as they are implanted in conscious and unconscious life. A word like perversion, she notes, tells you what to think, not what to do.

GENDER AS AN ATTRACTOR

As I listen in the study group to the way we play gender and play with genders and the way gender and desires play us, the application of the principles of chaos theory or nonlinear dynamic systems theory, to use Thelen and Smith's (1994) preferred term, seems increasingly apt. Gender systems come in multidimensional forms, interlocking at the level of history, family, subculture, and individual. I find it increasingly useful to think of gender as "softly assembled," more wetware than hardware.

Gender and sexual identity might be constructed of variable, locally particular subcomponents with much potential for distinct constellations and organizations.

This view of sexuality and gender is not new to psychoanalysis. An emergent and potentially novel interrelation of gender and desire is always one reading of Freud (1905) in the *Three Essays*. This idea is core to some classical analytic theories, particularly the French world (Laplanche, 1989). At the same time I think it fair to claim that more elaborated implications of this point of view have been developed in relational psychoanalysis by Muriel Dimen (1991, 1995a, b; 2002), Elise (1997, 1998), Layton (1998), and Stein (1998a, b), and in the culture studies of Sedgwick (1990). These theorists, strongly influenced by postmodernism, have been keeping an eye on the sources of distortion and social construction in any theory. Together, these theorists expand our understanding of the forms and the functions of sexuality. Sexuality expresses and contains multiple functions: self-regulation, interpersonal regulation, distancing, bridging. Sex may seem like the conditions for safety or the occasion for powerful and deliberation destabilizations. Sexual life may be in the service of courting excitement or danger or of sealing off such states. Forms and functions of desire thus do not have an obvious or unremarkable relationship to gender.

Psychoanalytic feminism exploits this kind of multifunctional analysis for gender as well as desire. The assemblage of gendered experience in sexual life is contingent on many interlocking contexts and is emergent, not preprogrammed. Desire and gender may be set up antagonistically or seem seamlessly enmeshed and obvious. Gender will be softly assembled as a body state, affective experience, ways of talking and thinking, and ways of loving or hating. Gender and desire would come into their unique and particular forms only in context, widely construed. As such, gender and sex are inseparable from the interpersonal fields in which they are embedded.

Waddington (1966) used a spatial metaphor to model what he termed epigenetic landscape. He imagined development as a kind of mountain down which many pathways of water flow. The local conditions shape and affect the pathways and intensity of the flow. Large tectonic forces (like the culture) have impact as well. Beginning at a common source, the endpoint is unpredictably but describably different. Landscape is an interestingly ambiguous term. The epigenetic landscape described the locally emergent variations in an individual's development. But these variations emerged from variations in the contextual constraints within which the individual grows. These contextual constraints are both within the individual and within the larger systems in which the individual is embedded. Embeddedness is the phenomenon that makes for patterns and for unique solutions.

Gender's Multidimensionality

If gender is to be softly assembled, perhaps the first question is, assembled with what? What features of experience might come into this construction? And while compiling lists of the components, we have to keep in mind the key principles of chaos theory: the emergent nature of a system, the focus on process not structure, and the multiple pathways in most developmental processes. This model of creative and constructive dynamic interaction of constitution and environment looks through a new lens at the thick descriptions of gendered and sexual life with which our field is brimming. We behold not one story but many.

There have been some interesting candidates for forms of systemization. Lewes (1988, 1995, 1998), imagining a variety of pathways through oedipal thickets and obstacle courses, draws up a list that includes object choice, forms of attachment and identification, and polarities of passive or active. This expanded systemization is Lewes's (1995, 1998) corrective to the normative forms of oedipal crisis and resolution that privileged one form of being and one form of desiring. Chodorow (1992) used this analysis to put in question heterosexuality, to suggest that even the most orthodox, "natural" sexuality could have a soft assembly. Perhaps compromise formation per se is a kind of soft assembly.

To the list of processes Lewes and Chodorow organize one would want to add sex of subject and the person's unconscious fantasy of the gender of all participants in sexual life. Additionally, from the work of Dimen (1991, 1995a, b, 1999, 2003), Elise (1997, 1998), Sedgewick (1990), and others, we would want to expand our understanding of the functions and forms of sexual desire. Sexuality is evolving from a simple drive tethered to reproduction, into a variety of human and interpersonal functions. Sexual experience lives in dissociation. Sex can be used to enable or to shore up splits in the self. Sex may fragment the self or be a kind of psychic bonding that parents fragmentation and psychic invasions. Sexual practices can be interpersonal glue or powerful intrapsychic fortressing. Sexual life and anxiety can be powerfully interwoven to protect a person from impingements, from loneliness and abandonment fears.

From particular clinical experience, we know that sexual experience is a way of achieving intimacy and for others a way of ensuring its absence. These contradictions argue for a multifunctional model for sexuality and one where sex and gender co-evolve and co-construct in quite unique ways. Sexual excitement may defend against gender fluidity or fragility or, alternatively, excitement may be derailed by that fluidity. Questions about the interrelation of sex and gender must be answered locally, not generically.

Fritz Klein (1990) proposes a multidimensionality for homosexuality that might easily be expanded to encompass many sexualities. He identifies attraction, lifestyle, fantasy, emotional preference, social preference, and self-identification. It is no accident that many of these reframes of gender and desire, this move to multiplicity and multivariate pathways, have come from queer theory, albeit a queer theory inflected through psychoanalysis. Being on the margins, feeling deeply and personally the wounds of normative categorizing of identity, offers a unique perspective that can help deconstruct those categories. It was the inadequacy and the necessity (political or personal) of categorical public identities that produced queer theory out of the practices of liberation and identity politics.

The features outlined by Lewes (1995, 1998), Klein (1990), Chodorow (1992, 2002), and others concern the child's elaborated and multiply gendered relation to sexual life. Another aspect of gender's soft assembly would take up the question of identifications. Drawing on Schafer's (1968) taxonomy, we could add incorporative, projective, and introjective identifications to our list of the modes of internalization of our experience of the gender of another person and how that person mirrors and construes our gender. To draw on the unique interpretation of introjection and incorporation developed by Abraham and Torok (1994), we could look for the melancholic, sequestered, incorporative features of gender or for the wider, more fluidly libidinized internalizations of gender identity. For some, gender may live as a traumatic encapsulation; for others, a seamless, ego-syntonic state imbricated in many self-states and experiences.

Butler (1993, 1995a, b, 2000b, 2003) has pursued this line of thought in proposing that gender has, inevitably, a melancholic structure. Gender will always contain and express disavowed loves lived as identifications.

The elements of desire in this identification remain lost to awareness.[4] One of the values of Schafer's (1968) account of internalization is that it becomes possible to see the nuanced ways that partial identifications are lived out as incorporations, as introjections, or as seamlessly internalized aspects of self. Schafer did not explore the intersubjective dimension of these processes, but his expansion of the concept of internalization, together with work like that of Mitrani (1995, 1996) and Alvarez (1992, 1993, 1997), illuminates a picture of a manifold self, with levels of integration of self and other and with a permeability of inside and outside.

Seeing the complex possibilities of use of the other, we can pay attention to the permeability of exteriority and interiority. Genders, like minds, may be distributed across persons (Olds, 2000). This distribution takes different forms. Personally lived gender may require externally braced recognition from others. For some, gender sculpting may require severe and stark disavowal of whatever feels ego dystonic. Part of the contemporary deconstruction of masculine identifications focuses on this as an aspect of normative gender development. Masculinity is achieved by the shearing away of any maternal identification, indeed any signs of softness, gentleness, or receptivity.[5]

Chaos theory applied to gender and gender development would address the kinds of components that might make up anyone's gender, the kinds of variability in the pathway to that end state, and the functions of gender both in situ and in interaction. Seen from a distance, a person's gender might look unremarkably simple or single valenced. In psychoanalysis, terms like core or primary are asked to do somewhat contradictory service: to hold a continuity of body and mind, to describe summaries of experience, but sometimes inexorably to be bedrock. Observed as surface and style and self-presentation, many regularities of pattern and form might prevail as gender. Corbett (2001b) has written about the contradictory pull for tradition and convention, on one hand, and the recognition of uniqueness on the other. The rich stews of gender life, even in its more lurid and cartoony aspects, both conscious and fantastical, can make a person feel recognizable, comprehensible, coherent. But such summary experiences cannot fully encompass gender complexity. It is this paradox that chaos theory addresses as it maintains the tension between regularity of pattern and variation.

Coherence, including gender coherence, is one of those "necessary fictions" in psychic life and often a requirement of our theories. From various sources—cultural, psychoanalytical, and personal—tolerance for and interest in incoherence is on the rise (Butler, 1990, 1993; Dimen, 1991, 1995a, b, 1998; Fausto-Sterling, 2000; Fairfield, Layton, and Stack, 2002; Layton, 2002). From a more molecular, finely grained, experience-near vantage point, the forms of one's gender would be quite variable, depending on the task at hand, the context, and one's life history and experiences.

Becoming gendered would be like learning to walk. Or, to use a metaphor of Edelman's (1987), becoming gendered would be like buying a suit. While an ideal and perfectly specified suit can be ordered and made up, most of us buy clothing already available, and it is a "good enough" compromise of our needs, historical conditions, and life circumstances. Our solutions satisfy loose constraints, and the fit between individual and environment is ad hoc not optimal.

Edelman used this analogy to describe the workings of a biological system, antibody production. I think gender might be another such suit. Suits, like languages, are general and specific, public and private. Suits, like skins, face outward and inward. They are modes of fortressing the self and ways of connecting to others. And, like wardrobes, individuals may vary significantly in many suits, what is mixed and matched, what is seasonal, what is enduring. Genders, like suits, can be uniforms, costumes, or skins.

Gender and Desires without a Predetermined Outcome

In posing questions of motivation with regard to gender development or sexual development, one can see the rich potential for chaos theory in relation to sex and gender. By minimal initial biases, Ghent (2002), Thelen (1995); Thelen and Smith (1994), Elman et al. (1997), and others intend subtle simple capacities not yet loaded with motivational thrust or cultural signification for the child. Almost immediately two things happen. First, in a very few iterations, the behavior, and capacity and potential for meaning become exceedingly complex. Second, the cultural, familial, and interpersonal surround of the infant become saturated with meaning. Parents draw their experience of their infant and growing child through the multiple and particular lenses of gender that matter to them. Culture, historical epoch, and family and personal dynamics all contribute to the structure of these lenses and become part of the context in which emergent gender(s) are softly assembled.

Ghent's (2002) work on motivation identifies three elements in

Edelman's model[6]: (1) initial values or biases, (2) recategorization and reentry of experience to make for unique and complex internal processes, and (3) a system of mapping. The boundaries, contours, and contents of experiences will be both variable and unique to any individual in context. Ghent also made the point that, at the experiential level, the building up of "categorization on value" and mapping will draw on affects, anxieties, and bodily states.

I think that there could be a productive interaction between this way of modeling the evolution of motivational systems and the psycho-analytic work on the emergence of desire in the context of maternal or parental sexuality (Laplanche, 1989, 1997, 2002; Green, 1995, 1997; Stein, 1998a, b). From a chaos theory standpoint, Laplanche's concept of maternal enigmatic seduction is a kind of Lewinian field theory, with desire in the child arising from an experience of being desired, an experience that is only partially metabolizable.[7] Desire as an increasingly agentic lived experience of the child emerges from an intersubjective context. The complexity of these phenomena, putting in play the question of whose desire lives in whom, destabilizes any easy self–other distinction.

It is important from this perspective that gender does not, in its initial forms, predict its endpoint. One can easily retrospectively trace the emerging complex and multidimensional experiences and attractors through which genderedness is expressed, but the beginnings are both interpersonally worked and simple. When Beebe and Lachmann (1994, 1998, 2002) outline the very complex, multimodal, interactive capacities of children in the first year of life, they are speaking of levels of organization for phenomena like gender. Within the preverbal register there are sensory and conceptual representations, not yet coded symbolically as gendered, but cohering around some ongoing agentic experience. These experiences are then creatively remapped when speech comes on line and when the imaginative and symbolic representations of gender are elaborated between parent and child and within the child.

But within the dyad there is an already elaborated interlocutor, whose fantasies and expectations of gender are part of the inevitable projective material through which the child is seen. There is a rich, partially unconscious, elaborated soup of meaning enveloping any child, what Corbett (2001b) describes as an early relational excess. These meanings, uniquely and idiosyncratically organized into semantic attractors or gender attractors, evolve for the child. And the child's contribution? To answer this question, the expanded view of infant capacity, seen through the lens of nonlinear dynamic systems theory, seems crucial. The power of this perspective is that complexity is built very quickly out of simple primitives. Laplanche (1989), sounding very like Ghent or Edelman, names this archaic infant state very simply as "initial somatic receptivity" (p. 52).

Laplanche's account of the complex relation of infantile and adult sexuality centers on paradox, nonlinearity (*Nachtraglichkeit*).

> When it comes to his sexuality, man is subject to the greatest of paradoxes: what is acquired through the drives precedes what is innate and instinctual, in such a way that, at the time it emerges, instinctual sexuality, which is adaptive, finds the "seat already taken," as it were, by infantile drives, already and always present in the unconscious [p. 114].

With some emendations, I think the same case could be made for gender. In this formulation, Laplanche means by drive a matter quite different from instinct: experiences that are contingent, variable, and nonadaptive. What he has termed infantile sexuality is objected related as well as private. And while the object is imaginary, a crucial term for his perspective, we might note that imaginary objects lean on real objects and that this reliance goes in both directions. Parent and child live out cocreated experience in multiple registers, real, imaginary, and symbolic.

Laplanche's idea of drive is quite close to the chaos theory model of an open system, transgressing homeostasis so as to be endlessly replenishable. And, for Laplanche, a powerful force in the construction of evolving "desires" is the complex, always partially unconscious parental reveries (desires, constructions, imaginings) in which the child is held from the beginning. It is this complex match and mismatch between infant and parent capacities that gives the child an inevitable surplus of enjoyment, affect, and anxiety. Another crucial aspect of this model is the retrospective reorganization, the appearance of new organizations that reshape the past, *Nachtraglichkeit*. Complex, noncontingent, unpredictable patterns of aim and object lead to the reconstruction of an imaginary origin.

One of my patients, M, lived in such a strange, nonlinear grip of reverberating traumas (Harris, 1998a). An early serious injury that left scars and disfigurement was perpetuated and augmented by an ongoing sequence of reparative surgeries. These sequenced injuries became enmeshed with and elaborated around matters of gender. Stoic defenses designed to obliterate painful memories by the performance of painful rituals became woven into ideas of feminine maintenance and body regimens. Later in her development, M's deepening understanding of her parents' marriage and of her mother's depression, alienation, and humiliated state organized around these traumas. Femininity became organized as shameful, disfiguring, and painful. Gendered life was reworked as mastery over pain and control over need and impulse.

The earliest induction into this series—an accident quite unrelated to gender per se—lived on in procedural forms of knowing and being, the original event amplified retrospectively by the terrible routines of rehabilitation. The haunting presence of this nonlinearity worked, but a powerful pattern would be manifested in the summer months (the seasonal site of postaccident surgery), when M inevitably engaged in the most strenuous and dangerous practices, courting disfigurement as she attempted to master pain's resurgent memories.

Any developmental story like M's starts with initial biases in responsiveness, parental fantasy, life events, and landscapes of various kinds that are then subject to repeated retroactive reorganization. Finally a construction is cobbled together in multimodal organizations, with multiple time lines and constructed meanings that can accrue to matters of gender and sexuality. M was quite phobic about penetration. Sex, surgery, original assaults (in her case, by an animal), and family dynamics are all uniquely self-assembled. How, in any child's experience, gender and sexuality are interwoven makes for another unique constructive developmental narrative.

What gender is the child imagined to be in any particular family? What does gender mean, in fantasy and in conscious perception, to that child's family and significant others? The works of Coates and her colleagues (Bradley et al., 1991; Coates and Moore, 1998) on gender dysphoria and Goldner's (1999; Goldner et al., 1990) work on the communications about gender in families with spousal violence show us how complex these questions can actually be. How do gender meanings become linked to sexual intentions, infantile or otherwise? And how will parental fantasies or phobic anxieties about a child's gender and desires be creatively assimilated by the child?

Gender, from this point of view, may overlap with systems of memory, language, representation, and thought as well as somatic state, motoric experience, and ultimately complex experience of shared and unshared identities and sanctioned and forbidden desires. The assembly of ways of being and feeling gendered and the overlap of such being and feeling with modes of desire or modes of thought or modes of inter-action are unique and emergent, not preset. For each child these over-lapping organizations map differently, and within each system the attractors through which gender organizations are maintained and re-produced are shared by individuals in the larger family or cultural sys-tem but also are differentiated and unique. The molar-level gender identity of a child may seem to be shared and comparable to that of a parent or significant other, but the microorganization is more variably assembled.

ATTRACTORS AND DYNAMIC LANDSCAPES

In looking at gender development and sexuality from the perspective of chaos theory, I am concentrating on the crucial concept of attractors and dynamic landscapes. As always from the chaos-theory perspective, it is difficult to hold on to theoretical constructs that privilege move-ment and process over structure.

In applying chaos theory to an understanding of gender, gender would be seen as a kind of attractor involved in a variety of functions that will vary within one person's life and between people. Attractors is a term from chaos theory to which we have given both a formal and a phenomenological definition. To make this theory more accessible to clinicians, let me draw for the moment on the descriptive level. Think of attractors (and there are different types) as organizing the quality, the form, and the pattern of certain organized behaviors within par-ticular systems. Some attractors have a periodic or quasi-periodic struc-ture, like a pendulum, and we might certainly see the fierce polarities of many gender systems as falling under such descriptions. Benjamin's concept of complementarity in frozen and polarized gender relations is such an attractor. The transformation of these grinding, reciprocally triggering experiences of gender polarity can give way to more mobile, subject-subject interactions where gender is not caught in sadomasoch-istic patterns or in relations of exclusion and disavowal. These kinds of postoedipal experiences of gender fluidity (Fogel, 1998) or subject–subject intersubjective (Benjamin, 2002) gender multiplicity would be described as strange attractors.

Gender can function as a boundary, between persons or within one person. Gender can be an intropsyhchic or interpersonal organiza-tion functioning to regulate affect. Gender can be an idealization, or a way of suspending and/or bearing loss. Gender, functioning these multiple ways as an attractor, could manifest different organizations. These multiply configured gender attractors could be fluid and constantly re-equilibrating (chaotic or strange attractors) or they could be periodic and cyclical and very change resistant.

To reprise one of Piers's most striking metaphors: attractors are like the charred remains of a fire. The residue of ashes are the sign that a system has formed, transformed, and left its mark. Imagine gendered experience as this kind of ash. Conflicts and struggles of many kinds, in matters of relatedness or separation or desire or mastery could all leave their traces in the ash we call gender. Gender, by this light, would not be a reified thing, or an engine for growth and outcome, but the residue of complex processes.

Gender, both as a cultural system and as a lived experience, might be described as a type of attractor, a systematic pattern with a number of different forms: steady collector, homeostatic system, periodic or limit cycle, or more fractal, unpredictable conditions. The kind of rigid gender complementarity Benjamin (1990, 2000a, b) notes as a site of failed mutual recognition would be a kind of periodic, limit-cycle attractor, its patterns organizing rigidly around two distinct polarities, a kind of pendulum effect. We might see a culturally derived gender system (inside and outside individuals) as a pendulum organizing itself around two distinct spaces.

Alternatively, gender, in moments of historical change or more local microdevelopmental change, may operate like a fractal and disequilibrating pattern, the more volatile strange attractors. The states are variously susceptible to change. Perturbations, from many sources inside and outside a system, can destabilize a state depending on its internal characteristics.

What chaos theory introduces into the schemes and structures of gender is the intriguing distinction between self-similar (strange attractor) and self-same (periodic). In self-similar repetitions, some subtle variation is always in play. In self-same repetitions, the system moves inevitably toward increasing rigidity and stasis. This kind of variation in clinical experience stems from the gendered experience of the analysand and, perhaps inevitably, from the gender system of the dyad. One might think of certain gender polarities as kinds of clinical impasses, systems shut down and unavailable for novelty or change. Partners in a dyadic system that is caught in a transference or countertransference impasse live out a self-same polarity.

As a number of writers have noted (Flax, 1990; Dimen, 1991, 1995a, b; Goldner, 1991; Elise, 1997, 1998) gender polarities seem to exert complex pressures that organize and trap other polarities: active–passive, receptive–penetrating; soft–hard. The gender attractor, both in the larger cultural system and as a lived experience in the individual, may then pattern a number of experiences and ways of being that, in turn, become gendered by virtue of being caught in that individual's particular attractor basin or valley. Gender attractors both constrain how the individual experiences gender and also reflect the constraints under which the system is organized.

Strange attractors show the greatest potential for transformation and change. Such attractors are useful in modeling gender development and also in modeling the kinds of shifts in gender state that can occur within one person, gender fluidity. Strange attractors capture both the multiplicity of gender experience and the inherent potential for change. Kauffman (1995) places great importance on a phenomenon he terms "the edge of chaos." "Life exists at the edge of chaos," he writes (p. 26). That edge is a fulcrum point between too much random noise and perturbations on the one hand and too much rigidity on the other. Chaotic systems, Kauffman points out, are highly sensitive to small shifts, which can cascade into unpredictable but orderly novel patterns. This is Kauffman's felicitously phrased "order for free." Patterns emerge out of uniquely forming clusters that operate from constraints, but in random and unpredictable ways. Using Kauffman's model, gender has both generic properties and unique manifestations. Gender is highly individualized given the local constraints (family and individual experience), but gender also draws on the larger macrosystem in which it is also embedded.

This account of the functioning and development of gender as kinds of interacting attractors might describe many radical discontinuity and state changes, not only ones involving gender. It is in Bromberg's (1994, 1998a, 1999) work that we find many highly nuanced clinical examples of these kinds of state shifts, shifts that are both within and between people. Or we might call to mind Cooper's (2000; Cooper and Levit, 1998) work on the interplay of the experience of old and new objects. Certainly Pizer (1998, 2001), whose interest is in negotiated paradox, has deployed the concept of fractal states to model negotiated change.

Here I think the concept of quantitative change that can unpredictably involve a qualitative reorganization might be interesting to apply to those moments in experience when either being in gender or being comfortable in gender can shift in an instant. Too much affect—perhaps, in particular, aggressive affect for women and vulnerability or tenderness in men—may be the motility in the system that disequilibrates an attractor state and institutes a phase shift. Humor, too, the eruption of laughter, and jokes may be the light touch that sets a state in motion. But, of course, misapplied, affect and humor can lead to shutdown and rigidity. Cognitive developmentalists modeling the emergence of representation speak of "semantic attractors" (Elman, 1995; Elman et al., 1997). This conception seems to me well related to the work of Lakoff and Johnson (1980, 1999) on embodied cognition. Semantic attractor space is multimodal and multidimensional and can include affect states, bodily experience, and action schemes all bound together with categories of meaning that are uniquely configured for any individual.[8]

My patient Charles, whose gender theories and ideals I described in chapter 4, might be seen to have a very particular set of semantic attractors with which he thinks about and experiences gender. Men are calm, urbane, free from worries, rich, comfortable in their skins, and unsentimental. Woman are depressed, homebound if not bedbound, often crazy under their simple, attractive surfaces, narcissistic, and feelingful, but never feelingful with him.

Our lived experience sometimes confirms and sometimes violates these patterns. Our different, more related interactions and my attunement to his feelings and fears start to destabilize this attractor system. And as living and vital experiences enter the system, we experience moments like the edge of chaos, moments when the brittle, too cartoonlike rigidity of the gender attractors starts to crumble. Charles's gender attractors seem unusually brittle, and he knows this fragile coherence mirrors something he sensed within his family, that their polite, orderly surface behavior concealed tension and contradiction. I often think that Charles's gender system is held so rigidly because, in a way, his family was without rules or consequences. Gender strictness for Charles functions in lieu of the usual forms the superego might take. Goldner (1999; Goldner et al., 1990) has addressed these functions of gender orthodoxy in couples with histories of violence as extreme and rigid structures that bind anxiety. We see the traumatic consequences of normal masculinity.

When Charles's anxieties and needs well up, he cannot easily hold on to the simple oscillating periodicity of his gender patterns. This pattern looks like the process Kauffman described at the edge of chaos when a system's connections or complex regimens may organize and reorganize in novel ways. If Charles is needy and depressed, is he a woman? Is he like mother? Has he crossed the semantic divide that has both sustained and constrained him?

Fogel (1998) has been tracking such moments of change and reorganization in the living of masculinity in certain patients whose terror of feminization has kept them in a regimen of phallic monism that cripples even as it fortresses. In his model of postoedipal experience, gender is a kind of strange attractor—bisexual, flexible and fluid, yet not without pattern and order.

Along with the uniqueness of particular gender attractors in an individual, we can see how gendered life facilitates or inhibits interactions and interpersonal relatedness (Benjamin, 1988, 2000a; Dimen, 1991, 2003). Gender systems between individuals can become entrained in rigid or in flexible ways. Systems coevolve (Fajardo, 1998; Palumbo, 1998), and systems are nested in hierarchies.

CONCLUSION

Our study group discussions are set at a powerful and volatile moment of intersecting systems. Each of us is poised as a reader and a receiver of cultural, institutional, and personal messages about the meaning of gender. Thirdness functions in our group, as an anchor, sometimes as superego, sometimes as a temporary bridge for reflective activity. This situation is replicated in the clinical setting where all the multiple, interacting schemes and systems of gender and sexuality mix and match within the clinical dyad.

Clinical and theoretical writing sits also in its particular historical moment, reworking the past, breaking open systems, and transforming understanding. Nonlinear dynamic systems theory, as a model of an open system, or more modestly as a "theory-constituting metaphor"[9] opens any dyadic system to more interlocking and embedded systems. This requires various degrees of self-consciousness and ongoing reflection to keep process and dynamic change from defaulting into reification. Gender may be softly assembled, but it is also a work in progress.

CHAPTER 7

☙

Genders Emerge in Contexts

*M*oving from a one-person to a two- or multiperson, transpersonal psychology means that gender experiences must be imagined and understood in context. In the previous chapter, I speculated on the various assemblies of gender. Gender is personal and social, personal and political, private and public. Any individual experience of gender is rooted in personal history, collective histories, and the slowly but also rapidly evolving, historically shifting world of bodies, words, and material life.

In fantasy, in somatic memory, and in conscious categorizations, gendered life carries much social and personal history, from the effects of serious trauma to everyday cultural and social ephemera. One's "gender" experience seems to absorb many experiences that are not inherently gender salient. It is as though gender were often the point of maximal psychic vulnerability, a flash point for the construction and maintenance of subjectivity.

It has proved to be extraordinarily complex to think even about two-person interactions. The Beebe and Lachmann (1994, 1998) model for the coordination and integration of self-regulation and self–other regulation is actually a model of systems within systems. Qualitatively distinct kinds of entrainments, patterns, and gestalts of interaction, across multimodal and multivariate sensory systems (see Lyons-Ruth, 1991, 1999; Lyons-Ruth et al., 1992, 1993; Beebe, Jaffe et al., 2000; Beebe and Lachmann, 2002; Sander, 2002) display a picture of early emergent, highly complex systems of relatedness. This complexity and unpredictable patterning can only deepen our vision of the broad systems of family, culture, and history in which the clinical dyads we work in are so intensely embedded.

Theoretical attempts to open up wider social and politicized understandings of relational configurations are underway in psychoanalysis (Cushman, 1995, 2000; Altman, 1996, 2000a, b). This attunement to the larger world is central to feminist psychoanalysis and to queer theory (Corbett, 1993; Lewes, 1995; Blechner, 1998; Layton, 1998). Setting identities within networks of multiplicity and context is also found in studies of race and identifications and in theorizing postcolonial experience (Bhabba, 1994; Eng and Han, 2003).

Chaos theory models early emergent complexity as pattern that is orderly but unpredictable, and contingent on many individual, environmental, and social factors. Gender assemblies are but one outcome of this astonishingly rich and subtle systems development. We see the power of this model in situations where there are radical discontinuities as well as continuities in gender experience and in situations in which culture, class, and family dynamics intersect with and shape matters of gender and of sexuality.

Gender as battleground, as playground, as flash point, and as reified carapace is a powerful focus in a 2002 film, *Bend It Like Beckham*. In this joyous and deeply playful (in all senses) film, the constraints on the Indian heroine, Tess, are traditional and at the same time decidedly postmodern: Tess is forbidden to play soccer; her mother demands that she be able to make "full Indian dinner." She is intergenerationally traumatized by the colonial prejudice and postcolonial memory of her cricketer father, who is himself stung from the prejudice that denied him opportunities in English sporting clubs. He must hurt her to protect her from humiliation and suffering. Caste and class systems, informing her sister's personally willed but socially arranged marriage, work their imprisoning ways on this younger sister.

Class and class mobility are being judged here. This is a morality play set in newly bourgeois communities. The heroine is free to get a job in some demeaning mall, but she is not free to bring home a Nike soccer shoe. There is the transcultural pleasure young women can take in forbidden forms of agency and aggression. A slender, athletic white girl, a determined tomboy, sees the Indian girl kicking a soccer ball in a park, recognizes a soulmate, and brings her to join her team. There is the complex way the filmmaker eroticizes and offers for spectator pleasure an MTV-inflected view of the girls' soccer practices. These girls, multi/culti soccer babes, are objects and subjects of desire, not really in control of their image or their intentions. The two soccer-playing team-mates can shop together in utterly contented, sisterly pleasure but live in distinct cultural worlds. And yet, in both families, the terror of the homoerotic flares up.

The guru of the Indian family is a male figure prayed to, consulted for advice, and admired, not unlike the image of Beckham, the idolized English soccer star who peers down from Tess's bedroom wall. Looms over her bed, actually. Among the gender ironies or comedies, we can also remember that Beckham in reality, or at least in the tabloids, is known to be a passionate shopper, a metrosexual engaged in activities more usually coded as feminine.

In this same intricate, compact little film, we see the conflictual intersections of gender and desire. The contested desired man, the coach, drives a wedge into the cooperative, lusciously physical play of the girls. Gender is fluid and fixed, made in the crucibles of family, class, culture, and historical epoch but blasted and transformed as well by forces of migration, globalization, commerce. All these factors are colliding and transforming in individual lives, bodies, and psyches.

CONTEXTS FOR EMERGENT SYSTEMS

Dyadic Systems

The context most familiar to analysts is the two-person, dyadic system, a clinical context that has already been interpreted within a chaos theory perspective (Fajardo, 1998; Palumbo, 1998).[1] Developmental psychologists and clinicians who practice at the intersect of psychoanalysis and infancy already have a highly elaborated tradition of using nonlinear dynamic systems theory to imagine and frame the emergence of self in the dyadic context. Sander (1988, 2002), perhaps most explicitly, thinks of systems entrainment, the emergence of "transegrity" and rhythmicity in dyadic systems, as the key to the growth of self and self in relation to others. His work has been highly influential for infancy researchers and clinicians. Among many different interests and foci, what has generally emerged is a transactional, transformational systems model for emergent attachment patterns and emergent patterns of self- and other regulation.

At the heart of this body of work on early dyadic patterning is a very sophisticated intervention into the matter of origins and into the question of monadic versus dyadic experience. A systems approach, in particular, one with a commitment to indeterminacy and emergence, opts neither for an endogenous individual model nor, on the other hand, for a model of original object relatedness. Recognition, a sense of the otherness of the other, and the experience of self and other are emergent. Elements of paradox persist. The unit of mother and infant becomes organized, always already bearing levels of recognition, some mutual, some asymmetrical. The infant mind emerges in the context of an expanded, two-person consciousness but also in the context of unconscious forces in the adult that impinge in novel ways on the infant and lead to unique organizations of excitement, affective tone, and relatedness.

A developmental account of identity formation must elaborate the dialectical and paradoxical idea that self, including a gendered self, emerges from an interaction in which the child is always already interpreted, experienced, and understood. The experience of being mirrored becomes an inextricable element in the child's internal self-schemes in a way that forever blurs the distinction between an experience's beginning inside or outside. Indeed, mirroring arises in the context of experiences before self and other are even precipitated out (Loewald, 1962a; Mitchell, 2000). Mirroring is the site of emotion contagion, now moments, affect transmission, rupture, and repair. We think of this process as providing a template for mutual regulation, self regulation, self–other differentiation, and many other negotiations of interpersonal experience with all their intrapsychic consequences. These ideas are well established in the infancy research literature and its clinical applications (Beebe, Jaffe, and Lachmann, 1992; Fonagy, 1997, 2001; Beebe and Lachmann, 1998; Lyons-Ruth, 1999).

Lyons-Ruth's (1991, 1999; Lyons-Ruth et al., 1992, 1993) research program has addressed a particular dyadic pattern, disorganized attachment. Her relational diasthesis model is actually a model of multiple pathways to particular outcomes. In those outcomes, distinct and different strategies for managing internal states in the caretaker, particularly those shaped by trauma, create a contradictory, fear-laced, hostile, and also often passively withdrawn adult mental context in which the infant develops distinct patterns of relatedness. Lyons-Ruth, compatibly with a chaos-theory approach, notices the way early patterns create in child and caretaker internal contexts for high degrees of vulnerability to subsequent trauma. The complexity of these early adaptations—their brittleness and fragility—organizes patterned ways of being in the child. Attachment patterns are kinds of attractors, with a variety of interactions leading in manifold ways to organizations that may be increasingly hard to disequilibrate and transform. Lyons-Ruth describes characteristic outcomes of disorganized attachment in which helplessness and hostile control flip back and forth in difficult and constricting forms, mutually regulating but in sharply and often dangerously rigid ways.

Within this systems approach to early, preverbal identity, gender and sexuality are not prominent, but there is ample indication that the particular meanings of gender, bodily life, and desire within this dyadic system must also be part of these complex transactions. Mirroring, of course, does not quite do justice to the constructive transformation or the misrecognition in this process. In thinking more broadly of the landscape of dyadic life, perhaps, like Alice, we must be interested in the space behind the mirror. The reflecting other, usually a parent, the mother, or primary attachment figure, sees an already gendered being. That embodied child is already charged with affective meaning as a body, as a gendered being for that mother, and so is already recognized and misrecognized along the lines of her own and others' collective and unconscious gender fantasies and gender perceptions.

Mirroring as a conceptual term seems to have been superseded by several other conceptual terms, such as scaffolding and reflective functioning. At a cultural, social level, theorists speak of interpellation, although this is often a brutal colonizing of the other by the forces of culture and social formation. In thinking of the development of unique ontogenetic landscapes in early dyadic life, I want to link up parental reverie, mentalization, and maternal seduction to provide a framework for imagining one phase of gender's soft assembly. Dyadic and intersubjective processes are a key site for gender transmission and thus provide part of the context in which any individual child's gender can be assembled. A number of theorists (Eigen, 1986; Fonagy and Target, 1995, 1996, 2003; Grotstein, 1999) draw on Bion's concept of maternal reverie and mentalization to augment our understanding of the dyad as a site of mutual and self regulation. Parental reverie as a presence in a child's experience may be capacious or constricted, flexible or rigid (Seligman, 1999a, b). The absence of such reveries, Fonagy (Fonagy and Target, 1995) argues, is an absence of mentalization about the child that creates a deeply violent experience for that child, a violence that retrospectively can seem as intense as physical attack. Alternatively, he argues, maternal projections can be violent impingements if evacuated into the child. When using terms like evacuation, we register the coercive ways of seeing and interacting with a child that enter the child's organization of self-states, including gender organization.

One may reasonably ask which aspects of seeing a child as gendered may produce such violent absences or impingements. One might think of certain forms of gender precocity imposed on children. This pseudomaturity, which might include a sexualized formation, could be resisted or introjected. A notorious case of a murdered child comes to mind. Jon Benet Ramsay, a young beauty pageant contestant, was often presented in very adult styles of clothing and projecting a very sophisticated gait and posture. One telling detail in the wake of her murder was that she was a bedwetter. The imposition of adult formations into this child was resisted at least at some somatic level.

Fonagy (Fonagy and Target, 1996, 2000) identifies the necessity of being mentalized with the ability to think and create, whereas Laplanche (1989) connects the power of being libidinized with the origins of desire in the child. These processes, which have their similarities and differences, seem closely akin to Bion's overarching concept of parental reverie, a concept in which the parent's thought, imagination, and fantasy have the potential to function as a container for the child. Bion was actually thinking more of a dialectic between container and contained in which the child's activity is (in ideal situations) absorbed into the parent's experience, metabolized, and reoffered in titrated form to the child.

Bion developed Klein's idea of projective identification as defense into a concept that was more active and more interactive. Bion was observing and theorizing that mother and child engage in multiple transactions through which the child's experience is scaffolded and enhanced through the sustaining mind of the parent. Projections by child or parent are, in this view, communications. One can be interested in the capacity of both to make space to receive input, to be inhabited by another's experience in order to find and connect to that other. And, to be faithful to Bion's understanding of the absolute interpenetration of thinking and feeling, what permits this fluid process of transactions (and assemblies) is some freedom to feel, think, and desire on the part of the parent.

Brought into an intense, embodied responsiveness and contact with the material world, caught up in the conscious and unconscious reverie of parents, prenatally already an object of intense fantasy, a child finds the experience of self within a relationship in which he or she is already seen and "recognized," and in some particular way this construction will draw on some parental ideas and fantasies about gender. Gendered meanings (first for the parent, then for the child) may begin to accrue to such densely agentic experiences as regulation of other and of self. The internalization (as incorporation or interjection) of the gender/body mirror becomes a part of the child's procedural knowing, available for many complex remappings and reassemblies in the course of development.

Does desire incite shame or guilt? What does being or giving birth to a boy or a girl mean? Whatever the unique configuration of these processes, whatever the fantasies of bodies, desires, and genders that the thinking, feeling, desiring adult brings to the interaction, collectively these experiences in the parental mind form another kind of dynamic landscape. Constraints in the child and in the parental system become part of the context in which the child begins to construct gender assemblies unique to his or her experience. A crucial element in any child's construction of gender and sexuality would be the adults' comfort or discomfort with his or her own desires, homoerotic or heterosexual, sanctioned or transgressive, evolved or primitive, aggressive or receptive.

In integrating the ideas of Bion, Laplanche, and Fonagy, I want to draw attention to the potential for a rich, flexible transitional space in which a gendered and desiring child emerges, shaped inevitably by the personal fantasies and representations that accrue from these intricate transpersonal settings. Within this complex situation, it is the place and potential for desire that is often the most provocative element in the system. The constituting potential of parental desire, itself the intersect of social and intrapsychic forces, is present from the beginning of human relatedness and, as Davies (2003) has been developing, this aspect of parental libido gets a powerful spike in the child's adolescence. Desire within dyads and within families or any intensely integrated system is perhaps inevitably one of Davies's "hot potatoes," an absolutely crucial ingredient for development and at the same time very hard to handle.

In this nonlinearity effect we can also see the working of *Nachtraglichkeit* in soft assembling, the way remapping and functional reorganization can traumatize the "old" experience as it is integrated into certain ongoing experiences. This kind of reentrance, rerepresentation of mapping makes nonlinearity possible and the forms of gender or desire unpredictable from the earliest adaptive forms of reactivity in the child.

In the literature on the transgenerational transmission of trauma, we can begin to see more of the concrete, procedurally carried modes of interaction and communication through which this transmission takes place. Seligman (1999a, b) and his colleagues have been developing fine-grained observations on mother–child and parent–child transactions through which subtle reorganizations and remapping of experience occur. They chart the way traumatic histories, incompletely metabolized by the parent, are transmitted to the child through ways of holding, speaking to, and interpreting the baby. Gender must inevitably be an aspect of parental reverie and parental mentalization and so is conveyed in these transactions laden with fantasy and meaning. It is in such particular environments or landscapes that the child takes in genderedness in self and in the other in a creative way, drawing experience into knots of meaning and signification. The fate of any such transaction or transmission depends on many factors: the levels of anxiety percolating through the system, the affective charge, and the draining of affect.

A child's emerging experience of self, what Palumbo (1998) has termed the infantile attractor, will be organized out of a variety of unique experiences of being treated, imagined, held, and reacted to as an already gendered individual. If a girl is the object of phobic anxieties and projections of a degraded experience of femininity (projected from either parent), an early, procedurally experienced sense of shame or badness could be organized quite seamlessly into her gendered life in the course of ongoing interactions with family and culture. In this way, forces of culture and social life, whether subtly nuanced or brutally powerful, come to live in the child's personally willed ways of loving, being, and knowing. And, as Laplanche (1989) argues in considering enigmatic seduction, these forces often remain unsymbolized though deeply lived in the body states, fantasies, and procedural modes of knowing of the child.

Bowlby's (1940) very early account of the environmental contextual effects on self-states in children describes a girl's severe anxieties about sexuality and masturbation. He links the child's affective state to the mother's obsessive washing of the girl's genitals and her anxious, penetrating surveillance. One of Seligman's observations is of a young father quite brutally shaking his newborn, purportedly to toughen him up, but, as Seligman shows, inexorably transmitting a single traumatic experience into the next generation. This process is not expliclty flagged as a gender phenomenon, but gender meanings do accrue to this transaction.

In both examples we see the kinds of gendered experiences and meanings that can sediment into particular attractor basins, linking up the unique anxieties and preoccupations of the family and dyadic system as a deep part of the child's state, including the child's experiences of gender.

Along with the study of these animations of gender in early infant experience, there is a renewed attention to the eroticized elements of attachment. The project of rehabilitating maternal erotics (Stein, 1998a, b; Corbett, 2001a; Elise, 2002; Harris, 2002, 2003; Davies, 2003; Goldner, 2003) allows us to watch the complex pathways of activation in which gender and desire are organized. The theoretical work now opening up focuses on expanding our perspectives on the multiple so-cial, sexual, and relational arrangements that create contexts for indi-vidual experiences of being and loving. Child sexuality and maternal sexuality are both charged and contested spheres. Recently Malone and Cleary (2002), bringing a critical eye to the contemporary empirical research on lesbian families, have noted the tendency among research-ers to "desex" (both as gender and as sexual) the scene. To match the pattern of bourgeois Western heterosexual structure, erotics and female homoerotics have been airbrushed out.

Cultural Formations and Regulatory Practices

When thinking of how gender is softly assembled within interpersonal spaces and as an individual intrapsychic matter, we also have to attend to the complex cultural spaces and systems in which gender is pro-duced, reproduced, and disseminated. This is one of the most difficult problems for a psychoanalytic theory that wishes to see how culture becomes embedded in psyche (Dimen, 1991, 2002; Layton, 1998). Gen-der systems and gender attractors are social as well as personal. The interrelation of psyche and culture in gender are multidirectional and multidimensional. Gender arrangements live in cultural products, and theorists who seek to interweave culture and personhood have the task of imagining and tracing the various transactions in family and dyadic systems and in individual intrapsychic life through which these trans-missions occur.

These preoccupations have been at the center of the work of Chodorow (1992, 1994, 1999), and others. The interweaving of culture and psyche has been a maverick part of psychoanalysis from its begin-nings (Fromm, 1941; the Frankfurt school, etc., see Jay, 1973).

Chodorow's (1999) review of the anthropological literature criticizes its thin psychology and, turning to psychoanalysis, she sees there the impoverished view of external reality. These concerns have guided a great deal of Lacanian-driven theorizing (Zizek, 1989).

Cultural formations are local and hegemonic. A whole terrain of material historical forces contribute to the construction and assembly of gender, as a set of categories, a set of images, a structure of being in the world. Some of these historical conditions are global, some local; some forces are volatile and transformative; others seem sluggish and rigidly constricted.

In the light of thinking about transgenerational transmission, it is worth proposing a long intrapsychic shelf life for macroprocesses that arise or are lived out at the social level. We have now interesting histories of the body (Shorter, 1982; Laqueur, 1990; Paster, 1993) histories of manners and advice to women (Ehrenreich and English, 1978), histories of reproductive management (Gordon, 2002), and histories of women's health (Oakley, 1993) and of the management of sexuality (Fausto-Sterling, 2000).

A number of authors have traced the century-long debates about the nature and form of different and nonnormative sexualities (e.g., Katz, 1976; Boswell, 1980, 1990, 1994). There are the microhistories of homophobia and reparative therapies (Drescher, 1998). These debates occur in the context of an evolution of practices, social formations, and community-building experiences. There are distinct and particular timelines for these changes in gender ideology, in sexual stigmatization, and the like. Compare those changes with the more volatile change in the discourse and practice around intersex persons and transgendering. The trajectory from individual voice to collectivity, from witness to protest, and then to action (legal and medical), is enabled both by the context of heightened awareness or disavowed voices and experiences and by the technological advances of the Internet.

Then there are the unique familial and individual translations of cultural codes or registers. The landscape for gender and for desire is a thicket of "no's" and prohibitions as well as rich sources of "yes." It is the particular insight of psychoanalytic theory that the very existence of the "no" may signify a node of excitement and meaning.

These historical accounts illuminate the large-scale forces that influence the particular thinking, feeling, and microlevel experiences of gender. Particularly, I have been interested in the deformations of misogyny that enter and stain our experience of femininity:

The early transactions of mother-child carry history as well as endogenous process. The mother who loves, leaves, libidinizes, contains, or fails at any or all of these projects is not everymother but a particular mother, in history, carrying both consciously and unconsciously the experiences (health, legal, economic, work-related, interpersonal) through which women are constituted. Third, there is the power of patriarchal structures that draw out and capitalize on these deeply emotional feelings that women in various incarnations evoke in all of us [Harris, 2003, p. 264].

In considering a complex phenomenon like gender to be a softly assembled system, we take up gender's meanings within any individual and familial system, its function and form with respect to specific tasks in specific environments. Gender meanings are carried in the unconscious life of the family and the individual. Goldner (1991, 2003) has excavated the often highly contradictory fantasies of gender in couples with histories of violence.

But the cultural environment or landscape in which gender and sexuality emerge is criss-crossed in grids with power of many kinds. Some of the best work on gender and sexuality holds a place for cultural imperatives as part of intrapsychic and sexual life (Lewes, 1988, 1995; Butler, 1990; O'Connor and Ryan, 1993; Magee and Miller, 1997; Layton, 1998; Schwartz, 1998). Internalized homophobia, the exhausting requirement of secrets, and hidden lives and misogyny are phenomena never solely outside, but deeply carved into the internal worlds and bodily states of individuals. At the same time, it is worth remembering that phobic hatreds usually contain hidden reserves of desire (Harris, 2003).

Thirdness as a Strange Attractor

Another way to consider the complexity through which gender is constructed is to think of how thirdness enters and alters the soft assemblies of gender. It may do so in a number of ways. Thirdness is certainly a concept with its own distinct and changing evolutions. Thirdness can represent or carry community norms, values, and attitudes that may be local or may be more general, institutional, professional, broadly held cultural beliefs and traditions with which the analyst is in complex conversation (Crastnopol, 2001; Greenberg, 2001; Spezzano, 2001). Thirdness is in this sense chaperone or superego, harsh and virulent or amiable and helpful. In different ways for analyst and analysand, the third is another, silent but potent partner in the conversation. Thirdness brings into the dyad the conventions and values in respect to gender and sexuality. It creates prisms of meaning or filters through which the analytic work and the gender arrangements of the participants are seen. Thirdness is thus the placeholder for gender norms; it operates as a kind of living gyroscope in the sailing and steering of the analytic boat.

But thirdness may be something else as well. Thirdness is perhaps at the edge of chaos, simultaneously an element in the general system and an aspect of the organized configuration of gender. Thirdness may have the potential or be the site of a potential to open a closed, periodic, oscillating system. Polarities like male–female, kill or be killed, eat or be eaten, passive–active, may line up in a lethal series and all may be organizable as gendered (Dimen, 1991, 2003). Thirdness opens a system and offers the potential for a more fractal strange attractor organization to emerge and reorganize. Thirdness, in this sense, may contain both the dominant hegemonic discourse and its potential for deconstruction.

For a number of theorists, thirdness is the particular property of fathers and of masculinity. It draws on the ties between patriarchy, masculinity, law, and the symbolic register. In psychoanalytic developmental theory we have tended to genderize thirdness; we have made the father the agent of individuation, the potential for opening space. But Kristeva (1980), Benjamin (1998), and others suggest that we look for the potential for thirdness in maternal reverie, in the way the mother inducts the child into language and language into the child.

Benjamin and Aron (1999) tie thirdness to intersubjectivity, but see an evolving process whereby a certain kind of recognition and a certain kind of difference or alterity come into being within and between people. This account of thirdness would fit quite well with the notion of strange attractors, a state on the edge of chaos. Benjamin's model of complementarity (1995, 1998) suggests that development, when it does not default into archaic polarities like active–passive, male–female, and self–other, opens up an interesting living dynamism. Her terms are usually tension and paradox. A recognition that does not cannibalize, an internalization that preserves the permeability of self–other boundaries, a negotiation of agency and subject position: these depend on an opening of intersubjective space, a lowering of omnipotence. This focus on recognition and reflection ties her work to that of Fonagy (Fonagy and Target, 1997; Fonagy et al., 2002). Thirdness is a property of internal mental reflection, itself an outgrowth of ways of being mindful and minded while being with another.

Ogden (1994) uses the concept of thirdness with a slightly different inflection. Thirdness, for Ogden, is the ground in which intersubjectivity grows. It constitutes the unique, cocreated relationship fostered in the analytic dyad. The work of analysis is often a sorting out of yours, mine, and ours (the analytic third), but work in that project entails a certain level of reflection, an inhabiting of the depressive position, even if transient. So, in a way analogous to the thinking of Benjamin (1998,2002) and to that of contemporary Kleinians like Britton (1989), thirdness emerges in conditions of reflective functioning.

I have in mind a kind of dialectical process. Currently, thirdness emerges in cultural and scientific discourse on gender and the body by way of discourse on intersex and transgender, in many different registers. It may be one intriguing feature of open or openable systems that it is the voice at the edge that often sparks the disequilibrium. The polarized attractors in the cultural gender system are opened up, and so a new kind of tradition or theory of gender becomes part of the analyst's sense of the third. A theory of multiple gender positions opens a space in individuals and in clinical dyads for disequilibrium and change.

The notion of thirdness is particularly interesting in a systems perspective because it is a space through which one can move and shift among levels. Thirdness carries the cultural system, its values, its norms, its rules into the mind/body of the individual and of the treating analyst. It is a potential in any subjectivity. It shimmers in and around analytic pairs as the following clinical vignette suggests. It is both a clarifying and an enigmatic structure.

James arrives for his session trembling and fearful. He is today, as he often is, caught between a need to say how uncertain and alone he feels and a wish not to burden me, a desire to convince me he is fine. We are approaching a break in sessions, but we are also at a familiar fulcrum point at which we have arrived again and again, he with disappointment and shame, I with curiosity. It is interesting to me that in these moments I feel the excitement, the wish to know, and he feels the terror of ravishment and abjection. One of us wants to penetrate a mystery (curiosity and the wish to ease suffering: how do I know the difference?). The other waits in dull terror for a bad experience to be over. He will be all right; but actually, his analysis is his determined and courageous attempt to disrupt his usually powerful intellectual defenses against this state. He knows he is not all right.

The moment that seems novel to both of us is his *spoken* wish not to be abandoned, his articulation of need for care and safety. But this moment is always interwoven with an older moment, when he was in greatest danger from the one who promised help. In an early archaic moment, seduction and greed begin in the mind and body of the other but migrate to him. Many scenes are engaged and transmuted when he arrives for the session. A sibling crawls toward him for comfort from a dangerous parent. But, in the ensuing confusion does James do something bad? As he works on his experience in analysis, the expansions in mentallization and imagination help him to live more in his body, but when that happens and when the delight is expressed to me, something very bad and sulphurous threatens him. A potential for preoedipal play and nourishment or oedipal longing converts without warning to a scene of perversion and confusion. Our task is to make and remake narratives and meanings of these mysterious drops and reversals from pleasure to terror.

James reports a dream. His friend (a doctor) is lecturing on mathematics. On the board is an equation in which she is interested. James is seated, looking at his piece of paper. His equations are entirely different from the ones on the board. He can't even understand how he got his forms and symbols from hers. In the corner of the blackboard is a big projector, which James calls a projection. It is a swirling design that threatens to pull him into a big, moving hole.

He rushes to tell me all the details, to lay out all his associations quickly and without interruption. He is fearful that, if I don't hold all he has to say, he will be panicked. He wants not to be crazy and not to be so frightened. How are women's equations mapped to men's? What swirling hole does he fear or want? What if his system of wants and equalities were like his mother's? Would he be a girl? Would he want her lovers? Or she his? He has used his mind to claim separation, but something did not work.

Am I stuck in formulas for desire and identity? Is the math a stand-in for the law? How many mathematical systems can you have? Can you break the law and make your own law? Are my reflections about me, about James, about our work together? He has been involved in a scene with someone who represents to him the need to keep sex and love separate. He cannot do it; they are interlaced. Is he mad or what? Is this scene a representation of his analysis or an episode from his life outside analysis?

The paradox here is that thirdness (the math formula on the blackboard) is both a site of control and a site of freedom. Relations of desire and passion are expressed as equations. How to learn math without being colonized? How to map your math to the other's? We could be talking about words as well as mathematical symbols. The third threatens and calmly invites. There is the black hole of projection and the orderly system of mathematics. Subjectivity is uniquely possible and under threat. Gender protects and threatens, makes distinctions and blurs them.

When James really needs to convey to me how frightening his early experience and his current internal worlds can be, he evokes the threat of terrorism. Not hard in New York. F-16's overhead, the drone of helicopters, siren sounds floating through the day and the night. James draws on these sounds to speak about his fear that we might be incinerated right here in the room, right now. He is convinced that the catastrophes ahead are inevitable and unstoppable, perhaps even now are underway.

This communication works extremely well, I notice. I feel myself sinking into the thick, visceral fear that has visited and revisited in these past two years. He is apologetic, but I realize as I sit in a numb, scared state, that he has at least actually conveyed to me what he is feeling. Thirdness as a space for reflection seems to have disappeared. Certainly my reflective functioning is stalled. Much later I think about saying something about the meaning of being incinerated together in my consulting room, a kind of suttee perhaps. But in the moment I just feel terribly frightened. James and I now come to sit numbly under the powerful control both of state-generated and privately generated fear. In the sense of a principle of a, dare I say it, "perverse" thirdness that does not allow reflection, we are both in that moment bereft and unthinking.

In Ogden's (1994) terms, the moment of jointly experienced terror is the analytic third. It is a thick, softly assembled moment of his, mine, ours, and it is also a moment deeply constructed by external forces. I see thirdness in the moment of being joined together as beings interpellated by the state. It is a moment of being entered by the other, entered because of the unique and willing personal receptors we bring to that situation.

But we work around and with terrorism in odd ways. James has a dream that I am an FBI agent (I hear this hoping to be Clarice Sparling, but later I find myself wondering if I'm Hannibal Lecter). I have an assistant. Perhaps it is James. But there is a terrorist bent on doing damage, and that man has an assistant, too. Definitely James. So we toggle back and forth between James as the assistant to the one that pursues and disarms terror and James the assistant to the one that deals it out. There is an odd detail in this dream. I have access to a light switch which, at the moment I turn it on, will illuminate everything and the terrorist and James will be killed at once by the teams of sharp-shooters I have deployed. So James is enigmatically the junior killer and the junior policeman who will be sacrificed in the wake of illumination. He is inside and outside the law. The third may be the malevolent terrorist or the sharp surveiller. In the scheme of *The Matrix*, who is in whose mind and where has thirdness disappeared to?

At many other times in the analysis, James and I live in an imaginative world recognizably bourgeois, in conventional dyadic pairings and familial triangular patterns. We have come through a rocky patch in relation to his difficult, painful family. He dreams I am driving in a car to his house. He is not exactly in the car, not exactly anywhere. He is speaking instructions to me over his cell phone. The directions are for a scenic route. Then he is looking from the back seat of a car out the back window through a rainy, grey scene that recedes as the car drives away.

Another kaleidoscopic, reversing dream. He is the voice in my mind, giving directions. He is the child in the back seat of a car on a family outing. So the dream is his imagination of my fantasy of him. I am in the driver's seat, holding him in mind. But he holds me in mind, sends instructions by cell phone. And the third here? Each of us provides a refuge of thirdness for the other. Perhaps there is also thirdness in the missing father, but perhaps also in the voice on the cell phone giving instructions. A precocious third, a child who has to enact parental authority in the absence of real relatedness and real paternity.

Thirdness should not just be a third. Otherwise we have set up a system isomorphic with the bourgeois family, a regulating thirdness with its inevitable nods to patriarchy and heterosexuality. Thirdness needs to migrate across genders, characters, settings. Thirdness operates sometimes as the frame, the context, the bracing reference points. Sometimes thirdness is the hinge for change, for disequilibrium. And we cannot leave out that thirdness is of interest to the state and the police, and that being gendered and having desires in whatever form they may evolve, fluid or fixed, take some shape from regulatory potentials of thirdness.

❧

CHAPTER 8

Chaos Theory as a Map to Contemporary Gender Theorists

A review of contemporary work on gender is deeply amenable to a conversation with chaos theory. I use the vocabulary and vision of chaos theory to read this work of psychoanalytic feminism, relational psychoanalysis, and queer theory in the spirit of dialogue and not appropriation. The developmental implications of chaos theory and nonlinear dynamic systems theories ventilate the kinds of transitional spaces in which theories and clinical observations come into play. Phillips (2001), in praise of Emmanuel Ghent and the relational turn, speaks of a theoretical practice not "hellbent on telling me the truth about human nature, as much as producing interesting descriptions of what they thought was going on" (p. 2). Chaos theory is not a deductive, predictive, top-down systemization. Its aim is to describe dynamic but unpredictable unfolding.

INTERSUBJECTIVE AND INTRAPSYCHIC

In the past decade there has been a growing consensus across different theoretical schools that some kind of interaction of internal and external forces comes into play in the development of selves, subjects, and genders. The more interesting questions are how this mix arises, what is in the mix, what is prominent, and what is background. The question of the permeability of the divide between internal and external experience has been a project in psychoanalysis for a long time (Freud, 1914;

Schafer, 1978, 1992). How stable are boundaries within and between persons? These questions, surrounding the transpersonal nature of affective states and intersubjective experiences of identity and longing, lie at the heart of the relational project (Mitchell, 1993, 2000; Spezzano, 1993, 2001; Pizer, 1998, 1999).

Jessica Benjamin's still unfolding work on subjectivity exemplifies a double focus on intrapsychic and interpersonal processes. What is productive of personhood and an experience of self and self and other, including gendered selves, is a capacity to live in a fulcrum state in which one's sense of identity neither depends on the acquisition or use of an other nor lives effaced in relation to that other. Benjamin's (2000a, b; 2002) most recent work is informed by her belief that many aspects of our internal and interpersonal worlds require the same maintenance of tension that earlier served in her analysis of gender.

Benjamin is interested in moving beyond the questions that have trapped an earlier feminist and psychoanalytic community. Is sexual difference a given, an achievement with variable constructions, or a stumbling block to be worked through for maturity and adult relatedness? Given that, as she notes (Benjamin, 1995, 1998), there needs to be a central structuring principle, what might that be if we unyoked sexual desire and subjectivity and allowed gender more variability? Benjamin develops the critique, which has been a strong aspect of feminist psychoanalytic work, that the standard issue oedipal theory supports a defensive masculinity (Freud's, patriarchy's, or individual's).[1] The question to ask is how difference is established and sexuality organized without recourse to the extremes of essentialism or deconstructionism.

Benjamin's (1995) strategy is to approach the metalevel of gender categories. "Let us say that the binary gender categories are analytically necessary to explain deeply embedded psychic experiences, but what fundamental reality they refer to remains unclear" (p. 38). The necessary fiction of these categories can be traced through a variety of other configurations: active–passive, sexual difference as a byproduct or as a linked and necessary precursor of heterosexuality, the tie of oedipal logic to a "naturalized" perspective on gender. Thinking of gender as constructs with variable content leads to multiple developmental pathways and to a developmental trajectory—preoedipal, oedipal, postoedipal—that has some of the fluid movement between inclusion vs. exclusion or difference vs. commonality.

Benjamin (1998, 2002; Benjamin and Aron, 1999) is opening up another view of intersubjectivity as a site of agency and emergent subjectivity. Here her work approaches that of Fonagy and Target (1996, 1997, 2000), and in the background we might also see Bion (1962).[2]

One of the experiences that leads to an appreciation of difference and of agency is appreciating an other that survives destructive impulses and actions. That other is a *minding* object, an object with its own center of regard, thinking, and intentionality in relation to you, the subject. Parental reverie and parental reflection are crucial aspects of child mentalization (Fonagy et al., 1997). The interpersonal, bidirectional relational crucible for self-emergence arises in a particular experience of otherness. Recognition of the other's otherness, his or her distinct will and intention, allows a break in omnipotence, brings relief from one's own destructive fantasies and brings a dawning sense of the theory of "others' minds." I have been interested in how hard this developmental trajectory is for girls laboring under the conventions and restrictions on aggression within a particular cultural, historical context (Harris, 1987, 1997, 1998b).

These developmental processes in which subjectivity emerges from unique forms of intersubjectivity, with a wide variety of distinct structural outcomes, draw on the microdevelopmental theories of Werner (1957), Vygotsky (1962, 1978), and others. When intersubjectivity is an outcome not a given, the chaos theory perspective, with its strong commitment to complexity as an emergence from primitive cascades, offers an interesting vision.

Ghent's (2002) work on motivation is relevant here. Motives to attach, or indeed any other articulatable motivational system, are the outcome of initially very simple processes of interaction. Ghent, following Edelman, called them biases or values. Projects of becoming gendered, sustaining attachments, knowing and being known are outcome motivational systems, emerging from highly complex and multiply distributed patterns of interaction. We can substitute the term "preferences" for Edelman's "bias" and "value." At the beginnings of experience a "preference" can be as simple as turning to warmth or light. From that simple transaction, complexity is a fast-emerging, online, real-time outcome.

This perspective on motivation can also be linked to Loewald's (1949, 1980) notion of early subjectivity. Neither primary narcissism nor early object relatedness dominates, but a system of individually experienced linkage produces a primal density neither solely narcissistic nor solely object related, from which an experience of self and object emerges. This perspective was a foundation to Mitchell's (2000) thinking about development. Using Loewald's concept of primal density from which object, subject, and drive emerge keeps the tension Benjamin is interested in as a potential. It is also a perspective that offers a third way into the contemporary debates over the primacy of object love or desire (Widlocher, 2002).

In this model, subjectivity, in its gendered aspects, has both agency and authorship. Benjamin (1998) has linked the project of feminism and the project of psychoanalysis as sites where women seek voice. Recognition and a speaking subject are linked experiences. She glances at the particular link the Lacanians make between gendering and language. I think that the problematics of language and speech need more integration into our ideas about subjectivity in relation to gender. From the chaos theory perspective a somewhat different take on speech is emerging. I take up this subject in greater detail in chapter 9, but note now that from the Lacanian perspective, the onset of language is akin to castration, a moment of disruption of narcissism and symbiosis, a claim by the symbolic, standing in for the law and the father. This is a view of language still caught in the male imaginary. I will argue that there is a view of speech and language in which symbolic, subsymbolic, and body-based private and public forms evolve. Lawfulness in speech is both emergent and imposed (Litowitz and Litowitz, 1977; Lakoff and Johnson, 1980, 1999; Karmiloff-Smith, 1992; Olds 1992b, 1994; Bucci, 1997, 2001, 2002).

There is perhaps no more crucial question at a personal, social, or global level than how respect for otherness and subjective agency co-exist. Through the tightly-grained psychoanalytic lens we can observe the complexity of how a sense of personal agency evolves (not seamlessly but transformatively) into an experience of partially alienated subjectivity. The paradox is that this evolution inevitably makes internal what was originally an experience in or of others. There are many dangers along the way to understanding this process. Various default positions have been proposed. There are what we might term paranoid theories of the subject that focus on the emptiness of base identity and the constructed aspects of self (Lacan, 1977; Borch-Jacobsen, 1992).

From an opposite perspective, there is a determination to claim primariness for femininity, to counter the focus on autonomy and bounded individuality with primary relatedness. Benjamin (1988, 1995) and others (Irigaray, 1985, 1990; Goldner, 1989, 1991, 1998; Dimen, 1991, 1995b; Layton, 2002) argue that these projects either erode any notion of motivation or agency or leave the framework of gender identity still firmly cast within the male imaginary.[3]

A strong feature in much feminist psychoanalytic work (Benjamin, 1987, 1988, 1992a, 1995, 2002; Flax, 1990; Dimen, 1991, 2000; Brennan, 1992; Elise, 1997, 1998; Layton, 1998; Harris, 2000, 2002) is that the terms of analytic theory seem driven by patriarchal demands and defenses. The splits in the conception of maternality and femininity, Benjamin (1995) argues, evacuate from child identity, and in particular masculine identity, all the dangerous experiences of vulnerability to maternal power. In earlier work Benjamin (1988) proposed paternal identificatory love as one antidote to this splitting. A number of critics have noticed that both heterosexual and paternal privilege is still maintained here and the splits in the maternal object remain unhealed (Magee and Miller, 1997). Brennan (1992, 1993) observes that this fantasy of autonomous egos and separateness requires the evacuation of passivity, tenderness, and relatedness into women and into the concept of femininity.

All these writers maintain a double vision, examining the theories and at the same time using theory to watch men and woman, boys and girls, in the throes of these negotiations of boundedness and connection, recognition and subjectivity (Layton, 1998; Dimen, 2000). This political and psychoanalytic perspective, conscious and self-conscious, always in tandem, is a hallmark of this body of work.

Two figures that practice more border-jumping, interdisciplinary work are Nancy Chodorow (1994, 1999, 2002) and Jane Flax (1990). Each has been concerned with making theoretical space for cultural and historical forces alongside the unconscious, fantastical elements in an individual's psychic life. Though they differ on the value of adding postmodernism to the mix, they undertake projects of synthesis, drawing mostly on the object relations tradition in psychoanalysis.

Chodorow's immersion in Loewaldian ego psychology leads her to privilege unconscious phenomena, and in particular emotion and affect, at the "core" of individual experience. Situating herself both as anthropologist in the field and clinician in the consulting room, she demonstrates how much observation, understanding, and meaning making is done through the prism of personal, subjective, affectively centered experiences. Walking an interesting tightrope, she insists on the primacy of personal meaning yet also on a constitutive, rather than reductive, role for cultural formations. She makes space for specific subjective translations of culture and for the objective material conditions of cultures. Like Flax, she sets us a problem rather than a solution: the difficulty of maintaining a tension between cultural forms and conditions and the personal (which for her must privilege the unconscious).

Chaos theory holds a similar tension. It is a theoretical commitment to both pattern and uniqueness. At the global level, or more macrolevel, one can imagine gender as robust and coherent, perhaps unitary or partaking of stereotype. At the microlevel, gender is more fractal and variable, appearing along unique and multiple pathways. In thinking of gender experiences as attractors, we might consider how unique and unpredictable meanings of many kinds might be folded into any network. Semantic attractors in multidimensional space, made in unique constellations and contexts, allow gendered life to be constituted in personal and generic forms.

Flax (1990) walks a different but related tightrope. She pays attention to the power in forms of knowledge. No conceptual prism we use to understand human functioning is clean of its place in history and in culture. In particular, where gender is considered, our language, our concepts, our whole perceptual and analyzing instrument have been forged in knowledge structures that are patriarchal and reason dominated and carry hierarchies of value with respect to gender, class, and race. Flax is examining the way political and social constructions shape theory, a process pursued in different ways by Brennan (1992, 1993), Wolfenstein (1996), Irigaray (1990), Benjamin (1988, 1992b, 1997), Dimen (1991, 1995), and cultural critics like Kauffman (1995). Wolfenstein's (1996) summary term, "the male imaginary," is one I have adopted. Flax (1990) reminds us that this designation needs to be made more specific and that class and racial implications cohere as well.

Flax positions herself in between worlds, in the interstices of postmodernism and feminism and psychoanalysis. She proposes that any of these discourses is both transitional and partial. Postmodern critiques of the fetishizing of the Enlightenment's overvaluation of reason and of coherent subjects shake us free of certain hierarchies of functioning that organize various inequalities presented as unremarkably grounded in science or observation.

But, as is now much debated among postmoderns (Butler, 1990, 1993; Benjamin, 1997; Layton, 1998, 2002; Fairfield, 2000a, b; Fairfield, Layton, and Stack, 2002), a purely decentered subject, produced as it were as a kind of textual effect only, has erased the emerging agentic self and collapsed any distinctions between self and subjectivity. Layton (2002), Benjamin (1997, 2000a), Chodorow (1999), and so many others insist on a deep and crucial space for subjectivity. Many analysts working in the more classical and neoclassical tradition in psychoanalysis have kept alive the vital elements of fantasy, body, and sexuality. We may argue about the kind of body we are theorizing or taking note of clinically, but the body as pressing, unmetabolizable presence is as necessary as the conditions of attachment, containment, and relatedness. I am arguing that Benjamin, Chodorow, and Flax, in different ways, are promoting a model of gender development in which the dynamic complexities of psyche, individuality, historical force, and intersubjective field are all in tension. It is this kind of thinking that is particularly conducive to a chaos theory perspective, in which gendered experiences are, like attractors (strange or periodic), susceptible to dynamic reorganization and transformation through the intersection and interaction of multiple and distinct forces inside and outside the individual.

GENDER PAIN, GENDER DYSPHORIA

The usefulness of the model of softly assembled genders in theorizing gender development in the context of attachment is illuminated by Susan Coates's (Coates, 1990, 1995; Bradley et al., 1991; Coates, Friedman, and Wolfe, 1991) work on gender identity disorder. In the first presentations of her work, she and her colleagues cast the femininity of the boys she treated as a complex, interactional outcome of four factors. First, she pointed to parental dynamics. Here she was primarily interested in what we might better term gender identity disorders in the parents and family. Those disorders are often expressed in the unconscious wishes and needs of the adults in the family system and are played out in the meanings the parents assign to, construct, and perceive in their child's bodily and psychic gender. Second, there is in that child a particular sensitivity and reactivity that seems constitutionally given. These two factors then coincide with two others: the appearance of a crisis in the primary figure of attachment and a critical point in the construction or consolidation of gender.

As Coates's work has developed, she has become interested in the transgenerational transmission of trauma, a process widely conceived to go beyond questions of gender (Apprey, 1996). Coates (Coates and

Moore, 1998) has made a complex examination of the subtle ways parental dynamics in context, and lived in various attachment patterns,
become part of the internal material of child knowledge and child fantasy. This approach is similar to that developed by Abraham and Torok
(1994), who speak of encrypted identifications, which carry projective
material from the earlier generation and embeds secret and unconscious
conflict in the child. Gender meanings transmitted intergenerationally
may carry these encrypted identifications.

I want to highlight the relational nature of the crisis Coates describes and to deconstruct the term constitution. The material conditions of the child—the body, the sensory apparatus, the responsive
capacities, the child's thresholds of reaction—are certainly elements in
the constitutional contributions the child brings to the primary relationships of attachment and identification. These material conditions,
the physiological substrate of the child's functioning, are the raw material available for parental fantasy and parental need with respect to
gender.

The body and the psyche of the child operate as projection sites,
material body forms made meaningful within the parents' psychic meaning system and already interpreted through the meaning systems and
narrative threads in parent, in family, and in the wider culture. A heightened sensitivity and reactivity in the child then undergoes social and
relational construction in particular interactive matrix of the parents
and child. A child's intense responsiveness, a lowered threshold to stimuli
of all kinds, is made meaningful by construing the child as empathic,
attuned, or creative. In our particular cultural setting, that attunement,
so highly available and so meaningful to the parent, is almost emblem-
atic of the feminine. Thus the sensitivity of a boy-child in this matrix
may become coded as an aspect of his feminization (from the parental
perspective) and perhaps from both sides of the relationship, those of
parent and of child—a necessary element in the management of the
parents' or the family's crisis and suffering.

A girl's response to a comparable crisis in her primary parent might
be similarly to have her bodily, sensory, and perceptual experiences
used to sustain the demoralized or shaken identity of the mother. A
tomboy self in this regard would enliven and excite, carrying for the
mother her own lost phallic identifications, perhaps replacing a disap-
pointing mate. This particular outcome would be understood only by
elaborating the maternal fantasy about the child and the integration
the child made of that fantasy as it was communicated consciously and

unconsciously. In an early rapprochement tomboy we may see the living evidence of fantasies, shared and unshared, conscious and unconscious, between parent and child.

Coates and her colleagues (Bradley et al., 1991; Coates, Friedman,
and Wolfe, 1991) were describing the suffering and anxiety of children
in reaction to the threat of collapse or abandonment by a parent. These
children, whether feminized or masculinized in this process, do not fail
in the transition to gender. They evolve a highly imaginative but apparently exhausting (reciprocally partnered) performance of adult identity.
Gender is not a problem but a brilliant solution. A child's solution to
the relational problem of sustaining the parent is lived excruciatingly
on the child's body and in the meaning of that body to the child.

The gender identity of some tomboys could be involved in such a
project of material preservation. My patient Jamie's fantasies that she
was loveable only as a boy were certainly lived out between us. She
despaired that my interest was only flamed up by masculinity—in the
man in the waiting room, in the books by men she imagines are on my
bookshelf. She had grown up imagining a kind of idealized dream lover
for her mother, a beautiful young man who would bring her mother to
life. And she began, even as a child, to imagine herself as that vital
figure, breathing life into a depressed and empty-feeling mother.

A similarly distorting conviction dominated another woman's sense
of her mother, although for that young woman the outcome was overt
despair and depression and a secret life as an alter ego who lived out
vital, sometimes murderous, sometimes rescuing fantasies. For both these
women, yet with quite different outcomes and organizations, gender
was obstacle and yet solution, carrying unintegratable psychic projects
in relation to a precious figure of attachment.

Transgenerational transmission of trauma—the haunting of a person by ghosts, demons, transmitted in some way well below the radar
screens of conscious reflection—may find in the structures of gender a
particularly vivid and well-elaborated host. I would like to think of it as
the "haunting of gender" in a wide variety of experiences of gender
development, lived out as aspects of incorporated (rather than fully internalized and metabolized) experience of the gender meanings of self
and of other and of self, in relation to other.

Drawing on the model of softly assembled behavioral attractors,
we see that gender, while diagnostically and perhaps socially problematic, has been recruited in the service of a particular skilled[4] task that
the child needs to resolve. Building a gendered self is one way of securing

stable interactions with and internal stability in another person. Some aspects of gender identification may, indeed, be the only available skills for such a task in such an environment. Gender may be the preeminent site of this type of relational negotiation because of its social and familial salience as well as its potential for malleability and fantasy. Gender, in this model, is distributed across persons. It arises in a particular intersubjective context in which its organization within one individual belies its relational webbing. Herzog's (2001) many clinical examples of work with children are bursting with the multiple gender plays and gendered characters through which conflict and danger are negotiated between child and analyst.

The difficulties for the child may be less in the realm of gender nonconformity than in the intensity of the cannibalization of the child's body and self for parental need. These may be needs for the child's attunement, needs for the child as an object to merge with, or needs for that child to contain a parent's dissociated self-states.

From these extreme situations, these emergencies of gender, we might extrapolate to see all gender and body ego gender constructions as forms of compromise formation. Parental fantasies about a child's gender would draw on and be structured through the parents' own experience of gender, the power and dangers of their own desires, and the prohibitions through which desire is installed and elaborated. The unique dialectic in any parent's experience of body, gender identity, and desire—how and why these experiences are linked or dissociated—will contribute to the interactive, intersubjective experience in which the child comes into his or her own understanding of these dynamics.

Another slant on this process is offered in Corbett's (2001a) analysis of the function of degraded gender categories as a defense in the development of a masculine identity often too brittle in its insistence on potency, bigness, and autonomy. Corbett notes that, for many of his boy patients, a too cartoonlike experience of phallic potency and mastery shores up very uncertain and vulnerable self-states. This vulnerability and many attendant feelings of shame are evacuated into the other, called "faggot," who must hold the anxieties and shame of losing and smallness.

Again we note the use of gender and sexuality in these projects of self-management and self-regulation. Interestingly, as Corbett works out the dynamics and family dynamics, he begins to feel that "faggot as loser" is also a kind of solution to the problem of neglect. Gender deformations, as Coates also sees them, are the outcropping of disruptions in attachment and the related conditions of failure to mentalize the other. Brittle masculinities reflect many processes. Like omnipotence, with its own shaky and overly dramatic qualities, a gender identity can be cobbled together (or stolen, as Corbett suggests in his case material) to cover drifting, open gaps in experience. Neglect and withdrawal by a mentalizing, imagining parent can be layered on previous, preoedipal structures as well as later, more oedipally based exclusions.

Corbett captures in clinical detail the theoretical idea that Butler (1997b) develops regarding power and regulatory practices. Regulatory ideas are never achievable. There is so much instability in any identification that enforcement is always ongoing. This enforcement is manifest in social pressure, in the idea of faggot = loser, and in internal beratement and shaming.

MULTIPLICITY OF GENDERS: "MANY-DRAFTED BODIES"

In the past decade psychoanalytic work on gender multiplicity, gender fluidity, and cross-gender identifications has undergone a great sea change. Fluidity or multiplicity can be a matter of subject position(s) (Butler, 2000a, b), a matter of fantasy and unconscious process (Chodorow, 1999), a theoretical position claiming multiplicity as normative of mental life (Fischer and Ayoub, 1997; Davies, 1998a; Bromberg, 1999; Pizer, 2001), a cultural description (Sedgewick, 1990; Garber, 1995; Eng and Han, 2003), or a political understanding (Rivera, 1989; Haacken, 1994).

This double or tripled vision (intra-, inter-, and meta-) characterizes most contemporary gender theorists, in cultural studies (Sedgwick, 1990; Butler, 2000b) as well as in psychoanalysis across various orientations (Corbett, 1993, 2001b, c; Chodorow, 1994, 1999, 2002; Davies, 1994, 1998b, 2001b; Dimen, 1996a, b, 1998, 2000; Elise, 1997b, 2001; Fogel, 1998; Layton, 1998, 2002; Stein, 1998a, b, 2002, 2003). Davies (2001b) and Dimen (2000) on the body and sexuality, Layton (1998) and Elise (1997) on bisexuality, are theoretical jugglers, able to keep a lot of balls in the air. The move from gender binaries to multiple subject positions and "the logic of many" varieties of oedipal, preoedipal, and postoedipal configurations allows a new set of questions. In a sense, gender is only one (although a powerful one) aspect of the larger and deeper question of identity and otherness with which relational analysts are now engaged.

Layton (1998) argues that within psychoanalysis there is often a collapse of two distinct experiences: the production of subjectivity, including gendered subjectivity, and the reproduction of subjectivity. I think she means that one needs to keep in tension two different experiences of gender, a point Chodorow (1999) has also developed. Culturally mediated gender inequality is installed in subjectivity (reproduction) and at the same time specific and unique, context-sensitive gendered subjectivities are intersubjectively and relationally produced.

This tension seems to be at the heart of my construal of tomboy experience as gender conformity and gender rebellion. Masculinity in a woman may draw on gender polarities or defy them. Tomboys, in a sense, live out the conflicts that have bedeviled cultural theorists and feminist psychoanalysts. Do we accede to the dominant terms of gender organized within a system of the male imaginary? Does resignifying or revalencing terms that are drawn from a patriarchal system reinvigorate and reframe identity?

It is in the synergy of feminism, relational theory, and postmodernist thought that the whole binary system of gender is addressed and critiqued (Dimen, 1991, 1996a, b; Goldner, 1991; Harris, 1991, 1997; Flax, 1993; Layton, 1998; Wilkinson and Gabbard, 1998). From this point of view, the rigidity and overdetermination of various binaries that, like barnacles, accrue to gender binary is put in question (Dimen, 1991). Gender practices and sexual practices then become multifunctional, in the service of relational as well as intrapsychic needs and agendas (Goldner, 1991, 2003). The focus on performance in postmodernism is quite often misunderstood as acting, role playing, or the voluntary taking up of a gender role (Harris, 1997).

Dimen (2000) uses the felicitous phrase "many-drafted bodies" (p. 11) to open up a view of body that is determinedly complex, multifaceted, and softly assembled. The protean versatile experience of one's body, including experiences and fantasies of inside and outside, allows for multiple deployments of identity and assigns multiple functions to longing, sex, or desire. As in Sedgewick's (1990) idea of gender saturation, one imagines distinct kinds of body–mind saturations, such as the dancer whose self-state is as her body. Or, equally poignantly, a young woman remembered that her favorite stuffed toy had been a giraffe.

She loved it and identified with it because the head was so far from the body. It is a figure in which gender is insignificant or ambiguous.

Dimen (1996b, 2000) notes something fascinating about how we construct our bodies—as minds, as genders, or not. Our bodies are the sites for complex struggles for freedom, and they are bulwarks against domination. And, of course, it cannot be a fully successful struggle. Cultural constraints and cultural readings affect gender in many ways, and yet each person makes a creative compromise, keeping and giving away oneself in an endless negotiation with self, other, and culture.

Clinicians working with patients with eating disorders know this in a daily way. The body is braced to reflect memory and to eclipse it, to carbon date a trauma through gesture and style. The body may be one way we evacuate affect into an other, setting off feelings of desire or disgust or horror or longing by the way we shape and carry bodily selves.

Dimen (2000, 2002, 2003) and Layton (1998, 2002) are each sensitive to another force within this experience of body–mind as softly assembled in a relational matrix. Cultural imperatives make their presence known in subtle and unsubtle ways. What feminists have articulated persistently is that women carry a variety of shames, mysteries, and gaps that, more properly named, are simply human. Within feminist theory this is the particular asymmetry of emotional labor under patriarchy. Interestingly, this perspective can be found among Lacanians as well (Brennan, 1992; Mieli, 2000). The feminine—the carrier of gaps, excesses, and the impossibility of speaking and desiring—is not an essence, as it has so often been in classical psychoanalytic theory. It is a construction softly assembled to carry feelings and states of mind deemed intolerable, the unconscious of the other. The gender divide continues the cultural work of sequestering frightening aspects of humanness.

In chapter 4 I argue that a tomboy identity, with its elements of protesting and envying, may accept or reject the divide. What differentiates the tomboy from the character Annie Reich (1953) theorizes in her paper on women who realize phallic aims and ideals through alliance with an intense, but secret identification with a highly phallic man? The latter is engaged in a kind of projective identification, disavowing but secretly, vicariously indulging masculine potency, even if idealized and mostly in fantasy. Has the tomboy been the object of another's projections? Is she unable to process her own excitement and agency separate from a male or boyish mimesis?

Perhaps some tomboys can push the envelope, transgress, and yet still have some access to power because the tomboy inhabits a valued identity, one less feared than femininity. She contains less of the regressive pull of the fully feminine, less the preoedipal mother. It is a matter of Artemis rather than Medusa. And Minerva and Artemis, those active, hunting, thinking boy-girls, were not mothers.

It is interesting to reflect on Corbett's (1999, 2001a) clinical and developmental work, its trajectory from girlyboys to phallic pleasures, all in the context of increasingly complex and multiply configured family arrangements. His space-opening, mind-opening projects are indebted to chaos' theory and nonlinear dynamic systems theory. Imagining the gender play in various family configurations, seeing how complexly gender is a tool or a solution to experiences of narcissistic wounding, neglect, and affective chaos, led Corbett (2001b) to what he terms quasi-axioms. He notes the term's oxymoronic status, capturing the tension in chaos theory, what Kauffman (1995) calls "order for free," the commitment to pattern but not to a deterministic outcome.

The difference between axioms and algorithms is crucial. By reconfiguring gender as multiplicity, by keeping the tension between chaos and coherence, by watching the bidirectional, dynamic pressures towards recognition and limit breaking (the mutually constituting pleasures of routine and freedom), a chaos-theory perspective places process and paradox centerstage. This is the terrain of much relational theory (Bromberg, 1993, 1996b, 1998a, b; Davies, 1998a; Pizer, 1998). The approach is not top-down or deductive, but productive of interesting descriptions, ways of watching and listening.

Chaos theory, without simply presenting a utopian prospect for multiplicity, would be a perspective from which phallic positions can be gendered or ungendered. A phallic position—playful, penetrating, aggressive, assertive, empowered—could become an aspect of identity constellations that may be rigid and brittle or playful and fluid. In another context, Bromberg (1996b) identifies the freedom to speak coherently while standing in many spaces, to act whole while being many. This kind of model of psychic life has for Bromberg elements of speech, of body state, of fantasy, and of dream state. This kind of soft assembly would encompass multigendered life as well.

Thinking of gender multiplicity takes one inevitably into an examination of bisexuality. There is perhaps no better roadmap into the history and theoretical thickets of this concept than Chodorow's (2003, in press) essay on bisexuality, a paper she perhaps means to be read in conjunction with her earlier work on heterosexuality as a compromise formation (Chodorow, 1992). In this essay, Chodorow makes a historical map locating the tension in Freud between the normalizing impulse of sexuality and an emerging understanding of sexuality as unhinged from its objects, always bisexual in potential, plural and multiple in its forms and meanings, constitutive but not exhaustive of subjectivity and identity. We can read in Freud's (1905) "The Three Essays" what Chodorow and others have noted: a radical statement of body, desire, and identification as uniquely configured *outcomes*. It is this commitment to emergent phenomena that makes for a good match with chaos theory.

In some of the classical and Kleinian psychoanalytic literature on bisexuality and cross-gender identifications, there is often slippage and contradiction as to whether masculinity or bisexuality is a matter of gender or of sexuality and how gender and sexuality are or are not linked. Birksted Breen (1993) argues that gender is the outcome of a psychosexual pressure, that sexuality shapes gender.

The relational literature (Dimen, 1991; Harris, 1991, 1997, 2000; Benjamin, 1997), with its focus on the object relational history of the person, often seems to privilege gender over sexuality. I find it interesting that, from a strongly classical perspective, gender fluidity and bisexuality are found within the province of unconscious fantasy and the intrapsychic. Gender binaries are located unremarkably in the body, which then offers itself to mind to be metaphorized. The politics of subject reproduction are, to an extent, mystified or hidden in a body that is somehow viewed as existing outside history and politics.

Chodorow's (2003) account of the fate of Freud's conception of bisexuality as a site of multiplicity and creativity is instructive. We need a social analysis as much as a psychoanalysis to understand the harnessing of psychoanalytic theory to normative accounts of sexuality that privilege by naturalizing heterosexuality and masculinity. As she notes, feminist and queer theory fueled interventions in psychoanalytic theorizing by taking up this radical Freud. Drawing on these traditions (queer theory and feminism), Chodorow elaborates the deep complexity of sexualities as amalgams of subjective desire, erotization, object choice, internal worlds of fantasy, and sexual orientation as a public, culturally mediated position.

Another key figure in the theorizing of bisexuality is the cultural theorist Marjorie Garber. A writer who can shift across disciplines and literary forms, Garber (1995) speaks for the cross-dresser, the bisexual

as a site for transgression, a refusal of definition.[5] Her concerns for pre-
serving a space (real, cultural, theoretical) for excess, for liminality, for
marginality are relevant to theory making in psychoanalysis. She is interested in how identities confound categorization and how, in particular, bisexual identities are lived between categories, inside and outside
regulated forms of life. We might wish that Garber were as unconven-
tional a reader of psychoanalysis as she is of literature and culture. This
notion of life between the spaces is deeply a part of relational theory in
the work of Bromberg (1993, 1996b, 1998a), Pizer (1998), Dimen (1994,
1996a, 1998), Davies (1994, 1998a), and others.

Garber's (1995) analysis of sexual "excess" and transgression as
necessary for human life and culture alerts us to a continuing unresolv-
able paradox in psychoanalytic work. Listening for multiplicity, fluidity, and refusal in our patients' material and our responses to it will
powerfully transform ways of working. Opening space in theory, between analyst and patient and within the fantasy and experience of
patients, creates just the kind of volatile hot spots that disequilibrate a
system. Yet clinical listening will inevitably also be regulating. How can
we listen to a tomboy without taming her?

A chaos-theory perspective suggests that we think of these contin-
gencies not as fixed, alternative pathways but only as exemplars of the
variable pathways development can take. Bisexuality would not be an
innate organization or even an innately prefigured potential. If the interrelationship of desire and identification is not predetermined and if
gender is lived in multiple registers (symbolic, metaphoric, iconic, embodied, fantastical, and concrete), and if sexuality serves intrapsychic
but also interpersonal functions, then many possibilities for variation
are opened up. "Masculinity" could be an aspect of gender or an aspect
of sexuality, a link between desire and identity or a brake. These meanings will be made in the crucible of individual and social/cultural life
(Chodorow, 1994, 1999).

Bisexuality as an endpoint, rather than as initiating force, has a
place in the new discourse on postoedipality. A potential for the fates
and consequences of desires and identity is possible if one unyokes, or
at least unsolders, gender from body and from desire. Chodorow's (1992)
essay on heterosexuality clarifies how rarely psychoanalysis has
problematized heterosexuality. If we place on an equal plane of possibility negative and positive oedipal identifications, multiple and complex characterizations of parental objects and selfobjects, and if we refuse

to genderize or normalize active and passive sexual aims, many possible forms of sexuality appear.

Chodorow's point that the term bisexuality seems best to stand in for multiplicities of gender and desires is a good segue to the work of Jody Davies. For over a decade, her theoretical and clinical work on sexuality as a lived aspect of transference and countertransference matrices has been joined with an investigation of oedipal and postoedipal dynamics. Her postclassical model of oedipality keeps a bidirectional focus (Davies, 2003). Libidinization of a child by the parental couple, by each parent, or by the family system is a lifelong process (Laplanche, 1997, 2002; Stein, 1998a, b; Slavin, 2002). Davies's (1998b, 2001b, 2003) clinical work and her theorizing are among the best answers to the usual classical and sometimes European-inflected critique of relational and interpersonal theory. That is, it is often thought that a focus on interpersonal transactions is shallower than a focus on individual intrapsychic interior life and worlds. Davies's work illustrates a wide variety of clinical situations in which the lived interpersonal dynamic creates a deeply intense, risky, and affectively charged interaction. The matrix of transference and countertransference, reproducing in unique forms the matrix of deadness or aliveness in the original worlds of attachment for the analysand, must be inhabited in states of often radical uncertainty.

A chaos-theory perspective would see the matrices Davies is describing as kinds of strange attractors, fractal structures that can disequilibrate and reform with dazzling unpredictability. Unpredictability does not mean an absence of pattern or regularity. Davies's (2003a, b) work takes up the need for some encounter with a structuring process but leaves open the variety of routes through crisis and resolution. One question that Davies and others wrestle with is that of language. When is the theory so altered that new conceptual terms are required, and how much does the preexisting language aid or inhibit? Can "oedipality" expand to this new bidirectional matrix for sexuality and identifications?

For Benjamin (1998), Bassin (1994, 2002) and, in a different tradition, Fogel (1998), bisexual identifications have the potential to help protect gender complementarities from rigid polarization. Bisexuality is thus an adjunct to sustained intersubjectivity; it keeps the tension between self and other as objects and as subjects. Fogel has proposed that fantasies of interiority and femininity can signal in men a capacity to tolerate intimacy and relatedness with women, because there is less terror with respect to femininity and so less need to evacuate dangerous feelings and fantasies into women. These theorists are following and extending Fast's (1984) Piagetian/Freudian model of gender development as a process of generalization and differentiation. All are making crucial theoretical moves to extricate the mother from the preoedipal soup she is too often trapped in and to let femininity and masculinity circulate and integrate in mature psyches. An enormous step forward, and yet it is hard not to feel that all our models are still haunted by heterosexuality and binaries.

Davies, Cooper, Corbett, and others are pursuing variations and elaborations in the conventional ideas of oedipal triangulation (Davies, 1994, 2003a, b; Corbett, 2001a, c; Eng, 2001; Cooper, 2003). Triangulation and bidirectional, coconstructed desires are essential components of oedipal resolution distinct from the particularity of the oedipal constellation. Any particular oedipal or postoedipal resolution arises in multidimensional complex spaces. Such solutions are kinds of attractors, hopefully strange attractors, reflecting the unique integration of agency in the individual, contextualized parental desires and a libidinized environment that makes space for rather than colonizes the growing individual. The outcomes of loving and being someone is orchestrated in the emergent and unique organization of parental management, including renunciation and pleasure. These unique organizations arising in the family overlap with attractor regimes organized through cultural and local cohort formations.

Butler (2000a) seems to mean something slightly different regarding multiplicity. She seems indebted, despite her critiques, to Lacanian ideas of desire as the desire of the other. When a desiring parent is encountered—the enigmatic seduction that Laplanche (1997, 2002) elaborates, enigma has many meanings. There is the quality of enigmatic desire in its overwhelming, swamping aspects (Stein, 1998a); there is enigma at the level of meaning. But another source of enigma is whom does the parent desire? Is the mother's desire for the child reflected in desire for her partner? Do you love the object or the object's desire? Or both? Desire is always multiple desires.

Butler (1990, 1995a, 2000) has been a powerful voice engaged with yet critical of psychoanalysis and psychoanalytic feminism. In her debates with Benjamin (2000b) she probes the limits on recognition. Recognition, she argues, is never fully free of misrecognition. She is interested in the particular forces that do not simply socialize but subjugate. She asks the difficult question, can we actually fully distinguish compliance and love? For feminist psychoanalysts with whom she is engaged, Butler holds the place for a certain kind of ambivalence in regard to gender performance and gender identity. Part of the debate is the question of whether gender is built out of foreclosure. If it is, how brittle is gender? How transient and how transgressive?

For Butler, no discussion of gender or desire, and in particular of gendered bodies, can occur without reference to power. Genders are not merely constructed but compelled. Femininity arises in what Butler (1990) dramatically terms a "zone of uninhabitability." Melancholic genders, particularly feminine ones, carry unliveable and therefore ungrievable loves, and so abjection and self-beratement inevitably curdle gendered life. We can catch the clinical relevance of this idea in a footnote to Corbett's essay "Faggot = Loser." He describes a moment in his work with a child when a parent accused him of pedophilia. Although his language is simple and straightforward, I found it moving and painful to read his description of a kind of internal management that went well beyond the usual vicissitudes clinicians are asked to absorb:

> There is, however, an extraordinary vulnerability for men working with children, which is even greater for gay men working with children . . . my experience has led me to reflect on how this vulnerability, built as it has been on my own experience of being hated, requires a particular kind of countertransference forbearance—a particular capacity to sustain multiple states of mind that allows me to experience the shame of being hated while simultaneously (or most likely retrospectively) thinking through the shame of being hated [Corbett, 2001a, p. 11].

TRANSGENDER AND INTERSEX

The radical edge of psychoanalysis is one spot from which to listen to the inaudible, see the less visible presences in psychic and cultural life. We are currently listening and responding to a new series of voices from the edge, a place where the avant garde in theory and in practice can meet (see Denny, 2002, of a biographical essay on transgendering; see also Feinberg, 1993; Bornstein, 1994, Eliot, 2001). In a kind of double whammy, these voices shake the logic of binaries by asking us to think about both/and and at the same time neither/nor.

The intersex community (new even as a community) speaks for the need to leave ambiguous bodies unbinaried. The transgender community speaks for the opposite perspective, that fantasy and mind can deeply require particular bodies. Gendered bodies and gendered minds are potentially assembled in various ways. These voices break with and still also reflect all the dominant voices (including our voices in psycho-analysis) who are in the business of constructing and observing subjects.

Keeping the complexity of bisexual, multiply-drafted, transgender and intersex experience requires that we think of gender in relation to sexuality in an irreducibly paradoxical way. Gender as a category is both empty and full, fluid and rigid. Dyess and Dean (2000a) are developing a critique of social constructionism and relational psychoanalysis that might be pertinent here. Much of my book and much of my understanding of the experience of "gendered" individuals take up gender as a big, imaginative playground in which to work out social and intrapsychic life. The potential for gender to soft assemble seems crucial to many of our gendered experiences. But Dyess and Dean (2000a, b) argue against the idea that a category could ever exhaust meaning, particularly where unconscious process is involved. They point to the elements in any gendered life of "its constitutive failure as a communicative process" (p. 746).

Following Dyess and Dean (2000a) and others (Zizek, 1989), I want to counter and augment the idea that gender is constructed relationality, with an alternative idea, namely that gender resists relationality and resists full representation. The struggles to be and live gender in all of us, most powerfully articulated in transgender and intersex experience, open to more understanding if we see in these gendered "constuctions" the impossibility of fully inhabiting a gender position, the limits on representation and on rationality. From a non-Lacanian perspective, Slavin and Kriegman (1992) built a comparable argument, the resistances to connection and to subjectivity in discourse. Gender is an assembly that is perhaps always potentially a strange attractor because of this matter of limit and of the resistance to sociality in unconscious life. Gender contradictions include contradictions between signification and gap, trauma and sociality, inchoate and coherent expression. This builds into gender assemblies the kind of potential for destabilization that strange attractors have.

Is a gender construction sometimes deployed as an unusually elaborate and subtle security operation? Over a decade ago, before the articulation of a transgender community and its multiple voices, I did separate consultations with two young women, who, although quite different in a number of ways, were seeking gender surgery. Each approached this possibility with some trepidation.

Each had implacable and bedrock reasons to say that, from her experience, it was degrading and dangerous to be a girl. A boy identity was literal and psychic survival. Terror at passivity and incorporation, terror at violation and vulnerability, could be allayed only by change in body character. In these cases a defense against annihilation apparently required extreme forms of concrete identity fortressing. Schafer (1968) points out that incorporation involves a concrete fantasy of taking on or becoming, in an embodied way, the corporeal elements of another. Gender as such a corporeal formation may be used to regulate an anxiety lived in relation to the body, its conflicts, and its safety.

We find another kind of haunting in the appearance of a silenced voice in the case of John/Joan, a case of gender reassignment that resurfaced several years ago and has been the subject of extended debate in the sex research and gender studies worlds. In this case, a genitally injured male infant (one of male twins) was reassigned as a female and reared as a girl through a very troubled adolescence. In the wake of intense new scrutiny of sex reassignment and an ongoing professional conflict, the detailed circumstances of the case came to light close to 30 years after its occurrence.

The case was initially presented as a seamless and appropriate sex-reassignment matter. John Money (Money and Eckhardt, 1972) used the material to argue for the power of cultural assignment and the relative plasticity of biology. But the clinical and social truths are more complex. The reassignment was made after a traumatic accident when the child was eight months old. Reassignment was at two years old. The family trauma was devastating: maternal depression, alcohol dependency, and serious instability in the "intact" twin. The individual's self-report (in young adulthood) includes an inchoate sense that something was wrong, a dogged refusal of therapeutic intervention (interventions that were grotesque and perverse in relation to sexuality), a long involvement with drugs, and a final disclosure of the original secret in adolescence (by the boy's father).

It might be useful to view this case through the prism of nonlinear dynamic systems. The gender identity of this child would seem to be a strange attractor, the instability of gender being held in parent and family memory, perhaps in some procedural forms of knowing by the child; in the mixed and variable communications (at myriad levels) to a boy-now-a-girl, a damaged boy, a "girl" at least in performance, a troubled adolescent, a misfit child harassed in her social milieu.

And yet all this was lived out in the 1960s in rural Western Canada, where gender was also a fixed-point attractor with sharp, deep basins such that genders could not blend. The category representations and experiences—bodily, genital, social—were like a powerful periodic structure, binary and mutually exclusive. One could make the argument that a boy without a penis could survive as a girl only in a certain system. Our own incredulity and horror at this case is at least in part influenced by the recent emergence of a powerful communication from the intersex community regarding sex assignment or reassignment (Kessler, 1982). The seedbed for this emergence is, I believe, over a quarter of a century of thought and action on the matter of sexuality and gender.

Contextualizing this narrative is not to airbrush the terrible clinical violations that occurred. In the reopening of this case, there is a danger of moving from pro nurture to all nature and biology. The voices and stories of the cast of characters suggest more nuance and complexity. At the level of fantasy and imagination there were probably many sites in which no gender reassignment had occurred.

The case of John/Joan occurred 40 years ago. Consultations on transgendering done over a decade ago seem antiquated and outdated. Fausto-Sterling (2000) has traced two centuries of slow, methodical movement, sometimes progressive, sometimes reactionary in appreciating the complexity and variability of sexed bodies. The history of the emergency of homosexuality as category, as person, as community is a comparably slowly evolving process (Boswell, 1980, 1990; Katz, 1976). That contemporary transgender and intersex communities are communities is actually a strikingly swift evolution. The movement from isolation to voice to community has actually been quite rapid. At the technological level the Internet and other spurts in technology have enormous potential for establishing links and coherence for voicing and protest. At the social level, the last half century of evolving consciousness of collective and individual voices of protest has created many pathways to activism.

CONCLUSION

A shift from contents and stages to processes and transformations makes developmental gender theory a new kind of project: what variable aspects of experience enable any person to live either happily or unhappily under the gender umbrellas, large and small, that we all must carry?

We would be less interested in how well our patients fit some norms of development and more interested in the unique constructions that draw on and transform public meanings and personal agendas.

In thinking of gender as a soft assembly, whether bound in a fixed-attractor system of rigidity and polarization or recombinant in unpredicable and multiple ways, the demand on clinicians is to keep a lot in play. We must pay attention to the body, to the cultural significa-tion, to the interplay and transactions in which gender is expressed or evaded by and between people. And always we have to pay attention to the complex categorical system that we use and are used by. When at work on gender's soft assembling, we have to watch our words.

The power of gender words and gender categories has been a cen-tral part of Butler's (1997a, 2000b) ideas about resignification. From psychoanalysts the criticism is that Butler is insufficiently attentive to agency within subjectivity. But interventions in discourse are ways of disequilibrating a system.

Chaos-theory models entail new models of speech practices, se-mantic attractors, speech performance, and speech competence. Speech is never free of public stain, never exhausted by it. Gender identities are shaped through processes and transactions that play havoc with the orderly notions of external and internal. Identity always involves com-plex, creative kinds of place changing and reversals. Dyadic life, one site for gender construction, is porous, permeable, entrained, and in-terdependent. Notice that none of these transformative theories does away with conflict and crisis, but the pathways to and through organi-zation and reorganization are multiple and variable.

Butler (2000a) does a wonderful riff on multiplicity, thirdness, and enigma in a dialogue with Benjamin in which she wants to make sure that there is room for desires to mutate from and with each other in unpredictable ways:

> Imagine she is bisexual and, putting off for a while her desires for women which tend to be desires to be a bottom, has sought to have a relationship with man No. 1. But instead of finding a woman as the third, she finds a man and "tops" him. Let us say, for argument's sake, that Man No. 1 would rather die than be "topped" by his girlfriend, since that would be too "queer" for him. He knows that she is topping another man, perhaps penetrating him anally and he is furious for several reasons. But what is she after? If she is bisexual she is a bisexual who happens to be "doing" a few men right now [p. 280].

Butler then goes on to generate a dizzying and plausible set of dynamic projects embedded in women's sexual practices, choices, and fantasies. And we, as readers, can watch this play and chime in with our own riffs. Just following what terms Butler decides to put into quotation marks suggests another thread all its own. Butler is theorizing and resignifying, but the terms of signification are an increasingly unstable strange semantic attractor, ready to reorganize into new possibilities. And, of course, as Butler (and others, such as Dimen and Stein) would immediately add, none of this is outside culture, prohibition, or suffering.

We have theories claiming that we own language and others that claim language owns us. Much potential space is opened up for a more complex relationship of concepts to objects and to speakers if we imagine that we rent words, to draw on Michael Holquist's (Bakhtin, 1981) apt concept. To return to Edelman's metaphor of the store-bought suit, the best we can say of our reconciliation of intention, expression, and communication is that the fit is good enough. Words' histories and our histories will mix and match in interesting ways. We are renters of representation, renters of gender and of identities. We have long-term and short-term leases and sometimes multiple habitations. These images allow for both stability and many changes of address.

Developmental Theory and Research

Developmental Applications of Nonlinear Dynamic Systems Theory: Learning How to Mean

*I*n this chapter and the next I explore several applications of chaos theory and nonlinear dynamic systems theory. Acquiring a language; gaining mastery over and access to your own body; learning about your own mind and the mind of others; and becoming a self, establishing identity or identities, learning how to know and regulate your own and others' internal states—these problem areas, formerly discrete domains of research and theory, are increasingly being treated as interdependent phenomena.[1] As these developmental tasks are more and more seen as mutually coconstructing and as susceptible to multiple pathways and trajectories, it is possible to draw on the utility and perspective of the nonlinear systems approach.

In this chapter I concentrate on the fascinating problem of how a child enters and is entered by the worlds of words, icons, and symbols. Although I am focusing on the development of speech and meaning, my interest ultimately is in looking at how semantic attractors and the strange attractors of gender might be linked. Learning to make meaning through speech or sign is one aspect of the complex process of what I have been calling the soft assembly of gender. In thinking of what is softly assembled to constitute gender experience, I include body states,

affective patterns, dyadic coupled systems attractors, individual translations of cultural proscriptions, concepts or schemes of gender meaning,
and modes of speech and thought. Language and gender development
are constituted in multicomponent systems uniquely open to external
and internal sources of information. I am arguing that both the process
of acquiring a speech system and finding a place in a gender system are
interdependent hot spots for change and for meaning making.

The great paradox in regard to both gender development and language development is that in both domains growth leads to freedom, to
powerful structures of fantasy and imagination, and at the same time to
social management. Speech rules and gender rules free the mind to
build novel worlds and representations of self and other, but these tools
also carry the constricting and categorizing aspects of culture (Harris,
1979, 1992).

I have several reasons for focusing on an intersect of the development of self, speech, and social cognition. First, I am interested in picking
up the story later in a person's toddlerhood, when more elaborated
forms of language come online. The integrators of infancy research
and psychoanalytic theories of development do not for the most part
focus on the period of toddlerhood and early childhood that Meltzoff
(1990, 1995) characterizes as "the dark ages." Yet toddlerhood and post-
linguistic childhood in a speaking community of family and culture are
fascinating, if less well known, sites in which to view key transformative
processes. By looking at current developmental work on a child's evolving
capacities to represent experience, including the transformations in the
child's theory of mind, of intentionality, and of self-representation, we
can see how processes identified from infancy work (e.g., Beebe and
Lachmann, 1994, 1998) as crucial to individual growth are shaped by
encounters with the system of signs and speech codes, matters where
the public and the private spheres become powerfully and inextricably
entangled.

Toddlerhood and, later, childhood are important sites to watch for
the interdependence of fantasy and history and of social formation carried in the ideology and formats of stories, meaning ascriptions, and
scripts (Nelson, 1985). It has certainly been a hallmark of Lacanian
psychoanalysis to tie up gender, subjectivity, and the symbolic register
in a heated knot of cocreation and constitution (Lacan, 1977). It has
also been the experience of generations of analysts of many persuasions
that the preverbal, nonverbal, and experiential wash of relationships

and bodies in relationships must be part of this coconstruction (Bucci, 1997, 2001, 2002; Astington, 2000).

It is increasingly clear that the child's emerging "theory of mind" is a complex multimodal process in which bodily awareness, agency, desire, communicative competence, and beliefs about self and other evolve in real time over the first three years of life. While the study of individual differences has for the most part been neglected or relegated to the extremes of psychopathology, it seems inevitable that integrating clinical and developmental sensibilities will demonstrate the subtle ways gender (whether as a body state, a belief, a semantic attractor, or a representational scheme) enters into a child's theory of mind.

When language comes online, new levels of metaconsciousness develop and take on prominence. Reflexivity, the shift from representation to instrumentality in mental activity, is a process whereby a child comes to be able to take one part of the mind instrumentally to work on another. While these capacities are built on earlier modes of mental life (Fonagy and Target, 2003), reflective capacities are enabled in a new and powerful way through speech. But speech is also a powerful vehicle for the installation of social normativity into private psychic life. Social mind and computational mind coconstruct with social forms, regulatory practices, and ideologies to become seamlessly aspects of self experience and modes of thought (Furth, 1987).

HISTORICAL ANTECEDENTS

Baldwin, Cooley, James, Mead, Peirce

To set the stage for a look at contemporary psycholinguistics, I want to call up some historical figures whose ideas animate so much of the way development is currently being imagined. Interestingly, some of these figures are important to the historical background of relational thinking.

For most of the last century, developmental psychology, the spheres of personality, cognition, and representation, had independent lines of inquiry and different traditions of empirical investigation. This phenomenon was connected to the powerful individualism in developmental psychology (see Chapman and Dixon, 1987, for critique) and to the legacy of Cartesian thought that kept separate mind and body, thought and feeling. In the past two decades, a profound change has occurred in the study of child development that is variously connected to social constructionism, contextualism, and pragmatism.[2] In Chapman and Dixon's (1987) account of the broad set of interests defining what they term "contextualism" in developmental psychology, they identify the following parameters:

> From this perspective, many psychological constructs are viewed as *multidimensional,* with *multiple directions* of change patterns. . . . Furthermore, empirical and theoretical emphasis is given to both interindividual and *intraindividual* variation, a conception reflecting the large differences in the life-course change patterns of individuals, and *intraindividual plasticity* [p. 51].

One of the leading figures in the study of child mind and intentionality, Inge Bretherton (1993), notes that the problems of interest to developmentalists at the turn of the 20th century are being taken up again with new precision and new methods of study. This theoretical turn is occurring after a century-long preoccupation first with behaviorism and then with technical information-processing models of cognitive and language development. The field is moving toward models in which the complementarity of external and internal experiences are more prominent. This move has led to the recovery of earlier influences in child development and in psychology in general. From these early figures (Baldwin, 1904, for example) there was a frank and clear appeal for interdisciplinary approaches and collaborations.

From the constellation of figures writing at the turn of the last century, an interesting network of ideas and conceptions emerges. Many of these ideas are familiar to relational analysts. In James (1890, 1910) and Baldwin (1904) one notes the move from faculty psychology to functionalism and a dialectical approach, by which we mean a treatment of child consciousness and mind that is emergent and is linked to processes of social action and interaction. Here self and other engage in a circular process of perceiving, imitating, and attributing within a bidirectional social field.

Baldwin is perhaps the figure most germinal for theories of developmental process, though not so prominently drawn on as Piaget. He believed that understanding children's minds requires attention to social, cognitive, affective, and interactional experiences. According to his social theory of mind, child subjectivity is never isolable but is emergent in social interaction.

At the turn of the 20th century he was articulating, albeit in speculative form, what has become axiomatic in much contemporary social theory as well as psychological and psychoanalytic theory: the route to the self is through the other. The child is caught up in activities that Baldwin termed "projecting" and "ejecting." Others were known to the child first as "projects," but later aspects of the child's experience were ascribed to others who were "ejected." The child's experience of self "goes out by a sort of return dialectic to illuminate the other person" (Baldwin, 1904, p. 185). At the same time, the child acquires a self by imitating the other, an imitation that is an active mimesis not a simple copy.

From our psychoanalytic perspective, the interdependence of these processes is quite familiar. We have long understood the back and forth fusion of self-states with other and of other states with self. This process is captured in Schafer's (1968) conception of the ebb and flow of interiority. Indeed a modern psychoanalytic reader of Baldwin cannot help but think both of relationality (Mitchell, 2000) and of Klein's (1977) models of early object relating with a stress on the bidirectionality of the process. The child is taken up as an intentional, meaningful emotive self in an act of parental reverie, seduction, or mentalization. Simultaneously the child ascribes self-states, what Baldwin (1904) termed the "raiment of the self," to the partner in the dyad. Such "sharing of self-states is variously described as attunement, contagion," now moments, amplification, and primary intersubjectivity, but inevitably it conveys a sense of coconstructing and bootstrapping.

William James (1907, 1910; Bird, 1986), writing on pragmatism, on the experience of the self, and on his theory of "radical empiricism," produced an influential network of ideas that are equally familiar to relational analysts. Distrusting abstraction and rationality, he focused on experience, and experience not simply of things but of things and their relations. This focus, along with his attention to the hermeneutical circular relations among belief, desire, and action, must strike a psychoanalytic reader as familiar. But what makes James an even more intriguing ancestor both to these social/cognitive theorists in developmental psychology and to relationalists in psychoanalysis is his "radical empiricism." This phrase connotes his project to understand the multiple intersections (his term) among an individual's knowing of objects, the public, shared nature of that knowing, and the problem of how one mind knows another.

Amid ongoing controversies about adjudicating and verifying truth and meaning, James (1907) provides a powerful statement in support of both perspectivalism and a pragmatic, narrative theory. "Truth in science is what gives us the maximum possible set of satisfactions, taste included, but consistency with previous truth and with novel fact is always the most imperious claimant" (p. 106). For James and later pragmatists truth was identified with expediency and utility. For James, however, this stance also had as a corollary an openness to revision and error. Hence his acute opposition to any notion of foundational, absolute truth that was separate from individual experience.

There are other historical influences, drawn from pragmatism and from the symbolic interactionists: Peirce (1955), Mead (1956), and Cooley (1909). For Mead, the self was a social phenomenon that would develop out of interactions and the integration of both self-reflection and the multiple positions in which the child was experienced by others. The developmental movement that interested Mead was the process of internalization, whereby the experience of being seen, interacted with, socially held, and controlled becomes part of the dynamic internal dialogue. Thinking, perceiving, and acting all had, for Mead, a distinctly social, dialogic quality—an inherently split and multiple subject, the I-self and the me-self, constructions of subjectivity found in James and Mead. The inherently and complexly multiple selves can be conflictual (James) or fluid (Baldwin). A commitment to a social origin of self is found in all these authors. Each, in his own way, undermined the idea of the autonomous individual or of development as endogenously driven. Cooley (1909), for example, asserts the twinned primacy of the individual and the social: "I do not question that the individual is a differential center of psychical life, having a world of his own into which no other individual can enter; living in a stream of thought in which there is nothing quite like that in any other stream" (p. 9). Yet that individual is constituted and encompasses experiences of being the object of another's reflection.

Finally, no discussion of the intellectual roots of a relational model of meaning making and representation is complete without attention to C. S. Peirce (1955).[3] The power and relevance of "other minds" in Peirce's (1955) system is palpable, with semiotics teaching us of the deep sociality of mind. Litowitz (1977, 2001) and Olds (2000) have proposed that Peirce's triadic theory of meaning and his notion of the multiple aspects of signs (index, icon, and symbol)[4] is of interest to clinicians precisely because of the social nature of meaning that is intended, the way signs carry and evoke affects and anxieties, and what infancy researchers call "now moments" (Stern et al., 1998). From Peirce's semiotic perspective, meaning is made between speaker and interpretor. It is the implicated presence of another listener that contributes to the heightened, amplifying affect, the multiple meanings, and the levels of symbolization that accrue to signs.

If we see words as having not only a symbolic, reflective function but also indexic and iconic functions, and if we follow Peirce in connecting a sign with its context, its speaker, and its listener, then we end up with a view of language as carrying procedural memory, intersubjective process, and "thirdness." Many interesting new ways of thinking about speech pop up: transference, *Nachtraglichkeit*, and signal anxiety are all newly animated when approached from this semiotic perspective.

Vygotsky's Developmentalist and Social Constructionist: Minds in History

For a theory in which the power of language as a material, cultural, historically shaped tool is absolutely central, I turn to Vygotsky (1962, 1978).[5] In a brilliant recasting of Vygotsky's work for contemporary cognitive science, Frawley (1997) poses the challenges of child language studies in the following ways: How do we integrate social mind and computational mind? How do we pay attention to the deeply private and internal experience of much conscious and unconscious experience and also attend to the powerful impact of social experience, and culture, and history on mind?

For Vygotsky (1978), speech and language were poised on the edge of the mind-world line, facing outward and inward. His work powerfully conveys the idea that the forms of social regulation carried in speech are internalized and become aspects of self-regulation. He charts for a later point in development the working assumptions of contemporary infancy studies: that self-regulation, affective states, and social interaction are grounded in dialogues (see Beebe, Jaffe, and Lachmann, 1992, for a compatible perspective).

Vygotsky sought to stay alert to the tension of public–private or internal–external when it came to speech and word meaning. What something means is "indigenous but not endogenous" (Frawley, 1997). Speech mediates mental life, bringing history and culture irrevocably into psyche. Yet psyche retains its own deep, internal processing. Minds need other minds to evolve and function. Hence mind becomes a kind of transpersonal phenomenon, flourishing in interaction and in conversation.

It is true that Vygotsky could not encompass a theory of the unconscious into his work, but he did think it important (van der Veer and Valsiner, 1991). He also began to frame a theory of emotion but it remained schematic. His use of emotion is immanent in his writing about psychotic speech, and his model for distortions and deformations in such speech parallels Bion's (1954) work on psychotic language, especially in "Attacks on Linking" (1959), a paper of central importance in contemporary Kleinian child analysis.

Vygotsky saw psychotic thought as an altered form of conceptualization, ruptured by some trauma or shock or emotional trigger, in which word meaning (for Vygotsky a complex coconstruction of social and intrapsychic) was altered. In psychotic speech there was a concretization, a collapse of the symbolic, which leads to the interesting speculation that a child's relation to his words and speech may illuminate other kinds of relatedness. This experience with language has less to do with mastery of structure than with our functional relationship to language. One of the confusing experiences in clinical work may occur when a patient's use of language suggests some mastery of the symbolic form, but speech use is in the service of some hidden but powerful primitive function. In many clinical situations it is much more useful to think that words are being used to cajole, seduce, scald, penetrate, disorganize, or arouse than to attend to meaning and symbolic content (Schafer, 1997; Harris and Gold, 2001). Words may also be deployed to destroy meaning and interaction (Bion, 1959).

A PSYCHOLINGUISTIC TOOLKIT
FOR PSYCHOANALYSTS

I want to introduce clinicians to the fascinating empirical world of child language research, where many intriguing demonstrations and studies are building a rich picture of children's capacities. Because this domain of theory and research is vast and technical, I present here a summary of 10 interesting ideas and concepts that grow out of a review of developmental psycholingistics. I think of this list as a toolkit, prepared for analysts to use in clinical listening and in their own conceptual work. I am drawing on models of language development that stress the primacy of function in development and in multivoicedness—a polylog of speech and a model of speech and thought as forms of embodied cognition.[7] From this perspective, the capacity to speak emerges out of the relational/social context and out of consequent functions—to represent, to describe, to be instrumental, to communicate, and to regulate. Collectively these functions make speech ride piggyback on intention generally and on a capacity for meaning making. We are dealing, in what follows, with the "meaning potential" in speech (Halliday, 1973) and "meaning readiness" (Bruner, 1986, 1990).

1. "Fast Mapping": Word Learning as One Ground for Intentionality

There is that delicious moment for doting parents when their child, usually sometime around the end of the first year of life, articulates his or her first word, that is, the first recognizable, public sign appropriately mapped to a person or object. Magical. Looked at with a psycholinguist's eye, this scene seems even more astonishing. As speakers, we hear digitalized units of words, phrases, sentences. But acoustically, speech sounds stream continuously. We actually live in "acoustic baths" (Harris, 1998a) as well as worlds of speech and meaning. Out of a sensory wash of continuous sounds, social process, and objects, the child has to figure out (1) that sound bites may have some property of "aboutness," (2) where to segment the continuous stream, and (3) what a particular sound bite maps to. No wonder it seemed easier to sidestep the whole question of development and just assume a kind of unfolding, innate competence.

But, as language studies have shown, word learning is not a magically emergent process but a laborious and intricate one that is unimaginable outside the social dyadic life of child and parent. Word learning takes place in the context of the development in each partner of an intentional stance (Feldman, 1988, 1990; Dennett, 1991). Intentionality as a property of words and intentionality as a property of minds bootstrap each other.

It is through various kinds of interactional processes, all carefully observed and described in the domain of infancy research (Tronick, 1989; Beebe and Lachmann, 1998; Sander, 2002), that a child gains the capacity to extract units of sound that can be mapped to objects. Thinking about the kind of a theory of mind this development calls for, Paul Bloom (2000) comes up with a variety of processes: monitoring the emotional cues of the adult; mutual gaze; social referencing; following the line of regard of the parent; the shift from pointing as an extension of looking to pointing as a functional act to compel attention in the other; the development of means–ends connections and goal-directed experiences (Piaget, 1924). The child's theory of mind in the context of word learning escalates as the child becomes sensitive to the other person's attention, mood, and gesture.

All these possibilities are the context in which very young children make the move to producing and using single words. This process, studied by Carey (1985) and others (Carey and Bartlett, 1978; Heibeck and Markman, 1987), occurs in what she calls "fast mapping," a highly efficient, almost error-free mapping through which a child can parse a running stream of sound, find the relevant unit and its boundaries, and connect to an object similarly extracted from the stream of experience with boundaries and conditions.

Jusczyk's (1997) account of the development of speech perception adds another element to this complex picture. He stresses early infant capacities to conduct a kind of innate guided learning that builds on modes of perceiving and on producing speech. These two systems gradually coordinate such that each bootstraps the other. There is an echo here of one of Vygotsky's (1962) central ideas about speech and language, namely, the reversibility of speech as simultaneously heard and spoken, potentially tying speaker and listener.

Quite casually in his discussion of this powerful early process in child development, Jusczyk (1997) notes, "The desire to have one's intentions understood is likely to be an additional impetus to achieve closer coordination of the two systems" (p. 209). But the crucial insight that the acoustic signal is also the voice of the beloved and powerful parent remains unexplored.

Dare Baldwin (1993), for example, locates the capacity for fast mapping in the context of a child's emerging grasp of his or her mind and the mind and focused attention of others. It is just this relational and intersubjective process that breaks developmental psycholinguistics out of its canalized pathways and offers a way to see how richly emotional, social, and intersubjective learning to speak must be. One could certainly also speculate that, if fast mapping is acute for salient, socially referenced meanings, gendered categories and concepts are acutely likely to be fast mapped. So gender's unique meanings for any child within the dyadic and wider familial context are embedded in the earliest acquisition of meaning and symbolization but in very individual and highly charged ways.

Bloom (2000) and Jusczyk (1997) would, I think, agree with Locke's (1993) judgment that emotion is to speech what motivation is to learning and that the process of induction into language nests in the deeply cathected attachment relation of parent and child. Bloom is responding to the formerly dominant Chomskian (1988) tradition according to which the task of speech acquisition is so difficult and happens so inductively and often indirectly that it must be a domain-specific, innately triggered capacity, a grammar gene (Pinker, 1994, 1996). Bloom's response is fascinating. He argues that language learning is both slower and faster than we imagined and that we need a multifactorial account of the process to make sense of anything this complex.

Although not yet well spelled out in Bloom's or others' accounts, a variety of social, affective, and intersubjective factors must be in play. This is where psychoanalysts can profitably enter the conversation. It seems clear that the process of acquiring speech entails powerful computational tools embedded in equally powerful social, emotional, and intersubjective processes. Speech building on, and also deepening and elaborating, preverbal and early dyadic experiences carries all the residue of emotion and relatedness, in part because of the unique properties of speech: its reversibility, its mix of voice and representation, and its emergence and consolidation in the wash of materiality: sound, touch, vision, holding.

But we need also to see the cutting edge of speech, its reliance on and transformation of internal computational skills. Learning to speak draws on a child's salience for base-level objects, an object bias. Later the child's capacity for pattern perception reads like the list of *gestalten*: seeing objects with common fate, with continuity, and, most crucially, organizing the world as patterned coherences.

2. Grammar: Running the Show, or a Dynamic Strange Attractor?

Thelen (Thelen and Smith, 1994) has been working on the use of nonlinear dynamic systems theory to model the development of symbolic thought. She connects her work in dynamic systems to that of Karmiloff-Smith (1992) and Lakoff and Johnson (1999), who argue against an exclusively rationalist understanding of symbolic thought. All these theoretical innovations oppose the more popular idea that language is driven by an innate "grammar gene," a concept, popularized by Pinker (1994, 1996) and deriving from the dominant mid-20th century model of language, Chomsky's (1957, 1965) generative transformational grammar.

These two ideas—that the acme of speech is its abstract rational component, its grammar, and that this uniquely human capacity is innate and under direct genetic management—have dominated both the popular and the specialized literature. By the age of three to three and a half, a child's competence for complex grammatical structure is so astonishing that it has been tempting to foreclose the question of development. Countering this tendency, Thelen and Smith's (1994) idea is that symbolic thought is an "activity-driven, reentrant, high-dimensional cognition." Comparably, Karmiloff-Smith (1992) calls cognition "realized in distributed processes of highly connected components, whose global properties get redescribed in symbolic terms—representational redescription" (p. 18).

Grammar, by these definitions, is an emergent, *functional* solution similar to that proposed, for example, for vision. In the latter instance, we are exposed to three-dimensional experience in the world that is mapped to two-dimensional spaces in the visual system, and yet we experience a reconstructed three dimensionality. The solution to this problem in the visual system is a set of emergent structures that are unique to particular visual domains, or problem spaces. This functional solution handles an emergent problem of informational overload by a streamlined reorganization, essentially a more economic system of perceptual categorization.

In the domain of grammar we find a similar story: "The grammars of natural languages may be thought of as solutions to an even more daunting dimension reduction problem, in which multi-dimensional meanings must be mapped onto a linear (one-dimensional) output channel (the mouth)" (Karmiloff-Smith, 1992, p. 62).[6]

This is a very difficult idea to grasp. Structure is a temporary outcome of process, not the spymaster or the executive control causing performance. A. Stein (1999), in an interesting but conceptually demanding application of chaos theory to Winnicott's (1971) model of potential space and representation, argues against the idea of internal representations as things or reified structures. And Moran (1991) argues similarly in elaborating a version of chaos theory in which unconscious fantasy is termed a strange attractor, a scheme or regimen of meanings elaborated in vivo (including the transference).

3. Intentionality Is Emergent, Not Built In

Bretherton (1988, 1992, 1993; Bretherton and Beeghly, 1982) views intention and intersubjectivity as emergent, not prewired or given. Bretherton follows Trevarthen's (1993; Trevarthen and Hubley, 1978) model of primary and secondary intersubjectivity, the latter arising with some metacognition, that is, the capacity to think about thinking. It requires a capacity to ascribe intentions, beliefs, and desires to self and other. But she breaks with Trevarthan in imagining these processes, even during primary subjectivity, as having a developmental trajectory.

Most researchers seem to agree that the initial theory of other minds that the child acquires is a 'naïve' one. Certainty and belief precede doubt and differentiation (Chapman and Dixon, 1987; Bloom, 2000). Just as procedural memory or organization of attachment patterns creates a powerful template for development, so the early "construction" that the child places on experience, emotion, desire, and intentionality receives a potent organizational shove from the adult (and other family figures) with whom the child is interacting (Dunn, 1982). When language comes on line, it is possible to see this fusion of public into private, of culture into psyche, in increasingly explicit and elaborate forms. Networks of meaning as expressed in speech constitute a kind of fractal organization in which procedural memory, narratives, and semantic attractors organize and reorganize in endlessly more complex and interesting formations.

Jerome Bruner (1986, 1990), Carol Feldman (1989, 1990; Feldman and Kelmar, 1996), and David Olson (1988, 1994), among others, have over several decades developed a deep understanding of learning "how to mean" and of the transformation in a deep semiotic capacity to link "aboutness" to signs. The two senses of intentionality are getting linked together, and learning to make meaning with words or signs emerges from, and is productive of, the experience of intending something in oneself or another.

Feldman (1989) has identified two processes in early child speech that reflect and produce an evolving theory of mind. She observed children as young as two years old beginning to speak about mental states, that is, to speak with what she terms "an intentional stance." Use of verbs like want and believe, and use of modal verbs like would and could, demonstrates the child's emerging experience of mental states with some representation. Feldman also observed and described a developmental process in which children, in her words, "go meta"; that is, they take their own words and concepts as objects of reflection. She sees this process in the changing use of a very common structure in early child language → topic → comment. Feldman (1989) watched the change in the conversations of very young children, between two and three years old. A topic is articulated, then commented on, and then the comment becomes a topic in its own right. The child has created a new object of thought from an earlier one.

Feldman tracks the transformations in micro- and in macrostructures. She watches how transformation is achieved within a sentence, how the topic of one utterance becomes an object of reflection and construction in the next.

But this creative construction occurs in the move from dialogue to monologue. Feldman writes about a little girl, Emily, who engages in complex negotiations with her father not to be left alone to nap. Father and daughter play with the possibility that everyone could come into Emily's room to nap—mother, father, brother, grandmother. She is warding off separation in this dialogic play. Then, alone in bed, she falls asleep through the following monologue:

> Sleep good. And so sleep a lot right there. Mommy there. Daddy there. And Mormor [her grandmother] there. Stephen there and Carl there and Daddy. And Stephen I c- Carl wa—come there. Carl was in there cause his mommy and daddy . . . fell down so, so he got to sleep in my bed with me. And also he's been sleep . . . way up in the ceiling. Mormor you can sleep on the ceiling a little bit away from Uncle Don and Carl . . . cause . . . cause I wanna play with Uncle Don . . . : Carl coming and Carl brought two bags. One for um, one for candy, for Uncle Don and one for grapes for him. . . . You know why the. . . . I don't have anything because I'm going to sleep. Just the other people brought a picnic, but they don't put it. So they put it, the bags, up there. So they could sleep and see the . . . [p. 115].

This is a fascinating and rich moment of creation, pretend, self-soothing, and elaboration. There are dialogic moments—"Mormor you can sleep on the ceiling"—and reverie and fantasy. And all this play occurs in the service of falling asleep alone. Note also that this comprehension and mastery of intentions is achieved transpersonally, that is, through dialogue as well as monologue.

From quite simple functions—calling, ostention, want, request, referencing—the child begins to put together narrative capacities in new and multifunctional combinations. Early narratives and early, simply structured speech reflect a growing capacity to think about self and other as objects of reflection. Minds, feelings, and mental states have a property of "aboutness." The fast-burgeoning capacities of speech, with its complex structures of syntax and semantic spaces, create new grounds for the ascription of intentional stances in self and in other.

A theory of mind takes on a particular density and shape as language emerges, but this theory has been brewing in the earlier processes of joint gaze, directed attention, and the patterning of production and perception. In this operation of bootstrapping, affect, thought, and speech together generate the capacity to know one's mind and to feel known by another.

4. Our Bodies, Ourselves: How Soma Shapes Speech and Representation

Lakoff and Johnson (1980, 1999), working on a model of the development semantics and what is termed "embodied condition," count as a profound influence the work of Varela et al. (1992). These three theorists are developing new models of word meaning and category formation that treat all categorization as degenerative, recombinant, and not susceptible to reified meaning systems. Rather, their ideas evolve in the social, intellectual, and somatic process of thinking, speaking, and interaction.

Lakoff and Johnson (1999) focus on representation and metaphor in which word meaning emerges from action, from body-based experience, from images, and unique ways of encountering the world of objects and the world of others. Word meaning and the surrounding aura of facts and associations would be clustered around some prototype affects or some prototype action schemes that are not pregiven but are motivated and emergent from the human interactions in which the term or category name is being applied. A categorization like girl or boy then grows out of a social matrix and out of embodied experience, another kind of attractor with its own basin, shallow or deep.

Semantic attractor systems involving gender are likely to have the complex hybrid structure that Bucci (1997), Olds (1992a, 2000), and Litowitz (2001) ascribe to language systems. Primary and secondary process coevolve in the development of word meaning. Meaning is never in isolation but is always contextualized, and context includes affect and body state. Indeed, the ability of words to carry "hidden regulators" or indexical or iconic force is what makes the talking cure possible.

In thinking about the function of representation as both organizer and reflector of desire, we can wonder how the gendered representation of body, particularly a sexualized body, will reflect the history of the handling of that body. The psychoanalytic tradition of core femininity could then be subjected to a linguistic critique as we wonder how much a woman's and a growing girl child's sense of sexual self is crafted through how she and others speak of her body. For example, the kinds of shame about body excess, about sexual desires of all kinds—experiences we see clinically in women at all ages will be both anchored and constructed through socially prescribed representation.

5. The Toddler as Analyst: Decoding Semantic Meaning, Pragmatics, and Deep Meaning

It has taken developmental psycholinguistics a long time to emerge from the domination of Chomsky's (1957, 1965, 1988) theory of generative grammar. Chomsky broke the stranglehold of behaviorism on studies of the psychology of language and gave generations of researchers extraordinary tools to describe the intricate rules of syntax that are operative in the speech of young children. But along with these powerful tools came a model of mind and of language in which language skills were almost sui generis, inborn, and scarcely even developmental processes. It has taken the generation of linguists (McCawley, 1968; Lakoff, 1987; Ross, 1985) after Chomsky to focus more on a multifunctional model of language, a recentering on semantics and meaning making as a primary motivation for communication and a richer interest in speech pragmatics, that is, the rules of speech usage. With that turn, contemporary developmental psycholinguistics can embed speech in the development of the self and in the complex social negotiations and constructions of children in their families and their culture.

This interdisciplinary project is by all accounts in its early stages.

How a child enters and is entered by a public–privatizable system of symbols and communicative devices is a formidable matter. In an overview of child language development, Locke (1993) proposes such an integration, though with a heavy emphasis on biolinguistic features. He does what is increasingly typical of child language researchers; that is, he places language learning in the longer standing, preexistent process of the child's discovery of intentionality in others, which subtends the child's theory of mind.

Children also develop good antennae for the subtleties of power and for the subtle way speech pragmatics display and disguise power. Children learn, for example, very early that interrogatives are not simply probes for information. They are often the subtle manifestation of power. "Whose boots are lying in the hall?" is a demand for action, not illumination, and very young children know this very well.

Urwin (1984) details a fascinating study in which children were set to ask each parent for something at mealtime, specifically a drink and some cereal. Asking the mother occurred simply and directly. Asking the father led each child into unique and striking strategies (rhetorical and regulatory) in order to achieve the desired result. A rather complex idea of relative power seems involved here. Your mother expects to serve your needs. You must convince or charm your father.

6. Voice: What a Great Place to Put Language— Speech and Affect

While acknowledging a powerful place for social interaction and attachment, Locke (1993) also notes that the explanation of affect still lags behind cognition in the study of child language. The absence of Tomkins (1962, 1963, 1992) as a figure in psychology's history is noteworthy. Locke notes the crucial features of dyadic life that language must capitalize on: interest, facial cues of emotion and focus, social referencing, and the subtle transformation of pointing into gesturing.[7]

Locke also calls attention to the deep connection of language to voice with his witty comment, "Voice, a great place to put language" (Locke, 1993, p. 332). There are powerful, affective layerings in voice, an archaic repository of memory, closeness, and material bodily infantile relational life. The partial nesting of language in voice pulls the child toward a powerful social and affective knot, just as the face draws the child to parental affect and thought. There is an inevitable concentration of voices and faces, as speech sound presents in the deeply engaged affectively rich face of the conversing participants. We can see, then, that, from the very beginning of life, speech has iconic and indexic potency, an interdependency of primary and secondary process (Ferenczi, 1931; Loewald, 1980).

Actually, of course, psychoanalysts have noticed some of this: it is at the heart of Kristeva's (1980) work on the tie to the maternal object as being a tie to semiotics (the material sensuousness of the body and voice) and to the symbolic register (words, concepts) (Clément and Kristeva, 2001). This idea likewise guides Horton's (1984) beautiful paper on language's solacing function, the capacity of the voice to carry regulatory power socially and intrapsychically.

7. Speech as Comfort Food: Language Solaces and Regulates

We need to integrate this picture of the speaking child into what Vygotsky (1962) felt was a critical development, namely, the evaluation of speech as an instrumental aspect of regulation. Frawley (1997) terms this "metaconsciousness," and I believe it to be one element of Fonagy's (Fonagy et al., 2002) concept of mentalization. Vygotsky was most interested in how a child came to turn speech from a representational to an instrumental function, from predicating or identifying to managing action, emotion, and thought. Wertsch (1985) terms Vygotsky's idea about speech a "tool to fix tools." As analysts and clinicians, we see the gradual and powerful use of speech to regulate affect. We are thus led to see speech as one tool in the stable organization of feeling and thought states whereby ideas and representations can be used and managed (what Frawley, 1997, classifies as computation). We see also that speech can be an element in self-soothing, in affect regulation (Harris, 1979; Horton, 1984).

Another important psychoanalytically relevant aspect of this work has to do with regulation. Luria (1957) produced a series of research demonstrations tracing the evolution of a child's capacity to use speech to self-soothe and self-regulate. The central idea was that processes of control begin on the social and dyadic level and are then actively internalized. This idea resonates with many ideas from recent infancy work and from the attachment literature (Lyons-Ruth, 1991, 1999; Fonagy, 1997, 2001) in which modes of knowing (procedural knowledge or organizing principles) emergent in dyadic life are seen to function as internal and integrative processes in the child.

In this context, contemporary researchers into the theory of children's mind stress the intricate relationship between a child's attribution of mental states in self and other and the emergence of the child's executive function. This relation draws together the two spheres of Vygotsky's (1962, 1978) work, the interrelation among speech, thought, and social process and the emergence of self-control as a relational byproduct. A link is also forged between the hidden regulators (Hofer, 1984, 1995, 1996) and entrainments (Sander, 2002; Beebe and Lachmann, 2002) and later emerging capacities for internal regulation, capacities that exploit representation and the dialogic elements of speech.[8]

What is intriguing in the integration of Vygotskian study of self-regulation with recent child-language work is that we can use language as one space in which to observe the interpenetration of subject position and self-regulation. Becoming self-regulating, as it emerges out of dyadic interaction, is one aspect of becoming a person. Thought as style, content, and emotion as regulated or unregulated components of psychic life—both are reflected in and altered through children's speech. It is here also that one can find a site for multiplicity of selves.

Drawing on the same data set of a young girl's monologues and dialogues used by Feldman (1989) and others (Nelson, 1989), Watson (1989) explored the emergence of regulatory capacities in the young child Emily's speech, one aspect of which became evident in dialogue. Recall that Emily was managed by her father, and, facing a pending separation (she was about to be put down for a nap), she used speech to attempt to forestall bedtime. Watson notes both the fragile nature of this negotiation and the complicated aspects of agency that occur. The talk between father and child seems to be about everything but bedtime. In Watson's narrative we hear, in the deep structure of the conversation, the attempts to manage an outcome. Later, alone, in bed, Emily uses speech, some of it hers, some mimetically rehearsed from her father, in an act of self-soothing. We see manifold selves, multivoicedness in the (not so) simple act of falling asleep. Emily is learning to regulate her own affect and anxiety states and hence to manage solitude.

It is possible to approach this integrated multifunctional set of experiences through a number of gateways: It is a speech phenomenon, it is about affect regulation, it is about the construction of thought and metaconsciousness or reflexivity. Emily's talk reflects her object relations. She speaks as and for her father and to herself. Dialogue is integral to a developing consciousness; it will be one of the building blocks of reflective functioning.

Emily's dialogues and monologues concern these various forces interlaced and mutually constructing. From the standpoint of Fonagy's (Fonagy et al., 2002) linkage of mentalization to dynamics and parental unconscious and of Vygotsky's (1962) model of regulatory functions arising socially before becoming intrapsychic, a powerful opening is made to personal dynamics and social forces as emergent properties of thought and of subjectivity. For the postmoderns among us it is a way of having one's cake and eating it too. There is no dearth of individuality and self not fully captured in cultural forms, but there are clear and researchable pathways for apprehending culture as an aspect of mind and psyche.

8. The Postmodern Toddler: Kids Speak in Many Voices

Dennie Wolf (1990) has made one of the most interesting integrations of speech and personality development in a research program in which she explores the powerful effect of multiple registers of speech. She argues that, as children between two and four master rules of syntax and many underlying competences on which language depends, they also begin to draw on multiple ways of speaking. Children begin, that is, to inhabit a multiplicity of subject positions, distinct "envelopes of experience" in which pretend play, speaking as another, shifting voices, and shifting roles all have a place. In her research young children were shown to produce different formats of the same event, giving distinct renderings to similar experiences. Interestingly, the children began to speak to themselves in what Wolf describes as an authorial voice. I think she is also describing the speech variations of regulation, the use of genres of speech (cajoling, excoriating, berating, soothing) to guide children's experience, their learning, and their interactions. This work seems a powerful example of Bakhtin's (1986) theorizing of speech's multivocal, multiregister character, the multiplicity of subject positions carried in speech and emerging in the earliest period of language development.[9]

Everything in observational studies of infant capacity suggests that infants are intensely responsive to pattern both in action and in sensation. Thinking clinically, one can imagine conditions of experience where the linking of pattern, tantamount to Winnicott's (1958) sense of "going on being," is disrupted or spoiled. And one can imagine as well the consequences of such disruption for the flexibility and integratability of distinct self-state experiences. Wolf (1990) speculates that these rudimentary self-states are transformed with an enhanced capability for speaking.

Two interesting phenomena occur. Between the ages of two and four, children begin to produce narratives, that is, to speak of an "I" who is telling a story. Second, Wolf tracks the appearance of acted scenes, of speaking as another, including many variants of a kind of verbal mimesis. It follows that speech does not fully constitute subjectivity out of absence but consolidates, shapes, and distorts self-states and experiences of speaking "others" in the performance of skits, scenes, and scripts (Nelson, 1985).

With language there is a concentration, a sedimentation of self in a particular voice or way of moving, that often has double or even multiple roles. Speech also evidences a divided self, a commentator and an experiencer. Wolf calls this "insider" and "outsider" talk as she notes very young children interacting and communicating and then offering a kind of commentary or reflective gloss on what is happening. We might think of this as a protoform of reflective functioning, drawing on this powerful property of speech: its multivocal character.

In work with a three-year-old, I followed the appearance of play scripts in which mother and child alternated speaking as themselves and as the other in the dialogue (Harris, 1992). In one scenario, the mother is holding a pretend birthday party. She speaks, altering her voice, intonation, and register of speech, sometimes as the child and sometimes as the child's favorite transitional object, a blanket to which she gave the name Blankie. Mother, child, Blankie, and an offshoot of the blanket, Tassle, are all animated through voice and gesture. In another scenario, the little girl speaks in an altered, high-pitched voice, pretending to be her new baby sister. She gets down on her hands and knees and carries a toy in her mouth, all the while making what she regards as new-baby sounds.

This work on dialogues and monologues helps us to think of speech as transitional space, in which there is a multiplicity of self-states both as a social phenomenon (mother–child) and as a more fully internal one (shifting genres and registers in the child). Multiplicity and heterogeneity have roots in preverbal experiences and in social interaction, but language boots these experiences into new levels of fantasy and reflective potential.

9. Stories Are a Primary Act of Mind

Clinicians are very familiar with the concept of narrative structures as a central element in psychic life. Schafer (1992), most notably, has developed an extensive argument that psychanalytic work is, in part, the crafting and recrafting of stories.

Story telling and story making are ubiquitous in childhood. Narratives of varying complexity are a staple of parent–child dialogue. And there is plenty of evidence (e.g., Dunn, 1982, 1997; Kaye, 1982; Wells, 1986) that some aspects of narrative competence are reflective of differences in class, character, social power, and cultural specificity. Story reading turns out to have an expansive effect on children's social and linguistic competence, and these skills, as we have seen, are carriers of many children's theory of minds.

Stories also have a subtle but trenchant canonical aspect. They are an often delicious way in which normativity is elaborated seamlessly and unremarkably into daily life. This is yet another way to think of the term interpellation, as stories enable power relations and gender relations to become installed into psyche and into intersubjective processes between child and family, through scripts, schemes, and narratives.

Narratives, Bruner (1990) suggests, draw on four elements: an experience of agency[10]; a capacity for iteration or a sequence of repetitions; a sense of what is canonical (this is in reference to the social and to the physical world); and an experience of voice or perspective, an "I" who denotes. These narrative capacities, which are built on prior protolinguistic functions, become themselves aspects of other functions; that is, they are used rhetorically or descriptively. While all these aspects of speech use could become implicated and coordinated in a gender's strange-attractor regimen, it is perhaps most interesting to think of the experience of the "canonical" narrative or script as one conduit through which the unique but culturally laden aspects of gender may enter and disequilibrate an open system.

Nelson (1985) has studied the emergence of early forms of the canonical narrative in what she call "scripts." Scripts include narratives of how you go to school, what you do at birthday parties, how you sequence meals, family visits, indeed, scripts produce many of the rituals of social and domestic and institutional life. It is important to remember that narratives come with conventions of form (the arc, crisis, and denoument of a story) and conventions of meaning (moral tales, stories of consequence and responsibility) that, through speech practices and stories, become configured in subjectivities. There is the potential for multiple storylines, or for coercive, singular narratives with little flexibility in meaning, all dependent on and reflective of family and personal dynamics embedded in conventions of culture and place. Both in feminist and in queer theory writing, there has been a frank interest in resignifying, in structuring narratives with space for difference. These strategies are based on our appreciation of the great constitutive and constructive power of stories.

There is also fascinating evidence of the healing power of narrative, that is, evidence beyond the usual accounts of clinical outcome. We tend to view analytic adequacy in terms of the acquisition and acceptance of new narratives, new meanings, and new ways to tell one's story. But journaling in times of trauma (Pennebaker, 2003) and having opportunities to detail a story in the wake of accidents and rape (Bruner, 1990) organize experiences that are often so affectively overpowering as to be unrepresentable.

10. Speech Is Always Dialogic: Meaning Making Is Transpersonal

Chomsky's (1957, 1965) generative grammar focused developmental psycholinguistics on single minds and their astonishing capacities. But we now understand that one property of speech is its reversibility, its impact on speaker and listener. Self and other are necessarily implicated in any speech act; internalization takes as its referent a dialogue, a conversation.

Recently a patient described an experience she remembered from the time she was a quite young child caught up in a confusing and frightening experience with her mother. She was often told by her mother and grandmother that she (the child) was too critical, that *she* seemed so angry and rejecting of her mother. She was told that her mother's sense of her as a baby filled her (the mother) with fear and horror. Mysteriously but inexorably, it seemed, she was apparently a "bad" baby very early on. She remembers sitting on a bed with her mother. Her mother says to her, "You are turning on me." The adult

patient remembers thinking, even then, as a child, that there was something wrong with this communication, that she was being accused
wrongly. But, eerily, as she absorbed the words, she realized that they
were becoming true. She did feel herself withdrawing and turning away,
trying to protect herself from what she experienced as projection and
attack.

Over time, just as inexorably and eerily as in the initial communications from her mother, the meanings and the speech style became
aspects of the patient's internal world and aspects of her speech performances. The angry, paranoid voice over time became too seamlessly
her voice, particularly acute in times of impending loss and crisis. And
inevitably this voice came as a gendered voice, part of what the patient
felt to be an alarming and terrible part of her femininity. We can hear
in this the ideas of Bernstein (1993) on the harsh maternal superego.
Clearly, speech is transpersonally a vehicle for forms of identification
and forms of self-beratement.

Meaning is made in interaction. Winnicott's (1971) concept of transitional space as a site for creativity and self-structuring depends on this
weblike transpersonal aspect of speech. Even the apparently monologic
aspects of speech in self-regulation carry a dialogic history. Hectoring
internal voices, Fairbairnian (1952) persecutory or tantalizing objects—
all carry an object-relational history in remnants that can remain virulent in the voices of beratement and self-attack through which one
self-regulates.

By thinking of speech as dialogic and as multivoiced and by thinking of the constitutive power of narrative we are very much in the theoretical purview of Bakhtin (1986), the linguist who paid exquisite
attention to double voicedness, the subtle shifts in register and genre
that occur in speech. All these capacities for meaning making, for story
telling, for shape shifting, and for inhabiting and being multiple, grow
in the early speech processes of very young children.

CONCLUSION

Developmental psycholinguistics began with a powerful commitment
to the discovery and elaboration of the general skills that underlie speech.
Yet inexorably, as the field evolved, we have seen that speech must be
saturated with social relations, individual fantasies about self and other,

somatic states, and histories of attachment. Speech thus saturates and is saturated by experiences of gender, both intrapsychic and intersubjective. Speech comes in registers, in genres, and thus is uniquely equipped to express the high individuality of gendered life for any child. Both speaking and living a gender are deeply performative practices, reflective of the particular meaning of agency, communication, representation, and interaction for any particular and particularly gendered child.

My hope is that this toolkit opens us to new ideas of how genders and forms of desires emerge in multiple, layered, and overlapping contexts. Genderedness—as lived, felt, embodied categories of experience—becomes part of self-representation and shared, symbolically sustained meanings. Inevitably there will be an interrelationship of gender as a set of softly assembled attractors and speech and word meaning as recombinant, multiply configured categories. Word meanings and speech practice, on one hand, and gender experience, on the other, are hybrids of body state, affective wash, and cognitive scheme. And both can be productively understood as function driven rather than as universal or innate underlying structures.[11]

Toddlerhood and the development of speech and thought in childhood are key sites in the evolution of an indissoluble paradox in human life, a paradox implicating both speaking and being gendered. As a child enters the speech system and the sex-gender system, there is a seamless enmeshment of public and private life and therefore the interweaving of "true" and "false" selves, private and public personas, that will take a lifetime to sort out.

I have drawn on the concept of interpellation to refer to the moment (many moments, of course) when the culture, through some powerful person in the child's experience, says some version of, "Hey you." It is a moment, or rather a series of moments, of being claimed, and often named, and begins the blurred experience of being public and private, recognized and mislabeled. Language researchers and clinicians chart the other side of this process, the deeply creative and always partially successful ways a child avoids full domination through language use and play that absorbs and alters the "Hey you."

A conclusion that any clinician might come to in reviewing these linguistic findings is that, as the understanding of learning to speak influences, and is influenced by, theories of intentionality, attachment patterns, affect, intersubjectivity, and the social context, speech will begin

to reflect important indices of individual, familial, and cultural variation. Getting away from the tendency to see language and speech as *sui
generis* phenomena unrelated to personality and social formation is a
welcome change. It opens the possibility of a genuine interdisciplinary
conversation, one in which psychoanalysts, who attend so acutely to
distinctions in the use and function of speech, should be participating.

CHAPTER 10

Dynamic Skills Theory:
Relational Mourning
as Shared Labor

*I*n this chapter I explore the clinical implications of the cognitive developmental theory of Fischer (1980; Fischer et al., 1997; Fischer and Bidell, 1998; Fischer and Watson, 2002)—dynamic skills theory—as an application of chaos theory. A dynamic systems theoretical approach (here, dynamic skills theory) is used to examine the development of thought and feeling in the microprocesses of a family's mourning.

Kurt Fischer's dynamic skills theory, first introduced in 1980, is a highly elaborated theory of cognitive development. Like Thelen's nonlinear dynamic systems theory, this is theoretical work with a strong empirical base devoted to exploring the manifold and multidimensional developmental spaces in which cognition, social relatedness, and emotion coevolve. Dynamic skills theory focuses on the local, context-sensitive emergence of experience and capacities. Development, from the chaos theory perspective, never just takes place according to a blueprint with an already prescribed endpoint set from the beginning. Growth is not a matter of innate competences that set off various kinds of performance. This is a theory in which development is not reified into ladderlike stages. One of Fischer's most felicitous metaphors is that of a constructive web.

Fischer's model commits to the interdependence of thought and feeling. What he terms skill is an amalgam of affect, appraisal, and action. That these are related phenomena is something that clinicians know intimately. Thinking something requires some emotional robustness; sometimes it requires more emotional capacity than we have available. Affect states and anxieties can deform and constrict thought and representation. Dynamic skills theory is built to maintain the kind of relational complexity that analysts live and work with.

One of Fischer's projects entails tracing out how a child maps the complexity of relational and kinship roles within a family, a mapping with social, emotional, and cognitive consequences (Fischer et al., 1997). As a psychoanalyst, I translate a term like role to include identifications, both conscious and unconscious, and a wide variety of relational patterns and self–other constellations in varying permutations that become part of intrapsychic life as an outcome of interpersonal experience. An added bonus to this approach is to disentangle oedipal constellations from heterosexual orthodoxy (Fischer and Watson, 2002). The constellation of representations organized, remapped, and reorganized is based on particular local kinship arrangements, which may vary across history and across cultures.

These "skills" are similar to Susie Orbach's (1999) concept of emotional literacy, the child's tracking of the conditions, and (I would argue) the supportive skills of the surrounding adults that allow a child to know her or his experience with nuance, robustness, and complexity. The dialectical aspect of this model is vital. Thought and feeling coevolve with each other.

This is the terrain of Vygotsky (1962, 1978) and of Tomkins (1962, 1963, 1992), the (not-so-well-known) theorist of the impact of emotion on relatedness and cognition. Emotions are phenomenal states as well as intentional states. They have particular, unique feels and tones, and yet they are *about* something. One of the intriguing aspects of this theory is that we get to see the bones of cognition in the flesh of emotion, and we get to see how much emotion glues and potentiates or constricts cognition. Affect, appraisal, and action coproduce and interact with each other in a dynamic, open system. Affect, as Tomkins and others argue, has the most powerful amplifying effects on cognition.

One feature of this model worthy of our attention is the different ways body and mind are conceptualized. Thought and feeling will be body based whenever one holds a theory that sees skill as the outcome of action, affect, and appraisal. The young girl in the case I describe in this chapter was three when her father died. Her representations of him at that point were multimodal and complex but very strongly body based. Being picked up and held, being bathed and dressed—her memories of her father lived in somatic and sensory forms as well as in stories and narratives and more symbolic formations.

Fischer could be described as a neo-Piagetian. He is not the Piaget of reified stages. His theory is more a process and dialectical Piaget, the Piaget who focused on the movement into and out of states of equilibrium. Fischer's affinity for and elaboration of Piaget is clear in his ideas of developmental range, of optimal and functional levels, and of gaps and ruptures in the growth of uneven masteries, of a dynamic mind in which feeling and thought both have the possibility of expanding or distorting each other. Fischer's (Fischer and Bidell, 1998) metaphor for the developmental process is of a web, not a ladder. Because there are multiple pathways through this web, with variations in how things are synchronized and how they are sequenced, this is a model wide enough and complex enough for the kinds of clinical data we routinely deal with.

Within Fischer's model, development proceeds along multiple pathways with many experiences occurring in particular domains. While there is an increasing capacity for integration, how well the "natural fractionating" mind knits together depends on many local, social, contextual factors. For Fischer, dissociation is not inherently pathological but, rather, a part of the skilled construction with which a child adapts to particular, demanding contexts. This view of dissociation as skill is important in thinking about grief, for example, or the conditions that permit a person to know pain and accept loss. In this process, one sees immediately how dependent thinking is on feeling. Mourning is often a matter of skilled pacing, titrating what is absorbable in manageable ways and moving through shock to new forms of knowing and representing.

Fischer describes stages in the child's emerging action and context-based capacities to know and inhabit roles and relationships. In psychoanalysis, we appreciate this capacity as part of the child's developing theory of mind. This capacity has been linked to the parent's ability to think and feel and bear complexity. From Bion (1962) and most recently from Fonagy and Target (1996, 1997; Fonagy et al., 2002), the capacity of parents to absorb projections or to metabolize them are seen to be the prerequisites for children's representational capacities. Translated into skills theory, this is the capacity of parents to bear representations of children's wishes, to know their children with all their complexity and nuance. Analysts make an important distinction between knowing someone and colonizing them.

Much recent focus in psychoanalysis has been on the complex experience of intersubjectivity, the process through which, gradually and only perhaps always partially, the distinctions of self and other and the representations of self and other as objects and as subjects are worked out (Benjamin and Aron, 1999; Gerhardt, Sweetnam, and Borton, 2000). Through many processes—attachment, the management of aggression and affective states, the establishment of differences alongside connection, the growing awareness of the other's mind and intentions—a child can come to know the limits and dangers of a colonizing intelligence of other people he or she lives in relation to and the uniqueness of all minds, including his or her own.

REPRESENTATIONS OF LOSS

The clinical material in this chapter is about the difficulties that children and adults have in mourning and accepting death. Death and loss always present cognitive and emotional challenges requiring a significant developmental leap. The severity of this developmental demand is captured in the distinction Freud (1917) made between mourning and melancholia. In melancholy, remnants of denial and continuing idealization of the lost love remain as a kind of haunting. Mourning is, most agonizingly, the work to accept death's finality and to metabolize the experience of loving and losing a significant person into a deep, loving, and loveable aspect of the self. Mourning, in these terms, is a kind of double loss. Finally, Freud argued, in the resolution of an act of mourning, even the vitality of the memorialized other is absorbed into the self. Only then is the mourner free to love again, though not without some lingering melancholic strain.

We have good psychoanalytic theory (Bion, 1962; Cain and Fast, 1973; Abraham and Torok, 1994; Fonagy et al., 1997, 1998; Britton, 1999; Benjamin and Aron, 1999) on the relation among mourning, the depressive position, the emergence of reflective functioning, and the capacity to tolerate the unknowable, unacquirable subjectivity of the other. We can infer the difference between mourning and melancholia is a difference in cognitive state, in capacities for abstraction or concreteness, in dissociation and disavowal, all deeply related to shared emotion and joint action.

Melancholy has the odd effect of foreclosing acceptance of loss by maintaining the bereaved person in a suspended state and being unable to invest love and attachment in new experiences and relationships. In melancholic grieving, the lost love is memorialized but also kept "alive" imaginatively and in fantasy. Abraham and Torok (1994) capture this process in what they term "the fantasy of the exquisite corpse," the potent conviction that the lost other is perfectly preserved somewhere, waiting to be found. These fantasies bind the mourner into an endless and sometimes endlessly self-berating transitional state, tied to the living dead, as Green (1970) describes in the case of the "dead mother."

What is required of a person to represent the lost object as lost? This is deep psychic work, entailing a thought process utterly dependent on emotional capacities in oneself and one's surrounding communities and family. There is a complex interweaving of melancholy and mourning, a shift from a state of acceptance to one of denial, an interweaving of fantasy and reality. Melancholic presences, nostalgia, and ghostly, sweet presences enrich psychic life. They are necessary and creative respites from the grueling ordeal of mourning.

In the case I describe, certain kinds of melancholic preoccupations—suspending reality for imaginative longing—were particularly crucial for the child's developing capacities to absorb loss. In fascinating ways children slide across symbolic and imaginary modes of thinking (see Fonagy and Target, 1997, 2003) on the movement between types of psychic reality, real and pretend). I suspect adults in the particularly acute stages of grief move into and out of the same kinds of unstable psychic spaces, often including a kind of double consciousness, a knowing and not knowing about the permanence of loss through death.

CLINICAL MATERIAL

I have been working with the mother of a three-year-old and a one-year-old, a family who lost their husband/father, who worked on a high floor in the second tower of the World Trade Center. Coming into therapy a month after 9/11, Pam was concerned with how to shape things for her children, Sarah and Catherine. Together we thought of our process as a way to find a space to hold memory and complexity for herself and her family. The work of Hofer (1984, 1995, 1996) on the biological consequences of bereavement seem particularly relevant in this case. The loss was to a family bound in close physical ties with a newborn, with the entraining sleep cycles and bodily interactions of parents, infant, and toddler. Loss was being registered at a quite material, creaturely level. It is a loss that, at the very least, will become part of the procedural memory within the family.

In the clinical material that follows I track both Pam's work to mourn and the work to steady and open spaces for her children, particularly her older daughter. One might think of her determination to have her children survive well, not to be damaged irreparably by the death of their father, as a complex mix of identification with her determined active husband and her own character and intersubjective history.

Pam's husband Chris had spoken to her twice after the first plane hit. He told her that others were leaving his floor but he was staying. She remembers urging him to "run." After the second tower was hit, she was never able to reach him on the phone again. Her initial shock response was to pack a suitcase and have a neighbor take a picture of her and the girls that might be shown to him if he were in a hospital.

Pictures are part of the way this family was to build and facilitate the complex representation of a father who was lost but whose influence and presence persist. After a very few days, she accepted that this fantasy of a man without memory or speech and lying on a hospital gurney somewhere was an empty hope. She described the unpacking of that suitcase as excruciatingly difficult. That act was perhaps the first representation of death. She did not want phone calls in the first weeks because she could not protect herself from the thought that it was he. Fantasy and reality ran alongside each other. Grieving, perhaps long term and certainly in the short term, entails living with some permeability in the boundaries between the experiences of life and death. In dreams, in fantasies, in some conscious representations, there are levels of "reality." Real, pretend, really real, and wished-for imagining all co-exist, coming in and out of focus for children and adults.

We are learning from studies of children with separation anxieties and traumatic loss how dependent their reactions are on the reactions of their parents, in particular on the parents' capacities to contain intense and terrifying affects (Bowlby, 1960; Frankiel, 1995; Fonagy and Target, 2000, 2003; Coates, Rosenthal, and Schechter, 2003). Pam had the daunting task of protecting her children from emotional flooding and from the anxieties that they might lose her to depression. She had to reach out and create means of expression for their feelings, while in great emotional agony herself.

I am going to draw on the work of Coates and her colleagues (Coates, Schechter, and First, 2003) at the Kid's Corner at Pier 94, where they interacted with and supported children and families who had lost family members in the World Trade Center attack. Out of their observations and interventions we have learned of the complexity of knowing and not knowing about the fate and death of someone in one's family. Coates and her coworkers describe many striking examples of the children's acute capacities to sense and understand what had happened to their lost parents. These capacities for imagination, reflection, and curiosity were not always recognized by the survivors. The opportunity to represent and give voice to losses and their unique and complex meanings needs a context. Parental mourning can shape the potential for integration or dissociation, as a child explores feelings, questions, and stray fantasies, however odd or unsettling.

Pam's is a somewhat religious family, and so her first way of representing and speaking with her children about the loss of their father was to make a mental, imaginative space called heaven, which interestingly was imagined as a space up high. This image seemed to me to carry the memory that Chris was on a very high floor but also captured this husband/father's function as overseeing and protecting. Pam, who is both spiritual and secular, made a "heaven" for herself and for the children. It was a Winnicottian transitional space surely, constructed and evolved through the talk and play of the family. It demanded of Pam a doubled consciousness of presence and absence, the kind of dual representations Fischer (in Fischer and Bidell, 1998) proposes as aspects of representations in transition.

Sarah, the three-year-old, has taken to this idea very intensely. She holds up pictures she is drawing for her father to see. She sings to him. She speaks to him. On her mother's birthday, she announced this news to her father. Throughout this early period, Sarah and her mother have talked about the father, the mother both eliciting and scaffolding memories.

Chris was a young father, highly enthusiastic about parenting, who had an active hands-on involvement with his children. He had taken his three-year-old to the rained-out Yankee game the night before the attack. This seemed to me a very telling detail. The game in question was widely seen as an important one, because the star pitcher, Roger Clemens, was expected to get his 20th win of the season. Dad was bringing his daughter to see this event. He expected to meet her after her first day at school. Sarah often speaks to him during her walk to school. From the beginning, there were many daily events in which his presence and participation must be remarked on, represented, and then represented as absent.

The family had traveled extensively, and now the mother and child revisit that last summer trip in conversations in which the child produces some details of narrative—"Daddy went for coffee across the street"—and the mother elaborates and scaffolds the child's experience. I use the term scaffold to evoke Vygotsky's (1962) zone of proximal development, his conception that developmental progression is facilitated by adult or parental aid and structure. This is an idea Fischer (1980) has also developed and that he terms bridging, the use of the structuring work of others to aid the child in integration and constructing higher level skills.

Pam is drawing on the natural forms of conversation that parents and children use as complex symbolic language comes online developmentally (Locke, 1993). Nelson (1985) uses the term scripts to describe the little scenes and stories that parents build with children to expand their children's knowledge and repertoire.

Pam and Sarah make a web of meanings and memories, the mother holding or elaborating the three-year-old's more fragmentary memories. Representations are mapped and woven in narratives and systems of meaning, and clearly this has enormous emotional resonance for mother and child. It must also be a very complex experience for Sarah, for these conversations and story tellings she is engaged in with her mother animate and sadden both of them. From the beginning of their mourning, holding together the experience of sadness and great love has been vivid in Pam's representations of her husband's death. It is an experience that contains enormous emotional demands. Over time, strikingly, Pam has made space for the children to join her and to be differentiated from her.

Green (1970), writing about the "dead mother," makes clear that he is speaking of a mother not actually dead but dead to her child. Caught up in a bereavement, the child finds her mother's vitality reserved for and channeled toward the lost object. Pam's daunting task was to express the deep engagement with her lost husband in a way that safely included her children, all the while firmly embedding them in a living world with her. There is the multiple consciousness of processing what is lost, what endures, and what thrives. There is the task of coordinating witnessing for others and making space for those aspects of loss that are contained in that part of the self Winnicott (1963) termed *incommunicado*, private but not isolated. There is the need to balance self and other. These dimensions of grief bring to mind the term relational mourning.

Pam has been worried about how to bring her younger child into this process. How will this girl bond without the shared experience of remembering, loving, and losing? She has put many pictures of her husband around the apartment, and certainly he is spoken of freely and frequently. Pam came across a picture of the baby taken from the front seat of the car when they were on a summer family outing. She saw how much this child looks like her father, and she wrote on the back, "This is what your father saw when he looked at you." These pictures and many other things Pam is saving are consciously thought of as material for the girls as they grow up. This particular representation of a father to a child who has had such slender direct experience of her father is very interesting to me. Pam is, in a sense, offering to her child a vision of a father who held her in mind, a vision of a parent who could recognize her, who thought about her. With each developmental milestone for both girls, Pam will evoke the pride and delight the father would have been feeling.

One day, still very early in the fall, Pam and Sarah, her older child, were still having a series of "When is he coming home" questions and answers. Sarah was in her bath, perhaps a setting where bodily memories of her father's presence could be conjured up, and she asked her oft-repeated question. The mother answered simply but with tears that he can't come home, that he was injured. She also said how much she wishes he could come back. Sarah then began to sing and clap and make up a song, "Daddy not coming back." It was a very complex moment. A defense against mother's affect? An anxious mastery? I am impressed (as I am much of the time in this treatment) by the mother's ability to tolerate all the modalities her child uses to absorb this new reality. Pam has been able to let Sarah find a modality to represent her experience, an experience that has its own history, a resonance with her mother's but also some difference. It may be that the game and song is a way to titrate the mother's affect, to be with her but not flooded.

One evening Sarah asked her mother if there is a door in heaven. The mother, somewhat uncertainly, said, "Yes, there could be." The child then said, "Well, if there is a door, couldn't Daddy open it and run out?" My thinking is that she has held in mind her mother's alarmed command to her husband to "Run," something she said to him on the phone on the day of the attack. Sarah seems to have held that intense, affect-laden expression and integrated the detail with what she also knows of her athletic, vital father. He is represented, even in heaven, as he was in life. Working with experience she has held from the beginning of this trauma, Sarah is trying to work out what is possible and what is not. This seems to me precisely the hard work of mourning.

But later Sarah saw a dead squirrel on the road and asked what was the matter with it. Now the concepts of dead, heaven, injured came up again. How would she parse out these competing representations? Is her father dead like that squirrel? Her mother answered briefly and, as she does on other occasions, focused the child on happy memories of the father. Pam, who is attuned to her own use of language and its impact on others, tells me she is trying to be careful with verb tenses. She has over and over to make decisions about what is spoken of as past and what as ongoing. How subtle these representations of the father and their family situation are.

Mother and child are beginning to coordinate experiences initially mapped distinctly. Animals, running, dying, father, husband. These representations have elements that can barely be tolerated as integrated ideas. This is cognitive work, of course, but there are critical and intense emotional and social braces that must undergird these thoughts. The conception or representation of Daddy—husband and father—is very complexly living and not living, injured and whole, remembered and missing. We might see this as a kind of semantic strange attractor, volatile, disequilibrating, and filled with elements and ideas and feelings that are terrible to tolerate in an ensemble.

In this family, there is a representation of a continuing father who loved, encouraged, protected. Robert Pynoos (2001), discussing the impact on a child of the violent loss of a parent, describes that loss as the tearing off of a parental shield, a loss of a protective capacity. Pam conjures a protective husband/father for herself and her daughters, a theme of ongoing love and pride, but also alongside this is a representation of her continuing sadness at his loss (Hamilton, 1989).

As weeks go by, Pam is clearly taking on that protective role herself, using memory and representation to make a protective shield for herself and offering it to the children. Often the image of parental protection appears in dreams and in action as an arm wrapped around a shoulder. One day at lunch when Pam found herself tearful Sarah put her arm around her sister and said "Mommy, Catherine and I miss Daddy, but we are not crying." Sarah is almost like an adult in the way she talked and in the protection she offered her younger sister.

For Pam it is important to represent both love and loss, so she acknowledges that she is crying and in simple terms she tells the girls why. Later she found herself crying as she walks down the street. Then she imagined Chris holding her hand and putting his arm around her. Often in her fantasies of him he is encouraging her, telling her he is proud of her. This is calming. Later, in session, as she is weeping and telling me these experiences, she remembers the girls holding hands in the back seat of the van when her husband was driving, and she feels soothed.

More and more she is the competent protector. She is the driver, in the front seat. After a difficult day and troubled sleep she had the first dream in which her husband appeared. In the dream he said to her, "Who will we give the crib to?" She reminded him whom it belongs to. In our session she associates to the girls growing, to the question of who will disassemble the crib. But the dream is set as a scene in the future when the one-year-old has outgrown her crib. This is a future she can only sometimes carry her husband into. Also hidden in the dream is the realization that there will be no more babies, and, although this was their plan, that idea now holds her grief and sense of loss.

There are complex layers of protection and containment operating. One of my containing functions, I believe, is to tolerate myself and to help Pam tolerate the deep contradictions and rapid shifts in her states. One minute she is a highly competent parent; the next minute she feels numbed and bereft. She is genuinely grateful for the outpourings of help, yet she can resent and feel swamped by these gestures. She may be angry at the indifference in the world or awed at the smooth ease of intact families.

Shopping in a supermarket late one evening, she found herself weeping as she walked through the aisles. She noticed someone looking at her and shouted angrily, "I am crying because my husband died, OK?" We decided that under the circumstances it was all right to shout in Gristede's. People have doubtless shouted in the grocery store before. Perhaps she will shout there or somewhere else again. We are making complex representational spaces, jointly imagined scenes and narratives, in which a kaleidoscope of feelings, wishes, and thoughts can coexist.

The capacity and opportunity for the children to know is encouraged but not, I think, made an obsession. And there are limits. There are certain doors shut in Pam and in me. In the first year of Pam's grieving, we rarely talk about the circumstances of her husband's death or of what happened after the second plane hit, an event she saw on television but one she cannot yet represent or map and integrate with other representations of him.

One of the most useful of Fischer's (Fischer et al., 1997) conceptions of development is seeing dissociation as a skilled adaptation not a pathological regression. Pam's process of mourning has its own timeline. Mourning, perhaps inevitably, has multiple timelines and multiple narrative sequences. Some aspects of the death of Pam's husband and the losses are sequestered. Some experiences have been fresh and intense from the beginning. And, paradoxically, as Pam moves into the world, takes up tasks, and begins new work projects, new experiences open new aspects of loss and fresh understandings of the degree of devastation. In the early months she experienced missing her husband during the quotidian domestic work of child care. She wishes, at a most concrete but deeply emotional level, for an extra pair of hands loading the van or shepherding children to their activities. These activities were undertaken in conditions of great shock, when very basic facts were still too raw to absorb. Later she has had to organize the experiences of being dressed in business clothes or going to a meeting without him as a dinner companion, as someone she would be meeting up with after work. She walks on the street looking with longing at couples dining in restaurants. Paradoxically, as the shock wears off, there is the more exacting cognitive/emotional demand of integrating the representation of her own survival and her loss. The mappings become more complex as Pam lives and functions in multidimensional spaces and often has to move along multiple timelines.

At Christmas, when the time came to hang the stockings, Sarah wanted to include one for her father. Together mother and child imagined the scene: tree, stockings, presents. In the morning when they speak of the stockings, Sarah asked if there would be presents for Daddy. Pam decided to say no, that Daddy is in heaven and is not able to be with them. Then she asked if the child thought that her daddy has a stocking in heaven. The child said "No." The interesting question here is what fantasy is tolerable and what is not? Does the closing of imaginative space—my father is here and we could open his stocking—shut down the child? Is there a loss that eclipses fantasy, a moment when sadness and pain break through? Pam and Sarah had made a transitional space in which the father could participate in this ritual. Had that space collapsed for the child? Or was the image of stockings in heaven too abstract for the child to represent?

Several months later a powerful episode took place at the doorway to the family apartment. There were sounds in the hallway, and Sarah went to the door with her sister. She said to a neighbor passing in the hallway, "Catherine thinks when there is noise in the hallway that Daddy is coming back. I know he isn't 'cause he was in World Trade Two." Pam scooped up the children and told her neighbor ruefully that she hoped she was not too freaked out. She felt a little embarrassed but, as she and I work in the session on this experience, we can talk of the skill displayed in this fractionated organization.

An aspect of mourning that is worth thinking about here is the odd ways that shame can accrue to loss. Pam has some worries about how she is seen, what people make of her experience and the children's. Our work has been to support and contain her intuitive capacities to let the children feel and speak. She and I talk about the individuality of mourning, the deep privacy of personal grief, its unique forms and meanings. Often we try to hold together the incredible contradictions in this experience. Sarah may have projected a hope she fears is baby-ish into her little sister and kept for herself what she feels is a more grownup experience. Pam says at the end of the session, "But that is me too. I have those thoughts. I have that split in me." Dissociation is a skill, Fischer (Fischer et al., 1997) argues. Splitting is a crucial aspect of the psychic work of mourning. Bearing absolute loss must be dosed, particularly with children, whose narrative memories of the lost parent must be simultaneously built and grieved. Insight and reality are won and lost hour by hour, day by day.

Pam accepts and organizes these contradictory states in which Sarah oscillates. But part of this reflective capacity is to see the con-tinuing aspects of denial and disbelief and the slow pace of accepting reality. Loss remains known and not known, held and resisted by her and by Sarah. Pam lives in a kind of double consciousness. At one level of representational mapping, Pam knows of this split. There is a nonlinearity to this process. Dramatic shifts in consciousness wax and wane. One feature of this shifting, even adaptive, dissociation occurs in Pam's experience of time. Sometimes there seems to be no future, only an endless, repeating, numb present. There is a rich past approached with longing and with pain, but it is a past also used to bear the present. Sometimes, for Pam, it is the future that seems long and endlessly empty. There are glimpses of potentials to come, unknowns that could be in-teresting. There is Pam's body state and body ego, which can feel to her sometimes static and sometimes living and vital. Bromberg's (1998a, 1999) work on shifting self-states and dissociation seems relevant here. Pam has the particularly arduous task of standing between and within starkly distinct and conflictual self spaces.

There is in Pam a sensitivity to the children's pacing. This is a family that grieves yet lives. Children go on play dates, spend weekends with family and friends. They have lessons and do sports. Pam had determined to spend these early years as a young family primarily at home, and she now orchestrates those old plans with the needs for some more child care and more time for herself. Sarah learned to ride a bike this year and to do cannonballs at the lake near the family vacation home. The youngest child, who was still breastfeeding on September 11, is an active toddler, so there are time-outs and plenty of moments of exasperation.

Pam has the normal exhaustion of a mother of young children. But her exhaustion is also shaped by the extreme psychological demands on her. One day, as Pam was recounting a particularly ragged week for herself and the children, it was clear that part of the raggedness came from the particular and terrible pain of emptying a chest of drawers that held Chris's clothing. This task brought her back to a more intimate connection with his body, stirring up a lot of memory and sadness. My role here was as protector and as guide, helping her to make a space for herself, for the unique and delicate feelings that can arise, almost without warning, from the many expected and unexpected tasks of mourning.

Throughout the work with Pam I have been very mindful of the thin line between the living and the dead that exists in the representations of loss in early stages. In an early dream, Pam was set to walk down a nearby street. Her husband appears to tell her not to walk there. When I asked her about this street, she told me it was very desolate and even dangerous, and we talked about her sense of having, in her husband, a guide through a desolate path. Talking about this dream then reminded her of an experience in her local playground. She had arranged a play date and then had gone with a father and his child to have pizza. The playground stirred up sadness and anger in Pam. She watched other children playing with the fathers, particularly in the kind of roughhouse play she associated with her husband. Anger is not prominent in Pam's experiences and reveals itself most usually in the context of watching or interacting with people or families whose lives have gone on, relatively undisturbed. She is angry at feeling caught up in and by a historical event she wanted no part of.

At the pizza restaurant, surrounded by intact families, Pam feels tearful. She imagines Chris sitting close, talking quietly into her ear, comforting her. Her tears fall and she sees that the father who is sitting with her is discomfited. She looks away but does not banish the fantasy or her feelings. Her anecdote makes me think of Loewald's (1980) deeply imaginative sense of the interweaving of fantasy and reality. In the process of mourning there is (perhaps always to some degree) simultaneously the need for acceptance and for creative denial. Chris "lives" as a voice in her ear, a presence at her shoulder; and at the same time he is dead and she is grieving.

Around the six-month anniversary, Pam goes to have a drink with some neighboring firemen. She has wanted to ask about the conditions of death by smoke inhalation. A door is opening as she begins to try to represent the circumstances of her husband's death. What the firemen tell her brings some relief. One of them describes loss of consciousness and a process of dying that is more peaceful and contained than the fantasies or images of burning, of falling, of pulverized, bodies. Pam had begun to worry about the details of her husband's last hours, sometimes thinking and sometimes not thinking about what had happened. Throughout these ruminations she was most haunted by what she imagined to be his fear in those last moments. The idea that loss of consciousness precedes death by smoke inhalation brought her relief. At the same time, she is aware that she is practicing some denial. She approaches these matters at her own pace.

As they were sitting and enjoying some wine, one of the men leaned back and raised his arm behind his head. Pam tells me that she felt a rush, a suddenly unexpected and startling twinge of pleasure. She gasped inwardly. Flesh, male arm, muscle. (She and I are laughing when she tells me this.) Then she walked back to her own apartment, smiling, a little buzzed. At home, seeing a picture of her husband, she immediately begins to sob. She describes "tumbled feelings." As we sit together in the session, our eyes fill with tears.

Pam is moving through complex contradictory representational states. She has to organize a system of representations with yes and no, bodily death and bodily life. There is a fascinating trajectory in this episode. What to think of the sequence of increased knowledge that allows her to imagine her husband's bodily death, a reaction of arousal to a new, living body, and then back to grief? Desire arises from the ashes and opens one again to pain and loss. No linear-stage model could do justice to the complexity and asynchrony of this process. The shifts in state and thought are paralleled in our session. Weeping can quickly follow laughter. Chaos theory, nonlinear dynamic systems, dynamic skills theory—these models are capacious enough for this degree of complexity.

As the process evolves for this family, there is increasingly a nuanced appreciation of sameness and difference. Pam is sensitive to what is not shared as much as she creates a space for connection and shared knowing. After the family had been out listening to some music, Sarah was jumping around, playing air guitar and making up a country and western type song about her daddy. Picking up on the song Sarah is inventing, Pam said that she "really, really" missed her husband and that she "really, really" loved him. Her daughter paused and then responded, "I don't *really really* miss Daddy. I just really miss Daddy. That's because I love you, and you didn't die." Pam was startled but attentive. Sarah is noticing an important difference between her experience and her mother's. Her loss and her mother's are not identical. Different perspectives and different subjectivities are dawning here, and Pam makes space for this new evolution.

In doing this work, I think mostly of my ability to create a setting for such affect-laden thought, the hard work of mourning. Mourning, I try to convey to Pam, is, in part, a matter of pacing. A friend said to her, "Your world did not end." And Pam and I talk together about how this is true and yet not true. She often finds great difficulty in simply representing how she is. She is fine. She is not fine. A world did end. A planned world of that foursome did end. A new family goes on. And Pam goes on or, as she says, "endures." She needs to allow for multiple spaces for the representation of systems—roles, relationships—that are often not synchronous. She is living in multiple timelines, along multiple narratives and inhabiting multiple psychic spaces.

As you might imagine, I am often tearful in sessions. The skill of grieving—of bearing the thought, of knowing loss—is made possible by someone else who creates space for your thoughts. Empathy and "sharing" are not exactly the right words. Empathy is here an imaginative construction that includes my own history of losses. Thinking in this way, employing the skills of representation, requires a landscape of others' emotions in addition to your own. I make kaleidoscopic space with Pam, or, to use Fischer's (Fischer and Bidell, 1998) metaphor, Pam and her family and Pam and I construct a web of meanings. But I am aware how much my colleagues hold open a complex landscape and constructive web for me. A skill like grieving, with its strange asynchronies and integrations, takes collective work as well as individual emotional and cognitive labor.

Many aspects of human functioning make this work difficult. There is the shaky status of subjectivity itself, the permeability of boundaries and identifications. Grieving requires that the intensity of that love object be held in mind together with a comparable sense of loss (see the discussions of safety and danger in long-term relationships in Mitchell (2001). This act of great vulnerability requires a representation that is perhaps inherently unstable, prone to disorganization and fracture, and filled with contradictions.

Fifteen months after Chris's death, Pam and her daughter left a holiday party. In a quiet, contemplative moment of a shared reverie on the ride home, Sarah said, "Mom, I want to say 'Dad.'" What does she mean, exactly, her mother wondered. "I want to say 'Dad' and have Dad pick me up." Pam realized that amid the active party Sarah probably watched a number of children ask to be picked up by their fathers. Pam said she missed Chris too and wished he was there to talk to. They drove home in the dark.

In that very affectively charged communication, Sarah did something that I believe is quite extraordinary. She was able to represent a wish, an envious feeling about the happiness of others, a lost hope, and a memory. Included in the memory was a sense of herself and her father that was embodied. When Pam and I discuss this experience, we remember another incident when Sarah asked her mother tearfully how tall her father was. Implicated in that question was a memory of being very small and holding her father's hands and having him support her while she walked up his body and sat on his shoulders. Somehow her tears are coming from her struggle to remember and reimagine that experience. What is represented as "Dad" is a body to climb on, an experience of being held and lifted, a unique kind of semantic sensory attractor.

Recently, an analysand told me ruefully, "I made an executive decision not to feel longings." The potential for disappointment, for pain, and for shame is too dangerous. Sarah does not have to make such an "executive decision." Because her surviving parent absorbs, tolerates, and thinks about her child's experiences, Sarah has the confidence that her expressions will meet with empathy and containment. As a consequence, her capacities to think with feelings are expanding. Affect enmeshed with cognitive schemes is among the core aspects of subjectivity. Sarah's subjectivity is becoming multifaceted and manifold.

In our theories and in our culture, we often speak of closure and working through. We have a concept of pathological mourning as somehow protracted and interminable. But the longevity of grief needs more distinctions. A supervisee describes a case about which she frequently feels so hopeless. A woman in early middle age remains suspended and remote from any personal intimate life. Her interior world seems haunted, magical, vampiric. Her father died suddenly and unexpectedly when she was four, and from that moment his name was never mentioned and all pictures disappeared. She never saw a picture of herself with her father until she was an adult.

Recently, Pam provided me with a different example of the long shadow of parental loss. She ran across an old friend, also a woman in early middle age. The woman had approached Pam to offer condolences and to tell her that she, like Sarah, had lost her father when she was very young. Pam watched her friend's face and said to her that what her friend told her has relieved her greatly because the woman's face had been lit up and emotionally opened when she said "my father." For Pam that meant that love for a father could survive over a lifetime. To Pam's surprise, her friend wept, agreeing that something in that phrase and those memories was still deeply important to her.

Here we can see Hofer's (1984, 1995) "hidden regulators," the powerful affects and somatic resonances, evidence for which surfaced in the particular way the words "my father" triggered states in the speaker and in the listener. Think of Margaret Little's (1985) frank statement, "Mourning is for life." We also see what Litowitz (2001), Olds (2000), and others find so useful in the semiotics approach. Here words have iconic, embodied, and index effects along with the more expectable symbolic features.

Of course, grieving is never solely a matter of a person's character or strength or heroism. When I think of what contributes to Pam's particular capacities, a number of things come to mind. She felt herself to be in a genuinely good and auspicious marriage. She married in maturity, after a satisfying, interesting, and varied professional life. She has sometimes worried about the sin of pride, the secret feelings of great good luck in her marriage. She and her husband were feeling confident of themselves as parents of a young family. She lived within a strong and supportive extended and immediate family. Before 9/11 she felt herself to be living a coherent, narratizable life. It is paradoxical, but certainly true that, when you have to hold a terrible rupture in life, the goodness and coherence of the lost past may be easier to hold, despite the rupture, than would be a past shaped by disappointment or difficulty. There are dangers of idealization and nostalgia that suspend current existence in an endless melancholy, but I have tried to argue here that one of the multiplicities in grieving is to hold the melancholy preservation of the lost love alongside the work of representing loss.

Another aspect of her mourning work is that, from the very first day of 9/11, Pam wrote. She kept journals. She wrote in a kind of epistolary form to her husband. He continued to be her interlocutor in this text for months. Bruner (1990) and Pennebaker (2003), among others, have studied the mutative and containing power of journals, narratives, and writing. Held by the mentalizing capabilities of others (including her therapist), Pam also inhabited her own networks of mentalization, creative representations, and constructions of what was happening to her and what it meant.

In what helped Pam bear her and her family's experiences, there is the important phenomenon of a vast and intense public representation of the catastrophe in which Pam's husband was killed. This is part of the relational field in which grieving and mourning are potentiated. There has been a distinct and imaginative public capacity to mentalize loss and absence. Although Pam was not active in the public activities around 9/11 and its aftermath, she may have benefited (although ambivalently) from the public expressions of loss and outrage. Many losses are not held in the collective mind. And some losses are held ambivalently. Think of the public silences in the wake of Vietnam. And loss through divorce or other kinds of social ruptures is often not collectively imagined in the same way or with the same degree of sympathy as 9/11.

In Pam's experience there are layers of holding environments for her and for her family, and in the clinical context there are holding environments for me. Yet, with all these relational webs and layered mentalizations, what Pam faces is excruciatingly difficult to bear. In a certain way, I have potentially set an idealized vision of how to mourn or to enable children to mourn. I think this vision may distort the enormous variety of pathways through grief and the huge psychic demands of Pam's situation. Many aspects of human functioning make this work very difficult.

In Pam's family there is a constructed web of representations of many experiences. The father, who is at the center of many of these representations, is energetic, loving, and vital. Grief here requires that the intensity of that love object be held together with a comparable intensity of loss. This requires a representation that is perhaps inherently unstable, prone to disorganization and fracture, and filled with contradictions. One sees here the intense degree of context dependence in emergent thought. A covering layer of mentalizations ring and contain the children in this family as they struggle to come to terms with their father's death. Progress is nonlinear and context dependent.

A GRIEVABLE LIFE:
RELATIONAL CONTEXTS OF MOURNING

This clinical experience has made me think of the work of Butler (2000b, 2003) on what makes for a "grievable" life. For a number of clinicians and mental health workers (Coates et al., 2003), the terrible experience and aftermath of 9/11 has necessitated a focus on mourning and trauma. From this tragedy has come the possibility of extending our understanding of the stress on families and children to other situations, other children at risk (see Cournos, 2003, on the foster care system) and other situations of loss.

Butler's (1990) work on gender centers on the particular fate of disavowed loss. She has extended this question to grief for AIDs deaths, and to mourning more generally. Hence her question, What makes a grievable life? The answer is that it must be narratizable, coherent, recognized, not disavowed. To connect to the psychoanalytic theories explored here, the life and subjectivity must be mentalized within narrow as well as wide relational nets. Individual representations of loss are aided by a mentalizable social surround, relational contexts that honor the depth and complexity of losing someone beloved.

Melancholy is an aspect of grief. Melancholy can, of course, represent sidetracked and blocked grieving, grieving distorted because the loss and often the love that underwrites loss has been disavowed. But melancholy is also the site of imagination, fantasy, and passion. It is an integral set of elements in the nonlinear project of bearing loss. Lost or absent objects are softly assembled, mixing the concrete, the imaginary, the symbolic. Such representations are complex, fractal, and nonlinear and are braced or disavowed in the transpersonal worlds of the mourner.

Endnotes

INTRODUCTION

1. The relation of feminism to relational theory is intriguing. Do both partake of a common change in our social-intellectual landscape? Aron (1996) has argued that the influence is more direct, that many feminist ideas were an integral part of constructing the relational approach. It is also worth noting that Mitchell's (1978, 1981) earliest writing was a very sophisticated reclamation of a psychoanalytic and nonmoralizing approach to homosexuality (see Chodorow, 2002b, for a discussion of this work).

2. Relational theory (Greenberg and Mitchell, 1983; Mitchell, 1988, 1993, 1997; Mitchell and Aron, 1999) is at the center of a debate about what can be construed as a paradigm shift within psychoanalysis. Certainly relational theory evolved in connection with compatible movements in philosophy and social theory.

The relational perspective has inspired theoretical and clinical innovation in practice (Hoffman, 1992; Renik, 1993; Aron, 1996; Gerson, 1996; Pizer, 2000), models of mind (Bromberg, 1991, 1994, 1998a; Spezzano, 1993; Davies, 1996a, 1998a) the nature and function of gender (Dimen, 1991; Goldner, 1991; Harris, 1991, 1996a, b; Benjamin, 1988), of sexuality (Davies, 1998a, b; Dimen, 1995a, 1999), the status of psychoanalytic knowledge and action (Ghent, 1989, 1992b; Pizer, 1990, 1998; Ehrenberg, 1992: Gabbard, 1994, 1995; Hoffman, 1998; Mitchell and Aron, 1999), and ways to consider the body (Aron and Anderson, 1998).

3. This work, inevitably influenced by my training and my temperament, is a project that crosses intellectual worlds and languages in attempting to hold in focus both psyche and society. Chodorow's (1999) work on the power of personal meaning draws on her coordinated and braided history as a psychoanalyst and a sociologist-anthropologist. My parent disciplines are developmental psychology and psycholinguistics, areas that make an important synthesis with psychoanalytic theory and clinical work.

4. Piaget is a complex figure. He is associated with quite reified state theories but also with a dialectic model for changes in thinking. Figures in the Piagetian dialectic tradition, less well known to contemporary psychoanalysts, are Sylvan Tomkins (1962, 1963, 1992) (an influence on some of the researchers of face-to-

face play in infancy, such as Ekman [1994, 1997] and a figure reintroduced to psychoanalysis by Virginia Demos [1992a, b]), Arnold Sameroff (1983), Peter Wolff (1960, 1996, 1998), Hans Furth (1987), Melvin Feffer (1988), and Willis Overton (1998).

   5. Rorty's pragmatism (1979) takes a relational approach to the nature of mind and of mind-object ties. Giving up what is for Rorty an unnecessary and misleading distinction between "real" objects and intentional objects allows a cascade of other distinctions to fall by the wayside: scheme-content (the distinction between what language contributes to the object and what the world contributes); the truly objective and the merely intersubjective; a description and a fact.

   "The interesting differences between them (objects) will be those made by our (often fluctuating) notions of what is relevant and irrelevant to the truth of beliefs about each sort of object. These notions will not be responsible to something called 'the intrinsic character of the object in question' but only to the ordinary process of reweaving our webs of belief and desire, often in unpredictable ways" (Dahlbom, 1993, p. 190).

   6. In cognitive developmental work, see Bruner (1986), Case (1992), Fischer (1980), Olson (1988), Tomkins (1992), Sameroff (1983). In developmental psychopathology, see Harter (1998), Cicchetti and Cohen (1995), Meyes (1990). In language development, see the work of Bretherton (1988, 1993), Bretherton and Bates (1985), Bates (1976), Bloom (2000), Lakoff and Johnson (1980, 1999), Karmiloff-Smith (1992, 1999).

   7. There is a well-developed body of work critiquing the use of Darwinian evolutionary theory as the backbone of developmental theory (Dimen, 1995a; Schwartz, 1995). There are critiques of Cartesian preoccupation with Reason (Gilligan, 1982; Feffer, 1988, 1999), and the prefiguring of particular adult forms of life within such theories (Harré, 1984; Phillips, 1993, 1999, 2003). Most crucially, these critiques have focused on the homophobic and pathologizing features of psychoanalytic theory in regard to gender identity and sexual orientation (Domenici and Lesser, 1995; Magee and Miller, 1997, Schwartz, 1999). Broughton (1987) drew together a number of these concerns. In England, Harré (1984) and Walkerdine (1984) have been prominent in this tradition, which is often a kind of ideology critique. It is one of the main arguments of ideology critique that special interests are presented as universal and inalienable. The relationship of theory to various forms of power and the presence of social theory and values, often disguised as a value-free method (or, in the case of analysis, of analytic neutrality) remain mysterious and unacknowledged. Perhaps the best known variant of this form of critique is Cushman's (1995) analysis of the social formations and historical pressures on theories of the self. Jonathan Silin (1995) examines the way developmental theory is used as a kind of gate-keeping operation to maintain discretion and control over the culture's discourse on sexuality.

   8. These debates have now given way to a new wave of theorizing about the interplay of infant observation and adult treatment (Beebe and Lachmann, 2002)

   9. To use a term from linguistics, masculinity and heterosexuality are the *unmarked* forms. George Lakoff (1987) has described the effects of markedness on certain words. The "neutral," unmarked form in any category, structure is always assumed to be the cognitively simple, normal form. In other words, there are pro-

totype and stereotype effects in language, and these reflect cognitive and social processes as well as linguistic ones. "Markedness is a term used by linguists to describe a kind of prototype effect—an asymmetry in a category, where one member or subcategory is taken to be somehow more basic than the other" (p. 60).

10. There are also what one might term epistemological-ideological objections, a critique of the project of hunting for origins (Butler, 1993; Grosz, 1994). This critique addresses psychoanalytic accounts of development as well as certain elements within feminist theory in which an Ur-femininity, an essentialism, a naturalizing of the female body, whatever its strategic and political purchase, lands its practitioners in various epistemological soups.

11. One of the interesting debates in developmental psychology and in psychoanalysis concerns universality. Are there transcultural or transhistorical experiences that would aptly be described as universal? Attachment, separation, the organization of sexuality: these exceedingly broad and abstract processes seem more aptly studied in their specific ecological, social, and historical niches. See Henriques et al. (1984), Harré (1984), and Broughton (1987) for discussions of this problem.

12. Strange attractors are spaces rather than things, knots of experience assembled in variable and multiform ways, susceptible to change and transformation rather than rigid canalized structures.

13. I think there was always a developmental process embedded in Mitchell's ideas about analysis and technique. He certainly thought that analyst and analysand had to develop together into the unique project they were undertaking. Coconstruction of meaning and the emerging intersubjectivity within the analytic process would have their own developmental history. A developmental theory is implicit in relational analysis (Aron, 1996, 2001; Pizer, 1999), but, initially, in Mitchell's work, it was an aspect of technique.

CHAPTER 1

1. Mitchell (1993) worked out ideas of manifold selves in *Hope and Dread*. In that book he was working with the fractionating mind that Sullivan imagined as having elements of me, not-me. These formulations have their own history in such earlier thinkers as Mead (1956) and Peirce (1955).

2. Multiplicity is not unique to relational theory, but it tends to be a less prominent perspective in ego psychology (for an exception, see Akhtar, 1995).

3. Fairfield (2001) has challenged relationalists to think more carefully about multiplicity. In her view, simply making a distinction between one-person and two-person psychology is insufficient. She adds a postmodern perspective, a point of view that relentlessly interrogates subject position, the presence of ideology in our theories, and the reification of identities, singular or multiple.

4. Ogden (1989) also conceives a less unitary subject. His innnovation within the Kleinian theory of paranoid schizoid through depressive stages has been to develop the concept of "positions," which are less hierarchically reorganized stages than they are states of self and social intersubjectivity, organized around certain constructions of self and other. Intrapsychic life as well as social interaction thus always contain certain transactions that may, or must, coexist and fluctuate. This is another account of multiplicity as a condition of psychic functioning.

Mitrani (1995, 1996), building on the tradition of Tustin (1981) and Klein (1977) and Grotstein (1999), following Bion, are also describing models of psychic functioning that imply various degrees of multiplicity in "position" or mental state.

5. One method of working in psychoanalysis but distinct from the relational tradition that is most like Dennett's (1991) heterophenomenology would be Schafer's (1992) work on narrative action as the best description of analytic work and of human subject formation. Relationists would see in that model a multivoiced and multiselved narrator. See also Spence (1994).

6. Like many psychoanalysts writing on affect, Damasio (1994, 1999) and Schore (1994) have been very influential in designing a picture of psychic functioning in which affect is the glue for cognition, rather than some kind of add-on. We cannot think in a manner that is distinct from intrapsychically and interpersonally braced feelings.

7. I think that, as we absorb new models for development from developmental psychology—analysts have important ideas to offer back, above all in the realm of sexuality. Granted that psychoanalysts sometimes get in trouble holding on to a theory of childhood sexuality, much recent work is devoted to reviving the ideas of maternal seduction and the sensuality and erotic potential in parental management of children over the course of childhood, and Davies (1998b, 2001a), Cooper (2000), Slavin (2002), and Stein (1998a) are all revitalizing the concept of childhood sexuality. Debates about Ferenczi (see Aron and Harris, 1993) about sexual trauma and overstimulation of children need to hold their place, but I would engage a term like skill in thinking about sexuality and intimacy as these become organized through complex identifications and representations and through bodily life and action that are always both social and personal, public and private.

8. In drawing together Benjamin's (2000b) work and Butler's (2000a), I collapse a useful debate between these writers, joined also by Layton (1997). It is a wonderful example of a kind of interdisciplinary conversation in which the analyst's insistence on attention to fantasy, an internal world as a residue of a relational world, meets in a productive encounter with the philosopher's questions about subjects made under the law.

9. Descriptively and diagnostically, multiple identities, splits in the subject, have a long history. Ian Hacking (1991) has tracked the changing definitions and descriptions of splits in subjectivity throughout the 19th century. He notes, without much interpretation, that, in the medical and psychiatric literature of the time, the idea of divided selves (first described as divided consciousness and then as divided personalities) was more usually attributed to women's experience, whereas the notion of the double, a twin outside the self, was more usually thought to be a man's experience.

10. Feminist considerations of multiple personality disorder (MPD), for example, have sometimes viewed that diagnosis as an iatrogenically driven organization of women's' experience through the pathologizing texts of psychiatry (Haaken, 1994, 1999). Haaken actually argues a subtle middle position, moving us beyond the impossible binary of "true" and "false" in respect either to multiple self-states or alters or the relationship of multiplicity to incest and abuse: "The multiple is an empowered hysteric who is no longer paralyzed" (1994, p. 207).

This feminist position on MPD views multiplicity as a style or means of expressing suffering and distress, a vehicle for women's enactment of their experience of damage as well as a vehicle for healing. In this way, forms of femininity and forms for the expression and communication of suffering and trauma may be historically or socially and culturally contingent and yet genuine. This perspective would alter some of the feminist ideas about hysteria as a refusal of signification. Perhaps madness, too, has elements of performance and these are shaped by many interpersonal and historical forces as well as by the dynamics of the patient.

11. Cognitive psychologist and memory researcher John Kihlstrom (1990) has speculated on the self-structuring feature of memory. In thinking about what is stored in episodic memory, memory of events and activities and streams of experience, he speculates that the event, some representation of agency, and an affective state are all features of the constellation of a particular memory. If we, as it were, personalize memory, one form a personalization might take is as an alter. Alters and separate-feeling and separate-seeming personalities are speech performances but for that no less authentic.

12. Winnicott (1971) rather famously articulated this approach to gender multiplicity by describing a clinical moment in which he found himself saying, "Who is this girl I am talking to in this man?"

13. In a posthumously published essay on the concept of the environment in child development, Vygotsky (van der Veer and Valsiner, 1994) spoke of a relational conception. Environment is not a static or unchanging given but is constructed as the child evolves. Similarly the child's changes occur in response to internalizations of the social context. Vygotsky presents what amounts to a clinical vignette, perhaps invented for rhetorical purposes. Three children in an abusing family (a mother is troubled, addicted to alcohol, and physically violent). One child is described as collapsed and traumatized, unable to process or react to the family's experience. A second child is torn by a conflictual mixture of attachment and terror, a condition Vygotsky terms *Mutter-HexeKomplex*, a mother-witch construction that sounds to a psychoanalytic listener like a description of split objects, a paranoid-schizoid position. The third child is described as precociously adult, the symbolic parent in the family, already thoughtful about his mother's predicament (he is described as nine or ten years old). He appears pseudostupid intellectually but acutely vigilant with regard to his parent.

14. Our most powerful language theories have tended to underestimate this aspect of language use. Chomskian (1957, 1965, 1988) linguistics, like Piaget's (1924) developmental theory, stress universal, transcultural phenomena. They focus on grammar and syntax rather than the subtle ways all speakers shape their discourse to the setting, their own state, and their experience of their listeners.

15. The psychoanalysts to whose work this project comes closest are probably Bion (1959, 1962) and Matte-Blanco (1988), both formalists who describe the contradictory levels of mental organization, and biologics, in which all human experience partakes. Matte-Blanco's concept of internal worlds stresses, along with the dynamic features of mind, the capacity to discriminate and to categorize. This capacity is organized with either symmetrical or asymmetrical relations. From the clinical examples he gives, these clearly seem to be variations of *pars pro toto* (symmetrical) and hierarchical (asymmetrical) schemes. If anything, Matte-Blanco's model allows for multiple levels of functioning, including moments when both

potential relations cooccur. Transference regressions, for example, are perhaps always to some extent contradictory experiences either simultaneously or sequentially oscillating between symmetrical and asymmetrical. The analyst is the same as the parent (a *pars pro toto* structure), and the analyst is differentiated from the parent in a structure of hierarchy. Note also that these activities follow Heinz Werner's (1957) orthogenetic principle where development emerges in moments of consolidation and of differentiation.

16. Interestingly, in Lakoff and Johnson's (1980, 1999) work on category structures and language, a central metaphor and language structure is that of the container. The container is an image scheme, more particularly a kinesthetic image scheme drawn from embodied and active experience. The vicissitudes of the polar relationship of the container and the contained, so fully elaborated in Winnicott's work and in post-Kleinian conception of fluctuating and conflicted object relations and internal object worlds, perhaps find particular salience in the image and structuring of the container–contained dialectical relations.

CHAPTER 2

1. I can see that whenever time experience is evoked there is an inevitable mixing of temporal and spatial metaphors. As Piaget (1955) noted, when he studied children's experiences of time, measures of time and space are wildly interrelated. We are all at least partially Cartesian and post-Cartesian. We are used to spatializing the mind, to using metaphors of structure and three dimensionality to describe psychic experience.

2. In many of Bromberg's (1998a) clinical examples, temporalities live in distinct ways. A shift in state brings with it its unique time dimension, often signaled by a change in the analyst but also by a change in the voice and pattern of the patient, as though several developmental timetables were in play.

3. Dennett was an important influence on Mitchell's thinking about consciousness and multiplicity.

4. These temporal age markers are highly susceptible to historical and cultural change. The aging mad star in *Sunset Boulevard*, a film made in 1950, is revealed to be 50 years old. In Sinclair Lewis's *Dodsworth,* written in 1929, the hero, described as an old man shepherding a young wife around Europe, is revealed to be 48.

5. Drawing on the ideas of Davidson (1980) here, we might think of time experience as lying within a web of beliefs and experiences both objective and subjective. Cognitive studies of time perception (reviewed in Friedman, 1990; Neisser, 1982) suggest a complex interaction between any internal metric marking and thinking, perceiving, and integrating other experiences, feelings, and thoughts. Our ability to orient temporally, to know how much time has passed, to locate ourselves and experiences on a timeline, is highly subjective. Physical body changes, temperature, filled and unfilled experience, meaningfulness, and trauma all affect time sense and time structure.

6. The phrase fort/da appears in "Beyond the Pleasure Principle" (Freud, 1920b). It is the term Freud gave to the action he observes in his young grandson who bears up under the absence of his mother by throwing and retrieving a little toy cotton reel, with each gesture saying fort—gone—and da—there. He captures

in the repetitive rhythm of throwing and recovering, a certain kind of sometimes obsessional, sometimes dissociated action with which the psychic management of loss and abandonment is processed. I use the term here to describe the same kind of repetitive action that I think is manifesting or expressing reversals in consciousness, shifts in state in this particular patient. I think it is a process and rhythm that appears in many different kinds of situations and persons, a repetition of reversal and psychic alteration, often more as an oscillating closed system than as an emergent transformation. Benjamin (1995, 1998) describes this process in terms of complementarity in relationships—doer/done to.

7. Winnicott (1958) captures the enormous stabilizing effect of feeling that one lives in sequential time with his phrase "going on being" describing the quite basic, nonverbal, somatically grounded experience that there is coherence and sequence and that one's self experience is not riddled with gaps and frightening precipices.

8. For almost anyone thinking about psychoanalytic accounts of trauma and repetition, "Beyond the Pleasure Principle" (Freud, 1920b) is a text that both in its structure and its topic register Freud's trauma.

CHAPTER 3

1. This distinction, between the strong claims of an alternative and more exhaustive metapsychology, on the one hand, and more moderate claims of an alternative point of view, on the other, is argued by David Olds (1994, 2000) in respect to semiotics and information theory as a model for organizing the communicative aspects of human interaction. Chaos theory allows a mode of thought about development that would coordinate with a variety of other perspectives and approaches.

2. In an introduction to chaos theory written for the general public, James Glieck (1987) describes an address to a collection of biologists and psychiatrists on a chaos-theory model of the functioning of one symptom of schizophrenia—atypical eye movement. The debates were over the adequacy of a simple model of nonlinearity to a phenomenon like schizophrenia: "The choice is always the same. You can make your model more complex and faithful to reality or you can make it simpler and easier to handle" (p. 278).

3. The use of a term like learning perhaps needs some exploration. Juarerro (1999), along with a number of theorists (see Elman et al., 1997) have taken pains to distinguish their model of learning from experience from behaviorism. Drawing from Edelman's (1987) weighted connections and using processes like feedback (backpropagation) and drawing on Hebb's (1961) original ideas about neural networks, the connectionists (Elman et al., 1997) produce concepts very different from the linear and predictive S-R behaviorist models. Their model has hidden levels that affect outcome, and is not a deductive form of explanation.

4. Juarerro (1999) is comparing complexity theory or chaos theory modes of explanation with behaviorism, a form of theory whose axioms and principles are proposed as "covering laws," that is, rules that deduce and predict learning processes. At the heart of chaos theory is the assumption of order without prediction, of emergent, immanent structure as an outcome of reorganization that itself arises from activity and interaction.

5. Kauffman (1995) uses the phrase order for free to describe the liberating effect of pattern and its connection to unpredictability. Juarerro (1999) similarly uses the notion of contraints to suggest the power of organization or, if you like, the power that is liberated through the economies of reorganization.

6. This is an important issue because there have been many seriously argued claims (Chomsky, Foder, Pinker in the realm of language, for example) that complex behaviors are set up as built-in to specific special purpose structures. The idea that there are some high level cognitive skills for which context is irrelevant has been a crucial element in Chomskian theories of language competence and Foder's (1983) work on language and mind.

7. Marchman (1993) and others propose the terms "hard" and "soft" maturation to introduce more complexity into the critical stage notion. In soft maturation, limits to change and growth may not exactly be limits of time but limits of learning space. A particular form of behavior reaches a limit in its development because the learning capacity has been used up, circuitry has become dedicated and is unavailable for novel events.

8. Juarerro terms this phenomena "coarse coding." This term is used to mean that there is not a one to one mapping of input to output. The integrations arrive in multiple layers and directions. It is this intriguing integration of noise and hierarchy, slop and specificity that makes for plasticity and emergence.

9. Working with the data from a number of developmental studies that focused on one crucial developmental shift in the construction of early object knowledge (the change when an infant can look for hidden objects in a new hiding place, the fourth substage in Piaget's [1924], sensorimotor thinking), Thelen (1995) demonstrates how new knowing emerges from the interaction of local subsystems, systems that are already intrinsic (from earlier actions and searchings) in the repertoire of the child, from the context, and from the preceding events. "Everything we know about biological development—from gene expression, to embryology, to neural and behavioral development—indicates that there is no such thing as a non-experiential component to development . . . relevant experiences for developmental processes are not there by designed solution to some set of prescribed and pre-known tasks. Rather, developmental process involve whole organisms as complex systems interacting with their environments" (p. 309). It is activity, in real time, that constitutes the driving force of change.

10. It is very interesting that the theoretical developments in understanding and modeling neural nets hark back to the work of Hebb (1961), work that, in its time, was buried under the avalanche of Skinnerian behaviorism and information-processing models. Hebb's is a learning theory, but with a difference. It is a speculative model of how a person acquires an experience of pattern and an internal model of increasing complexity and anticipatory capacity. Hebb is the originator of the model of pattern detection, synaptic weighting that can be based on excitation or inhibition, feedforward capacities, and crucially a reverberating and cycling capacity in the network that leads to "cell assembles" of increasing organization. Synchrony, anticipation, indefinite memory, and hierarchy are the outcome of emergence not of preplanning.

11. Kohler's (1947) account of the dynamic properties of knowing and meaning making written has a wonderful and eerie resonance with chaos theory and

dynamic systems modeling. Both in describing events and in describing mental events, Kohler and the Gestaltists assumed inherently patterned equilibrating activity and systems that function on principles of equilibrium and self-distribution (Lewin, 1943).

12. A key figure to introduce in this context is Tomkins (1962, 1963, 1992). It is not always clear whether to place Tomkins as a historical or a contemporary figure. He is, rather, the hidden hero (Demos, 1992b) in relation to the study of face-to-face play. His students are rather more well known than he: Ekman (1994, 1997), for example, on face-to-face play; and Beckwith and Rodning (1991) on emotional bootstrapping. Tomkins is a critic and a reviser of Piaget and a vital figure in integrating social cognition, affective and emotional development, and the emergence of subjectivity, particularly through the powerful interpersonal effect of emotional amplification as the ground for emerging subjectivity and reflection.

CHAPTER 4

1. The confusion goes back to the very beginning of psychoanalytic theorizing, as Jacqueline Rose (1978) has argued in considering the Dora case. Around the conflicts, person, and bodies in Dora's life Freud constructed and deconstructed his theories of sexuality. The tensions in mother–daughter life, in preoedipal experience, he seemed finally to understand, utterly complicated any simple account of oedipal sexuality. Women's difficulties, often confounded with men's difficulties with women, came to seem embedded in the very theory of sexuality.

2. Lampl-de Groot was analyzed by Freud and in a retrospective revisit to her own work (1982) claimed Freud's imprimatur for writing about femininity from her own experience. What to make, then, of this comment later in the same paper: "It is well known that active wooing may be used to effect a passive feminine orgasm" (p. 12)? Here Lampl-de Groot seems to be alluding to the compromises in female pleasure neccessitated by its integration into heterosexuality, a topic recently revived and expanded by feminist psychoanalysts considering the constriction of female pleasure both in our theoretical imagination and in women's experience (Elise, 1998, 1999, 2002; Dimen, 1999).

3. Brierley (1936) makes a subtle distinction from Kleinian orthodoxy to consider the interlocking of environment, drives, and ego capacities and has interesting speculations on a girl's fear of her aggression, her fear of injuring or having injured the mother.

4. In his paper on Leonardo da Vinci, Freud (1910) says: "The love of the mother for the suckling whom she nourishes and cares for is something far deeper reaching than her later affection for the growing child. It is of the nature of a fully gratified love affair, which fulfills not only all the psychic wishes but also all physical needs, and when it represents one of the forms of happiness attainable by man it is due, in no little measure, to the possibility of gratifying without reproach also wish feelings which were long repressed and designated as perverse" (pp. 92–93). The reference to all bodily needs may be taken as a hint that pregenital and genital desires find fulfillment in the care of the infant. The mother's bliss in caring for her infant, regardless of sex, seems dependent on the child's smallness and helplessness. Freud's remarks can be developed further to mean that mothers enjoy the care of their infants in substitution for their early repressed wishes to handle

their own genitals. I suggested a similar interpretation of a mother's need for a small child, in the hypothesis that early undischarged vaginal excitations are the basic source of the girl's need for a child (Kestenberg, 1956b, p. 258).

5. While this review has focused on the American contemporary work on core femininity, there is a rich vein of work in France that critiques phallic monism and has been highly influential for American neo-Freudians (Chasseguet-Smirgel, 1970, 1976; McDougall, 1980, 1989).

6. Thomas Laqueur (1990) describes fascinating historical transformations in understanding sexual experience, along with radical transformative consequences to how male and female bodies are treated and understood. Edward Shorter's (1982) account of the history of obstetrics and gynecology paints very powerfully the dangerous and difficult history of women's experiences in childbirth. Control over fertility and a sharp drop in maternal mortality are 20th-century developments.

7. I see in this work in philosophy and in the work of developmental theorists I have been describing a shared intention to heal the splits in intention and action, subject and object, body and mind that have dominated our models of psychic life. Many of the developmental theorists I am considering address one aspect of our particular intellectual legacy, the Cartesian split between the subject and object of knowledge. We strive to know the world and ourselves through our experience, and there is an irreducible indeterminacy in that activity. There is no mind before experience and no known, cognized objects separate from or before interaction.

8. Against the legacies of Cartesian dualism, particularly the machine metaphor for the body, Grosz (1994) proposes the philosophical lineage from Spinoza's materialist and monist theories. Rather than seeing the body as a machine for which fuel is provided from outside, she casts Spinoza's idea of the body's metabolisms as a self-constituting process inherent in the organism. Particular forms of bodily identity arise in the concrete interactions with tasks, environments, other beings. Identity's permanence is not as a substance or structure but in the relation of a person to other persons and things in history. This is a philosophic description of Thelen's project regarding motor development and cognition. It is also at the heart of relational psychoanalysis with roots in earlier forms of psychoanalytic theory (Ferenczi, 1911, 1931, 1932; Winnicott, 1947, 1950, 1958; Loewald, 1962a, b).

9. Grosz (1994) also draws on Merleau-Ponty (1962, 1964) and Foucault, a particularly interesting combination. Merleau-Ponty's (1964) phenomenology stresses the lived body, the body as immanent not as a given or a carapace for the vital mind; rather, the body is "the condition and context through which I am able to have a relation to others" (pp. 3–4). In a description that sounds remarkably like a radical constructivist account of sensorimotor thought, Grosz (1994) says, "The relation between the subject and the object is thus not causal but based on sense or meaning. The relations of mutual definition governing body and the world of objects are 'form-giving' insofar as the body actively differentiates and categorizes the world into groupings of sensuous experience, patterns of organization and meaning" (p. 89).

10. This phenomenon might be one way to think about the experience, possible and implausible, of passing. This experience can have a gendered meaning

(Fausto-Sterling, 2000) or be conducted in the realm of race or ethnicity (Bhabha, 1994; Cheng, 1997; Eng and Han, 2003). As bodily identities are shaped and claimed within histories and within social formations, we might think that any identity requires both individual and social collusion, agreements as to what bodies mean. Gender's "passing" must also take particular shape in particular historical periods, perhaps occurring most seamlessly in periods when identity markers for race and gender were not a focus of conscious social work.

11. This line of thinking is strongly influenced by the work of Coates and Moore (1998), Apprey (2003), and Seligman (1999a, b, in press) on the transgenerational transmission of trauma. See also Scarry (1985).

12. The proposed framework suggests that a girl's genital sexuality is central to the elaboration of her femininity. There is psychoanalytic literature in support of that view. Jacobson (1968) suggests that it is a girl's discovery of her own genitals that permits her to give up the notion of having a penis. The girl's libidinal cathexis of the vagina and her energetic investigation of her genital and masturbatory satisfaction contribute to the development of an active-genital relation to her sexual partner. Kestenberg (1956a, 1982) points to the girl's sense of a "productive inside" as playing a role in her development. Erikson's (1963) studies of girls' and boys' play suggest that girls have a "productive sense of inner space." Torok (1970) emphasizes the importance of girls' genital satisfaction in developing the capacity for orgasm and in establishing the groundwork for heterosexual competence.

13. What is interesting to contemplate is the *mutual* influence of these two enterprises—psychoanalysis and feminism. In the mid-1970s the ideas that underwrote women's liberation were behavioral or cognitive, centering on roles and changes in surface conditions and behavior. After that period, through the work of Juliet Mitchell (1974), Nancy Chodorow (1976, 1989) and Dorothy Dinnerstein (1975), this situation was radically altered. The use of psychoanalytic ideas to understand the deep, unconscious processes in gender and sexual life transformed a social movement and its social theory, and the resultant impact in intellectual and personal life is enormous. But the transformation worked in the other direction as well, fleshing out consideration of gender centered solely within family and intrapsychic life and demanding attention to the normative and dominating aspects of theory making itself. While this influence permeated the psychoanalytic world in the 1970s, its most concentrated forms have come from work embedded in the object relational, interpersonal, and relational worlds.

CHAPTER 5

1. The critique of heterosexist bias in Benjamin's (1988) model of gender complementarity has also been developed by Magee and Miller (1997) and by Corbett (2001c).

CHAPTER 6

1. This five-part organization distinguishes males and females and then includes various forms of hermaphroditic structures, delightfully called herms, merms, and ferms (Fausto-Sterling, 2000, p. 48).

2. This tension is at the heart of all of Benjamin's work on intersubjectivity

and the pressure to move beyond gender complementarity. It is also at base in the theorization of a relation to otherness in Levinas (Levinas and Lingis, 1974) and others (Ricoeur, 1992).

3. Laplanche, for example, has developed a complex nonlinear model of the origins of phantasy in papers on sublimation and on maternal seduction (1989).

4. See Butler (1990, 1997c), Dean (1993), and Layton (1997) for extended discussions of the place of identity politics, essences, social construction, and theories of subjectivity. I am occluding here the debates involving Butler (1997c), Benjamin (2000b), Layton (1997), and others about the role of agency in Butler's model. As Benjamin argues, the passionate attachment, disavowals, and splits in Butler's model of homosexual development require an extradiscursive, motivated self, even as there remain important distinctions between self and subjectivity.

5. This critique of normative masculinity began with the work of Dinnerstein (1975) and is elaborated in the work of Teresa Brennan (1988, 1992).

6. Edelman's term here, values, is not used in its conventional meaning. Here it is used only to describe subtle functional changes in neural cell assemblies that in short order become highly complex and unpredictable so. Reentrant remapping as a process has some affinity with the dual action of assimilation-accommodation in Piaget's (1924) theory in which the evolving internal scheme reconfigures action and reaction and interaction.

7. The contributors to Widlocher (2002) debate the question of what is transmitted, what we may adultomorphize, what is remapped as desire, and how these experiences are lived in object relations and in child fantasy.

8. Karmiloff-Smith (1992) draws on this process in thinking about symbolic representation. Her model, representational redescription—a phase model not a stage model—describes the gradually and idiosyncratic, context-sensitive reorganization of information through procedural to more explicitly symbolic forms. This process is emergent and on line, and occurs in real time.

I am thinking of gender in its symbolic and presymbolic forms as a forming categorization along these principles.

9. I also think that this motivational model is close to an analysis of gender that results when Lacan meets queer theory. Dyess and Dean (2000a, b) keep gender difference in the imaginary and in the symbolic register and then in the register of the real; gender does not yet penetrate, though the individual would be prey to its effects.

CHAPTER 7

1. The kind of shared process of entrainment and mutual coevolution that Palumbo (1998) and Fajardo (1998, 2000) propose to account for clinical process and therapeutic movement is an apt model of the clinical process detailed by Beebe and Lachmann (2002) in adult treatment. The understanding of adult treatment is as a mutually regulating dyadic system, one drawing on but transforming patterns of parent–infant regulation.

2. Transegrity is a term Sander (2002) imported from microbiology and systems theory to capture the self-generated capacity of a system (here a two-person system) to stabilize and balance in a dynamic, continuous open process. The key features here are dynamism and balance.

CHAPTER 8

1. The critique of masculinist and heterosexist bias in psychoanalytic theory is longstanding, from Horney (1926), through Kofman (1985), Irigaray (1990), to Magee and Miller (1997), Schwartz (1998), and Benjamin (2002).

2. Bion's (1962) theory of the container and the parental mind's containing function is a seminal influence in these contemporary psychoanalytic writers. This concept of container is given a more dynamic and dialectical reading in Vygotsky's work on the social origins of thought, a perspective on mind and thinking as transpersonally or intersubjectively developed.

3. This core insight of Brennan and many postmoderns reveals that the polarities of masculine/feminine; active/passive; eternal/timed; imaginary/symbolic maintain an oscillating complementarity. Among other matters, patriarchy is unchallenged.

4. Skill is a term I use here deliberately to engage with the developmental theory of Kurt Fischer (1980), which stresses skill as a mixture of social cognition, thought, emotion, and appraisal.

CHAPTER 9

1. The network of researchers in contemporary developmental psychology practicing such integrative work includes infancy researchers (Stern, 1977, 1985; Tronick, 1989, 1998; Lyons-Ruth, 1991, 1999; Beebe and Lachmann, 2002), language researchers (Nelson, 1985, 1989; Bretherton, 1993; Dunn, 1997; Bloom, 2000; Zelazo, 2000), workers at the intersect of social cognition, affect development, and cognition (Bruner, 1986, 1990; Astington, 2000; Olson, 1988; Feldman, 1988, 1989; Meltzoff, 1990, 1995; Baldwin, 1993; Trevarthan, 1993; Cicchetti and Cohen, 1995; Harter, 1998). It is this integrative spirit operative within a number of spheres in developmental psychology that makes for a unique opportunity for dialog with psychoanalysis.

2. The borderline between the domains of psychoanalysis and developmental psychology is a long one, although some crossing points are well traveled (Overton, 1998). Infancy work in particular has been the site of an intense and fruitful collaboration between empirical researchers and clinicians. Some border spots seem more neglected or even antagonistic. Gender development, for example, seems much more richly understood in psychoanalysis and in culture studies than in psychology at the moment. Gilligan's (1982) work, which began in the context of her work on moral development, has really migrated in more clinical psychoanalytical directions (Gilligan, Lyon, and Hanmer, 1990; Gilligan and Brown, 1993).

3. Peirce's (1955) semiotics and his triadic theory of speech and signification are becoming increasingly relevant to psychoanalysis. Ringstrom (2001a, b) has integrated double bind theory into his understanding of therapeutic impasses. Olds (2000) and Litowitz (2001) are developing a semiotic model of mind.

4. These terms—icon, index, and symbol—capture functional aspects of word meaning. See Horowitz (1972) on modes of representation. Icon is the least mediated experience of semiotic meaning. Index embeds meaning in context, in a system of referents and often in a highly affective chain, as Damasio outlines in his theory of emotions as the glue of cognition (Damasio, 1994, 1999).

5. Vygotsky (1962) was first read in English in a translation of a set of essays, some of which may have been lecture notes posthumously organized by his students. So it was as a contributor to cognitive and linguistic theory that Vygotsky was first assimilated into American developmental psychology. The researchers who made use of his work (Wertsch, 1985, and Bruner, 1986, 1990, primarily) were particularly taken with his account of the coevolution of speech and thought and the interpenetration therefore of social and psychic.

6. Forms of speech, thought, and affective state are functionally interwoven and related. This was an idea of an earlier generation of linguists, the first generation after Chomsky (1957, 1965), generative semanticists like Bates (1976) and McCawley (1968), and by British linguists like Michael Halliday (1973) and Basil Bernstein (1971), whose influences were anthropology, sociology, and literary studies.

7. For Locke (1993), an important determinant in thinking about the social/ affective/biological context for language development is that our species is what he terms perceptually precocious and motorically immature. So facial cues, voice, and mimicry assume great power and importance as vehicles for mastery and connection. Locke asks the hard question, which child language researchers and analysts must answer: "We might ask how much conceptual sophistication is needed to respond empathically. Presumably one must be able to sense what another individual is experiencing. But is this deeply analytical or superficially contagious" (p. 353). It is just this problem that has been compelling the study of "now" moments (cited in Stern et al., 1998).

8. Vygotsky (van der Veer and Valsiner, 1991; Frawley, 1997) had a complex relationship to psychoanalysis. In the Foreword to "Beyond the Pleasure Principle," which he cowrote with Luria, he admires Freud for courage, for taking a revolutionary path frightening to many of his followers. He reads this work of Freud as speculative, dialectical, a work "of metapsychology not metaphysics" (van der Veer and Valsiner, 1991, p. 101). Vygotsky views Freud as a materialist as well as a dialectician. He sees the interplay of destructive and libidinal action as a lifelong psychic process and claims for Freud, in this work, a renewed attention to the social in interaction with the intrapsychic. A relational Freud through a Marxist lens.

9. This material on multiple voices raises interesting theoretical and ethical problems regarding authenticity. One of the compelling debates in child research on social cognition is how early and in what way children figure out deceit or falsehood either in their own experience or in others. This kind of data and theorizing creates new difficulties for thinking about the true and false self that Winnicott (1971) proposed; now one must imagine a range and multiplicity of performed selves that function and feel variously authentic and vital. Yet a sense of falseness, deceit, and nonengagement in experience is also palpable to very young children.

10. See Halliday's (1973) concept of learning how to mean from learning how to act or Austin's (1962) interest in how to do things with words for models of how language functions in the service of and as an elaboration of intentional acts of mind.

11. A focus on gender, body ego, and the emergence of speech adds to the discussion of the development of reflective functioning, affect states, and self-structure, all of which are central to the theoretical work of Fonagy and Target (2003). Dialogue and the emerging capacities to represent in language are key sites for observing the presence of reflective functioning, and it is in toddlerhood, in the matrices of affective intensity and a dramatically increasing power over symbolic representation, that these capacities are transformed.

References

Abraham, K. (1923), Contributions to the theory of the anal character. *Internat. J. Psycho-Anal.*, 4:400–418.

Abraham, N. & Torok, M. (1994), *The Shell and the Kernel*. Chicago, IL: University of Chicago Press.

Agamben, G. (1999), *Potentialities: Collected Essays in Philosophy*. Stanford, CA: Stanford University Press.

Akhtar, S. (1995), A third individuation: Immigration, identity, and the psychoanalytic process. *J. Amer. Psychoanal. Assn.*, 43:1051–1084.

Althusser, L. (1971), *Lenin and Philosophy, and Other Essays.* London: New Left Books.

Altman, N. (1996), *The Analyst in the Inner City.* Hillsdale, NJ: The Analytic Press.

—— (2000a), Black and white thinking: A psychoanalyst reconsiders race. *Psychoanal. Dial.*, 10:589–605.

—— (2000b), Reply to commentaries. *Psychoanal. Dial.*, 10:633-638.

Alvarez, A. (1992), *Live Company*. London: Routledge.

—— (1993), Making the thought thinkable: On introjection and projection. *Psychoanal. Inq.*, 13:103–122.

—— (1997), Projective identification as a communication: Its grammar in borderline psychotic children. *Psychoanal. Dial.*, 7:753–768.

Anzieu, D. (1989), *The Skin Ego.* New Haven, CT: Yale University Press.

—— ed. (1990), *Psychic Envelopes.* London: Karnac.

Apprey, M. (1996), *Phenomenology of transgenerational haunting: Subjects in apposition, subjects on urgent/voluntary errands.* Ann Arbor, MI: UMI Research Collections.

—— (2003), Repairing history: Reworking transgenerational trauma. In: *Hating in the First Person Plural,* ed. D. Moss. New York: Other Press.

Arlow, J. (1984), Disturbances of the sense of time—With special reference to the experience of timelessness. *Psychoanal. Quart.*, 53:13–37.

—— (1989), Time as emotion. In: *Time and Mind: Interdisciplinary Issues, Vol. 6,* ed. J. T. Fraser. Madison, CT: International Universities Press, pp. 85–96.

279

Aron, L. (1991), The patient's experience of the analyst's subjectivity. *Psychoanal. Dial.,* 1:29–51.

—— (1992), Interpretation as expression of the analyst's subjectivity. *Psychoanal. Dial.,* 2:475–507.

—— (1996), *A Meeting of Minds.* Hillsdale, NJ: The Analytic Press.

—— (2001), Intersubjectivity in the analytic situation. In: *Self-Relations in the Psychotherapy Process,* ed. J. C. Muran. Washington, DC: American Psychological Association, pp. 137–164.

—— & Harris, A. (1993), *The Legacy of Sándor Ferenczi.* Hillsdale, NJ: The Analytic Press.

—— & Anderson, F. (1998), *Relational Perspectives on the Body.* Hillsdale, NJ: The Analytic Press.

Astington, J., ed. (2000), *Minds in the Making.* Malden, MA: Blackwell.

Austin, J. L. (1962), *How to Do Things with Words.* Cambridge, MA: Harvard University Press.

Bakhtin, M. M. (1968), *Rabelais and His World.* Ann Arbor, MI: University of Michigan Press.

—— (1981), *The Dialogic Imagination,* ed. & trans. M. Holquist. Austin: University of Texas Press.

—— (1986), *Speech Genres and Other Late Essays.* Austin: University of Texas Press.

Baldwin, D. (1993), Infants' ability to consult the speaker for clues to word meaning. *J. Child Language,* 20:395-418.

Baldwin, J. M. (1904), *The Story of the Mind.* New York: McClure, Phillips.

—— (1906), *Social and Ethical Interpretations on Mental Development.* London: Macmillan.

Balsam, R. (1996), The pregnant mother and the body image of the daughter. *J. Amer. Psychoanal. Assn.,* 44(S):401-427

—— (2001), Integrating male and female elements in a woman's gender identity. *J. Amer. Psychoanal. Assn.,* 49:1335–1360.

Bartlett, F. (1923), *Psychology and Primitive Cultures.* London: Cambridge University Press.

Bass, G. (2002), Something is happening here: Thoughts and clinical material regarding multiplicity, gender and touch in a psychoanalytic treatment. *Psychoanal. Dial.,* 12:809–826.

Bassin, D. (1994), Maternal subjectivity in the culture of nostalgia: Mourning and memory. In: *Representations of Motherhood,* ed. D. Bassin, M. Honey & M. Kaplan. New Haven, CT: Yale University Press, pp. 162–173.

—— (2002), Beyond the he and she: Toward the reconciliation of masculinity and femininity in the postoedipal female mind. In: *Gender in Psychoanalytic Space,* ed. M. Dimen & V. Goldner. New York: Other Press, pp. 119–179.

Bates, E. (1976), *Language and Context.* New York: Academic Press.

—— Bretherton, I. & Synder, L. (1989), *From First Words to Grammar.* New York: Cambridge University Press.

Beckwith, L. & Rodning, C. (1991), Intellectual functioning in children born preterm: Recent research. In: *Directors of Development,* ed. L. Inokagaki &

R. J. Sternberg. Mahwah, NJ: Lawrence Erlbaum Associates, pp. 25–58.

Beebe, B., Jaffe, J. & Lachmann, F. (1992), A dyadic systems view of communication. In: *Relational Perspectives in Psychoanalysis,* ed. N. Skolnick & S. Warshaw. Hillsdale, NJ: The Analytic Press, pp. 61–81.

—— —— —— Feldstein, S., Crown, C. & Jasnow, J. (2000), Systems models in development and psychoanalysis: The case of vocal rhythm coordination and attachment. *Infant Mental Health J.,* 21:99–122.

—— & Lachmann, F. (1994), Representation and internalization in infancy: Three principles of salience. *Psychoanal. Psychol.,* 11:127–165.

—— & —— (1998), Co-constructing inner and relational processes: Self and mutual regulation in infant research and adult treatment. *Psychoanal. Psychol.,* 15:1–37.

—— & —— (2002), *Infant Research and Adult Treatment.* Hillsdale, NJ: The Analytic Press.

—— —— & Jaffe, J. (1997), Mother–infant interaction structures and presymbolic self- and object representations. *Psychoanal. Dial.,* 7:133–182.

Benjamin, J. (1986), The alienation of desire: Women's masochism and ideal love. In: *Psychoanalysis and Women,* ed. J. Alpert. Hillsdale, NJ: The Analytic Press, pp. 113–138.

—— (1987), The decline of the Oedipus complex. In: *Critical Theories of Psychological Development,* ed. J. M. Broughton. New York: Plenum Press, pp. 211–244.

—— (1988), *The Bonds of Love.* New York: Pantheon.

—— (1990), An outline of intersubjectivity: The development of recognition. *Psychoanal. Psychol.,* 7(S):33–46.

—— (1991), Father and daughter: Identification with difference—A contribution to gender heterodoxy. *Psychoanal. Dial.,* 1:277–299.

—— (1992a), "Father and daughter: Identification with difference—A contribution to gender heterodoxy": Reply. *Psychoanal. Dial.,* 2:417–424.

—— (1992b), "The relational self: A new perspective for understanding women's development": Discussion. *Contemp. Psychother. Rev.,* 7:82–96.

—— (1995), *Like Subjects, Love Objects.* New Haven, CT: Yale University Press.

—— (1997), *The Shadow of the Other.* New York: Routledge.

—— (2000a), Intersubjective distinctions — Subjects and persons, recognitions and breakdowns: Commentary on paper by Gerhardt, Sweetnam, and Borton. *Psychoanal. Dial.,* 10:43–55.

—— (2000b), Response to commentaries by Mitchell and by Butler. *Studies Gender & Sexual.,* 1:291–308.

—— (2002), Sameness and difference: An "overinclusive" view of gender constitution. In: *Gender in Psychoanalytic Space,* ed. M. Dimen & V. Goldner. New York: Other Press, pp. 181–206.

—— & Aron, L. (1999), *The Development of Intersubjectivity and the Struggle to Think.* Spring Meeting, Division (39) of Psychoanalysis, American Psychological Association, New York City, April.

Bernstein, B. (1971), *Class, Codes and Control I.* London: Routledge & Kegan Paul.

—— (1993), *Female Identity Conflicts in Clinical Practice*. Northvale, NJ: Aronson.

Bhabha, H. (1994), The other question: Stereotype, discrimination and the discourse of colonialism. In: *The Location of Culture*. London: Routledge, pp. 66–84.

Bion, W. (1954), Notes on the theory of schizophrenia. *Internat. J. Psychoanal.*, 35:113–118.

—— (1959), Attacks on linking. In: *Second Thoughts*. Northvale, NJ: Aronson.

—— (1962), A psychoanalytical theory of thinking. *Internat. J. Psychoanal.*, 43:306–310.

Bird, G. (1986), *William James*. New York: Routledge.

Birdwhistell, R. (1970), *Kinesics and Context*. Oxford, UK: Ballantine.

—— (1974), The language of the body: The natural environment of words. In: *Human Communication*, ed. A. Silverstein. Mahwah, NJ: Lawrence Erlbaum Associates.

Blechner, M. (1998), Maleness and masculinity. *Contemp. Psychoanal.*, 34:597–614.

Bloom, P. (2000), *How Children Learn the Meanings of Words*. Cambridge, MA: MIT Press.

Bollas, C. (1987), *The Shadow of the Object*. New York: Columbia University Press.

Borch-Jacobsen, M. (1992), *The Emotional Tie*. Stanford, CA: Stanford University Press.

Bornstein, K. (1994), *Gender Outlaw*. New York: Routledge.

Boswell, J. E. (1980), *Christianity, Social Tolerance, and Homosexuality*. Chicago, IL: University of Chicago Press.

—— (1990), Social history: Disease and homosexuality. In: *AIDS and Sex*, ed. B. R. Voeller, J. M. Reinisch & M. Gottleib. Kinsey Institute Series, Vol. 4. London: Oxford University Press, pp. 171–182.

—— (1994), *Same-Sex Union in Premodern Europe*. New York: Villard Books.

Botticelli, S. (in press) The politics of relational psychoanalysis. *Psychoanal. Dial.*

Bowlby, J. (1940), The influence of early environment in the development of the child. *Internat. J. Psychoanal.*, 21:154–178.

—— (1959), The nature of the child's tie to his mother. *Internat. J. Psychoanal.*, 39:350–373.

—— (1960), Grief and mourning in infancy and early childhood. *The Psychoanalytic Study of the Child*, 15:9–52. New York: International Universities Press.

Bradley, S., Blanchard, R., Coates, S. & Green, R. (1991), Interim report of the DSM-IV subcommittee on gender identity disorders. *Arch. Sexual Behav.*, 20:333–343.

Breen, D. (1993), *The Gender Conundrum*. London: Karnac.

Brennan, T. (1988), Controversial discussions and feminist debate. In: *Freud in Exile*, ed. E. Timms & N. Segal. New Haven, CT: Yale University Press, pp. 254–274.

—— (1992), *The Interpretation of the Flesh*. New York: Routledge.

—— (1993), *History After Lacan*. London: Routledge.

Bretherton, I. (1988), How to do things with one word: The ontogenesis of intentional message making in early infancy. In: *The Emergent Lexicon,* ed. M. D. Smith & J. L. Lock. New York: Academic Press.

—— (1992), Social referencing, intentional communication and the interfacing of minds in infancy. In: *Children's Theories of Mind,* ed. D. Frye & C. Moore. New York: Plenum Press.

—— (1993), From dialogue to internal working models: The co-construction of self in relationships. In: *Memory and Affect in Development,* ed. C. A. Nelson. Mahwah, NJ: Lawrence Erlbaum Associates, pp. 237–263.

—— & Beeghly, M. (1982), Talking about internal states: The acquisition of an explicit theory of mind. *Develop. Psychol.,* 18:906–921.

—— & Bates, E. (1985), The development of representation from 10 to 28 months: Differential stability of language and symbolic play. In: *Continuities and Discontinuities in Development,* ed. R. N. Emde & R. J. Harmon. New York: Plenum Press.

Brierley, M. (1932), Some problems of integration in women. *Internat. J. Psycho-Anal.,* 13:433–448.

—— (1936), Specific determinants in feminine development. *Internat. J. Psycho-Anal.,* 17:163–180.

Britton, R. (1989), The missing link: Parental sexuality in the Oedipus complex. In: *The Oedipus Complex Today,* ed. J. Steiner. London: Karnac Books.

—— (1995), Psychic reality and unconscious belief. *Internat. J. Psycho-Anal.,* 76:19–23.

—— (1999), *Belief and Imagination.* London: Karnac.

Bromberg, P. (1991), On knowing one's patient inside out: The aesthetics of unconscious communication. *Psychoanal. Dial.,* 1:399–422.

—— (1993), Shadow and substance: A relational perspective on clinical process. *Psychoanal. Dial.,* 10:147–168.

—— (1994), "Speak! That I may see you.": Some reflections on dissociation, reality, and psychoanalytic listening. *Psychoanal. Dial.,* 4:517–547.

—— (1996a), Hysteria, dissociation and cure: Emmy von N revisited. *Psychoanal. Dial.,* 5:55–71.

—— (1996b), Standing in the spaces: The multiplicity of self and the psychoanalytic relationship. *Contemp. Psychoanal.,* 32:509–535.

—— (1998a), *Standing in the Spaces.* Hillsdale, NJ: The Analytic Press.

—— (1998b), Staying the same while changing: Reflections on clinical judgment. *Psychoanal. Dial.,* 8:225–236.

—— (1999), Playing with boundaries. *Contemp. Psychoanal.,* 35:54–66.

—— (2001a), Treating patients with symptoms, and symptoms with patience: Reflections on shame, dissociation, and eating disorders. *Psychoanal. Dial.,* 11:891–912.

—— (2001b), Out of body, out of mind, out of danger: Some reflections on shame, dissociation, and eating disorders. In: *Hungers and Compulsions,* ed. J. Petrucelli & C. Stuart. Northvale, NJ: Aronson, pp. 67–78.

Broughton, J. (1987), *Critical Theories of Psychological Development.* New York: Plenum Press.

Bruner, J. (1986), *Actual Minds, Possible Worlds.* Cambridge, MA: Harvard University Press.

——— (1990), *Acts of Meaning*. Cambridge, MA: Harvard University Press.

Bucci, W. (1997), *Psychoanalysis and Cognitive Science*. New York: Guilford.

——— (2001), Pathways of emotional communication. *Psychoanal. Inq.*, 21:40–70.

——— (2002), The referential process, consciousness, and the sense of self. *Psychoanal. Inq.*, 22:766–793.

Burch, B. (1996), Between women: The mother–daughter romance and homoerotic transference in psychotherapy. *Psychoanal. Psychol.*, 13:475–494.

Butler, J. (1990), *Gender Trouble*. New York: Routledge.

——— (1993), *Bodies That Matter*. New York: Routledge.

——— (1995a), Melancholy gender—Refused identification. *Psychoanal. Dial.*, 5:165–180.

——— (1995b), Keeping it moving: "Melancholy gender—Refused identification": Reply to Adam Phillips. *Psychoanal. Dial.*, 5:189–193.

——— (1997a), *Excitable Speech*. New York: Routledge.

——— (1997b), *The Psychic Life of Power*. Stanford, CA: Stanford University Press.

——— (1997c), Response to Lynne Layton's "The doer behind the deed." *Gender & Psychoanal.*, 2:515–520.

——— (1998), Analysis to the core: Commentary on papers by James H. Hansell and Dianne Elise. *Psychoanal. Dial.*, 8:373–377.

——— (2000a), Longing for recognition: Commentary on the work of Jessica Benjamin. *Studies Gender & Sexual.*, 1:271–290.

——— (2000b), *Antigone's Claim*. New York: Columbia University Press.

——— (2003), Violence, mourning, politics. *Studies Gender & Sexual.*, 4:9–37.

Cain, A. & Fast, I. (1972), Children's disturbed reactions to parent suicide. In: *Survivors of Suicide*, ed. A. Cain. Springfield, IL: Thomas.

Carey, S. (1985), *Conceptual Change in Childhood*. Cambridge, MA: MIT Press.

——— & Bartlett, E. (1978), Acquiring a single new word. *Papers & Reports Child Language Devel.*, 15:17–29.

Caruth, C. (1996), *Unclaimed Experience*. Baltimore, MD: Johns Hopkins University Press.

Case, R. (1992), *The Mind's Staircase*. Hillsdale, NJ: Lawrence Erlbaum Associates.

Casti, J. (1994), *Complexification*. New York: HarperCollins.

Cavell, M. (1988), Interpretation, psychoanalysis, and the philosophy of mind. *J. Amer. Psyhoanal. Assn.*, 36:859–879.

——— (1993), *The Psychoanalytic Mind*. Cambridge, MA: Harvard University Press.

——— (1999), Knowledge, consensus and uncertainty. *Internat. J. Psycho-Anal.*, 80:1227–1235.

Chapman, M. & Dixon, R. A., eds. (1987), *Meaning and the Growth of Understanding*. Berlin: Springer-Verlag.

Chasseguet-Smirgel, J. (1970), *Female Sexuality*. London: Karnac.

——— (1976) Freud and female sexuality: The consideration of some blind spots in the exploration of the "dark continent." *Internat. J. Psycho-Anal.*, 57:275–286.

——— (1986), *Sexuality and Mind*. New York: New York University Press.

Cheng, A. (1997), The melancholy of race. *Kenyon Rev.*, 19:49–61.

Chodorow, N. (1976), *The Reproduction of Mothering.* Berkeley: University of California Press.

—— (1989), *Feminism and Psychoanalytic Theory.* New Haven, CT: Yale University Press.

—— (1992), Heterosexuality as a compromise formation: Reflections on the psychoanalytic theory of sexual development. *Psychoanal. & Contemp. Thought,* 15:267–304.

—— (1994), *Femininities, Masculinities, Sexualities.* Lexington: University Press of Kentucky.

—— (1999), *The Power of Feelings.* New Haven, CT: Yale University Press.

—— (2000a), Foreword to Freud's *Three Essays on a Theory of Sexuality.* New York: Basic Books.

—— (2002b), Prejudice exposed: On Stephen Mitchell's pioneering investigations of the psychoanalytic mistreatment of homosexuality. *Studies Gender & Sexual.,* 3:61–72.

—— (2002), Gender as a personal and cultural construction. In: *Gender in Psychoanalytic Space,* ed. M. Dimen & V. Goldner. New York: Other Press, pp. 237–261.

—— (2003), Les homosexualités comme formations de compromis: La complexité théorique et clinique d'une description et d'une compréhension des homosexualités. *Rev. Franç. Psychanal.,* 1:41–64.

—— (in press), Beyond sexual difference: Considerations of clinical individuality, constitutive components and same-sex cross-generation relations in the creation of feminine and masculine.

Chomsky, N. (1957), *Syntactic Structures.* The Hague: Mouton.

—— (1965), *Aspects of the Theory of Syntax.* Cambridge, MA: MIT Press.

—— (1988), *Language and Problems of Knowledge.* Cambridge, MA: MIT Press.

Cicchetti, D. & Beeghley, M. (1990), *The Self in Transition.* Chicago, IL: University of Chicago Press.

—— & Cohen, D. (1995), Developmental processes and psychopathology. In: *Development and Psychopathology, Vol. 1,* ed. D. Cicchetti & D. Cohen. New York: Cambridge University Press, pp. 3–20.

—— & Toth, S. (1996), *Adolescence.* Rochester, NY: University of Rochester Press.

Clément, C. & Kristeva, J. (2001), *The Feminine and the Sacred,* trans. J. M. Todd. New York: Columbia University Press.

Coates, S. (1990), Ontogenesis of boyhood gender identity disorder. *J. Amer. Acad. Psychoanal.,* 18:414–438.

—— (1995), What do I do on Monday? Paper presented at the conference at CLAGS "Sissies and Tomboys." New York City, February 12.

—— (1997), Is it time to jettison the concept of developmental lines? Commentary on de Marneffe's paper "Bodies and Words." *Gender & Psychoanal.,* 2:36–54.

—— Friedman, R. & Wolfe, S. (1991), The etiology of boyhood gender identity disorder: A model for the integration of temperament, development, and psychodynamics. *Psychoanal. Dial.,* 1:481–521.

—— & Moore, M. S. (1998), The complexity of early trauma: Representation and transformation. In: *A Stranger in My Own Body*, ed. D. Di Ceglie. London: Karnac.

——— (2000), On having a mind of one's own: Discussion of Fonagy and Target. *Psychoanal. Dial.*, 8:115–148.

Coates, S., Rosenthal, J. & Schechter, D. (2003), *September 11: Trauma and Human Bonds*, Hillsdale, NJ: The Analytic Press.

——— Schechter, D. & First, E. (2003), Brief interventions with traumatized children and families after September 11. In: *September 11: Trauma and Human Bonds*, ed. S. Coates, J. Rosenthal & D. Schechter. Hillsdale, NJ: The Analytic Press.

Cooley, C. H. (1909), *Social Organization.* New York: Schocken Books.

Cooper, S. (2000), Mutual containment in the analytic situation. *Psychoanal. Dial.*, 10:169–194.

——— (2003), You say oedipal, I say postoedipal: A consideration of desire and hostility in the analytic relationship. *Psychoanal. Dial.*, 13:41–63.

——— & Levit, D. (1998), Old and new objects in Fairbairnian and American relational theory. *Psychoanal. Dial.*, 8:603–624.

Corbett, K. (1993), The mystery of homosexuality. *Psychoanal. Psychol.*, 10:345–357.

——— (1999), Homosexual boyhood: Notes on girlyboys. In: *Sissies and Tomboys*, ed. M. Rottnek. New York: New York University Press, pp. 107–139.

——— (2001a), Faggot = loser. *Studies Gender & Sexual.*, 2:3–28.

——— (2001b), More life: Centrality and marginality in human development. *Psychoanal. Dial.*, 11:313–335.

——— (2001c), Sexuality/sexuality: Discussion of Deborah Waxenberg's "On not being supposed to." *Studies Gender & Sexual.*, 2:375–381.

——— (2001d), Nontraditional family romance. *Psychoanal. Quart.*, 70:599–624.

Corrigan, E. & Gordon, P. E. (1995), *The Mind-Object.* Northvale, NJ: Aronson.

Cournos, F. (2003), Lessons for high-risk populations from attachment research and September 11: Helping children in foster care. In: *September 11: Trauma and Human Bonds*, ed. S. Coates, J. Rosenthal & D. Schechter. Hillsdale, NJ: The Analytic Press.

Crastnopol, M. (2001), Commentary on Greenberg's "The analyst's participation: A new look." *J. Amer. Psychoanal. Assn.*, 49:386–398.

Cushman, P. (1995), *Constructing the Self, Constructing America.* Boston, MA: Addison-Wesley.

——— (2000), White guilt, political activity, and the analyst: Commentary on paper by Neil Altman. *Psychoanal. Dial.*, 10:607–618.

Dahlbom, B. (1993), Mind is artificial. In: *Dennett and His Critics*, ed. B. Dahlbom. Cambridge, MA: Blackwell.

Damasio, A. (1994), *Descartes's Error.* New York: Putnam's.

——— (1999), *The Feeling of What Happens.* New York: Harcourt.

Davidson, D. (1980), *Essays on Actions and Events.* Oxford, UK: Clarendon Press.

Davies, J. (1994), Love in the afternoon: A relational reconsideration of desire and dread in the countertransference. *Psychoanal. Dial.*, 4:153–170.

——— (1996a), Dissociation, repression, and reality testing in the countertransference: The controversy over memory and false memory in the psychoanalytic treatment of adult survivors of childhood sexual abuse. *Psychoanal. Dial.*, 6:189–218.

———— (1996b), Linking the "pre-analytic" with the postclassical: Integration, dissociation, and the multiplicity of unconscious process. *Contemp. Psychoanal.,* 32:553–576.

———— (1996c), Maintaining the complexities: A reply to Crews, Brenneis, and Stern. *Psychoanal. Dial.,* 6:281–294.

———— (1998a), Multiple perspectives on multiplicity. *Psychoanal. Dial.,* 8:195–206.

———— (1998b), Between the disclosure and foreclosure of erotic transference-countertransference: Can psychoanalysis find a place for adult sexuality? *Psychoanal. Dial.,* 8:747–766.

———— (2001a), Back to the future in psychoanalysis: Trauma, dissociation, and the nature of unconscious processes. In: *Storms in Her Head,* ed. M. Dimen & A. Harris. New York: Other Press, pp. 245–264.

———— (2001b), Erotic overstimulation and the co-construction of sexual meanings in transference-countertransference experience. *Psychoanal. Quart.,* 70:757–788.

———— (2003a), Falling in love with love: Oedipal and postoedipal manifestations of idealization, mourning, and erotic masochism. *Psychoanal. Dial.,* 13:1–27.

———— (2003b), Reflections on Oedipus, post-Oedipus, and termination. *Psychoanal. Dial.,* 13:65–75.

———— & Frawley, M. (1992), Dissociative processes and transference-countertransference paradigms in the psychoanalytically oriented treatment of adult survivors of childhood sexual abuse. *Psychoanal. Dial.,* 2:5–36.

Dean, T. (1993), Transsexual identification, gender performance theory, and the politics of the real. *Literature & Psychol.,* 39:1–27.

———— (1994), Bodies that matter: Rhetoric and sexuality. *Pre/text,* 15:80–117.

De Marneffe, D. (1997), Bodies and words: A study of young children's genital and gender knowledge. *Gender & Psychoanal.,* 2:3–33.

Demos, V. (1992a), The early organization of the psyche. In: *Interface of Psychoanalysis and Psychology,* ed. J. Barron, M. Eagle & D. Wolitzky. Washington, DC: American Psychological Association, pp. 200–226.

———— (1992b). Silvan Tomkins's theory of emotion. In: *Reinterpreting the Legacy of William James, Vol. 5,* ed. M. E. Donnelly. Washington, DC: American Psychological Association, pp. 211–219.

Dennett, D. (1991), *Consciousness Explained.* Boston, MA: Little, Brown.

Denny, D. (2002), A selective bibliography of transsexualism. *J. Gay & Lesbian Psychother.,* 6:35–66.

De Urtubey, L. (1995), Countertransference effects of absence. *Internat. J. Psycho-Anal.,* 76:683–694.

Dimen, M. (1991), Deconstructing difference: Gender, splitting and transitional space. *Psychoanal. Dial.,* 1:335–352.

———— (1994), Money, love, and hate: Contradiction and paradox in psychoanalysis. *Psychoanal. Dial.,* 4:69–100.

———— (1995a), On our "nature": Prolegomenon to a relational theory of sexuality. In: *Disorienting Sexualities,* ed. R. Lesser & T. Domenici. New York: Routledge, pp. 129–152.

———— (1995b), The third step: Freud, the feminists, and postmodernism. *Amer. J. Psychoanal.,* 55:303–319.

—— (1996a), Discussion of symposium, "The relational construction of the body." *Gender & Psychoanal.*, 3:385–401.

—— (1996b), Bodytalk. *Gender & Psychoanal.*, 2:35–53.

—— (1998), Polyglot bodies: Thinking through the relational. In: *Relational Perspectives on the Body*, ed. L. Aron & F. S. Andersen. Hillsdale, NJ: The Analytic Press, pp. 65–93.

—— (1999), Between lust and libido: Sex, psychoanalysis, and the moment before. *Psychoanal. Dial.*, 9:415–440.

—— (2000), The body as Rorschach. *Studies Gender & Sexual.*, 1:9–39.

—— (2002), Perversion is us? Eight notes. *Psychoanal. Dial.*, 11:825–860.

—— (2003), *Sexuality, Intimacy, Power.* Hillsdale, NJ: The Analytic Press.

—— & Goldner, V., eds. (2002), *Gender in Psychoanalytic Space.* New York: Other Press.

Dinnerstein, D. (1975), *The Mermaid and the Minotaur.* New York: Beacon.

Donzelot, P. (1979), *The Policing of Families.* New York: Pantheon Books.

Domenici, T. & Lesser, R. (1995), *Disorienting Sexualities.* New York: Routledge.

Dreger, A., ed. (2002), *Intersex in the Age of Ethics.* New York: University Publishing Group.

Drescher, J. (1998), *Psychoanalytic Therapy and the Gay Man.* Hillsdale, NJ: The Analytic Press.

Dunn, J. (1982), *Siblings, Love, Envy and Understanding.* Cambridge, MA: Harvard University Press.

—— (1997), Connections between emotion and understanding in development. *Cognition & Emotion*, 9:2–3.

Dyess, C. & Dean, T. (2000a), Gender: The impossibility of meaning. *Psychoanal. Dial.*, 10:735–756.

—— & —— (2000b), Relational trouble: Reply to commentaries. *Psychoanal. Dial.*, 10:787–794.

Eagle, M. N. (2001), The analyst's knowledge and authority: A critique of the "new view" in psychoanalysis. *J. Amer. Psychoanal. Assn.*, 49:457–489.

Edelman, G. (1987), *Neural Darwinism.* New York: Basic Books.

Eigen, M. (1986), *The Psychotic Core.* Northvale, NJ: Aronson.

Ehrenberg, D. (1992), *The Intimate Edge.* New York: Norton.

Ehrenreich, B. & English, D. (1978), *For Her Own Good.* New York: Anchor/ Doubleday.

Ekman, P. (1994), Strong evidence for universal in facial expressions: A reply to Russell's mistaken critique. *Psycholog. Bull.*, 115:268–287.

—— (1997), Expression or communication about emotion. In: *Uniting Psychology and Biology*, ed. N. I. Segal & G. E. Weisfeld. Washington, DC: American Psychological Association, pp. 315–338.

Elise, D. (1997), Primary femininity, bisexuality and the female ego ideal: A reexamination of female developmental theory. *Psychoanal. Quart.*, 66:489–517.

—— (1998), The absence of the paternal penis. *J. Amer. Psychoanal. Assn.*, 46:413–442.

—— (1999), Tomboys and cowgirls: The girl's disidentification from the mother. In: *Sissies and Tomboys*, ed. M. Rottnek. New York: New York University, pp. 140–152.

—— (2001), Unlawful entry: Male fears of psychic penetration. *Psychoanal. Dial.,* 11:499–531.

—— (2002), The primary maternal oedipal situation and female homoerotic desire. *Psychoanal. Inq.,* 22:209–228.

Elliot, P. (2001), A psychoanalytic reading of transsexual embodiment. *Studies Gender & Sexual.,* 2:295–326.

Elman, J. (1995), Language as a dynamic system. In: *Mind as Motion,* ed. R. F. van Gelder. Cambridge, MA: MIT Press, pp. 195–225.

—— Bates, K., Johnson, M., Karmiloff-Smith, A., Parisi, D. & Plunkett, K. (1997), *Rethinking Innateness.* Cambridge, MA: MIT Press.

Eng, D. (2001), *Racial Castration.* Durham, NC: Duke University Press.

—— & Han, S. (2003), A dialogue on racial melancholia. In: *Bringing the Plague,* ed. S. Fairfield, L. Layton & C. Stack. New York: Other Press.

Erikson, E. H. (1963), *Childhood and Society.* New York: Norton.

Fairbairn, W. R. D. (1952), *An Object Relations Theory of the Personality.* New York: Basic Books.

Fairfield, S. (2000a), Analyzing multiplicity: A postmodern perspective on some current psychoanalytic theories of subjectivity. *Psychoanal. Dial.,* 11:221–251.

—— (2000b), Analyzing multiplicity: A postmodern perspective on some current psychoanalytic theories of subjectivity. Reply to commentaries by Crastnopol, Goldman, and Mitchell. *Psychoanal. Dial.,* 11:807–822.

—— Layton, L. & Stack, C. (2002), *Bringing the Plague.* New York: Other Press.

Fajardo, B. (1998), A new view of developmental research for psychoanalysis. *J. Amer. Psychoanal. Assn.,* 46:185–207.

—— (2000), "Where are we going in the field of infant mental health?": Comment. *Infant Mental Health J.,* 21:63–66.

Fast, I. (1970), A function of action in early development of identity. *Internat. J. Psycho-Anal.,* 51:471–478.

—— (1978), Developments in gender identity: The original matrix. *Internat. Rev. Psycho-Anal.,* 5:265–273.

—— (1979), Developments in gender identity: Gender differentiation in girls. *Internat. J. Psycho-Anal.,* 60:443–453.

—— (1984), *Gender Identity.* Hillsdale, NJ: The Analytic Press.

—— (1985), *Event Theory.* Mahwah, NJ: Lawrence Erlbaum Associates.

—— (1992), The embodied mind: Toward a relational perspective. *Psychoanal. Dial.,* 2:389-409.

—— (1993), Aspects of early gender development: A psychodynamic perspective. In: *The Psychology of Gender,* ed. A. E. Beall & R. J. Sternberg. New York: Guilford Press, pp. 173–193.

—— (1998), *Selving.* Hillsdale, NJ: The Analytic Press.

—— (1999), Aspects of core gender identity. *Psychoanal. Dial.,* 9:633–662

Faulkner, W. (1931), *Sanctuary.* New York: Cape & Smith.

Fausto-Sterling, A. (2000), *Sexing the Body.* New York: Basic Books.

Feffer, M. (1983), *The Structure of Freudian Thought.* Madison, CT: International Universities Press.

—— (1988), *Radical Constructionism.* New York: New York University Press.

—— (1999), *The Conflict of Equals.* Goteberg, Sweden: Acta Gothoburgesis.

Feinberg, L. (1993), *Stone Bitch Blues*. New York: Firebrand Books.

Feldman, C. (1988), How to mean: Some simple ways. *Semiotica*, 68:159–164.

———— (1989), Monolog as problem solving narrative. In: *Narratives of the Crib,* ed. K. Nelson. Cambridge, MA: Harvard University Press.

———— (1990), Thought from language: The linguistic construction of cognitive representations. In: *Making Sense*, ed. J. Bruner & H. Haste. London: Methuen, pp. 131–146.

———— (2002a), Genres as mental and cultural models: Interpretation in a cultural community. In: *Une Introduction aux Sciences de la Culture,* ed. F. Rastier & S. Bouquet. Paris: Presses Universitaires de France.

———— (2002b), The construction of mind and self in an interpretive community. In: *Literacy, Narrative, and Culture,* ed. J. Brockheimer, M. Wang & D. Olson. London: Curzon.

———— & Kalmar, D. (1996), Autobiography and fiction as modes of thought. In: *Modes of Thought*, ed. D. Olson & N. Torrance. Cambridge, UK: Cambridge University Press, pp. 106–122.

Feldman, M. (1993), Aspects of reality, and the focus of interpretation. *Psychoanal. Inq.*, 13:274–295.

Ferenczi, S. (1911a), Introjection and transference. In: *First Contributions to Psychoanalysis.* London: Karnac, 1952, pp. 39–93.

———— (1911b), On obscene words. In: *First Contributions to Psychoanalysis.* London: Karnac, 1952, pp. 132–153.

———— (1931), Child analysis and the analysis of adults. In: *Final Contributions to the Problems and Methods of Psycho-analysis.* London: Karnac, 1955, pp. 126–142.

———— (1932), *The Clinical Diaries of Sándor Ferenczi*, ed. J. Dupont (trans. M. Balint & N. Z. Jackson). Cambridge, MA: Harvard University Press, 1988.

Fischer, K. (1980), A theory of cognitive development: The control and construction of hierarchies of skills. *Psycholog. Rev.*, 87:477–531.

———— Ayoub, C., Singh, I., Noam, G., Andornicki, M. & Raya, P. (1997), Psychopathology as adaptive development along distinctive pathways. *Develop. & Psychopathol.*, 9:749–779.

———— & Bidell, T. (1998), Dynamic development of psychological structures of action and thought. In: *Handbook of Child Psychology, Vol. 11,* ed. R. Lerner. New York: Wiley.

———— & Watson, M. (2002), Dynamic development of socioemotional roles and distortions in families: The case of the Oedipus conflict. In: *Risk and Development,* ed. G. Roeper & G. Noam. Frankfurt: Suhrkamp.

Flax, J. (1990), *Thinking Fragments.* Berkeley: University of California Press.

———— (1993), *Disputed Subjects.* New York: Routledge.

Foder, J. (1983), *The Modularity of Mind.* Cambridge, MA: MIT Press.

Fogel, G. (1998), Interiority and inner genital space in men: What else can be lost in castration? *Psychoanal. Quart.*, 67:662–697.

Fonagy, P. (1997), Attachment and theory of mind: Overlapping constructs. *Assn. Child Psychol. & Psychiat. Occasional Papers*, 14:31–40.

———— (1998), Moments of change in psychoanalytic theory: Discussion of a new theory of psychic change. *Infant Mental Health J.*, 19:163-171.

—— (2001), *Attachment Theory and Psychoanalysis*. New York: Other Press.

—— & Target, M. (1995), Understanding the violent patient: The use of the body and the role of the father. *Internat. J. Psychoanal.,* 76:487–499.

—— &—— (1996), Playing with reality: I. Theory of mind and the normal development of psychic reality. *Internat. J. Psycho-Anal.,* 77:217–233.

—— & —— (1997), Attachment and reflective function: Their role in self-organization. *Develop. & Psychopathol.,* 9:679–700.

—— & —— (2000), Playing with reality III: The persistence of dual psychic reality in borderline patients. *Internat. J. Psychoanal.,* 81:853–874.

—— & —— (2002), Early intervention and the development of self-regulation. *Psychoanal. Inq.,* 22:307–335.

—— & —— (2003), *Psychoanalytic Theories*. London: Whurr Publishers.

—— Gergely, G., Jurist, E. & Target, M. (2002), *Affect Regulation, Mentalization and the Development of the Self.* New York: Other Press.

Foucault, M. (1965), *Madness and Civilization*. New York: Vintage Books.

—— (1975), Surveiller et punir: Naissance de la prison/Michel Foucault. Paris: Gallimard.

—— (1980), *The History of Sexuality, Vol. 1*. New York: Vintage.

—— (1988), On power. In: *Politics, Philosophy, Culture*. New York: Routledge.

Frankiel, R. (1995), *Essential Papers in Object Loss*. New York: New York University Press.

Frawley, W. (1997), *Vygotsky and Cognitive Science.* Cambridge MA: Harvard University Press.

Freud, A. (1946), *The Psychoanalytic Treatment of Children*. New York: International Universities Press.

—— (1965), Normality and pathology in childhood: Assessments of development. In: *The Writing of Anna Freud, Vol. 6*. New York: International Universities Press.

—— (1966), *The Ego and the Mechanisms of Defense*. New York: International Universities Press.

Freud, S. (1905), Three essays on the theory of sexuality. *Standard Edition,* 7:125–248. London: Hogarth Press, 1953.

—— (1910), Leonardo da Vinci and a memory of his childhood. *Standard Edition,* 11:63–137. London: Hogarth Press, 1956.

—— (1914), On narcissism. *Standard Edition.* 14:67–104. London: Hogarth Press, 1957.

—— (1917), Mourning and melancholia. *Standard Edition,* 14:243–258. London: Hogarth Press, 1957.

—— (1920a), The psychogenesis of a case of homosexuality in a woman. *Standard Edition,* 18:145–172. London: Hogarth Press, 1955.

—— (1920b), Beyond the pleasure principle. *Standard Edition,* 18:1–64. London: Hogarth Press, 1955.

—— (1925), Some psychic consequences of the anatomical differences between the sexes. *Standard Edition,* 19: 248–260. London: Hogarth Press, 1961.

—— (1931), Female sexuality. *Standard Edition,* 21:225–246. London: Hogarth Press, 1961.

Friedman, L. (1999), Why is reality a troubling concept? *J. Amer. Psychoanal. Assn.,* 47:401–425.

——— (2002), "Cavell, Friedman, and objectivity": Commentary reply. *J. Amer. Psychoanal. Assn.,* 50:1312–1313.

Friedman, W. (1990), *About Time.* Cambridge, MA: MIT Press.

Fromm, E. (1941), *Escape from Freedom.* New York: Avon.

Furth, H. (1987). *Knowledge as Desire.* New York: Columbia University Press.

Fuss, D. (1991), *Inside/Out.* New York: Routledge.

——— (1995), *Identification Papers.* New York: Routledge.

——— (1996), *Human, All Too Human.* New York: Routledge.

Gabbard, G. O. (1994), Sexual excitement and countertransference love in the analyst. *J. Amer. Psychoanal. Assn.,* 42:1083–1106.

——— (1995), Countertransference: The emerging common ground. *Internat. J. Psycho-Anal.,* 76:475–485.

Galatzer-Levy, R. (1995), Psychoanalysis and dynamical systems theory: Prediction and self-similarity. *J. Amer. Psychoanal. Assn.,* 43:1085–1113.

Garber, M. (1995), *Vice Versa.* New York: Simon & Schuster.

Gatens, M. (1996), *Imaginary Bodies.* London: Routledge.

Gergen, K. (1985), The social constructionist movement in modern psychology. *Amer. Psychol.,* 40:266–275.

——— (1994), *Realities and Relationships.* Cambridge, MA: Harvard University Press.

Gerhardt, J., Sweetnam, A. & Borton, L. (2000), The intersubjective turn in psychoanalysis: A comparison of contemporary theorists. *Psychoanal. Dial.,* 10:5–42.

Gerson, S. (1996), Neutrality, resistance, and self-disclosure in an intersubjective psychoanalysis. *Psychoanal. Dial.,* 6:623–645.

Gesell, A. (1940), *The First Five Years of Life.* New York: Harper.

——— (1946), The ontogenesis of infant behavior. In: *Manual of Child Psychology,* ed. L. Carmichael. New York: Wiley, pp. 295–331.

——— (1948), *Studies in Child Development.* Westport, CT: Greenwood Press.

——— & Thompson, H. (1934), *Infant Behavior.* New York: McGraw-Hill.

——— & Thompson, H. (1938), *The Psychology of Early Growth Including Norms of Behavior and a Method of Genetic Analysis.* New York: Macmillan.

Ghent, E. (1989), Credo: The dialectics of one-person and two-person psychologies. *Contemp. Psychoanal.,* 25:169-211.

——— (1990), Masochism, submission, surrender. *Contemp. Psychoanal.,* 26:169–211.

——— (1992a), What's moving, the train or the station? *Contemp. Psychother. Rev.,* 7:108–118.

——— (1992b), Process and paradox. *Psychoanal. Dial.,* 2:135–159.

——— (2002), Wish, need, drive: Motive in the light of dynamic systems theory and Edelman's selectionist theory. *Psychoanal. Dial.,* 12:763-808.

Gilligan, C. (1982), *In a Different Voice.* Cambridge, MA: Harvard University Press.

——— Lyons, N. & Hanmer, T. (1990), *Making Connections.* Cambridge, MA: Harvard University Press.

——— & Brown, L. M. (1993), *Meeting at the Crossroads.* New York: Ballantine.

Gilmore, K. (1998), Cloacal anxiety in female development. *J. Amer. Psychoanal. Assn.*, 46:443–470.

Gleick, J. (1987), *Chaos.* Penguin Books.

Goldner, V. (1989), Generation and gender: Normative and covert hierarchies. In: *Women in Families,* ed. M. McGoldrick & C. M. Anderson. New York: Norton, pp. 42–60.

—— (1991), Toward a critical relational theory of gender. *Psychoanal. Dial.,* 1:249–272.

—— (1998), Theorizing gender and sexual subjectivity. Presented at annual meeting of the Division of Psychoanalysis (Division 39) of the American Psychological Association, Boston.

—— (1999), Morality and multiplicity: Perspectives on the treatment of violence in intimate life. *J. Marital & Family Ther.,* 25:325–336.

—— (2003), Ironic gender/authentic sex. *Studies Gender & Sexual.,* 4:113–139.

—— Penn, P., Sheinberg, M. & Walker, G. (1990), Love and violence: Gender paradoxes in volatile relationships. *Family Process,* 29:343–364.

Gordon, L. (2002), *The Moral Prospect of Women.* Urbana, IL: The University of Illinois Press.

Grand, S. (1995), Incest and the intersubjective politics of knowing history. In: *Sexual Abuse Recalled,* ed. J. L. Alpert. New York: Aronson.

—— (1999), *The Reproduction of Evil.* Hillsdale, NJ: The Analytic Press.

Green, A. (1970), The dead mother. In: *On Private Madness.* London: Hogarth Press, 1986.

—— (1995), Has sexuality anything to do with psychoanalysis? *Internat. J. Psychoanal.,* 76:871–873.

—— (1997), Opening remarks to a discussion of sexuality in contemporary psychoanalysis. *Internat. J. Psychoanal.* , 78:345–350.

—— (2000), Science and science fiction in infant research. In: *Clinical and Observational Psychoanalytic Research,* ed. J. Sandler & A. M. Sandler. *Psychoanal. Monogr.,* 5:41–72.

Greenberg, J. (1995), Psychoanalytic technique and the interactive matrix. *Psychoanal. Quart.,* 64:1–22.

—— (2001), "The analyst's participation: A new look": Reply. *J. Amer. Psychoanal. Assn.,* 49:417–426.

—— & Mitchell, S. A. (1983), *Object Relations in Psychoanalytic Theory.* Cambridge, MA: Harvard University Press.

Grosz, E. (1994), *Volatile Bodies Toward a Corporeal Feminism.* Bloomington: University of Indiana Press.

—— (1995), *Space, Time and Perversion.* New York: Routledge.

Grotstein, J. (1999), *Who Is the Dreamer Who Dreams the Dream?* Hillsdale, NJ: The Analytic Press.

Grunberger, B. (1966), Some reflections on the Rat Man. *Internat. J. Psycho-Anal.,* 47:160–168.

Guillaumin, J. (1990), The psychic envelopes of the psychoanalyst. In: *Psychic Envelopes,* ed. D. Anzieu. London: Karnac.

Haacken, J. (1994), Sexual abuse, recovered memory and therapeutic practice: A feminist-psychoanalytic perspective. *Social Text,* 18:115–145.

—— (1999), *Pillar of Salt.* New Brunswick, NJ: Rutgers University Press.

Hacking, I. (1991), Double consciousness in Britain 1815–1875. *Dissociation*, 4:134–146.

Halliday, M. A. K. (1973), *Explorations in the Function of Language.* London: Edward Arnold.

Hamilton, V. (1989), The mantle of safety. *Festschrift for Frances Tustin, Winnicott Studies No. 4.* London: Karnac, pp. 70–94.

Hand, S. (1989), *The Levinas Reader.* London: Blackwell.

Hanly, C. (1999), On subjectivity and objectivity in psychoanalysis. *J. Amer. Psychoanal. Assn.*, 47:427–444.

—— & Fitzpatrick-Hanly, M. (2001), Critical realism: Distinguishing the psychological subjectivity of the analyst from epistemological subjectivism. *J. Amer. Psychoanal. Assn.*, 49:515–533.

Harré, R. (1984), *Personal Being.* Oxford, UK: Blackwell.

Harris, A. (1979), Historical development of the Soviet theory of self-regulation. In: *The Development of Self-Regulation through Private Speech,* ed. G. Zivin. New York: Wiley.

—— (1985), Bringing Artemis to life. In: *Rocking the Ship of State,* ed. Y. King & A. Harris. Boulder, CO: Westview Press.

—— (1987), Women in relation to power and words. *Issues Ego Psychol.*, 10:29–38.

—— (1991), Gender as contradiction. *Psychoanal Dial.*, 1:107–244.

—— (1992), Dialogues as transitional space. In: *Relational Perspectives in Psychoanalysis,* ed. N. Skolnick & S. Warshaw. Hillsdale, NJ: The Analytic Press.

—— (1995), False memory? False memory syndrome? The so-called false memory syndrome. *Psychoanal. Dial.*, 6:155–187.

—— (1996a), Animated conversation: Embodying and gendering. *Gender & Psychoanal.*, 1:361–383.

—— (1996b), The conceptual power of multiplicity. *Contemp. Psychoanal.*, 32:537–552.

—— (1997), Envy and ambition: The circulating tensions in women's relation to aggression. *Gender & Psychoanal.*, 2:291–325.

—— (1998a), Psychic envelopes and sonorous baths: siting the body in relational theory and clinical practice. In: *Relational Perspectives on the Body,* ed. L. Aron & F. Anderson. Hillsdale, NJ: The Analytic Press.

—— (1998b), Aggression: Pleasures and dangers. *Psychoanal. Inq.*, 18:31–44.

—— (2000), Gender as a soft assembly: Tomboys' stories. *Studies Gender & Sexual.*, 1:223–250.

—— (2002), Mothers, monsters, mentors. *Studies Gender & Sexual.*, 3:281–295.

—— (2003), Misogyny: Hatred at close range. In: *Hating in the First Person Plural,* ed. D. Moss. New York: Other Press.

—— (2004), Discussion of the relational unconscious. *Psychoanal. Dial.*, 14:131–138.

—— & Aron, L. (1997), Ferenczi's semiotic theory: Previews of postmodernism. *Psychoanal. Inq.*, 17:522–534.

—— & Gold, B. (2001), The fog rolled in: Induced dissociative states in clinical process. *Psychoanal. Dial.*, 11:357–384.

Harter, S. (1998), The development of self representations. In: *Handbook of Child Psychology, Vol. 3.* New York: Wiley, pp. 553–617.

Hebb, D. (1961), *The Organization of Behavior.* New York: Wiley.

Hegel, G. W. F. (1807), The independence and dependence of self-consciousness: Master and slave. In: *The Phenomenology of Spirit.* Hamburg: Felix Meiner.

Heibeck, T. H. & Markman, E. H. (1987), Word learning in children: An examination of fast mapping. *Child Devel.,* 58:1021–1034.

Heidegger, M. (1962), *Being and Time.* New York: Harper & Row.

Henriques, J., Hollway, W., Urwin, C., Venn, C. & Walkerdine, V. (1984), *Changing the Subject.* London: Methuen.

Herdt, G. (1998), *Same Sex, Different Cultures.* New York: Perseus.

Herzog, J. (2001), *Father Hunger.* Hillsdale, NJ: The Analytic Press.

Hofer, M. (1984), Relationships as regulators: A psychobiologic perspective on bereavement. *Psychosom. Med.,* 46:183–197.

—— (1995), Hidden regulators: Implications for a new understanding of attachment, separation, and loss. In: *Attachment Theory,* ed. S. Goldberg, R. Muir & J. Kerr. Hillsdale, NJ: The Analytic Press, pp. 203–230.

—— (1996), On the nature and consequence of early loss. *Psychosom. Med.,* 58:570–581.

Hoffman, I. Z. (1991), Discussion: Toward a social-constructivist view of the psychoanalytic situation. *Psychoanal. Dial.,* 1:74–105.

—— (1992), Some practical implications of the social constructivist view of the psychoanalytic situation. *Psychoanal. Dial.,* 2:287–304.

—— (1998), *Ritual and Spontaneity in the Psychoanalytic Process.* Hillsdale, NJ: The Analytic Press.

Holland, J. (1998), *Emergence.* New York: Perseus Books.

Holtzman, D. & Kulish, N. (2000), The femininization of the female oedipal complex, Part I: A reconsideration of the significance of separation issues. *J. Amer. Psychoanal. Assn.,* 48:1413–1437.

Horney, K. (1926), The flight from womanhood: The masculinity complex in women, as viewed by men and by women. *Internat. J. Psycho-Anal.,* 7:324–339.

—— (1932), Observations on a specific difference in the dread felt by men and by women respectively for the opposite sex. *Internat. J. Psycho-Anal.,* 13:348–360.

—— (1933), The denial of the vagina: A contribution to the problem of the genital anxieties specific to women. *Internat. J. Psycho-Anal.,* 14:57–70.

—— (1934), The overvaluation of love: A study of a common present-day feminine type. *Psychoanal. Quart.,* 3:605–618.

Horton, P. (1984), Language as a solacing function. *The Psychoanalytic Study of the Child.* New York: International Universities Press, pp. 167–194.

Horowitz, M. (1972), Modes or representation of thought. *J. Amer. Psychoanal. Assn.,* 20:793–819.

Irigaray, L. (1985), *The Speculum of the Other Woman.* Ithaca, NY: Cornell University Press.

—— (1990), This sex which is not one. In: *Essential Papers on the Psychology of Women,* ed. C. Zanardi. New York: New York University Press, pp. 344–351.

Isay, R. (1996), Psychoanalytic therapy with gay men: Developmental consider-
    ations. In: *Textbook of Homosexuality and Mental Health,* ed. R. Cabaj & T.
    Stein. Washington, DC: American Psychiatric Association, pp. 451–469.
Jacobs, T. (1991), *The Use of the Self.* Madison, CT: International Universities
    Press.
Jacobson, E. (1968), On the development of the girl's wish for a child. *Psychoanal.
    Quart.,* 37:523–538.
Jaffe, J., Beebe, B., Feldstein, S., Crown, C. & Jasnow, M. (2001), *Rhythms of
    Dialogue in Infancy. SRCD Monogr. 265,* Vol. 66, No. 2.
James, W. (1890), *The Principles of Psychology.* New York: Henry Holt.
—————— (1907), *Pragmatism.* Cambridge, MA: Harvard University Press, 1978.
—————— (1910), *Psychology.* New York: Henry Holt.
Jay, M. (1973), *The Dialectical Imagination.* Boston: Little Brown.
Joseph, B. (1989), *Psychic Equilibrium and Psychic Change.* London: Tavistock/
    Routledge.
Juarerro, A. (1999), *Dynamics in Action.* Cambridge, MA: MIT Press.
Jusczyk, P. (1997), *The Discovery of Spoken Language.* Cambridge, MA: MIT
    Press.
Kahn, S. (1994), *Coming on Strong.* New York: Free Press.
Kaplan, L. (1991), *Female Perversions.* New York: Doubleday.
Karmiloff-Smith, A. (1992), *Beyond Modularity.* Cambridge, MA: MIT Press.
—————— (1999), The connectionist infant: Would Piaget turn in his grave? In: *The
    Blackwell Reader in Developmental Psychology,* ed. A. Slater & D. Muir.
    Malden, MA: Blackwell, pp. 43–52.
Katz, J. (1976), *Gay American History.* New York: Crowell.
Kauffman, S. (1995), *At Home in the Universe.* New York: Oxford University
    Press.
Kaye, K. (1982), *The Mental and Social Life of Babies.* Chicago, IL: University of
    Chicago Press.
Kessler, S. (1998), *Lessons from the Intersexed.* New Brunswick, NJ: Rutgers Uni-
    versity Press.
Kestenberg, J. (1956), Vicissitudes of female sexuality. *J. Amer. Psychoanal. Assn.,*
    4:453-476.
—————— (1982), The inner genital phase: Prephallic and preoedipal. In: *Early Fe-
    male Development,* ed. D. Mendel. New York: S. P. Medical & Scientific
    Books, pp. 81–126.
Kihlstrom, J. (1989), *Functional Disorders of Memory.* Mahwah, NJ: Lawrence
    Erlbaum Associates.
—————— (1990), The psychological unconscious. In: *Handbook of Personality,* ed. L.
    Pervin. New York: Guilford Press.
Klein, F. (1990), The need to view sexual orientation as a multivariate dynamic
    process: A theoretical perspective. In: *Homosexuality/Heterosexuality,* ed. D.
    McWhorter, S. A. Sanders & J. M. Reinisch. New York: Oxford University
    Press, pp. 277–282.
Klein, M. (1977), *Envy and Gratitude and Other Works 1946–1963.* New York:
    Delta Books.

Knoblauch, S. (1997), Beyond the word in the psychoanalysis: The unspoken dialogue. *Psychoanal. Dial.*, 7:491–516.

—— (2000), *The Musical Edge of Therapeutic Dialogue*. Hillsdale, NJ: The Analytic Press.

—— (2001), High-risk, high-gain choices: Commentary on paper by Philip A. Ringstrom. *Psychoanal. Dial.*, 11:785–795.

Kofman, S. (1985), *The Enigma of Woman*. Ithaca, NY: Cornell University Press.

Kohler, W. (1947), *Gestalt Psychology*. Oxford, England: Liveright.

Kohut, H. (1977), *Restoration of the Self*. New York: International Universities Press.

Kristeva, J. (1980), *Desire in Language*. New York: Columbia University Press.

—— (1982), *Powers of Horror*. New York: Columbia University Press.

Kulish, N. (1991), The mental representation of the clitoris: The fear of female sexuality. *Psychoanal. Inq.*, 11:511–536.

—— & Holtzman, D. (1998), Persephone, the loss of virginity and the female oedipal complex. *Internat. J. Psycho-Anal.*, 79:57–71.

Kuhn, T. (1962), *The Structure of Scientific Revolutions*. Chicago, IL: University of Chicago Press.

Lacan, J. (1977), *Ecrits*. New York: Norton.

Lakoff, G. (1987), *Women, Fire and Dangerous Things*. Chicago, IL: University of Chicago Press.

—— & Johnson, M. (1980), *Metaphors We Live By*. Chicago, IL: University of Chicago Press.

—— & —— (1999), *Philosophy in the Flesh*. New York: Basic Books.

Lampl-de Groot, J. (1933), Problems of femininity. *Psychoanal. Quart.*, 2:489–518.

—— (1982), Thoughts on psychoanalytic views on female psychology 1927–77. *Psychoanal. Quart.*, 51:1–18.

Laplanche, J. (1989), *New Foundations for Psychoanalysis*. London: Blackwell.

—— (1997), The theory of seduction and the problem of the other. *Internat. J. Psycho-Anal.*, 78:653–666.

—— (2002), Infantile sexuality and attachment in metapsychology. In: *Infantile Sexuality and Attachment*, ed. D. Widlocher. New York: Other Press, pp. 37–54.

Laqueur, T. W. (1990), *Making Sex*. Cambridge, MA: Harvard University Press.

Laufer, M. E. (1996), The role of passivity in the relationship to the body during adolescence. *The Psychoanalytic Study of the Child*, 51:348–364. New Haven, CT: Yale University Press.

—— (1997), Interferences in the move from adolescence to adulthood: The development of the female. In: *Adolescent Breakdown and Beyond*, ed. M. Laufer. Madison, CT: International Universities Press, pp. 27–37.

Lax, R. (1994), Aspects of primary and secondary genital feelings and anxieties in girls during the preoedipal and oedipal phases. *Psychoanal. Quart.*, 63:271–296.

Layton, L. (1997), The doer behind the deed. *Gender & Psychoanal.*, 2:515–520.

—— (1998), *Who's that Girl? Who's that Boy?* Hillsdale, NJ: The Analytic Press, 2004.

—— (2002), Gendered subjects, gendered agents: Toward an integration of postmodern theory and relational analytic practice. In: *Gender in Psychoanalytic Space,* ed. M. Dimen & V. Goldner. New York: Other Press, pp. 285–311.

LeGuin, U. (1969), *The Left Hand of Darkness.* New York: Harper & Row.

Lesser, R. (1996), "All that's solid melts into air": Deconstructing some psychoanalytic facts. *Contemp. Psychoanal.,* 32:5–23.

—— (1997), A plea for throwing development out with the bathwater: Discussion of Jessica Benjamin's "In defense of gender ambiguity." *Gender & Psychoanal.,* 2:379–388.

—— (2001), Category problems: Lesbians, postmodernism, and truth. In: *Sexualities Lost and Found,* ed. E. Gould & S. Kiersky. Madison, CT: International Universities Press, pp. 125–134.

—— & Domenici, T., eds. (1995), *Disorienting Sexualities.* New York: Routledge.

LeVay, S. (1993), *The Sexual Brain.* Cambridge, MA: MIT Press.

Levinas, E. & Lingis, A. (1974), *Otherwise than Being.* Boston, MA: M. Nijhoff.

Lewes, K. (1988), *The Psychoanalytic Theory of Male Homosexuality.* New York: Simon & Schuster.

—— (1995), *Psychoanalysis and Male Homosexuality.* Northvale, NJ: Aronson.

—— (1998), A special oedipal mechanism in the development of male homosexuality. *Psychoanal. Psychol.,* 15:341–359.

—— (2001), Psychoanalysis, post-modernism and the lesbian rule. *Psychoanal. Dial.,* 11:131–144.

Lewin, B. (1946), Sleep, the mouth, and the dream screen. *Psychoanal. Quart.,* 15:419–434.

Lewin, K. (1943), Defining the "field" at a given time. *Psycholog. Rev.,* 50:292–310.

Lewis, S. (1929), *Dodsworth.* New York: Harcourt Brace.

Lichtenberg, J. (1993), Human development and organizing principles. In: *Hierarchical Concepts in Psychoanalysis,* ed. A. Wilson & J. Gedo. New York: Guilford Press, pp. 203–231.

Litowitz, B. (2001), On a semiotic continuum. Presented at the William Alanson White Institute, January 15.

—— & Litowitz, N. (1977), The influence of linguistic theory on psychoanalysis: A critical, historical survey. *Internat. R. Psycho-Anal.,* 4:419–448.

Locke, J. (1993), *The Child's Path to Spoken Language.* Cambridge, MA: Harvard University Press.

Loewald, H. (1949), The ego and reality. In: *Papers on Psychoanalysis.* New Haven, CT: Yale University Press.

—— (1962a), Internalization, separation, mourning and the super ego. *Psychoanal. Quart.,* 31:483–504.

—— (1962b), The superego and the ego ideal. *Internat. J. Psychoanal.,* 43:264–268.

—— (1962c), The superego and time. In: *Papers on Psychoanalysis.* New Haven, CT: Yale University Press, 1980, pp. 43–52.

—— (1972), The experience of time. In: *Papers on Psychoanalysis.* New Haven, CT: Yale University Press, 1980, pp. 138–147.

―――― (1975), Psychoanalysis as art and the phantasy character of the psychoanalytic situation. *J. Amer. Psychoanal. Assn.*, 23:277–299.

―――― (1980), Primary process, secondary process, and language. *Papers on Psychoanalysis.* New Haven, CT: Yale University Press, pp. 178–206.

―――― (1986), Transference-countertransference. *J. Amer. Psychoanal. Assn.*, 34:275–287.

Luria, A. (1957), *The Role of Speech in the Regulation of Normal and Abnormal Behavior,* ed. J. Tizard. New York: Pergamon.

Lyons-Ruth, K. (1991), Rapprochement or approchement: Mahler's theory reconsidered from the vantage point of recent research on early attachment relationships. *Psychoanal. Psychol.*, 8:1–23.

―――― (1999). The two-person unconscious: Intersubjective Dialogue, enactive representation and the emergence of new forms of relational organization. *Psychoanal. Inq.*, 19:576–617.

―――― Cicchetti, D. & Toth, S., eds. (1992), *Maternal Depressive Symptoms, Disorganized Infant-Mother Attachment Relationships and Hostile-Aggressive Behavior in the Preschool Classroom.* Rochester, NY: University of Rochester Press.

―――― Alpern, L. & Repacholi, B. (1993), Disorganized infant attachment classification and maternal psychosocial problems as predictors of hostile-aggressive behavior in the preschool classroom. *Child Devel.,* 64:572–585.

Magee, M. & Miller, D. (1997), *Lesbian Lives.* Hillsdale, NJ: The Analytic Press.

Malone, K. & Cleary, R. (2002), Desexing the family: Theorizing the social science of lesbian families. *Feminist Theory,* 3:271–293.

Mannoni, O. (1980), *Un commencement qui n'en finit pas.* Paris: Le Seuil.

Marchman, V. (1993), Constraints on plasticity in a connectionist model of the English past tense. *J. Cognit. Neurosci.,* 5:215–234.

Maroda, K. (1987), The fate of the narcissistic personality: Lost in time. *Psychoanal. Psychol.,* 4:279–290.

Massey, C. (1996), The cultural and conceptual dissonance in theoretical practice: Commentary on Rosemarie Perez Foster's "The bilingual self: Duet in two voices." *Psychoanal. Dial.,* 6:123–140.

Matte-Blanco, I. (1988), *Thinking, Feeling and Being.* London: Routledge.

Maturana, H. (1980), Autopoiesis. In: *Autopoiesis, Dissipative Structures and Spontaneous Social Order,* ed. M. Zeleny. Boulder, CO: Westview Press.

―――― (1985), The mind is not in the head. *J. Soc. & Biolog. Structures,* 8:308–311.

―――― (1999), The organization of the living: A theory of the living organization. *Internat. J. Human Computer Studies,* 51:149–168.

Mayer, E. (1985), Everybody must be just like me: Observations on female castration anxiety. *Internat. J. Psychoanal.,* 66:331–348.

―――― (1995), The phallic castration complex and primary femininity: Paired developmental lines toward female gender identity. *J. Amer. Psychoanal. Assn.,* 43:17–38.

McCawley, J. (1968), The role of semantics in a grammar. In: *Universals in Linguistic Theory,* ed. E. Bach & R. Harms. New York: Holt Rinehart & Winston.

McDougall, J. (1980), *Plea for a Measure of Abnormality.* New York: International Universities Press.

—— (1989), *Theaters of the Body*. New York: Norton.

—— (1995), *The Many Faces of Eros*. New York: Norton.

Mead, G. H. (1956), *On Social Psychology,* ed. A. Strauss. Chicago, IL: University of Chicago Press.

Meltzoff, A. (1990), Foundations for developing a sense of self. In: *The Self in Transition,* ed. D. Cicchetti & M. Beeghly. Chicago, IL: University of Chicago Press, pp. 139–164.

—— (1995), Understanding the intentions of others: Re-enactments of intentions in 18 month olds. *Devel. Psychol.,* 31:838-850.

Merleau-Ponty, M. (1962), *Phenomenology of Perception.* London: Routledge.

—— (1964), *Signs.* Evanston, IL: Northwestern University Press.

Mészáros, J. (1985), Ferenczi's pre-analytic world. In: *The Legacy of Sándor Ferenczi,* ed. L. Aron & A. Harris. Hillsdale, NJ: The Analytic Press.

Meyes, L. (1999), Clocks, engines, and quarks—Love, dreams, and genes: What makes development happen? *The Psychoanalytic Study of the Child,* 54:169–192. New Haven, CT: Yale University Press.

Mieli, P. (2000), Femininity and the limits of theory. In: *The Subject of Lacan,* ed. K. Malone & S. Friedlander. New York: SUNY Press, pp. 265–278.

Mitchell, J. (1974), *Psychoanalysis and Feminism*. New York: Pantheon.

—— & Rose, J., eds. (1985), *Feminine Sexuality*. New York: Norton.

Mitchell, S. (1978), Psychodynamics, homosexuality, and the question of pathology. *Psychiatry,* 41:254–263.

—— (1981), The psychoanalytic treatment of homosexuality: Some technical considerations. *Internat. Rev. Psycho-Anal.,* 8:63–80.

—— (1984), Object relations theories and the developmental tilt. *Contemp. Psychoanal.,* 7:473–499.

—— (1988), *Relational Concepts in Psychoanalysis*. Cambridge, MA: Harvard University Press.

—— (1993), *Hope and Dread in Psychoanalysis*. New York: Basic Books.

—— (1997), *Influence and Autonomy in Psychoanalysis*. Hilldale, NJ: The Analytic Press.

—— (2000), *Relationality*. Hillsdale, NJ: The Analytic Press.

—— (2001), The treatment of choice: Commentary on paper by Susan Fairfield. *Psychoanal. Dial.,* 11:283–291.

—— (2002), *Can Love Last?* New York: Norton.

—— & Aron, L., eds. (1999), *Relational Psychoanalysis*. Hillsdale, NJ: The Analytic Press.

Mitrani, J. (1995), Toward an understanding of unmentalized experience. *Psychoanal. Quart.,* 64:68–112.

—— (1996), *A Framework for the Imaginary*. Northvale, NJ: Aronson.

—— (2001), *Ordinary People and Extraordinary Protections*. New York: Brunner-Routledge.

Money, J. & Eckhardt, A. (1972), *Man and Woman, Boy and Girl*. Baltimore, MD: Johns Hopkins University Press.

Moran, M. (1991), Chaos theory and psychoanalysis: The fluidic nature of the mind. *Internat. Rev. Psychoanal.,* 18:211–221.

Müller, J. (1932), A contribution to the problem of libidinal development of the genital phase in girls. *Internat. J. Psycho-Anal.*, 13:361–368.

Muller, J. P. (1996), *Beyond the Psychoanalytic Dyad*. Florence, KY: Taylor & Francis/Routledge.

Neisser, U. (1982), *Memory Observed*. New York: Freeman.

Nelson, K. (1985), *Making Sense*. New York: Academic Press.

—— ed. (1989), *Narratives of the Crib*. Cambridge, MA: Harvard University Press.

Notman, M. & Lester, E. (1988), Pregnancy: Theoretical considerations. *Psychoanal. Inq.*, 8:139–159

Oakley, A. (1993), *Essays on Women, Medicine and Health*. Edinburgh: University of Edinburgh Press.

O'Connor, N. & Ryan, J. (1993), *Wild Desires and Mistaken Identities*. London: Virago Press.

Ogden, T. (1989), *The Primitive Edge of Experience*. Northvale, NJ: Aronson.

—— (1994), *Subjects of Analysis*. London: Karnac.

—— (1995), Analyzing forms of aliveness and deadness of the transference-countertransference. *Internat. J. Psychoanal.*, 76:695–709.

Olds, D. (1992a), Consciousness: A brain-centered, informational approach. *Psychoanal. Inq.*, 12:419–444.

—— (1992b), The physicality of the sign. *Semiotics*, 9:166–173.

—— (1994), Connectionism and psychoanalysis. *J. Amer. Psychoanal. Assn.*, 42:581–611.

—— (2000), A semiotic model of mind. *J. Amer. Psychoanal. Assn.*, 48:497–529.

Olivier, C. (1989), *Jocasta's Children*. London: Routledge.

Olson, D. (1988), *The Social Foundations of Language and Thought*. New York: Norton.

Orbach, S. (1999), *On Emotional Literacy*. London: Penguin.

Orgel, S. (1965), On time and timelessness. *J. Amer. Psychoanal. Assn.*, 13:102–121.

—— (1976), On the experience of time and its dynamics, with special reference to affects: Discussion. *J. Amer. Psychoanal. Assn.*, 24:377–382.

—— (1994), *The Words on Paper*. New York: Cambridge University Press.

Overton, W. (1998), Developmental psychology: Philosophy, concepts, and methodology. In: *Handbook of Child Psychology, Vol. 1*, ed. W. Damon & R. M. Lerner. New York: Wiley, pp. 107–188.

Palumbo, S. (1998), *The Emergent Ego*. Madison, CT: International Universities Press.

Paster, G. (1993), *The Body Embarrassed*. Ithaca, NY: Cornell University Press.

Payne, S. M. (1935), A conception of femininity. *Brit. J. Med. Psychol.*, 35:18–33.

Peirce, C. S. (1955), *Philosophical Writings of Peirce*, ed. J. Buchler. New York: Dover.

Pennebaker, J. W. (2003). Telling stories: The health benefits of disclosure. In: *Social and Cultural Lives of Immune Systems*, ed. J. M. Wilce, Jr. London: Routledge, pp. 19–34.

Perez Foster, R. (1995), The bilingual self: Duet in two voices. *Psychoanal. Dial.*,

6:99–123.

Person, E. S. (2000), *The Sexual Century*. New Haven, CT: Yale University Press.

Phillips, A. (1993), *On Kissing, Tickling, and Being Bored*. Cambridge, MA: Harvard University Press.

—— (1995), Keep it moving: Commentary on Butler's "Melancholy gender." *Psychoanal. Dial.*, 5:181–188.

—— (1999), *Darwin's Worms*. New York: Basic Books.

—— (2001), On what we need: A celebration of the work of Emmanuel Ghent. *Psychoanal. Dial.*, 11:1–21.

Piaget, J. (1924), *The Construction of Reality in the Child*. New York: Basic Books, 1954.

—— (1955), The development of time concepts in the child. In: *Psychopathology of Childhood*, ed. P. H. Hoch & J. Zubin. New York: Grune & Stratton, pp. 34–44.

Piers, C. (2000), Character as self-organizing complexity. *Psychoanal. & Contemp. Thought*, 23:3–34.

—— (in press), The mind's multiplicity and complexity. *Psychoanal. Dial.*

Pinker, S. (1994), *The Language Instinct*. New York: HarperCollins.

—— (1996), *Language Learning and Language Development*. Cambridge, MA: Harvard University Press.

Pizer, B. (2000), Negotiating psychoanalytic holding. *Psychoanal. Inq.*, 20:82–107.

Pizer, S. (1998), *Building Bridges*. Hillsdale, NJ: The Analytic Press.

—— (1999), Playing with technique—Trios and duets: Commentary on paper by Lewis Aron. *Psychoanal. Dial.*, 9:61-68.

—— (2001), The capacity to tolerate paradox: Bridging multiplicity within the self. In: *Self-Relations in the Psychotherapy Process*, ed. J. Muran & J. Christopher. Washington, DC: American Psychological Association, pp. 111–135.

Pollock, G. H. & Ross, J. M., eds. (1988), The Oedipus papers. *Classics in Psychoanalysis, Monogr. 5*. Madison, CT: International Universities Press.

Pynoos, R. (2001), When the bough broke. Presented at the Conference "When the Bough Broke." New York: Columbia University, November.

Reich, A. (1953), Narcissistic object choice in women. *J. Amer. Psychoanal. Assn.*, 1:22–44.

Reisner, S. (1999), Freud and psychoanalysis: Into the 21st century. *J. Amer. Psychoanal. Assn.*, 47:1037–1060.

Renik, O. (1993), Analytic interaction: Conceptualizing technique in light of the analyst's irreducible subjectivity. *Psychoanal. Quart.*, 62:553–571.

—— (1996), The perils of neutrality. *Psychoanal. Quart.*, 65:495–517.

Richards, A. (1992), The influence of sphincter control and genital sensation on body image and gender identity in women. *Psychoanal. Quart.*, 61:331–351.

—— (1996), Primary femininity and female genital anxiety. *J. Amer. Psychoanal. Assn.*, 44(S):261–281.

Ricoeur, P. (1992), *Oneself as Another*. Chicago, IL: University of Chicago Press.

Ringstrom, P. (2001a), Cultivating the improvisational in psychoanalytic treatment. *Psychoanal. Dial.*, 11:727–754.

—— (2001b), "Yes, and . . . "—How improvisation is the essence of good psychoanalytic dialogue: Reply to commentaries. *Psychoanal. Dial.*, 11:797–806.

Rivera, M. (1989), Linking the psychological and the social: Feminism, poststructuralism, and multiple personality. Dissociation: *Prog. Dissoc. Disorders*, 2:24–31.

Rivière, J. (1929), Womanliness as a masquerade. *Internat. J. Psychoanal.*, 9:303–313.

Rorty, R. (1979), *Philosophy and the Mirror of Nature*. Princeton, NJ: Princeton University Press.

Rose, J. (1978), Dora: Fragment of an analysis. M/F 2, 5–21.

Rosenfeld, H. (1983), Primitive object relations and mechanisms. *Internat. J. Psychoanal.*, 64:261–267.

Ross, J. R. (1985), *Infinite Syntax*. Northwood, NJ: Ablex.

Rothbaum, F., Weisz, J., Pott, M., Miyake, K. & Morelli, G. (2000), Attachment as culture. *Amer. Psychol.*, 55:1093–1104.

Sameroff, A. J. (1983), *Handbook of Child Psychology, Vol. 1*, ed. P. H. Mussen. New York: Wiley.

Sander, L. (1988), Reflections on self psychology and infancy: The event-structure of regulation in the neonate-caregiver system as a biological background for early organization of psychic structure. In: *Frontiers in Self Psychology: Progress in Self Psychology, Vol. 3*, ed. A. Goldberg. Hillsdale, NJ: The Analytic Press, pp. 64–77.

—— (2002), Thinking differently: Principles of process in living systems and the specificity of being known. *Psychoanal. Dial.*, 12:11–42.

Sapisochin, G. (1999), "My heart belongs to daddy": Some reflections on the difference between generations as the organizer of the triangular structure of the mind. *Internat. J. Psychoanal.*, 80:755–767.

Scarry, E. (1985), *The Body in Pain*. New York: Oxford University Press.

Schafer, R. (1968), *Aspects of Internalization*. New York: International Universities Press.

—— (1978), *Language and Insight: The Sigmund Freud Theoretical Lectures, University College London, 1975–1976*. New Haven, CT: Yale University Press.

—— (1992), *Retelling a Life*. New York: Basic Books.

—— (1997a), In the wake of Heinz Hartmann. In: *Tradition and Change in Psychoanalysis*. Madison, CT: International Universities Press, pp. 3–22.

—— (1997b), Vicissitudes of remembering in the countertransference. *Internat. J. Psychoanal.*, 78:1151–1163.

Schaie, K. W. & Baltes, P. B. (1975), On sequential strategies in developmental research and the Schaie-Baltes controversy: Description or explanation? *Human Devel.*, 18:384–390.

Schechter, D. S. (2003), Intergenerational communication of maternal violent trauma: Understanding the interplay of reflective functioning and posttraumatic psychopathology. In: *September 11: Trauma and Human Bonds*, ed. S. Coates, J. Rosenthal & D. Schechter. Hillsdale, NJ: The Analytic Press, pp. 115–142.

Schore, A. (1994), *Affect Regulation and the Origin of the Self.* Mahwah, NJ: Lawrence Erlbaum Associates.

Schwartz, A. (1998), *Sexual Subjects.* New York: Routledge.

Schwartz, D. (1995), Retaining the classical concepts—Hidden costs: Commentary on Lewis Aron's "The internalized primal scene." *Psychoanal. Dial.,* 5:239–248.

—— (1999), The temptations of normality: Reappraising psychoanalytic theories of sexual development. *Psychoanal. Psychol.,* 16:554–564.

Sedgwick, E. (1990), *Epistemologies of the Closet.* Berkeley: University of California Press.

Seligman, S. (1999a), Integrating Kleinian theory and intersubjective infant research observing projective identification. *Psychoanal. Dial.,* 9:129–159.

—— (1999b), Infant-parent interactions, phantasies, and an "internal two-person psychology": Reply to commentaries. *Psychoanal. Dial.,* 9:235–243.

—— (2000), Clinical implications of current attachment theory. *J. Amer. Psychoanal. Assn.,* 48:1189–1195.

—— (2001), The new baby settles in: Commentary on paper by Frank M. Lachmann. *Psychoanal Dial.,* 11:195–211.

—— (in press), Systems theory from behind the couch: Theory, technique and therapeutic action. *Psychoanal. Dial.*

Sennett, R. & Cobb, J. (1972), *The Hidden Injuries of Class.* New York: Knopf.

Shorter, E. (1982), *A History of Women's Bodies.* New York: Basic Books.

Silin, J. (1995), *Sex, Death and the Education of Children.* New York: Teachers' College Press.

Silverman, D. K. (1996), Polarities and amalgams: Analytic dyads and the individuals within them. *Psychoanal. Rev.,* 83:247–271.

—— (2000), An interrogation of the relational turn: A discussion with Stephen Mitchell. *Psychoanal. Psychol.,* 17:146–152.

—— (2001), Sexuality and attachment: A passionate relationship or a marriage of convenience? *Psychoanal. Quart.,* 70:325–358.

—— (2003), Theorizing in the shadow of Foucault: Facets of female sexuality. *Psychoanal. Dial.,* 13:243–272.

Slavin, J. (2002), The innocence of sexuality. *Psychoanal. Quart.,* 71:51–81.

Slavin, M. (1996), Is one self enough? Multiplicity in self organization and the capacity to negotiate relational conflict. *Contemp. Psychoanal.,* 32:615–625.

—— (2000), The drama within the womb: Reflections on the biology of mother–fetal interaction and the nature of intimate human therapeutic negotiation. Presented at the Spring Meeting of the Division of Psychoanalysis (39), American Psychological Association, San Francisco, CA, April.

—— & Kriegman, D. (1992), *The Adaptive Design of the Human Psyche.* New York: Guilford.

Smith, H. F. (1999), Subjectivity and objectivity in analytic listening. *J. Amer. Psychoanal. Assn.,* 47:465–484.

Snow, C. & Ferguson, C. (1977), *Talking to Children.* Cambridge: Cambridge University Press.

Spence, D. (1982), *Narrative Truth and Historical Truth.* New York: Norton.

——— (1992), Language games. *Psychol. Inq.,* 3:65–67.

——— (1994), *The Rhetorical Voice of Psychoanalysis.* Cambridge, MA: Harvard University Press.

Spezzano, C. (1993), *Affect in Psychoanalysis.* Hillsdale, NJ: The Analytic Press.

——— (2001), How is the analyst supposed to know? Gathering evidence for interpretations. *Contemp. Psychoanal.,* 37:551–570.

Sroufe, L. A. (1990), An organizational perspective on the self. In: *The Self in Transition,* ed. D. Cicchetti & M. Beeghly. Chicago, IL: University of Chicago Press, pp. 281–307.

Stein, A. H. (1999), Whose thoughts are they anyway? Dimensionally exploding Bion's double-headed arrows in coadapting transitional space. *Nonlinear Dynamics, Psychol. & Life Sci.,* 3:65–92.

Stein, R. (1991), *Psychoanalytic Theories of Affect.* New York: Praeger.

——— (1998a), The enigmatic dimension of sexual experience: The "otherness" of sexuality and primal seduction. *Psychoanal. Quart.,* 67:594–625.

——— (1998b), The poignant, the excessive and the enigmatic in sexuality. *Internat. J. Psychoanal.,* 79:253–268.

——— (2002), Evil as love and as liberation. *Psychoanal. Dial.,* 12:393–420.

——— (2003), Vertical mystical homoeros: An altered form of desire in fundamentalism. *Studies Gender & Sexual.,* 4:38–58.

Stepansky, P. (1999), *Freud, Surgery, and the Surgeons.* Hillsdale, NJ: The Analytic Press.

Stern, D. (1977), *The First Relationship.* Cambridge, MA: Harvard University Press.

——— (1985), *The Interpersonal World of the Infant.* New York: Basic Books.

——— Sander, L., Nahum, J., Harrison, A., Lyons-Ruth, K., Morgan, A., Bruschweiler-Stern, N. & Tronick, E. (1998), Non-interpretive mechanisms in psychoanalytic therapy: The "something more" than interpretation. *Internat. J. Psycho-Anal.,* 79:903–921.

Stern, D. B. (1996), Dissociation and constructivism. *Psychoanal. Dial.,* 6:251–266.

——— (1997), *Unformulated Experience.* Hillsdale, NJ: The Analytic Press.

Stimmel, B. (1996), From "nothing" to "something" to "everything": Bisexuality and metaphors of the mind. *J. Amer. Psychoanal. Assn.,* 44(S):191–214.

Stoller, R. (1968a), A further study of female gender identity. *Internat. J. Psychoanal.,* 49:364–368.

——— (1968b), The sense of femaleness. *Psychoanal. Quart.,* 37:42–55.

——— (1973), Overview: The impact of new advances in sex research on psychoanalytic theory. *Amer. J. Psychiat.,* 130:241–251.

——— (1976), Primary femininity. *J. Amer. Psychoanal. Assn.,* 24(S):59–78.

——— (1985), *Presentations of Gender.* New Haven, CT: Yale University Press.

Sullivan, H. S. (1953), *The Interpersonal Theory of Psychiatry.* New York: Norton.

——— (1964), *The Fusions of Psychiatry and Social Science.* New York: Norton.

Sweetnam, A. (1996), The changing contexts of gender: Between fixed and fluid experience. *Psychoanal. Dial.,* 6:437–459.

——— (1999), Sexual sensations and gender experience: The psychological positions and the erotic third. *Psychoanal. Dial.,* 9:327–348.

Taylor, C. (1989), *Sources of Self.* Cambridge, MA: Harvard University Press.

Thelen, E. (1986), Treadmill-elicited stepping in seven-month-old infants. *Child Devel.,* 57:1498–1506.

―――― (1995), Motor development: A new synthesis. *Amer. Psychol.,* 50:79–95.

―――― Bradshaw, G. & Ward, J. A. (1981), Spontaneous kicking in month-old infants: Manifestation of a human central locomotor program. *Behav. & Neural-Biol.,* 32:45–53.

―――― & Ulrich, B. (1991), *Hidden Skills. Monogr. Soc. Res. Child Devel.,* Serial 223, Vol. 56. Chicago, IL: University of Chicago Press.

―――― & Fisher, D. M. (1982), Newborn stepping: An explanation for a "disappearing reflex." *Devel. Psychol.,* 18:760–775.

―――― & Smith, L. (1994), *A Dynamic Systems Approach to Development and Action.* Cambridge, MA: MIT Press.

―――― & Corbetta, D. (2002), Microdevelopment and dynamic systems: Applications to infant motor development. In: *Transition Processes in Development and Learning,* ed. N. Granott & J. Parziale. New York: Cambridge University Press, pp. 59–79.

Tomkins, S. (1962), *Affect, Imagery, Consciousness, Vol. 1.* New York: Springer.

―――― (1963), *Affect, Imagery, Consciousness, Vol. 2.* New York: Springer.

―――― (1992), Script theory. In: *Personality Structure in the Life Course,* ed. R. A. Zucker, A. I. Rabin, J. Aronoff & S. Frank. New York: Springer, pp. 152–217.

Torok, M. (1970), The significance of penis envy in women. In: *Female Sexuality,* ed. J. Chasseguet-Smirgel. London: Karnac.

Trevarthen, C. (1993), The self born in intersubjectivity: An infant communicating. In: *The Perceived Self,* ed. U. Neisser. New York: Cambridge University Press, pp. 121–173.

―――― & Hubley, P. (1978), Secondary intersubjectivity: Confidence, confiding and acts of meaning in the first year. In: *Action, Gesture and Symbol,* ed. A. Lock. London: Academic Press.

Trofimova, I. (2000), *Nonlinear Dynamic Systems in Life and the Social Sciences,* ed. W. Sulis. Amsterdam: Amsterdam Press.

Tronick, E. Z. (1989), Emotions and emotional communication. *Amer. Psychol.,* 44:112–119.

―――― (1998), Dyadically expanded states of consciousness and the process of therapeutic change. *Infant Mental Health J.,* 19:290–299.

Tustin, F. (1981), *Autistic States in Children.* London: Routledge & Kegan Paul.

Tyson, P. (1986), Psychogenesis: The early development of gender identity. *Psychoanal. Quart.,* 55:691–693.

―――― (1994), Bedrock and beyond: An examination of the clinical utility of contemporary theories of female psychology. *J. Amer. Psychoanal. Assn.,* 42:447–467.

―――― (1997), Sexuality, femininity, and contemporary psychoanalysis. *Internat. J. Psycho-Anal.,* 78:385–389.

―――― & Tyson, R. (1990), *Psychoanalytic Theories of Development.* New Haven, CT: Yale University Press.

Urwin, K. (1984), Power relations in the emergence of language. In: *Changing the Subject,* ed. J. Henriques, W. Holloway, C. Urwin, C. Venn & V. Walkerdine. London: Methuen.

Van der Kolk, B. (1995), The body, memory and the psychobiology of trauma. In: *Sexual Abuse Recalled,* ed. J. Alpert. New York: Citadel Press.

—— (1996), The body keeps the score: Approaches to the psychobiology of post-traumatic stress disorder. In: *Traumatic Stress,* ed. B. van der Kolk, A. C. Mcfarlane & L. Weisaeth. New York: Guilford.

Van der Veer, R. & Valsiner, J. (1991), *Understanding Vygotsky.* Oxford: Blackwell.

—— & —— (1994), *The Vygotsky Reader.* Oxford: Blackwell.

Varela, F., Thompson, E. & Rosch, E. (1992), *The Embodied Mind.* Cambridge, MA: MIT Press.

Vygotsky, L. (1962), *Thought and Language.* Cambridge, MA: MIT Press.

—— (1978), *Mind in Society.* Cambridge, MA: Harvard University Press.

Waddington, C. H. (1966), *Principles of Development and Differentiation.* New York: Macmillan.

Waldrop, M. (1992), *Complexity: The Emerging Science at the Edge of Order and Chaos.* New York: Simon & Schuster.

Walkerdine, V. (1984), Developmental psychology and the child-centered pedagogy: The insertion of Piaget into early education. In: *Changing the Subject,* ed. J. Henriques, W. Holloway, C. Irwin, C. Venn & V. Walkerdine. London: Methuen.

Watson, R. (1989), Monolog, dialog and regulation. In: *Narratives from the Crib,* ed. K. Nelson. Cambridge, MA: Harvard University Press.

Wells, G. (1986), *The Meaning Makers.* Portsmouth, NH: Heineman.

Werner, H. (1957), *Comparative Psychology of Mental Development.* New York: International Universities Press.

Wertsch, J. (1985), *Vygotsky and the Social Formation of Mind.* Cambridge, MA: Harvard University Press.

Whitmer, G. (2001), On the nature of dissociation. *Psychoanal. Quart.,* 70:807–838.

Widlocher, D., ed. (2002), *Infantile Sexuality and Attachment.* New York: Other Press.

Wilkinson, S. & Gabbard, G. (1998) Nominal gender and gender fluidity in the psychoanalytic situation. *Gender & Psychoanal.,* 1:463–481.

Wilson, E. (1998), *Consilience.* New York: Knopf.

Winnicott, D. W. (1947), Hate in the countertransference. In: *Collected Papers.* New York: Basic Books, 1958.

—— (1950), Aggression in relation to emotional development. In: *Collected Papers.* New York: Basic Books, 1958.

—— (1958), The capacity to be alone. In: *The Maturational Processes and the Facilitating Environment.* New York: International Universities Press, 1965, pp. 29–36.

—— (1960), Egp distortion in terms of true and false self. In: *The Maturational Processes and the Facilitating Environment.* New York: International Unversities Press, 1965, pp. 140–152.

—— (1963), The development of the capacity for concern. In: *The Maturational*

Processes and the Facilitating Environment. New York: International Universities Press, 1965, pp. 73–82.

——— (1971), *Playing and Reality.* New York: Basic Books.

——— (1974), The fear of breakdown. *Internat. Rev. Psychoanal.,* 1:103–117.

Wolf, D. (1990), Being of several minds: Voices and versions of the self in early childhood. In: *The Self in Transition,* ed. D. Cicchetti & M. Beeghley. Chicago, IL: University of Chicago Press.

Wolfenstein, E. V. (1996), For I love you, O Eternity: Time and gender in Nietzsche's philosophy. *Gender & Psychoanal.,* 1:171–202.

Wolff, P. (1960), *The Developmental Psychologies of Piaget and Psychoanalysis.* New York: International Universities Press.

——— (1996), The irrelevance of infant observations for psychoanalysis. *J. Amer. Psychoanal. Assn.,* 44:369–392, 464–474.

——— (1998), The irrelevance of infant observations for psychoanalysis: Reply. *J. Amer. Psychoanal. Assn.,* 46:274–278.

Wolfram, S. (2002), *A New Kind of Science.* Champaign, IL: Wolfram Media Inc.

Wrye, H. & Welles, J. (1995), *The Narration of Desire.* Hillsdale, NJ: The Analytic Press.

Yates, S. (1935), Some aspects of time difficulties and their relation to music. *Internat. J. Psychoanal.,* 16:341–355.

Yovell, Y. (2000), From hysteria to posttraumatic stress disorder: Psychoanalysis and the neurobiology of traumatic memory. *Neuropsychoanalysis,* 2:1–18.

Zelazo, P. (2000), Imitation and the dialectic of representation. In: *Minds in the Making,* ed. J. Astington. Oxford, UK: Blackwell.

Zizek, S. (1989), *The Sublime Object of Ideology.* London: Verso.

Subject Index

Author Index

315